The pitm
of the
northern coalfield

Dedicated to
Wilfred Archer 1896–1982
Hilda Archer 1900–
George Colls 1901–
Doris Colls 1902–1973
and to
Rebecca and Amy

The pitmen
of the
northern coalfield

Work, culture, and protest, 1790–1850

Robert Colls

Manchester University Press

Published by Manchester University Press
Oxford Road, Manchester M13 9PL, UK
27 South Main Street, Wolfeboro, NH 03894-2069, USA

British Library cataloguing in publication data

Colls, Robert
The pitmen of the northern coalfield : work,
culture, and protest, 1790–1850.
1. Coal miners — England, Northern —
History — 19th century   2. England,
Northern — Social conditions
I. Title
307.7'66   HN398.E5/

Library of Congress cataloging in publication data applied for

ISBN 0-7190-2202-9 *hardback*

Printed and bound in Great Britain
by Billing & Sons Limited, Worcester.

Contents

Graphs, maps and tables

Glossary of terms
and acronyms

Terms

bank   above ground

base   estimated limit of annual output, set by coalowners' cartel in order to regulate markets

binding   agreement of pitmen with employers for one year's hire

board   ('narrow' or 'wide') − a unit of excavation into the coal cut by the hewers

bond   pitman's annual contract of hire

brattice   wooden partition placed in pit shafts, headways and boards to aid the flow of air

broken   area of mine which has already been worked with 'boards' left standing and 'pillars' to support the roof

cavilling   pitmen's quarterly lottery to allocate working places

chaldron   'Newcastle' chaldron, a measure of coal (217, 989 c.in.) containing approximately 53 cwt.; a 'London' chaldron contained approximately 28 cwt.

chingle   or chinley or shingly coals; when screened neither large nor small: see 'round' and 'small' coal

choke damp   or black or after damp; gas produced by the combustion of carburetted hydrogen: see 'fire damp'

corf   or corve; a basket for carrying coals from the face, gradually replaced in the nineteenth century by tubs

coursing   a more efficient conducting of air through the mine by means of partitions and stoppings

creeps   the lifting of the floor of the board under pressure from the pillars

dadding   dashing dusty pit clothes against a wall

Davy lamp   safety lamp invented by Sir Humphrey Davy in 1815 where the flame was insulated by a wire gauze

deputies   set of pitmen employed to set timber and draw props, gradually becoming responsible for safety supervision underground *double work* where two hewers worked simultaneously in a single board; extra payments might be agreed for the inconvenience

drivers boys who led horse-drawn full tubs along the main underground roads out-bye

face workings into the coal seam

fighting trade periods of non or partial regulation of output by owners

fire damp carburetted hydrogen gas which can become inflammable

fitters coal brokers who sold from colliery to shipper

foul air air in an inflammable condition arising from a concentration of fire damp gas

foul tubs containing quantities of coal or stone considered unfit for market

goaf collapsed, or collapsing, area of the broken and/or robbed mine

hand money extra money paid at binding to encourage and consolidate agreements

headways excavations at the coal face driven in the direction of the seam

hewers pitmen who won the coal at the face by pick, wedge, and gunpowder; usually over twenty-one years old

hinds male farm servants, Northumberland

holeing a communication passage between two places

idle-time clause in the bond promising payment for days not worked

in-bye underground, towards the face

issues collieries' fortnightly permitted output, decided by cartel, according to base multipliers and prevailing market conditions

judding system of mining where the second working (see robbing) followed closely after the first

keelmen men who moved coal from the staith to the ships in flat-bottomed vessels called keels

kirving wedged-cut into the lower half of the coal seam made by the hewer

longwall system of mining without pillars where all the coal is taken at the first working across an advancing face

multipliers proportions of base allotted to coalfield districts for representation within the cartel

out-bye underground, towards the shaft

overmen   supervisory grade beneath the viewer or underviewer responsible for underground workings

overs   and shorts; the over and under-production of collieries, relative to their issues

panel   separately ventilated district of a mine

pillar   mass of coal left to support the roof after excavation: see board

poss   wooden laundry implement used to pound soaking clothes

putters   adolescent boys who pushed or pulled full tubs from the board to the drivers

Restriction   pitmen's collective strategy for regulating production in order to control hours and conditions

robbing   partial excavation of pillars on a second working: see broken

rolley way   main underground road

round coal   large coals, separated from small either below ground, or after screening at bank

royalties   rights of mineral ownership vested in the freehold, and rents accruing from exploitation of that mineral

score   and score price; a number of corves and tubs, usually twenty, upon which hewers' and putters' prices were levied

screening   separation at bank of large and small coals by means of a grid iron frame, 3/8 to 3/4 in. width

seam   strata of coal

sinker   constructor of the pit shaft

small coal   coals of a certain size assessed after screening, or underground, and either wasted or sold cheaply, usually for export

smart money   negotiated payments made by employers to those injured while unable to work

splint   coarse coal

splitting   division of the incoming current of air into the mine

staith   riverside place for transferring coal from tubs to keels, and later directly into ships: see keelmen

thrusts   crushing of coal pillars by pressure from the roof

trapper   youngest of mineworkers, employed to open trap-doors to allow passage of tubs and close them to aid current of air

vend   cartel of coalowners, formally from 1771; replaced in 1805 by Joint Durham and Northumberland Coal Owners' Association

viewer manager of a colliery; or a group of collieries, head
  viewer
whole mine district of unworked coal

Acronyms

ASSI	Assizes
CEC 1842	Children's Employment Commission, Appendix First Report, Mines, Pt I, PP 1842 (381) xvi
CWS	Co-operative Wholesale Society
DCCA	Durham County Charter Association
DCRO	Durham County Record Office
FPU	Female Political Union
FS	Friendly Societies
HL	House of Lords
HO	Home Office
MH	Ministry of Health
NCB	National Coal Board
NCL	Newcastle City Library
NCRO	Northumberland County Record Office
NEIMME	North of England Institute of Mining and Mechanical Engineers
NMA	National Miners' Association
NPU	Northern Political Union
PLL	Picton Library, Liverpool
PMC	Primitive Methodist Circuit
PMM	Primitive Methodist Magazine
PP	Parliamentary Papers
PRO	Public Record Office
QS	Quarter Sessions
RC	Royal Commission
SC	Select Committee
SDUK	Society for the Diffusion of Useful Knowledge
SP	State Papers
SPCK	Society for the Propagation of Christian Knowledge
WCL	Wigan Central Library
WO	War Office

Preface and acknowledgements

This book has as its pride of place the pitmen of Northumberland and Durham. It is in this respect a history of labour. The book is also offered as a history of a society, for no history of the pitmen which confined itself to their 'labour', however defined, could do them justice.

The pitmen's labour was bought by other people from a wider society who looked in turn to a wider world for their business. What happened in places far away from the pit – in the coal exchanges, counting houses, and Trade offices – largely determined whether the pitman worked, and how he worked. The coal nexus was long, and involved, and owned by others whose hands were white. The labour of the pit was only where the nexus began. Equally, but from the other side, the pitman's ability to negotiate his part in that nexus rested in large measure on political and cultural resources which also existed away from the pit. Any history of the pitmen which stopped with their labour would stop short of their lives. Probably no life and labour has been more vividly imagined in British social history than that of the coalminer, but his labour depended upon the labour of others. The daily supply of men and boys was made possible by the work of women. Any history of the northern pitmen which stopped at the pit would misconceive the nature of labour as an exclusively male activity.

This book, therefore, centres on the pitmen but spreads its net outside the pit – into the economic, political, cultural and gender relations of the society beyond. It stands, then, as a history of labour which aspires to be a history of society.

The history is organised under three headings. Part One concerns changes in *work*; Part Two concerns *cultural change*, particularly that achieved by the Primitive Methodists; and Part Three concerns changing techniques of *protest*, the actions of the community to make things for itself. Parts One and Two are more structural, they track the major themes of the period; Part Three is more a straightforward narrative, pulling in the major themes as it proceeds.

Other historians have tried their hand before me. Richard Fynes, who lived some of it and then wrote about it, was first with his classic *The Miners of Northumberland and Durham* (1873). After him came the Hammonds with their two chapters in *The Skilled Labourer* (1919); Sidney Webb's tribute to his constituents, *The Story of the Durham Miners* (1921); Edward Welbourne's *Miners' Unions of Northumberland and Durham* (1923); Robert Wearmouth's sections in *Methodism and the Working-Class Movements of England* (1937); and Challinor and Ripley's *Miners' Association* (1968). An economic first cousin to these works is Paul Sweezy's fine *Monopoly and Competition in the English Coal Trade*, published in 1938. My book has a lineage. I feel a certain kinship with these historians. I see their works as 'family'.

My 'friends' have been inspirational. The writings of Asa Briggs, Eric Hobsbawm, Sheila Rowbotham, Raphael Samuel, Edward Thompson, Gwyn Williams, Raymond Williams, and Stephen Yeo have all saved me from the shrinking recesses of my own brain. And there are collectives to thank. History Workshop, *Past and Present*, The Society for the Study of Labour History, have been this apprentice's guilds.

Not quite 'family' and not quite 'friends' are two histories commissioned by the National Coal Board. Flinn and Stoker's *History of the British Coal Industry*, Volume Two, and Church, Hall and Kanefsky's *History*, Volume Three, are monumental works. Here, the industry is surveyed as a vast and complicated machine whose factors of capital, labour, and enterprise are inspected for working order. I have my quarrels with this new inspectorate, but for their scholarship there is gratitude as well.

All this is to sum up the book's objective and pedigree, as in the manner of prefaces. Just to have an objective and a pedigree might suggest a clear and unwavering project. But beware of retrospectives. There was little that was clear and unwavering about this project. Over a long period of research the project turned at critical moments. It began as a doctoral thesis stung into life by outrage, and perplexity, at Edward Thompson's view of Methodism in his wonderful *Making of the English Working Class*. This partly explains the concentration on Primitive Methodism in Part Two. Then, from the mid-1970s, there were difficult debates within the profession about historical theory. For a while the arguments over structure, narrativity, determination, class-consciousness, and culture overwhelmed the project. It only moved again when I stopped pondering and started to write. My *Collier's Rant. Song and Culture in the Industrial Village* (1977) helped me to restabilise the larger project by going outside it, and the strategy employed here — an attempt to combine structural analysis within a narrative of human actions — can also be explained in terms of this phase. Next there was the new enlightenment of feminism and women's history. A full history of the women of the coalfield awaits its author; my hope is that this book will help her. Finally, there was the miners' strike of 1984–5. I taught Leicestershire and South Derbyshire miners on day-release throughout that year, and their anxieties — with the State's war on the National Union of Mineworkers raging all around us — must have affected some of the writing.

So far I have tried to explain how this book was written. But why was it written? In one sense, there was little choice. I was brought up in the shadow of pits and shipyards, and talk of pits and shipyards. All my life these industries have been in decline. 'Decline' is nowadays the North-East's second sense. When I was born in 1949 there were four collieries in the vicinity of South Shields, and every night you could hear the screaming metal of the shipyards. Now, there is one colliery and the yards are said to be near the end. There comes a feeling in places like this that the past is the only reference. And as its present deteriorates and its future runs out, sometimes the finished-past seems to be all the town knows — the historical sense becomes ingrained.

Educated in such a company of historians, I was compelled to affiliate with the past early on. This may have been an error on my part — in Jack Common's memorable phrase, a Blunder By An Unborn Babe — but I can't tell for I had no choice in the matter. After the early affiliations came the professional ones. Academic scribbling is a lonely enough activity, God knows, but *historical* scribbling must be positively detrimental to one's health. How can this book mean anything to the sodium-lit motorways of modern Newcastle? What can Tommy Hepburn mean to un-employed young workers on the region's Manpower Services' schemes? In moments of such isolation from place and time I have to touch Jack Common for luck. His hero, Will Kiddar, who found that 'What is important about a man is not how able he is, nor how hard-working, but what's his luck', keeps staring back, a knowing grin on his face. Some things don't change.

Of course I want the book to be read and talked about. By whom, is a harder question. The people I most want to read it, the working-class people of the North-East, probably won't, not in any great numbers. This is not just a matter of price. It is really a matter of how we are educated, the class composition of 'higher education', and the way in which reading and writing is culturally and commercially directed. Perhaps adult education will find the book's true readership? If it cannot, and the book becomes the property of academics, there is a chance that over the years some of its findings will filter through. At the very least there is, I suppose, some solace in the fact that the book exists. Some solace.

On happier matters, there are many people to thank. First, the staff of those places where the research was done. Thanks to: the local history department of Newcastle Central Library; Northumberland County Record Office; the North of England Institute of Mining and Mechanical Engineers; Durham County Record Office; the Public Record Office at Chancery Lane and Kew; the Picton Library, Liverpool; the Methodist Archives, first at Epworth House and then the John Rylands Library, Manchester; Colindale Newspaper Library; and the libraries of the universities of York and Leicester. Thanks also to Wigan Central Library, the remnant of whose Pitmen's Strike Collection is now in the Record Office, Leigh (ref. DDZ/Z31). Second, thank you to all the people who talked and corresponded with me over the years. Such is my debt there are too many of these people to name, but special thanks to my teacher Eileen Yeo (whose teaching was the best), and to Philip Dodd, Ron Greenall, Royden Harrison, Norman McCord, Edward Royle, John Rule, and Jim Walvin. My brother, Graham Colls, has helped me out on various occasions after impossible requests for obscure references. Adele Jones and Pam Yorke typed and typed, and Angela Chorley drew the graphs and maps for not much reward but a lot of thanks, now made formal. Third, there are those who trusted me and my project with money. If the Social Science Research Council had not funded me for the first three years the work would have not been started. After the SSRC's touching faith, further good works came from the University of Leicester Research Board, the Twenty-Seven Foundation, the National Union of Mineworkers, Durham and Northumberland areas, and the British Academy. They helped me to finish it and MUP to publish it.

Most importantly I thank Rosie, my wife. Only I can know for how much.

The Pitmen of the Northern Coalfield is dedicated to my grandparents and to my children. Between the past and the future, which is the weave of all history, they live and have lived. This book reaches out to them.

Robert Colls
Leicester, January 1987

Map 1 The Northern coalfield: nineteenth-century development
Source: adapted from A. E. Smailes: *North England*, Nelson, London 1961,
pp. 164–5.

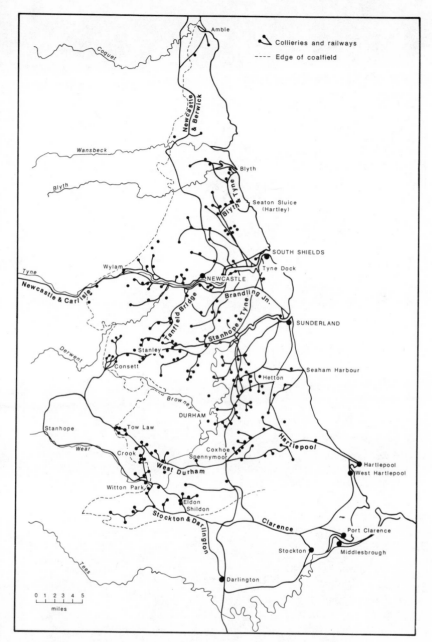

Map 2 The Northern coalfield: collieries and railways in 1850
Source: adapted from A. E. Smailes: *North England*, Nelson, London 1961,
pp. 164–5.

Introduction

'The general diffusion of manufactures throughout a country generates a new character in its inhabitants.'

(Robert Owen, *Observations on the Effect of the Manufacturing System*, 1815)

In 1817 the Newcastle Religious Tract Society was worried about the irreligious character of the pit villages:

> Were there not numbers of persons in the neighbouring collieries yet enwrapt in moral darkness, as profound and opake, as if they had been reared in a heathen or pagan country?

By 1904, the 'moral darkness' had disappeared; Revd J. Christie was concerned only to praise the pitman's religiosity:

> The pitman, as a rule, is a quiet living, religious, and godly man, who enters with the greatest heartiness into all exercises of the communion, which is generally one of the many Methodist bodies, and *par excellence* the Primitives.[1]

Between 1817 and 1904, it would appear that the northern coalfield, in Owen's words, had generated 'a new character in its inhabitants'.

The nineteenth century is full of the evidence and comment of social change. Much of this change − 'industrialisation', 'urbanisation' and the like − is measurable as a matter of social fact. However, within and alongside the evidences of this *factual* change is comment on change in the character of the people themselves. Seen as a category of 'qualitative' evidence and considered to be, in some profound way, about change in the character of human relations, it is a form of evidence harder to assess.[2] It was this to which Owen referred in 1815, and a simple juxtaposition of the quotations from the Religious Tract Society in 1817 and Revd Christie in 1904 would appear to yield evidence of this sort of change: brazen images from the troubled days of 1817, when the pit villages were a heathen camp without the walls of Heaven and Newcastle; to more stable Edwardian tones, when the pit villages were seen as a Methodist communion within the mansion halls of liberal capitalism. Within a hundred years, the men and women of the mining community would appear to have changed their social characters.

However, both comments have to be seen as *prescriptive* as well as *descriptive* accounts, and these two elements bear upon each other in complicated ways. The Tract Society and Revd Christie each had an interest in what should happen, as well as in what was happening, in the pit villages, and it is at this point that their language of prescription and description merges. One can see this in the rhetorical questioning of the Tract Society ('Where there not ...?'), and in the generalising of Christie ('... as a rule ... which is generally one ...'). In fact, as factual descriptions both comments are demonstrably inaccurate, but this is not to say they are worthless as evidence for, even if inaccurate, they are typical as expressions of feeling among certain groups for their own time. Thus, if it is inaccurate to claim, as Christie appears to claim, that most Northumbrian pitmen were Methodist communicants in 1904, it is nevertheless true to say that in 1817 there were no Primitive Methodist societies in the coalfield, whereas by 1904 the Primitives were its major denomination and that many people took comfort from that as an example of change and progress.

The idea of change in the social character of people is not then a simple or a neutral notion. The idea has to refer back to ideas of what went before, in relation to ideas of what was happening, and what should happen, in the present. Some of these ideas of change can be judged as matters of social fact, but all of them have to be understood as expressions of social feeling. And to complicate the issue just a little more, the 'feeling' of observers can be mobilised to intercept the 'fact' of change, as it happens. When consciousness is mobilised in this way, the 'facts' of change become themselves an area of contest. In the nineteenth century, opportunities for the perception and communication of feeling expanded, particularly for the working class. As these opportunities expanded, so did the areas of contest for the control of social change increase. That much of the feeling and contest centred on the matter of *social character* should not surprise us.

The northern coalfield in the nineteenth century was a notable example of social change because there the contest for its control was so great. The coalfield had to be changed because its product was the energy of national economic development. In addition, the people of the coalfield experienced aggressive forms of social manipulation because their character was felt to be a threat to the existing control and direction of that development. By the 1850s, the coalfield and its people were experiencing change and manipulation on such a scale that even some of the manipulators were calling for a halt. As Dr Wilson told his audience in 1863:

> I would say, then to the philanthropist – 'Let well alone' and do not interfere with the physical condition of the miner in our northern coalfields. A more useful and important aim would be to try to improve his moral state, although even in this respect he is better than he seems, and has been grossly misrepresented.[3]

Dr Wilson was calling for a change of emphasis in what people like him were wont to call 'improvement'. It is worth noting his confidence in the *manipulability* of the mining community. Such a confidence had not always been possible, but by the 1850s most of the mining community's actions against change over which they had little control had either been defeated, or were thought to have been absorbed. The owners, managers, and their advisors in the coalfield believed that a new era had begun – that a new system of productive and social relations could/would/should be developed. Central to their belief was the *feeling* (not yet a *fact*, but based on certain facts; not yet a description, but a prescription based on certain descriptions) that the mining community could be 'colonised'. This feeling was the result of contests over the previous sixty years. These years of contest, from the 1790s to the 1850s, for the control of social change in the making of 'a new character' in people, is the subject of this book.

The book is divided into three parts, *Work, Culture, Protest.* Each part very roughly covers the same sixty-year period, the period which could be called the first phase of the modern industrial era. This book will end where another book should begin for in the second phase, from the 1850s to the 1920s, the planned 'colonisation' was not achieved. What this failure meant it is hoped that this book will help the next book to explain for, in the first phase as in the second phase, no plan could survive the impact of battle.

Part one

Work

1
Economic development

From 1791 to 1843 the North East experienced three major cycles of industrial investment, all of which were closely connected with its coal industry. The French wars brought the first cycle which stimulated all sectors of regional industry (lead, iron, shipping, building, transport), but particularly the coal industry. Between 1791 and 1815 there were twenty-nine new 'winnings' of the larger and more important seasale collieries. The second investment cycle can be dated 1822–36, and was led by steam railway which absorbed investment at a rate of over £200,000 per year during the early 1830s, rising to some £350,000 per year during the late 1830s and early 1840s. By the late 1840s railway investment in the region had reached a staggering average of £846,000 per year. The considerable stimulation given by this railway investment was accompanied in the period 1836–43 by a speculative boom which in itself constituted the third major investment cycle. Across the British coal industry as a whole, 1831–54 saw unprecedented and not to be repeated levels of investment, over 6% per year increases in historic capital.[1]

Rising national consumption of industrial and domestic coal supplies, particularly in London and in the iron markets, the reduction and abolition of ancient coal duties (export duties in 1816, coastwise duties in 1831, 1834, and 1845), and the economic penetration of previously landlocked areas of the coalfield by railway, saw a corresponding major growth in the number of seasale collieries: from sixty-two in 1822 to 184 by 1850.[2] New deep-mines represented very large investments indeed, larger than in other coalfields and larger than the costs of comparably scaled investments in cotton mills or metal workshops. And the geological risks were enormous: Monkwearmouth was won in 1834 at a cost of £100,000, Murton in 1843 at a cost of £250,000.

In 1835 the Lambton collieries alone, in Durham, represented an estimated investment of £384,381. In 1828, total capital investment in the coalfield stood at about £2.25 m, and between that date and 1842 a further £7.75 m was invested. In 1855, contemporary observers reckoned that coalfield investments stood at about £14 m.[3] The very definition of the coalfield was changing. In the early and mid-eighteenth century the coalfield only extended along the banks of the River Tyne, above Newcastle bridge, with some scattered exceptions on the Wear. By the late eighteenth century, mining concentrations stretched below the bridge and in the hinterland of the Tyne, particularly in the North Tyne central basin, and on the Wear at Sunderland. By the 1820s new concentrations were developing along east Durham and in mid-Durham, mainly south of Sunderland. The 1830s saw further developments in west Durham.[4] Although it is difficult to trace genuine troughs and peaks in the trade cycles of the coal industry in the North East during the first half of the nineteenth century, in terms of investment, output, and recruitment, the graphs were rising continuously.[5]

Output rose from about 4,465,000 tons per year in 1801 to 10,500,000 tons in 1851. The decades 1826–36 and 1851–61 saw the largest percentage rises in tonnage, 62% and 85% respectively, in a century (1816–1911) which had an average tonnage increase of 30.8% per decade.[6] Coal output rose from the 1790s to the 1850s without any significant technological innovation at the point of production. Most of the engineering and scientific innovations involved either safety or haulage, especially haulage above-ground. Throughout the period coal was won by pick, shovel, and tired limbs. Although productivity rose slowly up to the 1820s, and dramatically in the 1830s, a good deal of the increased output was achieved by a corresponding increase in labour.[7]

At the beginning of the nineteenth century there were 11–14,000 men and boys, about one quarter of them above-ground, employed in the coalfield.[8] In 1807 Mr Thomas of Benton Hall thought that the work-force had recently increased significantly, but note that his estimate is deduced and not certain:

> ... the number increases cannot admit of a doubt since the quantity of Coal wrought amounts to 1/3 more than was wrought 20 years ago; *this added to the great advance in the wages of the Pitmen within that*

period must have occasioned a very considerable increase in their number.[9]

Between 1829 and 1844 – during the second and third major investment cycles – the total mining force increased by over 50%, from 21,000 to 33,000, and had increased to 38,000 by 1851.[10] These increases involved significant movements of people into and across the coalfield. During the period 1841–50 the percentage increase in net migration for the west Durham plateau was 24.9% (+ 6,560); for the north-west Durham plateau, 26.1% (+ 4,912); and for the mid- and lower Wear coalfield, 6.5% (+ 5,512). In these years only the Northumberland coalfield suffered a decline, a decrease of 5.4% (– 2,086). Most coalfield migration was short-distance, within Northumberland and Durham. Long-distance migrants were numerically insignificant. Most pitmen in the new colliery districts had been born and bred in the traditional areas of the coalfield. At the important Hetton colliery in 1851, 85% of miners had been born in the two counties, and most of them came from the old established coalmining parts, particularly lower Tyneside and the mid-Wear valley. Similar impressions have been found for the new (1840) colliery of South Wingate (72% born in the two counties), as well as the ancient pit village of Cockfield (84% born in South Durham). This is not to say that they had all been born the sons of miners. Church estimates that the industry as a whole recruited 30% of its adult labour force from occupations other than mining, particularly agriculture, between 1831 and 1860, and that in this, among the older coalfields, the North East was prominent. Poor Law explanations of the relatively high wages of agricultural workers in Northumberland and Durham in the 1830s attest to labour competition from nearby collieries. The absorption of 'outside' labour is a constant point of contention between owners and unions from the 1820s to the 1860s. These are powerful shaping themes in our narrative. However, when considering specific settlements, one has to bear in mind two subsidiary factors. First, one has to remember the diversity of employment opportunities, say between coal and agriculture, within the region. Tyneside and inland South Durham in the 1830s represented very different levels of opportunity. Second, one has to pose the possibility of casual transference from, say, pit-work, to other coal-related employment such as sea-going, to agriculture, and perhaps back to pit-work, depending on age, marital status, health, or market demand. These two factors may help explain the odd remarks of a leading coalowner in 1853 that there had been little entry into the industry by agricultural workers. For Hetton at least, in 1851 its mineworkers had closer connections with the old established mining areas than had its tertiary workers, who tended to come from more rural and distant parts.[11]

To sum up, the 1790s to the 1850s was a period of major economic development for the northern coalfield. Three investment cycles, each one shorter yet more energetic than the last, quickened the regional economy. Coal output grew with the number of collieries, the number of collieries increased with the spread of railways, and there were increases in the labour force without technological innovations at the coalface. The factors of production multiplied, but the organisation and methods of coalmining seem to have remained largely unchanged. Families migrated, but the shift appears to have been made by people from local mining areas.

For the historian these bare facts of economic development would appear to suggest changes in the size of the industry without significant changes in the industry itself – expansion without rupture. Coal poured out, and men and money poured in, but the pitman has been generally regarded as retaining his conditions and traditions as other workers lost ground in the 'heroic' period of 'Industrial Revolution'.[12] Other crafts and jobs may have been lost, but coalminers only grew in number – expanding nationally to over a million men by 1914; other communities may have had to fight for survival, but miners' disputes were only simple confrontations over wages by men already at the heart of society's industrial future.

This might be the impression, but it was not how the pitmen of the northern coalfield saw their situation. Ben Embleton told miners' union delegates in 1842 that

> ... if they did not unite and join themselves together for the protection of their trade, in a little time the pitmen would be in as bad a condition as the handloom weavers. These weavers were coming into the coal-trade, not weekly, but daily. And this was naturally to be expected from a class of men, nineteen thousand of whom were living, on an average, upon elevenpence per head in the week ... What were they to do to prevent the trade being ruined? They must adopt a plan which would enable these men and themselves to make their bread together ...[13]

The first resolution of this meeting was: 'We unite to save ourselves from destruction'. The pitmen were in fact uniting to save themselves as a regional labour-elite. The coal hewers, numbering between a quarter and a third of the entire work-force, were the core of this elitism. In 1809 there were only 1,980 bound hewers in Tyneside collieries, a corps small enough to be known by name, ability, and temperament by the agents who employed them.[14] The pitmen entered the century as something of a 'caste': skilled men whose practices were recognised as awesome and peculiar, and whose community was acknowledged as the custodian of those practices. Over the next fifty years economic development and attendant changes were to reorganise mining practices, and change the way the community was seen from the outside. Moreover, the importation and recruitment of 'outside' labour not only undermined the caste's notion of its own skill but also challenged the community's self-esteem. The beginning of the end of an elite was detected in 1832: a correspondent to a local newspaper wrote that 'Hitherto the pitwork has been a monopoly' but 'it is now thrown open to the world'.[15] The struggles over *work* between 1790 and 1850 can only be understood by realising that the pitmen sensed that the social standing of their labour was shifting against them. The quantative changes in economic development, in investment, output, and labour, were accompanied by simultaneous qualitative changes in work and social standing. After 1850 the caste of 'true-bred' pitmen was lost as surely as those of the stockingers or croppers or handloom weavers or any other human anachronism of the age. The fast pace of mining expansion before and after 1850 blinded society to this loss. The destruction of a community was blurred as a hereditary caste of skilled pitmen merged into a market of Victorian labourers.

2
Craft, conditions, and organisation

Edward Allen Rymer recalled the action of a 'bred' pitman in Durham in the 1840s:

> Coal-hewing in the North fifty years ago made many capital workmen, especially where picks, wedges, hammers, and drills had to be used. And to see THE REAL PITMAN STRIPPED TO HIS 'BUFF' in short breeches, low shoes, and cotton skull-cap, swinging his 5lb pick, while the sweat runs down his face, is a sight which can never be forgotten.[1]

These compact skills were not easily mastered. The 'true-bred' pitman considered himself to be a man trained in a craft. The craft was taught informally, through family and friends,[2] and guarded by the exclusivity of the mining community. Arguments over workmanship could involve insults to both, as for example at Benwell colliery in 1810 when two pitmen argued

> ... about which was the best workman ... that Walton said he was as good a Man as any at Heaton ... Walton said he could pay every Heron amongst them, James Heron said that he Walton could not, on which James Heron put off his Cloaths (sic) to fight ...

As a writer in the 1850s remarked, in miners' conversations 'the apple of discord' usually turned upon 'personal and professional prowess'.[3]

With the expansion of the industry through the nineteenth century the community's exclusivity declined and its valuation of the craft was increasingly difficult to uphold. But this was a slow process because hewing remained the premier skill and the family remained important in its transmission; as the industry stayed conservative in coal-face technique, the rapport between craft and kinship stayed strong. Hopton's famous primer of the 1860s, *Conversation on Mines between Father and Son*, was a book which in its title recognised the real medium of instruction. For as late as the 1890s, Jack Lawson could recall his new social and professional status on starting work:

> Still, I was a man, and I knew it. There was no more drudging at home … I sat up to the table with my elder brothers and father, black from pit, paraded my knowledge of pit technique, and generally tried to live up to my newly acquired status. It was worth getting up at five o'clock in the morning for that.[4]

The persistence of this rapport, compared to the ways in which economic development despatched a whole economy of other trades and other rapports, left miners with a certain ambivalence about their skill. Seen from without by the end of the nineteenth century as a market of labourers, they continued to see themselves from within as a community of the skilled. This has made for difficulties in classifying the historical skills and status of the coalminer. His skills were real, but not transferable; his craft was learned, but not apprenticed; his knowledge was demanded, but not much valued. Working coals, and bringing them out, was an athletic performance not necessarily reducible to words:

> A labourer of a very special kind, in the hierarchy of labour he defies classification.
>
> The legitimacy of his claim to be entered among those with the rank and dignity of 'craftsmen' has only recently been conceded …
>
> … the essence of a craft is its dependence on a precarious combination of manipulative skill embodying a physical training and judgement … the essence of a 'knack' is its difficulty of communication.[5]

'Essences' can be communicated by means other than words. The problem of identifying the pitman's standing is made more difficult because in his bearing, as well as in his work, the pitman declared his craft. True pitmen were bred as well as trained:

> I use the word 'pitman' in contradistinction to collier. If a man comes to me for a situation as overman, or any other situation of responsibility, my first question is, 'is he a regular-bred pitman?' We speak of a good pitman as we would do of a good seaman … A collier is a man who works the coals; therefore we have a middling good pitman, a thorough good pitman; and a pitman; which latter are the highest degrees.[6]

The word 'pitman' carried with it meanings of social bearing: other men were 'colliers' compared to 'pitmen', and others again were labourers compared to colliers. Note the scorn in this account of local men's attitudes to strike-breakers in 1831. In their very bearing, the strangers from the Midlands were considered to lack the dignity of pitmen:

> Lord! What poor wretches they were! They came trooping here, with an old flannel jock-a-piece, and a pit-cap without even a brim. They had no furniture to put in their houses; many of them had left their wives and children at home ... They had ... a log of wood to sit on, and a bundle of straw to lie on; they eat fat mutton and drank ale, and looked as black and melancholy as a tame raven with his wings clipped ... They seemed no better than Irish. They didn't understand this sort of coalfield neither ...[7]

The pitman's craft and identity was inextricably connected to his safety at work. When in 1823 John Peile, agent at Whitehaven colliery, wrote lamenting the cause of a recent explosion there, his description of Whitehaven miners is very similar to the description of Midlands strike-breakers:

> ... a great ignorance in the Workmen, indeed our Pitmen are a most ignorant race & few of them are regularly bred & the majority composed of Irish and other Trampers, that turn only to us when no other employment can be had, and it may be readily conceived how ignorant they must be of their own safety and how difficult to impress their minds with a proper sense of care & of dangers ...

Peile asked John Buddle, the North-East agent and entrepreneur, for 'regularly bred' pitmen 'from your numerous band' to come and supervise in Cumberland, but the following month Buddle himself lost fifty-nine men after an explosion at Penshaw colliery. Buddle, who was eager to equate pit-craft with the supervisory grades and make himself the judge of it, criticised supervision at Penshaw and called for pitmanship over friendship and family:

> ... none shall be placed or promoted, unless they pass a satisfactory exam as to pitmanship. Such valuable property & such a number of Lives must not on any acct. be entrusted to ignorance or imbecility. Friendship, or relationship must be put entirely out of the question, we must have fit men only.[8]

If skills were connected to safety, then safety was connected to a knowledge of the system of the mine. When William Lowrie of Coxlodge wrote in 1825 asking for work, he regarded himself as a man trained in a dark and complex system which had to tether the legs of its untrained child-workers for fear of losing them: 'I am a bred Pitman and by long experience I have obtained a

knowledge of the Pit System'.[9] The 1835 Parliamentary Select
Committee on Accidents recognised the interdependence of each
man and boy below ground for, on 'the daily unceasing, strict discharge of duty by every person ... depends the safety of hundreds ...
from minute to minute'.[10] The knowledge of the mine came from
long experience of mines. Boys starting work at ten years-old would
work for eleven years, from 'trapping' to 'putting', before becoming hewers. One had to be fit, quick-witted, and start young:

> During the first few weeks I worked at Leitch Pit, I had to learn the
> mysteries of underground life of men and horses. With great difficulty
> I got acquainted with the nomenclature of the mine, and had to adapt
> myself to the circumstances with which I was surrounded, defective
> sight causing me endless troubles ...[11]

Lord Ashley's 1842 Royal Commission on child labour forced the
coalowners into admitting the reality of this knowledge, and the
necessity of early induction. John Buddle explained to Lord
Lambton that he and his fellow viewers were 'decidedly of opinion
that if [boys] are not initiated before they are 13 or 14 – much
less 16, 17 or 18 – they *never will become Colliers*'.[12] Certainly,
Assistant Commissioner Leifchild did not doubt the reality of the
knowledge of the mine. He and his fellow Assistant Commissioners
found learning it difficult and exhausting. Apart from the athletic
performance which took its toll of Commissioners, there was the
old problem of putting it into words:

> ... the lads were necessarily in continual locomotion ... the numerous
> mining technicalities, northern provincialisms, peculiar intonations and
> accents, and rapid and indistinct utterance, rendered it essential for
> me, an interpreter being inadmissable, to devote myself to the study
> of these peculiarities ere I could translate and write the evidence.[13]

'Bred' pitmen were rapid and efficient workers as well as knowl-
edgeable and safe ones. The owners categorised hewers according
to their 'class' and when, in the early century, there were severe
shortages of hewers in the coalfield the agents accepted that they
could only recruit from *within* a community of quite specific skills:

> ... it is well known that *three* Strangers will not be able to work as many
> coals as *two* men who have been accustomed to work the Hartley Seam.

> I was bred a Forgeman to an Iron Factory in the Shire of Ayr North
> Britain, but the Factory was laid in, for reasons unknown to me, which
> obliged me to Travel South in order to get Bread for myself and Family,

accordingly I engaged myself the last Binding as a Pitman in your Lordship's colliery, but being an entire stranger to the Work I am not able to endeavour for a sufficiency for my said Family ...[14]

So ingrained were these skills in regional practices, that the Jarrow hewer John Atkinson, when questioned about inspectors of mines in 1849, could only envisage inspectors as 'bred and brought up to it', belonging 'to the county that they have to inspect in'.[15] The North-East coalowners used the fact of the pitmen's craft as a defence of their cartel, the Vend. Parliamentary committees were told that the break-up of the Vend would mean the demise of the hewing elite and the loss of irreplaceable labour skills.[16]

But the owners were not so loyal to their arguments in the coalfield as they were in Parliamentary Committee. Craft standards appear to have been waning since the 1830s. In 1842 Assistant Commissioner Mitchell had found lads hewing at eighteen years, and some even at sixteen years, instead of the traditional twenty-one. This was particularly prevalent at the new collieries, and old men like John Buddle did not approve. In 1843, as Lord Londonderry's chief viewer, Buddle defended George Hunter, Londonderry's agent at Penshaw, for his old age, and criticised the new 'Mushroom Collieries'. Hunter's breed, Londonderry was told, was getting harder to find:

Hunter's fort is that of *a Pitman* – and I do not know a better one ... There are plenty of *half bred Pitmen* – Young Viewers, which have been reared in the new *Mushroom* Collieries. But we require *a thorough bred* one of experience and resource with some Brains in his head.[17]

Here Buddle was criticising 'half bred' viewers and managers in private. In public, the 1830s and 1840s saw a mounting criticism of the pitmen's skills rather than those of managers, especially over the question of safety. There was more talk of the pitmen's ignorance and wilful disregard of safety measures. Miners' representatives rejected the charge as it stood, and blamed instead the falling valuation of the craft and the increasingly dangerous nature of the job.[18] The owners' importation of labour from outside the coalfield during the strikes of 1831–2 and 1844 was held as a vivid example of this.[19] The disastrous aftermath – four major explosions in six months (May to November 1832), and four major explosions in five months (July to December 1844) – offers some support for the 'true-bred' pitmen's claims.

Of course, idle pits are dangerous pits and the period after a return to work would have meant more danger, but there is evidence that local men blamed the 1844 explosions on unskilled labour working a system which it did not understand. An anonymous pamphlet which is plainly from the National Miners' Association (f. 1842), directly blamed a deputy, John Brown, for the October explosion at Coxlodge colliery. Brown, formerly an agricultural labourer, was 'a man who went down the pit at the time of the Strike' and who caused the explosion by entering an old working with a naked flame even though the working 'was considered by the regular pitmen "foul"':

> There is no doubt but the fault was in Brown's want of experience, had he been thoroughly acquainted with the state of the 'board' when he so daringly entered, he would never have taken a step towards it with a candle, both for his own sake, and for the sake of those who were working in the pit at the time.

The *Miners' Advocate*, newspaper of the union, backed this view in its editorial.[20] Haswell colliery had exploded, three weeks before Coxlodge, on 28 September 1844, killing ninety-five men and boys. The inquest was told that 'the "old men" complain[ed] that "new men" were employed in the waste. They said the strange men were not themselves aware of the danger ... The murmuring was ... the strange men ... might hazard their lives and all down ...' W.P. Roberts, the union solicitor, accused the viewer George Forster of neglect, the coroner's court of ignorance, and the owners of hypocrisy in allowing unskilled men to do what they knew to be a potentially lethal job:

> There is no more general cause of anxiety in a mine than the employ-ment of strange men in those parts which are so far dangerous as to require the use of lamps instead of candles. One of these three men was a stone-mason – another a watch-maker; none of them were ever pitmen before the strike in April last.

The union asked for an independent inquiry into the Haswell explosion, to be headed by Matthias Dunn, a local and well-respected viewer later to become one of the first government inspectors of mines. The Haswell viewer's objection to Dunn, 'on account of a private pique he has to me he might do an injury to the owners', was upheld. Another viewer, from Somerset, was appointed. The eventual verdict was 'Accidental Death'.[21]

After 1844 an open labour market gradually became the chief determinant of entry into the industry. Immigration and a huge expansion of the labour force demanded forms of safety which went beyond the old pitmanship. By 1866 Parliamentary witnesses were claiming that pit skills were *soon* learned by immigrants. By 1873 mining engineers thought that pitmen could be trained in twelve to eighteen months, while inspectors regretted the end of the 'Old Pitman' not so much for his skill as for his gentlemanliness. But for those who could remember the skill, and whose memories were sharpened by the rapid change around them, the immigrant miner was a threat:

> There are a great number who are reckless, but they are persons who have been introduced into the mines; they are not persons who have been brought up to mining under the tuition of their fathers or relatives.[22]

Fear of the threat of the 'introduced' rather than 'bred' miner was an understandable response in two generations of pitmen who had experienced rising risks of death by accident at work. The northern coalfield had had a reputation for gasiness since the seventeenth century. In 1816 J. H. H. Holmes made it clear that 'The mines on the Tyne and Wear are considered in a peculiar degree dangerous, from the quantity of gas yielded by their coal.'[23] This gas was of two kinds: 'fire damp' and 'choke damp'. 'Fire damp' was carburetted hydrogen which, when mixed with from five to fourteen times its bulk of atmospheric air, becomes explosive. 'Choke damp' (or 'black damp' or 'after damp') followed the explosion and was commonly known as carbonic acid gas, the product of the combustion of the carburetted hydrogen in the air. Fire damp killed by burning, choke damp killed by suffocating. On 28 June 1839 the St Hilda colliery at South Shields exploded killing fifty-one men and boys. Rescuers found them the victims of both gases:

> We encountered in one place the bodies of five men who had died from the effects of the gas, and had apparently died placidly, without one muscle of the face distorted. Then there were three more that had been destroyed by the explosion; clothes burnt and torn, the hair singed off, the skin and flesh torn away in several places, with an expression as if the spirit had passed away in agony. Going with a single guide, we encountered two men, one with a light, the other bearing something on his shoulders; it was a blackened mass, a poor dead, burnt boy he was taking out.[24]

In 1830 a Parliamentary Select Committee was told that since about 1820 deeper coal seams had been won with concomitant increases in capital expenditure, not least in ventilation costs. Most pits had to deal with a permanent yield of gas and as they plunged deeper then their ventilation needed to be more effective. Similarly, as pits deepened then the accumulation of gas in 'goaves' or isolated roads and workings became more frequent, and the need for effective ventilation was re-emphasised.[25] By the beginning of the nineteenth century the basic principles of ventilation involved a 'downcast' shaft, an 'upcast' shaft with a furnace at its foot, and a free passage in the workings for the entrance, transit, and exit of air. Air was to enter the mine randomly, wander the workings, and leave by the pull of the upcast shaft's furnace. In the 1760s James Spedding had introduced the method of 'coursing' the air. Here, the workings were 'coursed' into a unitary one-way air tunnel by a plan of doors and stoppings. This was an improved technique, but in the big northern collieries a single course could be many miles long and so much accumulated gaseous air streaming into naked contact with the upcast furnace carried obvious dangers. The dangers were partly met by 'splitting' the workings into districts where each district comprised its own course. This was common practice by the 1830s.[26] In 1831 John Buddle introduced the 'dumb furnace' (an extra passage to the upcast shaft which by-passed the open furnace), and it was he who gained the reputation for splitting his courses to an unprecedented extent. In 1839 the longest course at his large Wallsend colliery was a mere four miles.[27]

From fragmentary seventeenth and eighteenth century evidences it seems that the practice of basic ventilation principles had never been satisfactory, hence the traditional respect for craft, experience, and knowledge of the system of the mine. However, early nineteenth century deepening of shafts and expansion of workings were tending to increase the risk of explosion, and its fatality when it happened. Shafts were the biggest single item of capital costs – about half the cost of the entire plant – and it seems that in many mines the basic principles were not observed. Killingworth colliery in 1842 had one single air course 160 miles long. Instead of having a minimum of two shafts, downcast and upcast, many mines had a single shaft which was 'bratticed'. A brattice was a partition which divided the shaft to serve all purposes: downcast air, upcast gaseous air, men, and coal all came and went by the same shaft. Deeper mines tended to be hotter as well as more difficult to ventilate and made for headaches and nausea. In 1849 hewers at Hetton, Washington, Usworth, Seaton, Walker and Wallsend complained about the 'very bad atmosphere in the face', and the same Select Committee heard evidence that was uncompromising in its condemnation of single shaft pits. They were told that 'the chief causes of accident are, too few shafts, *narrow* shafts, constricted shafts, and badly constructed furnaces'.[28] As early as 1842 the gentlemen of the voluntary South Shields Committee on Safety had condemned most collieries in the coalfield, double shafted ones included, for insufficient ventilation, and had called for the immediate end of brattices:

> ... the system and rate of ventilation of the mines in this extensive coal district require a great and important change; for, if allowed to continue, there is scarce a single mine amongst them, with one or two rare exceptions, that in a day or hour may not be plunged by some easy contingency into a destructive explosion .[29]

The engineer Kenyon Blackwell was equally adamant in his 1850 report, as was the Thornley pitman who in 1844 specifically condemned bratticed shafts at the neighbouring Wingate, Trimdon, Coxhoe, South Hetton, and Quarrington Hill collieries. A witness to the 1849 Select Committee told how once he asked a passing pitman the way to Jarrow colliery: 'Sir, I do not know of any colliery; but there − (pointing me in the direction of the colliery) − is a butcher's shop'. The witness later discovered the remark to be an ironic reference to Jarrow's bratticed shaft.[30] In fact, it is possible to go back to the 1835 Select Committee to find questions about single shaft workings, but the problem of their lesser safety was answered by the special pleading of their greater expense:

> When Mr Taylor is recommending to that Committee more numerous shafts for ventilation, they asked him 'if he was aware that the *cost of sinking a single shaft would ... exceed £100,000?'*

Mr Garforth, a witness from Lancashire, claimed that *he* could sink a shaft eleven foot in diameter for 250 yards at a cost of £1500 − but was told '*that in many districts of the north a shaft of the same diameter, and to the same depth, would cost £50,000!'* Although this cost was a gross exaggeration (as the South Shields

Committee later pointed out), and although their report identified bratticing as extremely risky, the 1835 Select Committee were not inclined to make any recommendations to Parliament on the matter.[31]

Gunpowder for blasting the coal was first introduced into the coalfield about 1813. By the 1830s it was in fairly common use and being so rapidly adopted that by the 1880s, when it won 43% of output, neither Northumberland nor Durham could envisage profitable operations without it.[32] For blasting, a hole was bored with a drill, the powder charge was inserted and plugged with clay to be lit by a straw fuse. The blast would drop a section of the seam which the hewer had 'kirved', or wedged-out, along its bottom, driven about thirty-six inches into the coal and standing sixteen inches in height. Before gunpowder was introduced, the kirved section had been knocked out by wedge and mallet. Powder-blasting was an extremely hazardous practice in gaseous mines because it involved naked flame. Although, in the earlier nineteenth century, viewers could argue that the very dangerousness of powder-blasting made the pitman more alert in his skills, later that century, engineers and inspectors were growing suspicious of an industry which praised the Davy lamp but continued to tolerate the naked flame of blasting. It is likely that the worst explosion of the nineteenth century (at the Oaks colliery in Yorkshire, 12–13 December 1866: 361 killed) was caused by the ignition of powder-blasting.[33] In 1876 Her Majesty's Inspectorate of Mines were closely split on the issue: five were 'of opinion that explosives should be prohibited in mines where safety lamps are used'; six were against Mr Thomas Wynne for Staffordshire, the leading advocate of prohibition, who thought that 'to use powder where lamps are necessary is a farce' and insisted that this had been the unanimous view of the Inspectorate at their first meeting.[34] These fears, which continued into the 1880s,[35] hardly seem to have existed in the more carefree, and more dangerous, 1830s.

If gunpowder put men at greater risk in the 'whole mine' open workings, the Davy lamp led them into greater dangers in the 'broken mine' workings.[36] The whole mine was the district of coal which was intact; the broken mine was a district which had already been worked, and consisted of coal pillars left to prop up the roof. As pits deepened, thicker coal pillars were left to protect the workings from the 'creeps' and 'thrusts' of the roof pressing on the floor.[37] The pillars grew to be quite massive: from a 1765 estimate of about forty-five feet square, to around twenty to forty yards by twenty yards in the 1840s.[38] This method of mining in the northern coalfield was called 'board and pillar': the 'board' was the excavation, the 'pillar' propped it up; 'headways' led across the pillars to enable the coal to be transported from the face. But thicker pillars meant more wasted coal, and the first half of the nineteenth century saw the increased re-working of the broken mine. This 'robbing', as it was called, involved cutting at the pillars as far as was safe, and then withdrawing from them, surrendering the area to creeps and thrusts and water and gas. This broken, robbed, and collapsing area was called 'the goaf'. Robbing was no afterthought. Although it can be traced back to the 1760s, robbing became a major operation in the North East by the early nineteenth century. In 1812 Wallsend colliery, in the van of this 'new' practice as in so many others, hoped to take 45% of a seam at the first working, and 30% by robbing at the second.[39]

The introduction of Davy's safety lamp after 1815 had two indirect effects on this practice. First, it discouraged the proper ventilation of mines by more shafts, tending, as the engineer John Taylor testified in 1835, 'to make the owners of collieries not take the same pains for ventilation that they otherwise would do'. Secondly, the lamp encouraged increased robbing of the broken mine. The broken was notoriously gassy. The Davy lamp made it possible to work in this gas and rob the pillars on a greater scale than ever before:

> Do you not consider these lamps have enabled you to work where otherwise you never could have done so? – I think so; or else there would have been great hazard of men's lives.

It was this hazard which John Buddle was referring to when he answered the 1835 Select Committee:

> Is it your opinion that the loss of life in proportion has been much less since the introduction of the Davy-lamp? – No, I think not; but the causes of the loss, and the circumstances of the mines, are perfectly changed; the risk is very much increased.

As a substantial coalowner and the inventor of a safety lamp which rivalled Davy's, George Stephenson was a man of informed opinion. Before the same Committee, Stephenson supported

Buddle's view that the working of the pillars was the chief cause of accidents. This is Buddle again:

> ... until some effectual plan can be devised for dislodging and expelling the gas ... effectually from those lodgments occasioned by working the pillars, the chief cause of all our accidents will I fear remain unabated.

In 1842, two veteran pitmen, Thomas Batty and Ralph Hall, told the Royal Commission that they could remember no broken working in previous years, but Nicholas Wood, coalowner and viewer, had told the 1835 Select Committee that 'the value of the pillars [is] sufficient to the proprietor to justify him in encountering the danger'.[40]

There can be no doubt that extensive re-working of the broken heightened the risk of explosion. Goaves were ramshackled gasometers; gas accumulated in these idle and buckled workings, and, given that their proper ventilation was expensive, Davy provided the excuse not to try. Buddle reckoned that once an area had been made goaf then that area of 'the mine is then placed under circumstances beyond our control'.[41]

The re-working of the broken also increased the intensity of labour. Breathing became heavier as coal-faces pushed further and the air got thinner. Robbing was one of the most disliked jobs. As the pitman approached, 'the air stream is more languid, the warmth augments, the fire damp issues silently'. Dr Clanny testified to the 1835 Select Committee that

> ... the excess of foul air in such pits cannot but be detrimental to the workmen, for they have to breathe bad air, and sometimes work in it with Sir Humphrey Davy's lamp, when, they say, they are weakened by it. It is a peculiar affection, producing a sort of nervous attack, a loss of energy of the whole system.[42]

The risk was high in tentatively wittling down the pillars. The broken was always susceptible to roof falls, or 'thrusts', as they were known. As the depth of mines increased and the pillars were left thicker to take the added strain, then in some collieries the re-working became the most productive operation. Moreover, by the 1830s a new system was being adopted at certain collieries where pillars were re-worked within self-contained ventilated areas called 'panels' and then collapsed 'nearly simultaneously with the whole workings, or a very short distance behind them'. This 'drawing the jud', or 'judding', where pillars were robbed and supplemented by wooden props and then knocked away as the work moved on, was devised by the inventive Buddle. Depending upon how soon the second, broken working followed the first working, and in turn depending upon the prevailing geological conditions, especially the state of the roof, judding brought board and pillar close to the greater extractive yield of 'longwall' techniques – techniques which eschewed the second working by taking all the coal and allowing the roof to fall behind an advancing face. It raised Buddle's extraction rate from 48% with board and pillar at the first working to 63.5% after a second working, but it was a job 'the most hazardous in the pit'. Roof falls, but particularly the 'judding' operation, could compress and push out waves of fire damp gas from the poorly ventilated broken into the whole workings where gunpowder could be in use, with the chance of ignition and explosion.[43]

The Davy lamp had made this working in the broken more feasible, and the broken had intensified the labour and the risk of accident. The 1835 Select Committee regretted changes in practice and subsequent accidents through 'ignorance [fault of the pitmen] and a false reliance upon its merits [fault of the viewers]'; the 1836 Committee, set up to examine trade rather than accidents, nevertheless published the testimony of a witness who told them that they 'were induced by that invention to work under greater risk; we are working mines now which could not possibly have been worked without the assistance of the Davy lamp'. The philosopher and inventor William Martin, who had been advocating his own patent ventilator-fan since 1805, called Davy's invention a 'murder lamp'; and even Nicholas Wood, the first president of the North of England Institute of Mining Engineers, could admit in his 1852 inaugural address that he was appalled by the level of fatalities since Davy's introduction.[44] Broken working must be added to a devalued craftsmanship, deeper mines, more expansive workings, inadequate ventilation, and gunpowder, in promoting the atmosphere of increased danger in the northern coalfield in the first half of the nineteenth century.

Such statistics as can be reasonably relied upon do show very high – probably the highest ever – rates of death by accident in North-East collieries from the early century into the 1840s. However, all conclusions drawn from statistics during this period

must be tacit because the accuracy of the historical evidence affects
the received rates of mortality. In the first place, there was a
reticence among owners and viewers about fatality figures. In the
second place, most of the figures which we do have are underestimates of risk for pitmen because they include surface workers
with underground workers. Explosion details were first published
in local newspapers only in 1812, and after that only the major
explosions were listed. John Buddle thought that more men were
lost in the coalfield every year by small accidents rather than
major ones.[45] The 1835 *Report on Accidents* published returns –
elaborated by the Children's Employment Commission seven years
later – but P.E.H. Hair, the historian of the subject, demon-
strating that they were based on the list of a local historian who
took them from the newspapers, has said that 'No conclusions
about trends in mortality can be drawn' from them. More minor
blasts got into print after 1835, but the figure remained incomplete
until the returns of the Registrar General and the inspectors of
mines in the late 1840s and early 1850s.[46]

The best figures which do exist for our period come from two
sources. First, the coalowners took a private calculation, based
on a sample of collieries, for the years 1811–15. These show a
rate of mortality from all causes by violence at work of 8.1 per
1000 employed per year. Hair reckons the real figure was probably
higher, up to 10 per 1000 employed per year. Second, the coalowner
and safety campaigner T.J. Taylor, produced figures for the 1849
Parliamentary enquiry which, Hair says, 'may well be exact
statistics'. Taylor's figures are reproduced below, alongside later
figures from the inspectors.

TABLE 1   *Deaths from violence in 55 North-East collieries, 1839–45,
and in all North-East collieries, 1851–3 (per 1,000 employed
per year)*[47]

	Total Deaths	Explosions	Death from roof falls	Other accidents
1839–45	6·1	3·1	1·3	1·7
1851–3	3·5	0·9	1·1	1·5

One can see that during the 1840s, although there were marginal (and questionable) improvements in the rate of deaths from roof falls and other accidents, there appears to have been a marked improvement in safety relating to gas. Taken with the coal trade figures from 1811–15, a general rise in safety standards appears to have started in the 1820s. Of course, that there was an improvement is not to say that standards were good. Compared to the overwhelming majority of jobs, coalmining was a very dangerous occupation. Moreover, it is probable that all these figures, even the best ones, are underestimates. Nevertheless, one must try to explain the reasons for improvement. We have already seen strong criticism of ventilation practices during the period. We have already seen how the Davy lamp heightened dangers by making the broken workings more accessible. In the light of this evidence it might be useful to look to the organisation of labour rather than technology for reasons behind improved safety. The period saw efforts towards the greater systematisation of work and the better regulation of workers. It will be suggested that the resulting diminution in the volatility of their labour contributed to the mitigation of their risks. It will be further suggested that one of the major agents in this diminution was the unofficial action of the men themselves.

Coalmining remained a labour-intensive industry throughout the nineteenth century and although there were important technological innovations, and the industry is famous for them,[48] they had little direct bearing on the *system* and *organisation* of labour. Major innovations since the eighteenth century were in steam water-pumping, tram and 'rolley' ways, steam inclined plane and railway engines (above-ground), air coursing and splitting, safety lamps, gunpowder, iron tubs, long fuses, and wire ropes. Of these, as we have seen, safety lamps and powder-blasting had the most direct influence on the organisation of labour, and certainly increased the intensity of the work itself. Inadequate ventilation of deep mines and powder-blasting probably combined to increase respiratory difficulties. There was concern in the late 1840s about what constituted a comfortable current of air at the face: 8 mph was inconvenient; 4 mph was better. Observers noted the respiration of pitmen. The first English medical paper on 'Black Spots on the Lungs' was published in 1813 but it was not until 1831 that Gregory at Edinburgh related it to coalmining, and not until 1837 that doctors Stratton at North Shields and Thomson at

Edinburgh classically established it as a dust disease, 'anthracosis'
− later (1874) to be named *pneumoconiosis anthracosica*.
Advanced medical research was beginning to understand the illness,
but casual witnesses did not seem to know whether what they often
termed 'asthma' was a chemical or a physical condition of gas,
or dust, or both:

> ... the laborious work of 'hewing' ... excites, like other violent exercises,
> a great respiratory action; he breathes deep, and draws into his lungs
> with avidity this loaded mixture. His chest is bare, and the whole class
> of his respiratory muscles are in beautiful action; consequently he
> expectorates black matter; he breathes thick; and he is subject to
> asthma. If he has a consumptive taint, he speedily falls a victim to that
> disease, his breathing is rarely natural, that is, inaudible ...[49]

The other innovations were less important in their bearing on
labour. Water pumping innovations enabled mines to go deeper.
Air coursing and splitting created a new category of worker, the
'trapper', lowest in the hierarchy and responsible for keeping the
door-ways shut. Wire ropes were distrusted by some. At Wingate
Grange colliery in 1843 the pitmen were forced to accept wire ropes
against their wishes, wishes − 'on the ground of pretended want
of confidence in [their] safety' − which the viewers and owners
did not take seriously. Iron rails speeded underground haulage,
and the increasing use of pit ponies aided 'helping up', but there
is no evidence to suggest that they were unpopular with 'putters'
who hauled the trams and tubs. Although it is possible that the
intensity of the work increased − 'Thinks the boys now do,
perhaps, the same amount of work in less time' − it is also possible
that iron rails allowed the boys the opportunity of shorter hours,
and one former putter even wrote a poem in praise of them:

> But *heavy puttens* now forgotten,
> Sic as we had i former days,
> Ower holey thill and dyels a' spletten' −
> *Trams* now a' run on *metal ways.*[50]

The greater systematisation of the pitmen's labour is not explained
by technology; in the exhaustive detail of their work, that work
remained much the same:

> ... begrimed men, kneeling, sitting, stooping, sometimes lying, and
> hammering at the black wall of coal before them with short, sharp,
> heavy picks ... The pick and the spade are here the hewer's only

weapons; and the intensity of his toil is proportioned to the hardness of the coal and the shallowness of the seam. The best hewers are those who manage, by ingenious shifts of posture, and great endurance, to bring the coal rapidly and freely down ...
(Anon., *The Pits and the Pitmen*, n.d., 1850s, pp. 10–11)

Imagine a rough, pitch-dark tunnel, three feet wide and four feet high, through which, bent double all the way, and perspiring in a temperature of 75 degrees, you have to shove a wagon holding seven hundredweights of coal. (Children's Employment Commission, 1842)

'Boys must be employed to drive; and men to hew' and little could be done to change it.[51]

In a labour-intensive industry workers were systematised more by organisation than by technology. Board and pillar, and the single shift of about eight hours for hewers and twelve hours for boys, was the 'traditional' mode of operation in 1842, although there is some evidence that boys worked a regular fourteen-hour day prior to 1832.[52] In times of high demand, collieries would resort to mad bouts of production, lasting the equivalent of two or three stints, which the 1842 Children's Employment Commission condemned. The Commission referred to these bouts as 'double shifts', and particularly criticised them for putting people to work at night:

That in the great majority of these mines night-work is a part of the ordinary system of labour, more or less regularly carried on according to the demand for coals, and one which the whole body of evidence shews to act most injuriously both on the physical and moral condition of the work-people, and more especially on that of the children and young persons.

Against this charge, the proprietors replied that the 'double shift is now very rare'.[53] However, there was some confusion here. Lord Ashley, who led the 1842 Royal Commission, appears to have been talking of the 'ordinary system of labour' which always involved night work – hewers starting at about 3 am and boys at 5 am, on a single shift. But his later reference to night work 'carried on according to the demand for coals' was picked up by the proprietors as a reference to the mad bouts which could last the equivalent of two shifts and dismissed as exceptions to the rule.

In fact, a regular system of double shifts, involving two shorter, hewers' shifts of about six hours each, supported by one long boys' shift of about twelve hours, was becoming the rule in the 1840s.

There were two reasons for this new system. The first was the adoption of powder-blasting which raised productivity and had less use for two hewers in a board at the same time; and the second was the 'judding' technique in the broken:

> ... when there are two sets they work about six hours, one after the other ... When the pillars are removed, it is necessary to do it quickly, and therefore two parties are put on ... It is less dangerous work when it is rapidly done ...[54]

When Angus Reach visited the coalfield for the *Morning Chronicle* in 1849, he found 'A great number of the pits' working this double shift.[55] That he fixed the hours at eight, 'fore' shift 2 am to 10 am and 'back' shift 8 am to 4 pm, and the 1842 witness fixed the hours at six, suggests either a decline in hewers' conditions since 1842 or a misunderstanding about when shifts started and ended – 'bank to bank' or time at the coal-face? Whatever the exact hours, this double shift became standard practice in the northern coalfield and was one major determinant in the pitmen's ability to win for themselves a uniquely privileged position by the end of the century. During the 1850s (with the unions weak) hewers' hours were about nine, and the boys about twelve; during the 1860s hewers' hours fell to between seven and a half and eight; from 1871–3 hewers' fell to six and a half, and boys' to about ten. These gains were lost from the late 1870s into the 1880s, with the hewers back on seven and a half, and the boys on eleven. By the 1890s the hewers were down to six and a half to seven, and the boys down to ten hours. The hewers' hours in the 1890s were probably the shortest in the British working class.[56] Men in the 1840s were comparing their shorter hours with the situation 'fifty years ago' when labour was expected to meet what was for them the random demands of a market which could claim double or even treble stints: 'Not only has the severity of his labour been much lessened' it was said, 'but the duration of it has been considerably shortened' – 'by blowing the coal down with gunpowder ... the labour of the hewer has ... been much abridged.'[57]

However, the short double shift was relatively new in the 1840s, and its impact on the system of labour, certainly in terms of significantly reorganising that labour, is problematic. The pitman's own collective efforts were probably more important. Indeed, in the detail of the hewer's work, his own choice was the only feasible agent of significant change. At the coal-face, where the pick was thrown from the shoulder, the pitmen were virtually autonomous. Unlike factory workers, their labour was not open to constant supervision, and this autonomy the pitmen valued as a sign of their craft and as a mark of their status. They could produce, and they could not-produce. One of the problems of assessing hours, a problem shown in the inexactness above, is quite simply that hewers did not keep fixed, synchronic, hours. Within the broad span of a shift, they pleased themselves. Evidence from the whole of the nineteenth century testifies to this fact. The 1835 Select Committee were told that regular working was essential to the industry but 'it must be left to the general feeling of the workmen' for 'There is no time appointed'; the Board of Trade reported in 1891 that:

> It should, perhaps be stated that short time does not necessarily mean bad trade, the miners sometimes preferring to work less than the ordinary full time ... There is, however, no novelty about it, for in various reports about 50 years old, concerning the condition of the mining population, reference is frequently made to the same kind of thing.[58]

Much of the late century evidence about the pitmen's discretionary powers concerned the recent introduction of 'advanced longwall' techniques in Northumberland and Durham, techniques which meant a more closely supervised work-force. The pitmen's discretion was much older than the fifty years estimated by the Board of Trade, for it was connected to the board and pillar technique which, of all techniques, needed the least supervision.[59]

The growth of trade unionism in the coalfield from the 1820s[60] saw efforts to control this autonomy in the collective interests of the pitmen as a whole. The unions' primary case was that each hewer's autonomy had not acted in their collective interest; that autonomy had not brought independence but an anarchy of production where men and boys competed with each other in pride, for price, through a culture which celebrated the marks of manliness and skill as one. The unions expended their strength against this culture, the culture of the 'big hewer'. At Merrington colliery there was

> A HEWING MATCH EVERY DAY at this flat, and in order to satisfy the competitors and keep our turn, Bill and I worked like horses, going home after each twelve hours' shift with sore and tired bones. This kind of thing, which went on year after year amongst miners, broke

down strong men, and kept down the ... price in every district. In fact, it is only too true that this slavish, ignorant, and clumsy competition kept criminal passions predominant over the better part of the miners' natures.[61]

The northern coal industry in the first half of the nineteenth century suffered from over-expansion of capacity, and periodic gluts and shortages. The owner's cartel, the Vend, adjusted output to maintain market-share in London. As the market was considered under-supplied or over-supplied according to oligopolistic manoeuvre, then the mining community suffered feast or famine, mad bouts of work or short-time. Under such conditions, and learning from the regulatory lessons of their employers, the early unions called for prudence.

The first formal union in the coalfield was 'The United Association of Colliers' founded in 1825. One of its first deeds was to declare its principled opposition to the detail of the pitman's work. Whilst admitting the owners' case that some hewers (in some places at some times) could earn seven or eight shillings in a day, the union claimed such examples to be untypical. Some eccentrics of gigantic strength might earn high wages but at 'the leading collieries' excess earnings were now a 'moral impossibility':

> ... have the pitmen to bury themselves in the pit 12 hours per day, work like irrationals, gormandize like cannibals − then work little, get into their holes and live on their grease?

Once the collective principle had been established, it remained for the union to legislate for it. The United Colliers' *Rules and Regulations* stated that their four thousand hewers were not to work more than eight hours, or earn more than 4s 6d, in a day. If any hewer earned more than this then his union reserved the right to fine him the whole of his earnings for the day. As money made him irrational, so money could make him rational.[62] This was 'Restriction', the fundamental strategy of Northumberland and Durham miners' unionism in the nineteenth century. Restriction was preached and practiced whenever and wherever the union was strong enough: prior to, and during, the strikes of 1831−2; through the mid-1830s; prior to, and during, the strike of 1844; in the late 1840s as a central part of National Miners' Association policy; and in the early 1850s. The 1873 Select Committee noted, with regret, its continued operation, it seems to have been

the major determinant of falling levels of productivity from the
1870s; and the 1892 Royal Commission on Labour could not
break down John Wilson's or Ralph Young's cool defence of its
benefits:

> Then I gather that your Association is against men in the full vigour
> of life, working longer hours or ... being permitted to earn more ...
> than they otherwise would be quite willing and anxious to do? – Our
> Association thinks this, that taking the number of years the aggregate
> average result will be that the man will make as much by being restrained
> into a proper quantum of hours as he would if he had a free hand.
>
> The question of hours is therefore a question for a class? – Yes. Not
> for an individual? – No.
>
> There is no exception to your rule; that is to say, that a man, however
> able and willing to work longer, your Association would object to his
> doing so – Yes.[63]

So certain was the fact of the pitmen's discretion over the time
they worked, and so ubiquitous was the advocacy of Restriction
from the 1820s to the 1890s, it seems that less intensive labour
and/or a shorter working day was more a thing that the men took
than a thing they were given (by Act of Parliament), or negotiated
(as they did in 1871 and 1891). The taking was such a long drawn-
out, informal, and uneven affair that late nineteenth-century
miners' leaders appear to have been unsure as to its origins.
Testifying before the Royal Commission in 1892 Ralph Young
needed two answers before he could clarify his opinion:

> And have the hours of the workmen been shortened through the com-
> bined action of the men mainly? – Well, we have not anything very
> clear or specific, I am afraid, upon this point, but I think at one or
> two collieries one could almost say that it was by the action of the Union
> that the hours were shortened. But I am inclined to think that the
> introduction of the short-shift system was principally due to the
> introduction of blasting.
>
> Do you consider that the reduction in the hours, whether it is com-
> pulsory or by custom, has been brought about owing to the individual
> desire on the part of the workmen to limit their hours, or that it has
> been in consequence of a sort of generally recognized arrangement
> brought about by the Trade Societies? – I should think by desire
> on the part of the workmen to reduce their hours whenever it was
> opportune for them to do so. I think that the opportunity for reducing
> the hours was afforded them when the principle of blasting became
> general in the county.[64]

At least there was no doubt that Restriction policies had steadied and systematised the organisation of the pitmen's labour. In 1835 it was reported that the men 'do not work so hard now'; in 1836 it was lamented that the men do not 'put forth their powers as they could'; in 1842 the viewer of Urpeth colliery dated steadier working from 1832, 'Since the strike extreme labour would be scarcely tolerated', whilst the underviewer of Hetton colliery dated it from the 1820s, 'They were more headstrong men at that time; now they give themselves an hour or so longer, and work more regularly.' In 1844 a Thornley pitman wrote to state his thanks for the results of this dispersal of effort:

> Men and boys do not strive so much for the mastery as they formerly did. He was the best man that could perform the most work and get the largest sum of money. Hewing matches have been frequent, and very often followed up with fighting. These things have been the downfall of the Miners for many years but I feel very thankful that the Union and restricting principle (under the blessing of Providence) are doing away with these things.[65]

Given the hewer's autonomy, Restriction was a cultural assault which demanded the persuasion of individuals. Hewing matches were a fairly common feature of the eighteenth-century press. For example, in 1766 a hewer called Hatherick at Holywell Main colliery wagered he could cut a whole twenty-five hundredweight London chaldron in a single $9' \times 4\frac{1}{2}' \times 9'$ piece — and the epic 'big hewer' remained a potent source of pitmen's self-identity well into the nineteenth century. However, when John Temperley of Craghead, acknowledged 'big hewer' of the 1840s, restricted himself to do in two and a half hours what it took most men seven hours to hew, then the union had made a personal cultural conversion towards a collective salvation where 'we think it fair to stand by each other as a body, and not to go on competing'.[66] There were other, informal and personal benefits in Restriction, such as the 'carrying' of men who needed help, but it was essentially a union strategy: it was 'to the Union what the mainspring is to a watch' said William Cloughan, a district secretary, in 1846. On those occasions when Restriction was not observed at collieries outside the union's control, the union used shaming to enforce its influence. In 1843 six hewers had been sent from South Hetton colliery to begin new operations at nearby Murton. Although all six had abided by Restriction at South Hetton, they broke it at

Murton. The National Miners' Association reported their action and named names.[67]

This restricted working was necessary to a generation of pitmen who faced uncontrolled changes in the conditions and status of their work. Restricted, regulated, steadier labour was a way of imposing some control. Although it is difficult to make simple generalisations – work details varied with the twist and texture of seam and strata – by the 1840s the pitmen were conscious of a general deterioration in their conditions and status.[68] Using a different language, that of health and morals, a good deal of the 1842 Royal Commission's concern is about the nature and relationship of these factors. In March 1843 at a union meeting near Newcastle, speakers Pyle, Embleton, Watson, Brophy, Cloughan, and Swallow were all agreed on the matter of deterioration: on increased water and damp; increased gas risk and defective ventilation; increasing incidence of thinner, deeper, hotter, seams where men had to work naked and 'crawl to and fro in the tunnels like beasts of burden'.[69] They also noted the increasing intensities of a speedier productive operation, the consequence of short-time working – damaging to Restriction – where men were pressed to do three days work in two and, so it was claimed, do the work with bigger 'corves'. Corves were basket-tubs, traditionally holding about ten to thirty pecks and acting as the unit-measure of the hewer's pay. At the meeting, Ben Embleton told a tale:

> In one colliery, there was once a corf [alternative spelling] so big that it held 41 pecks; and woe to the poor hewer who got this unconscionable corf, for it was sure to clean him out! (Great laughter) At last, a sly pitman asked the viewer, as a favour, to make him a present of the corf, that he might use one end of it for a cow-byer, and the other for a piggery! [Roars of laughter] The corf never showed its face in the pit again.[70]

3
New disciplines

The double shift system and union Restriction policies were the beginnings of fundamental changes in the organisation of work. These changes were accompanied by a new disciplining of the workers.

The first public declaration that the pitmen were generically inadequate to their task was in 1813. On 25 May 1812 the Brandling Main colliery at Felling exploded and killed ninety-two men and boys. Revd John Hodgson, vicar of the parish, buried the dead and rebuked the living and argued that the traditional craft-sense of the pitmen could no longer be trusted by educated men who had read science. On the day after the explosion, pitmen from all over the coalfield assembled at Felling to suggest ways in which they could attempt a rescue of any victims who might be trapped. It was a matter of some urgency because the owners of the colliery were anxious to surrender hopes of rescue and block up the pit to extinguish the fires and save their investment. Of the assembled pitmen, Hodgson said:

> Every one had some example to relate of successful attempts in cases of this kind ... Their reasonings and assertions seemed indeed to be a mixture of those prejudices and conceits which cleave to workmen who experience has afforded a partial insight into the nature and peculiarities of their profession, and not to be grounded on any memory of facts, or to result from a knowledge of the connection between causes and effects.[1]

By the 1830s, Hodgson's sort of distrust had flowered into a full critique and displacement of the pitmen's craft. More and more, it was the viewers who were claiming the rights of pitmanship alligned with a true 'knowledge of the connection between causes and effects'. Their claim to this knowledge, as a band of experts, was given credence by the 'constant and continual succession of improvements, alterations, and adoptions of new systems, or modes of working' which they were busy introducing.[2] Also, the viewers were becoming increasingly important as consultants to floating capital which was permanently seeking lucrative investment opportunities and was in need of commercial and geological advice. Leading viewers like John Buddle valued their knowledge as 'capital'; it was entrepreneurial as well as scientific. Buddle's printed card set his fees on a scale from five guineas to one hundred guineas depending on the value of the pit, with two guineas a day expenses.[3]

Although the viewers' knowledge, transmitted through family dynasties and informal apprenticeships, was as much based on experience as the pitmen's, it was also acquiring the formalities of a profession. National mineralogical and geological societies were founded in 1799 and 1807; Adam Sedgwick turned the Cambridge Chair of Geology from a sinecure into a serious activity from 1818 and was not modest in lending his advice to pitmen and owners alike; Newcastle had a Colliery Viewers' Society from 1826 (although it was not initially well-supported); the Geological Survey was founded in 1835; in 1852 the North of England Institute of Mining Engineers was founded, in splendid premises with a splendid first President – Nicholas Wood, 'Member of the Institute of Civil Engineers, Fellow of the Geological Society, Mining Engineer and President of the Society'.[4] Although it was not until 1880 (first Chair of Mining, Armstrong College, Newcastle), and 1903 (first Home Office sanctioned degree for colliery management at Newcastle), that this fund of experience was formally recognised as knowledge, as early as 1838 it had been a professional academic, the Reader in Chemistry and Mineralogy at Durham University, who had called for scientific management:

> The management of large bodies of workmen is a subject of great importance. It is an art of great delicacy, which most people think very easy to be acquired, and yet which very few persons ever thoroughly attain. The first object should be to instruct them, so that when you appeal to their reason you may be certain of being understood.[5]

By 1852, the President of the Institute was claiming an exclusive responsibility for the 'Art and Science of Mining' for his own eighty members. In 'the Science and economy of mining,' he claimed for them the nomenclature of miners *and* professionals:

> ... it is an Institution of practical miners associated together, to
> endeavour by a combination of practical knowledge – by an inter-
> change of practical experience – and by a united and combined effort,
> to improve ourselves in the science of our profession.

When Sir Edward Harland questioned Ralph Young for the Royal
Commission on Labour in 1892 about University Extension courses
in the colliery villages, he was told about 'Science and Art classes'.
By this time, so complete was the displacement of professional
knowledge from the pitmen, Harland could hardly believe Young's
evidence, asking 'Are not those very big words, "Science and Art
classes" among the colliers?.'[6] Buoyed up by fifty years of State
recognition of their practices – good practices compared with the
managerial absurdities of the butty systems of other places – and
made confident by a professional identity going back even longer,
northern viewers in the 1880s were certain of their responsibilities
for what happened underground.[7]

The professionalisation of the viewers brought a new scrutiny
of the pitmen. In 1835, it was testified that what had once been
a simple job calling for burly strength and impetuous energy was
now a more complex and technical operation calling for thought
and system. The pitmen were guilty of 'a wanton neglect of
ordinary caution, and a recklessness of danger in defiance of common discretion'. One witness threw another light on these charges
by testifying that the recklessness only applied when their own lives
were in danger; for 'the lives of their comrades', they were 'very
particular'. In other contexts this could be called bravery, but in
this context it was worthy of condemnation. One owner reported
carelessness with gunpowder 'and my life has been put in peril by
such careless acts as one cannot suppose'; a scientist confirmed
that pitmen were 'extremely reckless of accident', whilst Nicholas
Wood concurred that few pitmen had knowledge 'about what is
going on in the pits; they exhibit a sort of indifference in that
respect'.[8]

By the 1840s this critique of craft had, in its turn, been
transformed into a total theory of class psychological instability.
Whether by neglect at work, or by political misleading, or by trade
union cupidity, or because of wilful ignorance, or irreligion, or
the wrong kind of religion, the mining community was diagnosed
as suffering from a taste for crimes of social *passion*. Scientists
Playfair and de la Beche identified the notorious 'thoughtless

daring' of pitmen, and Commissioner Seymour Tremenheere described the same disposition in his report on the 1844 strike:

> ... that there was no cause, in any of the grievances ... for a movement so injurious to others as well as themselves. The immediate and effective cause can only be found in the excitability of their peculiar tone and temper of mind.[9]

Owners and viewers came to demand the disciplining of this 'peculiar tone and temper'. The old method had been to prosecute offenders in court. This was rare, and always exemplary in intention. In 1832 Lord Londonderry prosecuted Robert Kennedy, a hewer, for rearranging brattices across air courses to stop his candle from going out:

> The present prosecution is instituted more for the sake of preserving regularity and preventing accidents ... than with a view of inflicting any severe punishment upon the prisoner. The workings of the Marquis' Collieries are so extensive, and the lamentable effects which might be produced in consequence of conduct similar ... has induced the Managers ... to take the present proceedings.

No doubt Mr Kennedy, who had first responded to the viewer's challenge by raising his pick, was suitably quelled by the court. The problem was that this half-system of legal threat and studied fortuity was coming to be seen as unfitting either to the scale of investments or to the psychological temper of the work-force. The new call was for 'an organised system of mining'.[10]

The theory and practice of colliery safety unfailingly pointed to the need for worker subordination. John Phillips had given his Royal Society opinion in 1850 that decent engineering alone 'will not ensure safety ... unless there be a vigilant administration, due subordination of authority, constant inspection, and effective discipline ...' Select committees and their witnesses underlined this opinion throughout the decade.[11] The Index to the 1835 Report had a large section on *'Lamp Discipline, and Punishment of Miners for using it improperly'*. Work-rules began to appear in northern collieries from the late 1840s – Robert Stephenson had printed instructions at his pits in the 1830s – and, under growing pressure from the government, the owners, and the inspectorate, uniform County Regulations were drawn up in 1854.[12] The 1855 Mines Act brought in *general* rules with an emphasis on engineering, to apply to all collieries, and *special* rules with an emphasis on labour discipline, drawn up by each colliery and checked by the Home Office. Here was an opportunity to clarify control without the usual negotiation. These regulations beat-out the correct *tempo* of the mine: constant control, proper posting, graded foremen, sober conduct, stringent discharge:

> Workmen and boys are also required to inform themselves of the rules, for which purpose each workman is furnished with a printed copy, which is to be taken care of, as the loss of it will be considered a delinquency.[13]

Castle Eden colliery drew up one hundred work-rules in 1847. In them, every movement and action of the pitman was to be predetermined and controlled; the regularity of all underground habits was stressed; all relationships between men and supervisory grades was defined; all job responsibilities, obligations, and duties were allotted. Under the rules, the aim of greater safety under more difficult conditions was not unrelated to the intention to break the pitmen's autonomy. Rule 19 made 'Restriction' solely the company's privilege:

> The overmen to regulate, at the commencement of each day, the workings of the different ways in each pit, and the quantity of coals to be worked by each man, so as to equalize as nearly as possible the earnings of the hewers.

Rule 37, in its statement of extra duties for hewers, denied union demands and insulted a whole culture of manhood and hewing:

> The hewers are to work the different seams according to the plan and in the manner ordered by the owners or their agents ... and are to do the business of the drivers, and set on tubs when it shall be requisite; and the hewers and drivers are, when required by the owners or agents, to put with trams or act as barrowmen.

Similarly, the County Regulations defined subordination and management and offence but, significantly, did not invite pitmen to the conference which drew them up. Owners, engineers, and inspectors met in London in May 1854, but only workers' petitions were accepted.[14]

Although the union accepted the need for safety rules – David Swallow said of the County Rules 'we embrace the whole of them' – the owners never failed to indicate equally that the government was wrong to expect either greater discipline or greater safety from printed rules alone. What mattered most was who enforced the rules. The union insisted that effective discipline rested in the character of deputies and overmen, and as long as these men lacked respect there could be no change. There was a gradual realisation of a direct relationship between danger and poor management:

> Although the actual occurrence of explosions may often be traced to the ignorance or carelessness of the subordinate agents, or of the workmen, their primary causes even in these cases, must be generally assigned to the want of skill and care in the management of the mine, which has produced the conditions that render this carelessness dangerous.[15]

A depressing picture of incompetence and victimisation emerges in the 1850s: of some supervisory 'safety' grades who were not good enough for complex mining; of miners who were not willing to trade their safety for company favour. As the trade unionist Martin Jude testified in 1853:

> It is generally well known to viewers what men in each pit are inclined to raise difficulties, and what men are not? − Yes,
>
> And when they find difficulties of various kinds arise they are very apt to pick out those men who they think have been at the bottom of these disturbances, or these combinations of men, and so forth? − Yes.[16]

Inspector of Mines Matthias Dunn rather attributed the resulting reticence 'to their not being sensible of danger', but it does seem that many deputies and overmen were picked as favourites rather than as able men, and Jude's phrase 'moral unfitness' well captures the contempt of men of his sort for men of that sort:

> In going to the pit was past Storey's house, and saw Bell, the overman, and Barras, a deputy, singing and drinking in the house. They would have to go down the pit between twelve and one o'clock that night. I consider the colliery generally to be in a bad state, and never in a proper state. (Robert Todd)
>
> Many of them do not attend to their duties; they drink with the overmen and deputies, and when the under viewer drinks, all the others must follow as a matter of course. (Martin Jude)[17]

Against such patronised incompetence, those men who were mindful of safety needed to be independent-minded:

> The fact is, that if we wish our fellow-workmen to unite in support of their interests, they tell us we are agitators, that they do not want us on the colliery, and that we must seek work elsewhere ...

... and as soon as the men attempt to combine the leading men of the combination receive notice to quit the colliery. In this way they are prevented from combining, and that is a pretty general thing throughout the county of Durham.[18]

The National Miners' Association was a staunch campaigner for a government inspectorate of mines. The 1842 Mines Act (5 & 6 Vict., c. 99) had appointed the first inspector, but Tremenheere was more an inspector of the conditions of the workers (under the Act), rather than the conditions of the workings. Tremenheere had a certain integrity and proved to be an influential educator, but he was neither a miner, nor an engineer, nor was his brief to report on the technical operations underground. In 1849 the Northumberland and Durham pitmen petitioned the Lords' Select Committee for 'properly qualified Inspectors of Mines (such inspectors being practical miners)', and Swallow and Jude testified for the union:

> What the colliers generally want is some one to point out the danger; and if the masters do not remove it, then subject them to a penalty; but give them the option to remove it.

The owners retorted that their viewers were talented and professional engineers and should not be forced to enjoy unsolicited government advice:

> I think that if an Inspector is appointed who has the power to go and order in any way, the mode of working the colliery, he then takes the responsibility, and then I think the mine-owner ought not to be liable for any accident which happens in the mine after such orders are given.[19]

The 1849 Report in fact recommended the appointment of qualified inspectors, and the 1850 Act for Inspection of Coal Mines in Great Britain (13 & 14 Vict., c. 100) appointed four. The 1850 Act, in the main, accepted the owners' plea and granted the inspectorate only powers of petty fining. However, by 1852 the Select Committee had come round to the union's 1849 position:

> To increase the power of the inspector is a ... delicate matter. To this some of the most intelligent of the managers of mines who were examined objected ...
>
> Your Committee therefore having full regard to the rights and privileges of private property, but at the same time forming, to the best of their ability, a due estimate of the value of human life ... consider that they should fail in their duty if they did not recommend that a power should be placed somewhere to enforce precautions and to facilitate

the exaction of penalties, where neglect of such precautions was pertinaciously persevered in; and that until those precautions were adopted, there should exist a power to stop the working of the mine.[20]

In 1860, after ten years of inspection, the Mines Regulation and Inspection Bill (23 & 24 Vict, c. 11) was passed. The Act not only increased the powers of the inspectorate but also legislated for fundamental changes in the operation of collieries, making them more uniform.

Those who called for new discipline also called for new schooling. John Phillips wanted mining schools for officials because 'knowledge is nowhere more powerful, obedience nowhere more necessary than in a coal mine'.[21] Education was to supplement discipline. An appropriate schooling would make for 'better management and care on the part of the overlookers' and 'less recklessness on the part of the workmen'. An early nineteenth-century distrust of the gifts of education was replaced by a mid-century theory of its uses:

> When we look at the enormous money value of the iron and coal ... the comparative expense of producing auxiliary schools in the country would be next to nothing.

And Inspector Mackworth, if he recognised education, he also recognised control:

> Do you think that education of the colliers and overmen would be the means of insuring better discipline? — I think that the education of both is of very great importance ... In the case of the collier, he becomes more careful and attentive; and by adopting a system of reward or promotion for education and intelligence, I think the best system of discipline may be introduced into the mines, ... Education is an instrument of great power for good which position has placed into the hands of the master if he will use it aright.[22]

Because 'the elder people are not so attentive to particular orders as might be expected', some mine schooling for children was also advocated. The union agreed that children might be socialised in the system of the mine but their concurrence on schooling was qualified in the same way as their concurrence on inspectors. As they wanted an inspectorate supported by and perhaps even re-cruited from their own ranks, so they also wanted pitmen on school committees and some working-class control over the style and content of education. Tremenheere, anxious to establish education schemes in order to heal class conflict, took the union's advocacy of schooling as a sign of common agreement in 'principle', but it is clear that the union's idea of education was different from the curriculum that was eventually adopted.[23]

From Tremenheere's and the experts' side, a properly constituted education was not to be about 'merely abstract things, but really valuable knowledge', and was presented as a way of adapting pitmen to their social and occupational place under changing conditions.[24] The socialisation of the schoolroom would counter the endemic instability of the community; it would condition the habits and responses of its young proletariat; it would train them in a proper proletarian temper by regularising their calendar:

> 'Idle Monday' is ... one of the greatest indications, of the general low condition of intelligence ... and long before there cease to be idle Mondays the population will be better educated, and that will lead to fewer idle Mondays ...;

by improving their punctuality:

> Discussing what this education should be, he enlarged upon punctuality in attendance as of great importance at mining schools ...;

and by making them sober, industrious, and 'redeemed':

> Educated boys would be less reckless and do better work, and when these boys become men their labour in the days redeemed from dissipation and idleness would more than recompense the employers for any sacrifice they have made in allowing them to school.[25]

This training in proletarian temper represented little more than property's taste in a new propriety for old pitmen. In 1849, Tremenheere, a zealous weaver of the State's expectations with capitalist intentions, praised the density of schools and churches in Consett, a new iron-making town on the Durham moors, as an example of what could and should be done to condition 'a whole adult generation ... grown up under a system of almost entire neglect'. Consett, and 'new industrial colonies' like it, would grow to be fireproof from the machinations of Chartists and trade unionists. Five years later Tremenheere had to concede that his expectations had yet to be achieved there, but he remained optimistic.[26] Working-class practices and ideas could and should be discounted. As 'Ignorance cannot detect its own wants', the real proletariat would have to surrender the right to its own authenticity:

> To teach children to read, to write, and to cipher, may be within the
> capacity of an ordinary labouring man, made into a schoolmaster after
> some accident disabling him from work. But all persons are now agreed
> that this is not education.[27]

'All' those persons who knew what education was, on the other
hand, had to try to provide it. There were limits to this of course
– in particular it had to be inexpensive. Nevertheless, in 1847
Tremenheere could report to the State on a virtual revolution in
northern employers' attitudes to education:

> ... an indication that practical men, having large capitals at stake, have
> had sufficient proof of the inconveniences and losses arising from the
> contrary principle of leaving those matters to the spontaneous efforts
> of the people themselves.[28]

What finer reference of a proper industrial temper than the
insurance companies? Dr Davidson testified in 1866 that whereas
in the past no insurance company would accept a pitman, they
were now canvassing the collieries for customers.[29]

The pitmen were increasingly the subjects of social and occupational regulation which, in turn, invited a changing perception of
their 'character'. In 1854 it was explained that the northern miners,
unlike Cornish miners, were straightforward wage labourers and
had 'to depend more upon other persons'. One year later, William
Whellan's topography celebrated the North's 'due subordination',
'constant inspection', and 'effective discipline':

> The great Newcastle mines may be said to be established upon a system
> of effective and excellent discipline, which has been arrived at by
> degrees, and has been much improved within a comparatively recent
> period.[30]

Those who traded in perceptions of this kind were confident of
the accuracy of this observation by the last quarter of the century.
Henry de la Beche saluted the new miner who 'works more as a
machine, or a soldier', and Revd Street said he had once heard
the mining community described as 'rude and barbarous' but now
'Never was there a greater libel published upon an industrial
class, so far as the miners of Northumberland were concerned'.[31]
In view of this it is as well to remember that at first, conservative
coalowners had opposed the growing faith in schooling on the
grounds that it was irrelevant and would damage the skilled line
of born and bred pitmen. The true pitman must start young:

'we cannot well dispense with the service of small boys'. John Buddle had regarded any outside − especially Metropolitan and State − interferences as likely to impair the skills needed:

> What we have to guard against is any obnoxious legislative interference in the established Customs of our peculiar race of Pitmen. The stock can only be kept up by breeding − it never could be recruited from an adult population. It is like bringing Lads up to the Sea − only the Pit Lad's Life is incomparably better and more comfortable than the Sailor's. But if our meddling morbid humanity mongers get it infused into their heads, that it is cruel, unnatural, Slavery to work in the dark − and to be imprisoned 12 hours a day in the Pit, a Screw in the system, will be let loose ...[32]

It was only a short time, some thirty years, between Buddle's perception of the pitmen as animals and later perceptions of them as machines. By the turn of the nineteenth century this bred and born 'stock' no longer existed; it had since been fitfully buried under an eventual 239,000 men, fifty million tons annually,[33] and the maturation of those work changes we have seen in the previous two chapters − loss of caste, shift work, Restriction, reorganisation, regulated and disciplined working. A community of men was declared to have changed its social character: 'the economy of the mine is not less perfect than that of any well-ordered establishment above ground', and the pitman was more and more seen as one of its operatives.[34]

4
The Bond and the Vend

The pitmen's contract of hire, the Bond, was the central article of labour regulation. A legal document of productive relations, the Bond also interpreted social relations.

The first recorded bond is for 26 November 1703 at Dawson's Pit, Benwell colliery, near Newcastle.[1] Complete bonds for the eighteenth century exist only randomly, and they are scarce until the late 1760s when sporadic examples begin to appear.[2] From the 1760s there are sufficient bonds to make analysis feasible and, in the early nineteenth century the character of the Bond changes so radically, and complementary evidences present themselves so readily, that the scarcity and randomness is no longer a problem. The origin of the Bond system is obscure. It did exist in other occupations, notably agriculture, and the most likely explanation for it is that it was a late seventeenth- or early eighteenth-century attempt by coalowners to stabilise their labour force.[3]

The form and function of the Bond had changed by the 1850s. This chapter will concentrate on the Bond itself, and Chapter Five will consider the history of the 'binding' from the 1790s.

Pay and bonds

The Bond determined how much a pitman could earn by his labour. It contracted rates of payment for coal extracted; rates of fine for absence or unsatisfactory work; and a mass of allowances and extras inserted by negotiated custom, such as the binding-day annual expense paid by Sir John Delaval at Hartley colliery in 1778 – plus 'Bedmoney & Lent money, the first of which is alwais given in the Coll^e, to all Young men & the latter is regularly taken off in the Bills Through the Course of the Year'.[4] Although bonds became more uniform in the nineteenth century, the rates of pay, fine, and allowance tended to vary according to seam, pit, and colliery. Given these differences in rates, and differences in the strength and skill of pitmen, the Bond is a necessary but in no way sufficient source for inferences about the community's standards of living.

Differences in places of work were the most significant variables. Hewers extracted the coal and were paid by 'score price', a score generally consisting of twenty tubs or 'corves'. Putters pushed the full tubs away from the face to the 'rolley ways', underground roads, and were paid by score and distance. Putters were adolescent lads pushing either singly or in pairs, whilst the drivers, who drove the ponies and carts along the rolley ways, were usually younger boys. Like the youngest 'trappers' who controlled the underground doorways, the drivers were paid by the day. Piece rates for hewers and putters were more variable than day rates for drivers and trappers. They could vary between different seams in one colliery, as at Denton and Kenton in 1804 when hewers' rates in the Low Main seam were 3s 1d per score, and 5s per score in the Benwell Main seam. Even a single seam could have different rates. At Bushblades colliery in 1766, as well as differences in rates between the Hutton and 'Top' or 'Hard' seams, there were differences between parts of the Hutton seam: 1s 8d per score in the North and Prosperous pits, 1s 11d per score in the Hopewell pit.[5]

Rates also varied between 'whole' and 'broken' workings. At Byker and at St Anthony's colliery in 1770 the rate was 2s 6d per score in the whole and 2s in the broken. At Denton and Kenton in 1804 it was 3s 1d in the whole and 2s 11d in the broken of the Low Main seam, and 5s in the whole and 4s 10d in the broken of the Benwell Main seam.[6] Whether the hewer sent up 'round' or 'small' coals also meant a difference to his rates. Rounds were big coals, and smalls were defined as inferior to rounds by those who sold them. At the Delaval pits in 1770 hewers received 2d per corve for rounds and 1d for smalls; at Byker Hill in 1773 the rate was 1s 3d per score rounds, and 1s per score smalls. By 1776 Lord Delaval had increased his rates to 2¼d per corve rounds, and 1½d smalls.[7] Although the 1703 bond contracted putters to be paid by the day (1s 10d), putters came to be as dependent as hewers on the physical features of their workplace. For instance, at Charlaw colliery in 1767 they were paid 6d per score for basic runs of sixty and a hundred yards, with 1d extra per score for

every twenty yards over that distance.[8] 'Headway' work advanced
the coal-face and it too was paid by the yard. At Burnmoor colliery
in 1787 hewers received 1s 4d per yard, and at Walker colliery in
1788 10d per yard.[9]

There were also differences between collieries in their tub
measures. Tubs at Penshaw colliery in 1793 were expected to
measure twenty pecks, one peck equalling an 'eighteen quart
Winchester measure'

> ... of Clean pure Coals both round & small (the round Coals not to
> exceed 14 or 15 Inches at most Square) mixed together & free from
> any Mixture of Top or Roof Coals.[10]

The discrepancy between Charlaw colliery in 1767 at 1s 1d per
score, and Byker in 1770 at 2s 6d per score, may seem enormous
until one notes that Byker used twenty-peck corves and Charlaw
used eight-peck corves. A uniform system of mensuration did not
begin to appear until the 1820s, and that was gradually replaced
by measurements in weight.[11]

A major earnings variable obviously was the difference in the
strength and skill of pitmen. Table 2 shows differences in pay
among those twenty-three hewers who worked every one of ten
working days, in what should have been a twelve working day
'fortnight', at Ouston 'B' pit from 28 October to 11 November
1834, with rates at 3s 3d per score.

Table 2   *Hewers' pay, Ouston colliery 'B' pit, County Durham, 28 October–
11 November 1834*[12]

	£ s d		£ s d
Edward Pigg	1 16 1	George Elliot	1 1 11
George Eddy	1 16 0	Ralph Maddison	1 19 9
John Banks	1 13 1	Robert Hall	1 17 3
John Bainbridge	1 12 0	Thomas Smith	1 13 11
William Bell	1 14 10	John Hall	1 16 4
Andrew Smart	1 15 7	John Ridley	1 18 8
George Dunn	1 13 11	Francis Carr	1 17 1
Thomas Davis	1 4 7	James Haswell	1 19 0
John Gray	1 14 10	Edward Hall	1 15 11
John Simpson	1 2 9	Edward Kennan	1 19 6
Robert Usher	1 19 6	Charles Mayson	1 18 3
John Carr	1 14 10		

What must be said at once is that it is not possible to know to what degree some of these men, or all of them, were restricting their output according to union policy. The union was not strong in 1834, so restriction is an unlikely variable, but collective strength could remain at colliery level even when the union was weak across the coalfield. The group's average pay for the ten days was £1 14s 6d. Significant differences in pay are noticeable, but it is difficult to unravel how much of this was due to strength and skill and how much was due to various allowances for difficult or extra work. Ralph Maddison at £1 19s 9d was the best paid: 1s 9d accrued from 'ramble', a thin stratum of shale above the seam which caused separation problems and earned 4d per score bonus; 8s 4d accrued from ten yards headway at 10d per yard. George Elliot at £1 1s 11d was the lowest paid: all of his pay, except one yard headway, accrued from straight score price. Headway prices increased from 10d to 1s to 1s 2d per score for 'wet work' (John Hall got wet, but was paid 3s 8d for his trouble), and 4d per yard extra was paid to pairs of hewers doing headway in one board – 'double work'. Extras, bonuses, and the coal itself differed from place to place. To ensure equal opportunity for good or bad places the pitmen would draw quarterly lots, called 'cavilling',[13] and within significant margins, pay would differ by this, the gamble of a lottery.

Although there was an element of chance, the pitman did charge a price for his craft. He laboured by a tariff of penny prices and feint extras which added up to a living, and the tariff stood by precedent and bargain. The bargaining was ceaseless as conditions constantly shifted but bargaining power primarily depended on local demand for pitmen. 'Binding money' seems to have been traditionally an annual sum of 1s or 6d to seal the agreement of the bond, but during labour shortages it was used to entice hewers to the colliery offering it. In 1766 Bushblades was a new excavation binding 'sinkers' and 'drifters' (a drift was an exploration, sinkers built the shafts) as well as hewers and putters. A new colliery demanded new labour and the binding money was extraordinarily high at £1 2s for hewers and 11s for putters:

67 @ 22s	£73 14s 0d
2 @ 31 s 6 d	£3 3s 0d
35 @ 11s	£19 5s 0d
1 @ 3s	3s 0d
To drink, Brid, & Cheese at Sundry places – to the 18th Novr. 1766	£10 10s 0d
	£106 15s 0d[14]

In 1762 the Delavals paid binding moneys at two rates over the six weeks 25 August to 8 October. The evidence is a mere scrap but, given the named importance of Thomas Dury, and the fact that only seven were bound at the higher price, we could be dealing here with a hewing elite enticed for two guineas:

14 bound @ £1 11s 0d	Aug 25 – 29
Thos. Dury bound @ £2 2s 0d on	Aug 29
7 more bound @ £1 11s 6d	Aug 30 – Oct. 1
3 bound @ £2 2s 0d on	Oct 2
10 bound @ £1 11s 6d on	Oct 2 – 8
3 bound @ £2 2s 0d on	Oct 8[15]

In assessing the moving arithmetic of the pitmen's pay it should be clear that the Bond is not too helpful when used by itself. No legal paper could be expected to be trusted for a labour process whose return was made by distance and volume, and whose quality could crumble in a second. Nevertheless, in spite of the inherent difficulties historians have tried to make general estimates of pay and standards of living in the eighteenth and nineteenth centuries.

On hewers' pay, there is some consensus about a gradually rising level up to the 1790s: Simpson's estimate was very gradual indeed – rising from about 1s per day in 1700 to about 2s per day by 1790; Flinn and Stoker's estimate was similar.[16] For the period of the Napoleonic Wars, from the 1790s to 1815, Simpson, and Flinn and Stoker stay close – between 4s and 5s per day – while Hair estimated pay rising to about 6s in 1808 from a level of 3s in 1800. After the Wars, daily pay was estimated at about the same level (Simpson, Flinn and Stoker), or falling (Hair), through the 1820s. For the 1830s, Simpson estimated pay as falling to 3s or 4s through to the early 1850s; Flinn and Stoker detected a definite drop in the early 1830s to between 2s 6d and just over 3s. On the other hand Hair estimated a definite rise from a low point of just under 3s in 1829 to just under 4s by the mid-1840s; Mitchell said there were definite cuts in 1832, which were followed by a pattern of 'widely fluctuating wage rates'.[17]

On hewers' pay set against general prices, Flinn and Stoker thought that wartime money gains, approximately double in 1815 the figure of 1800, represented real gains with inflation at around 70% to 80% during the War.[18] Hair was more ambitious. He set his daily wage graph against Silberling's cost of living index. Apart from the late 1820s and early 1830s, this showed daily wages to be generally (slight exception 1817–19) above costs throughout the first forty-five years of the nineteenth century.[19] However, Silberling's index was based upon inappropriate statistical assumptions about the British worker during the period, and cannot be trusted as a cost of living index at all. Working from a revised cost of living index set against hewers' weekly earnings for all British coalfields, Church has recently suggested quite desperate levels of poverty in the 1830s and 1840s. By his figures, hewers' earnings were consistently below cost of living subsistence levels (except for 1836–7) from 1830 to around 1847. A period of steep fluctuation, but decline, with an 1842 trough 14% below 1830, Church concluded that for real earnings this period was 'certainly the low point'.[20]

Nevertheless, for the northern coalfield there is no statistical knowledge directly to bear our research. Such statistical knowledge as there is – a variety of pay and cost of living indexes – are inadequate due to their variable subjects and evidences and the historian must treat them with caution. Instead, there are some random figures, and some intelligent money estimates, and they should be used with other kinds of evidence about the pitmen's economy. It is in view of the randomness and variability of evidence that the worth of a run of bonds, for Walker colliery 1780–98, makes itself felt.[21] Improvements in rates and extras over the period were matched by efforts towards greater control over production, and the breaking, by owners, of traditional obligations for 'idle time'. Thus, hewing rates rose from 2s 3d per score basic in 1780 to 3s per score top price in 1798. In 1783 the newly opened Gosforth pit entered at 2s 6d per score; the Henry pit in 1784 at the same rate; the Jane pit in 1792 at 2s 9d, rising to 3s in 1795 with the Gosforth and Henry pits following at 2s 9d. Putting and driving prices also improved: in 1795 horse drivers were introduced at 1s 4d per day, and 1797 putting prices rose to 11d per score. In 1792, headway, wall, and 'stentin' (an opening between two headways for air circulation) rates increased by 2d per yard, and board-work was reintroduced for the first time since 1781 at a 1d per yard more. In 1793 double-work extras rose from 2d to 3d per score, and to 4d in 1797. In 1797 extra payments were introduced for wet-work. All through the period fines remained stable.

Thus at Walker there were unambiguous improvements in the rates of pay, and in extras and allowances. Fines did not rise commensurately. However, on closer examination, three new clauses appeared in the bonds which were to have serious implications for the pitmen as contractors. First, in 1792 the pitmen undertook to separate round coals from smalls and 'kirvings'. This undertaking could have increased the incidence of measures considered to be 'foul' and the fining that accompanied it. Secondly, also in 1792, the owners extricated themselves from the payment of idle-time until fourteen days afterwards:

> ... do what ... shall think needful to be done in the said colliery ... from any length of time not exceeding in the whole space of fourteen days without paying. (1793 bond)

Finally, in 1797 the pitmen were made responsible for the refunding of lost or broken equipment.

High war-time demand for labour from the mid-1790s brought prosperity. This prosperity forestalled the implications of round and small separation and the idle-time agreements of the kind introduced at Walker in 1792. When, after 1815, these clauses were applied by owners as instruments for maintaining profitability under difficult market conditions, then they became major issues of contention. The reasons for post-war difficulties resided primarily in the structure of the Coal Trade itself.

Economic structure of the Coal Trade

The 'Coal Trade' was a generic name for the producers, shippers, and distributors of coal. Although there were substantial markets in the North East itself, and along the English coast, and abroad, the real nexus of the Trade was understood to be between Newcastle and London. Among the coal producers there had been a marked drive to oligopoly since 1711 when the five families of the 'Grand Alliance' had informally agreed (made formal 1726) to seek control of the ownership and output of South Tyne, above-bridge, 'seasale' collieries. The control of coal-bearing land, its wayleaves and leases, royalties and rents, by purchase and the due process of law, turned places into property and property into a coalfield.

The growth of the coalfield beyond the reach of old oligopolistic practices called for new forms of agreement between owners: the 'Vend' from 1771, and the Joint Durham and Northumberland Coal Owners' Association from 1805. By the early nineteenth century the northern coalowners comprised mainly landowners, speculators, partners from regional trade, manufacture, banking, and coal-related businesses, and 'professional' men from inside the industry. Viewers were often owners as well as managers and they, with their partners, presided over complex interlocking dynasties, – as with the Stella Coal Company, founded in 1835 with £26,000 put up by two viewers (John Buddle and T. Y. Hall) and one coal fitter (Addison Potter), being joined by a third viewer (Matthias Dunn) in 1839, and joined to a clutch of other collieries and enterprises through its partners' other, expanding, interests and connections. The northern coalowners operated largely by the re-investment of their own profits; they tended to recruit from their own number; they were bound together (and apart) by a financial and commercial interdependency manifest in genealogy, or private partnership, or public company – money bonds which might begin in the North East but which by mid-century could stretch across other coalfields and the world; and they sought, for most of the time, when private dynastic interests could permit, to control their markets through a cartel whose members ranged in size from giants like Lord Durham ('vended' in 1828 at 126, 484 chaldrons), to the handful of partners of Usworth colliery ('vended' in 1828 at 8,847 chaldrons). The great landowners – Londonderry, Durham, Ravensworth, Wharncliffe, and Bowes – were few in number but great in importance.[22]

If the producers lived by profits, others lived by rents on the Trade. Landowners in the coalfield, some of whom were also producers but the greatest of whom was the Diocese of Durham, leased their land and charged rents. These rents, or 'royalties', were partly a fixed payment, partly a payment according to output, and partly a payment for previous year's output, or lack of output not accounted for. They also charged 'wayleave' rents for the right to move coal across their land.

About two-thirds of output was sold to shippers or factors in the port of delivery. The most important port of delivery was London. Here, 'heavers' and 'whippers' unloaded the coal, 'lightermen' moved it to the wharf, 'meters' measured it, 'brokers' 'crimps' 'undertakers' and other factors bought it, and three tiers of 'buyers' bought it again and acted as wholesalers to the retail market.[23] Some coalowners had their own factors to safeguard their interests in an unruly market which lived off duty, tax, 'cuts', percentages, and speculative dealing – not to mention fraud, bribery, favouritism, and other sharp practices. The Coal Trade was a commerce in which everyone seemed to have their hand in the till. The State was no exception. For nearly two hundred years the Trade had been encrusted with private and public acts to raise revenue. 'King's Duty', 'Church Duty', 'Duke of Richmond's Duty', 'Orphan's Duty', duties to pay for City of London public works, export, and coastwise duty were among the scores of regulations which taxed and shaped the Trade. Acts in 1831, 1834, and 1845 reduced and abolished coast and export duty and the trend over the century was towards more direct dealing, but the production, shipping, buying, and selling of coal remained a complex and devious business.[24] Pit-head prices from the 1770s to the 1840s ranged from about 6s to 11s per chaldron. Between these prices and the wholesale market in London there was about an extra 18s per chaldron difference, and between the wholesale and retail markets about another 8s per chaldron difference. Over the period Londoners bought their coal at a rough average of 26s per chaldron more than it cost to produce.

'Vending' was the name given to the owners' limiting of output. Limitation was set by 'bases', 'multipliers', and 'issues'. The cartel would set an annual base for, say, Tyne seasale collieries at 800,000 chaldrons. A Newcastle chaldron was a measure containing fifty-three hundredweights. From this base, Wear and Tees collieries would be allotted a *multiplier* of it, say two-thirds Wear, and one-third Tees. The base was only an approximation of annual output, set for reasons of proportional representation. As the cartel developed in the early nineteenth century, the *actual*, permitted, output would be set by the executive, the United Committee, every fortnight. This Committee made *issues*: it had a fair idea of how much it wanted to release on the market, and controlled competition between collieries by the same system of base and multiplier. Thus, a colliery set at an annual base of 50,000 chaldrons would be issued at, say, 25: 1000, and permitted to produce 1,250 chaldrons for the fortnight. An account of 'overs' and 'shorts' related to what issues collieries were allotted every fortnight, and what they actually managed to over-produce or under-produce. Collieries with shorts were allowed to catch up, collieries with overs had to pull back.

Bases and multipliers between collieries were determined by their respective capacities, and, it was alleged, by the ascribed quality of their coal – 'best' or 'Wallsend' round coals, with inferior grades beneath. Coal prices ultimately found their level within a fettered market, but immediate prices were set by the bigger collieries for their best coals, with the smaller producers shuttling into line behind them. Disagreements between parties, usually about overs or shorts, were referred to the Owners' Committee for arbitration, and after 1833 a security of £20 per 1000 chaldrons was levied for fining purposes.

Although the northern seasale collieres dominated coastal and London markets, these markets did not dominate the northern coalfield. About one-third of their output was local 'landsale' and not subject to vending. The other two-thirds was vended: one-third for coastal, and one-third for London. From the 1840s these markets were changing. Coal for coking (especially south and west Durham), iron-making, and export rapidly increased its market share, and coal for domestic consumption declined. Nevertheless, during the period of this study London's domestic consumers remained the key, or pivotal, market. In London, the cartel was quite capable of raising prices with relatively little change in supply, but quick profits were not its objective. Vending was primarily intended to put the northern coalowners in a position of permanent domination. Levels of profit were not to be left to the vagaries of competition, nor to the guessing game of demand. Instead, these markets were to be regulated fortnightly. The fortnightly issue was set by comparing those prices fetched, say, in London, with the price asked at the place of shipment, plus the average freighting charge. Then, if the prices fetched were considered to be above a 'fair price' ('which is a price something below what the Coals from other districts can be supplied at')[25] then more northern supply was issued to move prices down, below 'that point which will just meet the competition from Scotland, and the other places'.[26] On the other hand, if fetched prices were considered to be less than 'fair', then less northern supply was issued, to move prices up.

At one time the northern coalowners gave the impression that regulation of output was simply about encouraging an adequate supply of best coals: the market had a taste for them, and prices were ordered to make sure that their production was remunerative.[27] However, under questioning, the owners had to admit that the real determinant of out-put was London price, not coal quality, and that the Committee, *not* the best coal collieries, had the power to 'say that the owner ought to charge his coal at a fair relative price':

> Does not the agreement which you have entered into keep up the price of coals to the consumer in London, to that point which will just meet the competition from Scotland, and the other places? – Exactly so ... The regulation proceeds upon the plan of assigning a certain quantity to each colliery, whether it be the best or whether it be inferior.
>
> Have you never heard it avowed as a principle for fixing the quantities, that the quality shall be an integral part of their consideration? – ... it may be a consideration on some occasions, but I think it is not an integral part.[28]

Because it already dominated the coastal and London markets, the cartel believed it could permanently keep other coalfields out by tipping supply this way and that, as it saw fit. In this way, the vend orchestrated the competition of its own members and manipulated the competitive opportunities of its rivals.

There was a second, closely connected, reason for the cartel. This was the need to try and keep the market regular in order to maintain steady working in the pits. Regular working for a regular demand at an optimum price did two things. First, it kept overhead unit costs low for an enterprise which was risky, long-term, and carried massive standing expenses on fixed capital depreciation (about three-quarters of all assets) and interest payments. Secondly, it was said by apologists for the coalowners to save the coalfield from the social disruptions of a freer market whose demand for northern coals might change from week to week. Unlike their argument that pricing arrangements were set according to coal quality by collieries anxious to ensure the supply of the market's preference for best, this argument had some truth in it. Here, the coalowners could admit, in private at least, that although their fixing was 'in its complexion ... contrary to Law', it was 'good in spirit and beneficial in its effects'.[29] In public, the coalowners used the argument about social disruption. Perhaps they felt it had more purchase on the State. In Select Committee, the industry's spokesmen spoke of 'the desultory nature of an open trade ... workmen are sometimes at full stretch, and making very high wages, whilst at other times they are reduced to the very lowest scale ... This causes dissatisfaction ... hence those ... strikes

... which have so frequently disturbed the public peace ...' If the cartel ceased to function:

> The public, in the meantime, would certainly get their coals cheaper; but there would be a transfer of the labour and capital from one district to another, which would materially affect the value of property within that district. To trace all the effects a violent measure of that kind would produce in the country is impossible ...[30]

All of these intensely material matters were held together by a key concept: the concept of 'best' coals. In order to understand how the concept of best acted as what one colliery manager called a 'pivot' for the system, it is first necessary to make clear that for the general uses of the market, best coal — although superior to its inferior alternative, 'second class' coal — was no better than its other alternative, 'small' coal. As Buddle admitted after some close questioning:

> Are you able to state whether there is anything in the state of what is called the small coal, that is, a coal partially pulverized, that renders it inapplicable to the ordinary purpose of fuel, or is it prevented only by artificial circumstances from being so applied? — It is only by artificial circumstances; the small coal of our collieries is of the best quality.[31]

Time and again, the Parliamentary Select Committees of 1830 and 1836 wanted to know why small coals were wasted or burned rather than brought to market. Could one buy small in the market? they asked — Yes, one could get it if one offered the same price as best, or round. But did not this 'practically ... prevent you' from selling it? — No, because coal is graded and sold at different prices. Why then is small coal not demanded and supplied? — because the market prefers best. But was it not better to sell small at any price rather than waste it? — It is sold abroad, and selling it at home depended upon its profitability. Then what price could it be sold at in order to render some profit? — It all depended upon each colliery. Then please give us an example of a colliery? — 'I cannot do it' Mr Brandling answered. Giving evidence before the 1830 Select Committee John Buddle was drawn into a closely questioned sequence about the concept of best and small. Buddle assured them that there was 'no prohibition to the sale of small coal' provided he received 'a remunerating price' for it. Other apologists would talk of a 'fair price'. Questioned further, Buddle answered that by 'remunerating' he did not mean cost price, or profitable price necessarily, but 'a price that would pay him as well as the large coal'. Apparently baffled by this, the Committee asked:

As a large proportion of this [small] is wasted, would not the smallest price he could realize beyond the expense of sending it to the spout be of the nature of a saveall to him? − Not, if it prevented him selling a chaldron of round coal.[32]

Asked if 'the refusal to sell the small coal force[d] the use of round coal in its stead?' Buddle replied that 'that certainly is our object'. Whereas Buddle claimed that small coal was in fact sold rather than wasted, it was mainly sold abroad at a cheap price to maintain its 'dumped' relationship to best. Six years later Thomas Wood affirmed that

... the coal-owner will sell under all circumstances, during a regulation, his small coals to go foreign (because they do not come into the vend) for a lower price than he would sell them to go to the English coast.[33]

Best coal, it is clear, was a concept which in its relation to small coal, was defined neither by aesthetic nor use-value, but by a two shilling 'question only of profit':

... if I am the manager of a colliery for any gentleman, he would expect me to make the most profit of it I could, and I certainly should not conceive I was doing him justice or conducting his concern properly if I sold an unprofitable article or an article upon which I could get only 6d instead of selling an article upon which I could get half a crown.[34]

The concept of best dominated the language and operation of the market to keep up prices, and served as a marker from which other coals, sometimes mixed with best, took their price. The marking of prices by best both kept small out, and raised to artificially high levels the price of inferior grades. Priced at about 2s per ton cheaper than best, the inferior grades were enjoying a rising market. Between 1833 and 1835 London imports rose from 2,003,010 tons to 2,294,554 tons. Out of this, only 66,427 tons were best. English consumers were paying high for inferior coal and being denied their full chance to buy good quality small coal.[35]

When Buddle was at his most dissembling, he had denied that the coal-owners looked to London prices in order to set their output − 'the shipowners are our customers'.[36] This was pedantry bordering on deceit, but it was nevertheless true that the concept of best against smalls worked equally to the advantage of the shippers and retailers. Until the 1831 Act which abolished the office of coal 'meter' and required coal to be sold by weight rather than measure, it was notorious that 'Coal occupies more space when broken than when solid'. Smashed coal meant more measure for the same weight. At every stage between pitbank screening of best and small, and metropolitan consuming, there was breakage; no 'consumer in London ever receive[d] one chaldron of coals in the same large state that it was when it was delivered to the shipowner'.

> When you say there is a taste in the market for the purchase of round coals, do you not believe it to be the taste of other persons than the consumers? — Yes, I conceive it to be the taste of the coalbuyer, because there is more scope for breakage; he can break down the large coal into chingle.[37]

The rounder the coals shipped, the rounder the profits made from their breakage.

The economic structure of the Coal Trade obliged the pitmen, on pain of fining, to produce 'that fictitious article'[38] of best coals where 'smalls' existed as a concept to provide the fiction of 'best', and best kept the price of inferior qualities high. By the 1830s the Trade was proving to be not only wasteful of natural resources (the Professor of Geology at Oxford and the Reader in Mineralogy at Durham fretted about this), expensive for the consumer, and overbearing on its workers, it was also increasingly beset by its own internal problems. An industry structured to restrict was expanding; and it was expanding not because it wanted to but because it needed to.[39]

For far, this chapter has referred to the industry's restriction as a 'cartel', but in fact The Vend was always less than a cartel though more than an oligopoly. Even when the northern coalowners could agree, competition from other coalfields meant that the market was supplied by a dominated oligopoly whose major producer was a cartel. When the northern coalowners could not agree, the question was for how long would intra and inter-coalfield competition last before the major coalfield regrouped to re-establish its domination? From 1819 the regulation of output was fragile as owners fought to raise their bases, increase their issues, sell cheap, sell over, hold up agreements for as long as it suited them, make and break alliances and form subregulations within the Vend. In 1824, 1826, 1828, 1829, 1832–3, 1840–3, and

1844 the industry failed to agree unanimously, leading to short-run scrabbling by some owners to make a run on the Vend, and long-run machinations by others to reorganise it.[40] In 'fighting trade', as bouts of non- or partial regulation were called, prices dropped dramatically as collieries competed one with another in games of internecine book-keeping. Between 1831 and 1833 the industry failed to regulate and prices dropped to just over half.[41] The main reason for this discord was the growth of new colliery ventures in the coalfields.

By 1829 the industry was becoming more attractive to loose, speculative money. In fact, little of this money came from public subscription or the banks, but this did not prevent established owners from being suspicious as to its stamina. Buddle regretted that there were only five family concerns on the Tyne and three on the Wear, 'all the rest are in the hands of lessees or adventurers'. To bracket lessees with adventurers in this way was a prejudiced gloss on affairs, but from the 1830s the pressure of venture capital increased: it poured into the inland coalfield in particular 'to accumulate adventure upon adventure, to add colliery to colliery'.[42] Some of these enterprises, like the Durham Coal Company (1836) and the Northern Coal Company (1837) were as disastrous as they were dishonest, but most of them, in the end, toed the Vend's line. Even the Hetton Coal Company, founded on London money in 1821 and a great exploiter of Vend disunity in its early days, combined with Lambton and Londonderry concerns in 1836 to block the purchase of nearby North Hetton colliery by joint stock companies. More distant, but no less threatening, Welsh coal was developing a seaborne trade with London; it was pointedly asked, if the Welsh could sell their 'culm', why could not the North East sell its small?[43]

This growth was locking the Vend into the contradictions of its own logic. In order to raise their output collieries had to expand their capacity well beyond what they would be allowed to produce. This was leading to a ridiculous state of affairs:

> Do you not consider, that having machinery to the extent of double the quantity of coal required to be raised is superfluous, and beyond what is really necessary for the good working of the pit? − I consider it judicious management, and it is what I should recommend.[44]

Newcomers to the regulation were allotted bases well below their real capacity. In this way the Vend stoked its own expansion to the detriment of its own *raison d'être*. In addition, the Vend could not control renegade capital. It did not enjoy open competition, either in the seasale markets or in its own backyard. At first, Tyne coal and shipping interests complained about the ancient taxes they had to pay, which the Wear also had to pay, although less, and which the developing Tees did not have to pay. Later, Tyne and Wear owners bitterly opposed railway building around the Tees, especially Stephenson's Stockton-Darlington line in the 1820s, and the Durham South-West Junction and the South Durham Railway in the 1830s.[45] Railway Acts placed a compulsory purchase order on land at a 'fair' valuation, thus drastically reducing the large permanent expense of wayleave rents which had to be paid by Northumberland and North Durham owners. These owners petitioned against the South Durham Railway bill of 1836 declaring that its passage

> ... in the present shape, without way-leaves, would be a most unjustifiable bonus to the Promotors thereof, subversive of the long established customers of the country, and unjust to the lessors and lessees of existing Collieries and Railways.[46]

Local pamphleteers revelled in the difficulties the old owners had in bringing the new ones into line. They caricatured the Vend as a 'Monster ... nearly one hundred years old' known to the pitmen as 'HALF MEAT – HALF WARK', the shippers as 'WORK FOR NOUGHT AND FIND YOUR OWN MEAT', and the shivering 'Cockneys' as 'HALF RAW – HALF ROASTED'. The Monster was now dying from the gluttony of trying too much:

> Excess of *Scotch Brose* and *Welsh Rabbits* brought on his first sickness. *A Darlington Dumpling* stuck in his throat and nearly choked him. Washing it down with *Tees Water* brought on his first *Shivering Fit*, to which he was ever after subject.[47]

In 1836 the Vend spokesman was breezily confident about absorbing newcomers and the sixteen collieries not yet affiliated. The Tees had been formally brought into regulation in 1834, but 1838–42 saw quite desperate moves to bring recalcitrants to order. To its own alarm, the industry was operating under conditions of huge excess capacity:

Table 3: *% increase in productive capacity compared with increase in Vend,*
1829–43[48]

	1829–36	1836–43
Approximate increase, productive capacity	40	60
Approximate increase, Vend	30	30

As capacity exceeded not effective demand, but the existing
structure of the industry, and as standing costs of an over-capacious
investment rose against a backdrop of gradually falling prices, it
is not surprising that the Vend was becoming more and more
difficult to hold together.[49]

Some owners of the larger and more efficient collieries, like
Thomas Wood, recognised the economic anachronisms of the Vend
and wished to end them. Wood sat happily at a confluence of
Political Economy and self-interest, and had ruthlessly exploited
the 1832–3 disorganisation with a thirteen month refusal to
regulate at Hetton. The Hetton Coal Company was the largest and
most flamboyant of the new capitals. It had been founded in 1821
with non-local money raised by an ex-colliery agent, Arthur
Mowbray, 'By dint of prowling round the Royal Exchange and
Stock Market'. The Hetton Coal Company grew rapidly in the
1820s to jostle the prestige, and squeeze the bases, of its two lordly
rivals on the Wear, the Lords Londonderry and Durham. Hetton's
cheap selling policies and coyness to regulate were much abused
by its rivals – 'a pack of madmen ... swords in their hands slashing
about them on all sides' – but this was a question of the pot calling
the kettle black.[50] In Wood's evidence to the 1836 Select Committee one can see the rationale of his actions at Hetton. He thought
the Vend a mollycoddler of weak capital at 'an extravagant rate
of profit', and wanted to drive inefficient collieries to the wall.
Selling their coals at what Matthias Dunn considered to be below
cost price, 'So that all now go, helter, skelter':

> The Hetton Co. seem determined to carry on with a view of driving
> certain people to a stand still ... In the meantime every Colliery
> is losing money and the Consequences will be ruinous.[51]

Asked to explain himself in 1836, Wood invoked the imperatives
of free trade and the hidden hand of perfect competition. Having

sold his share in Hetton for £324,000. Wood now owned and managed Thornley, a new, unregulated colliery in mid-Durham. His security was established; for the consumer:

> ... the security I should offer would be, that the districts which had other coals to supply, as soon as ever the price got up, to remunerate them for producing them, would immediately produce them. The owner of a coalfield would be naturally anxious to make something of it if it could be made, and he would be limited purely by the consideration whether he could sell to a profit or not.[52]

Profitability was a murky area then, and its calculation remains difficult now. In one sense, capitalism's own market dictums tell us all we need to know. The period saw record levels of investment in the coalfield, and we can only assume that those capitalists who did the investing did so after a rational consideration of profitability in coal against profitability anywhere else. Certainly, even the lowest estimates of clear profit are higher than the 3 to 4% yield which an investment in public stocks would have obtained at the time. Wood's contemporary but renegade view was that profits were high, between 12% and 25% or higher, per year. These were raw figures by a man with a grudge who happened to be adept at picking good investments, and they did not include depreciation of capital over the term of a lease. Buddle's figures did, and he estimated a profitability of about 5% after paying off the original capital. But Buddle was extraordinarily cagey on this figure. Under questioning, he would not guess at an average and, on reflection, said that 5% was 'only a very vague conjecture'. Among historians, Mitchell, Church, and Sturgess have all tended to Buddle's lower estimate, but Sturgess did make the point that coal did yield a larger return than could be accrued from comparable investments. Flinn and Stoker, on the other hand, have reckoned higher, an average of 28.3% of total costs per year for selected collieries 1717–1830, with 'immense profits' 1800–10, and coalmining 'generally a very profitable business'. Every colliery was different. For the big concerns and for those 'in the know', profits could be huge. Lord Londonderry made £45,000 from his collieries in 1836. However, there can be no doubt that for Londonderry, as well as for the smaller fry, profits were falling from the later 1830s as the Vend curbed output and capacity grew apace with the massive, unremunerative, standing charges which excess capacity meant.[53] Whatever their profits, the majority of northern coalowners saw only too well the hand of Wood's perfect competition. In 1830 the Select Committee was assured that only six Tyne and Wear collieries could survive a period of prolonged non-regulation.[54] Many owners would have agreed with Matthias Dunn's private remarks about Wood's 'brutral' approach, defending the Vend in public at least, as a guarantor of best coals and good employment. When its structure generated conflict with those who they claimed to be its most immediate beneficiaries, the pitmen, they blamed the pitmen.[55]

The hardships of the pitmen were cast, in general, as 'the penalty of Adam',[56] and, more directly, connected to those other lapses as identified by Revd Malthus. The Vend 'indulged' the pitmen 'with employment'; they suffered from declining wages and short-time because their wages had been too high and they produced too many children for the industry to absorb. In 1844 it was calculated that since 1830 labour had increased by 79%, but output only by 53%, and that in consequence the industry was carrying a surplus of 6,800 workers.[57] The owners argued that the pitmen's 'feelings of dissatisfaction' were not 'guided by a proper consideration of the real cause of depression' because the real cause lay in their own inability to adapt their numbers.[58]

Malthusian arguments were unjustified. They cannot be an acceptable explanation of an industry which had been recruiting workers from outside the mining community since the 1830s. Nor can they be acceptable comment from an ownership which not only vended coal, but which had also been vending labour since 1806.[59] Nevertheless, it was the pitmen who were blamed, and who took the brunt of the industry's gathering difficulties. Fining had long been a feature of Bond agreements. Small coals became a growing problem from the 1760s when robbing the broken was introduced. Broken working produced more small as a matter of course, but is also reduced the amount of underground space available to store it. Owners did not want small coal because their market was structured to take 'best'; nor did owners want small coal brought up the shaft because they had to pay for it as their leases included proportional rents on all coal brought to bank. Haulage was an added cost. It was best to leave it below, and the best way to do that was to fine the pitmen for poor separation of round and small. Screening of round and small, at the pit bank, appears to have preceded fining; fining clauses emerge from the late eighteenth century. By 1816 smalls accounted for about one-third of coal. Screening continued, to serve a growing export ('dumped') market, as did the fining — for separation, for 'bad' measure, and for stone. With wages at about 50% to 60% of working costs, fining became a central feature of cutting marginal, and not so marginal, costs.[60] So did the idle-time clauses of the Bond. One of the earliest, perhaps the earliest idle-time clause was 1s per man per day not worked, in 1770. This clause was made standard by Tyne and Wear owners in 1811.[61] However, the first half of the nineteenth century brought changes in the interpretation of idle-time as it did for fining. They both change, as the Bond itself changed, from considerations about the work into systematic instruments for greater exploitation. As fines were applied more strictly, and idle-time payments were avoided as the working-fortnight shortened, then the pitmen's earnings declined. This forty year deterioration was seized by crises in 1810, 1825, 1831, and 1844, and each crisis was brought on by the issue of fines, idle-time, and a fundamental shift in the nature of the Bond.[62]

Exploitation and Control

In 1810 the coalowners had tried to change the binding time from October to January. This was a deliberate move to reduce the pitmen's market advantage of bargaining just before the heavy winter demand for coals. The pitmen objected, and broke their bonds to leave work. On 10 January 1811, in order to resolve the dispute, the owners made an eleven point proposal about the terms of a new bond. Four of their points in particular did not accede to the men's demands. One point concerned the January binding (it was later changed to April where it remained until 1845), and another concerned arbitration procedures. The other two points of disagreement were about the increasingly vexed area of fines and idle-time. Whereas the pitmen rejected the idea of all fines, the owners insisted upon fines for bad measure, separation, and 'foul' splint or stone; whereas the pitmen wanted immediate payment from the day when the pit was idle, the owners insisted that payment (2s 6d per day for men, 1s per day for boys) should begin only after three days of continuous idleness. The owners were merely trying to intensify, and the pitmen to resist, a conventional mode of capitalist productive relations which operated by safeguards against embezzlement, fraud, and unsatisfactory work. After all, the entire Coal Trade, from coal seam to retail market, was permeated with the opportunity to chisel, and the pitmen and their employers were no exception.[63] In the end, the owners' terms prevailed, but compared with later arrangements when fines and short-time moved to centre-stage as owners sought to cut (flexible) labour costs, the 1811 terms were generous. The idle-time clause now applied to the whole labour force, comprehensive sick payments were incorporated, coal hewed would be paid for if the rejected amount was under four quarts measure, and pitmen were permitted to seek employment elsewhere if there was none available at their current place.[64]

In 1825 the United Colliers published their grievances. They believed their conditions had declined since 1811. The limit for refusing ('setting out') corves was now two quarts foul instead of four; there were now more fines for 'bad separation' of round and small coals; and fining for short measure was now more frequent. The working fortnight had been reduced to an average of nine days, rather than eleven or twelve, and owners were reneging on the idle-time payment. Men were systematically laid off for the three day period and re-employed on the fourth day to avoid contractual obligations. The union complained that the result was 'sometimes doing nothing, and then again working at extremity'.[65] The owners replied in terms of depressed demand and market preference for round, best coal − spontaneous factors conveniently out of their control.[66] The pitmen sensed more definitive reasons: 'Our bond is too rigorous', involving 'the removal of many of our privileges ... these things have all been by little and little taken from us'. They claimed that what had once been a bargain was now a fraud, and quoted Lord Thurlow's legal judgement that 'If it appear that the person did not understand the bargain he made, or was so oppressed that he was glad to make it knowing its inadequacy, it will show a command over him, which may amount to fraud'.[67]

The 1831 and 1832 disputes wrestled over the minutiae of fines and 'set outs', short-time and idle-time. During the 1829 failure to regulate, the medium and smaller collieries were hit so badly by the unrestrained cheap production of the larger collieries that they 'reduced their establishments and workings to the very lowest possible scale'. In 1830 a section of collieries withdrew their idle-time clauses altogether. In the punitive post-stike atmosphere of 1832 these clauses were dropped, to reappear in 1838, only to be dropped again after the 1844 strike when the owners were trying to divest themselves of all legal and contractual restraints.[68] The 1829 failure to regulate was eventually patched up, but the pitmen sensed deeper, qualitative, changes at work. The owners were warned over changes in their basic attitude to fining — 'the penalty is often too severe ... it seems ... quite evident ... no pitman will voluntarily send up a corf for which he is likely to incur any fine whatever' — and they were further asked to 'particularly guard against the too arbitrary exaction of the terms of their agreements'.[69]

The warnings were not heeded. The 1844 dispute involved the same issues. In December 1843 the Thornley Coal Company took to court three pitmen who had left the colliery and broken their bonds. These were intended to be exemplary cases because the whole colliery had been on strike since 8 November. The issues they raised were to be the issues which raged throughout the coalfield the following summer. Mr W.P. Roberts, solicitor for the National Miners' Association, defended the three men at the county court in Durham, and presented their defence on the grounds of recent changes in the interpretation of the Bond. Roberts submitted that to interpret the Bond to rule as the Company was doing was not in keeping with its traditional function. He also maintained that fining and laying off procedures had become so bad that the men could hardly earn a living. The solicitor had three hundred men ready to testify to the truth of this in the manner of John Cookson, first witness:

> I don't think a man can get a living if the Bond is to be carried out in its strictness. If a quart of splint is to be fined for, I am sure a man cannot get a living. I will go to gaol before I will go to work under such a bond.[70]

Roberts lost the verdict at Durham but took the case to the court of Queen's Bench where the defendants were acquitted. Testimonies like Cookson's could be heard in every colliery. In addition, prices were being reduced as fines were being increased. A joint audit by Thornley, South Wingate, Hetton, Haswell, Kelloe, and South Hetton pitmen calculated that since 1842 hewing prices had dropped by an average of 23%, putting by 26%, driving day rates by 10.5%, and trapping day-rates by 21%. The newspaper of the NMA, the *Miners' Advocate*, published colliery by colliery reductions through 1843 and 1844.[71] The owners represented the advances demanded as monstrous — an increase of 28% over 1843 prices. However, their figures did not allow for the slow fall in labour prices which had been going on for a generation.[72] The union replied with their familiar grievances — fines, set outs, short time, the sheer practical difficulty of sorting coals into rounds and smalls, stones and splints, in the dark of the face, at speed, perhaps by hewers who were not 'true-bred'. It was, they said, 'utterly impossible for the most honest and careful workmen to avoid sending up a small quantity of splint and stone'.[73]

The mining community could not experience a generation of contractual pilfering and remain indifferent to the ideology of labour value — that labour is the source of all wealth but is denied its surplus value. Chartism had gained a hold in the pit villages during 1838–40, particularly those clusters of raw, new capital around Bedlington and Hetton. Here were the networks of men and women who were most confident in their analysis. At South Hetton the pitmen simply presented their case as creditors: they were owed £204 15s for hewing, £136 10s for broken work, £93 3s 4d for losses on small coals, £27 14s 8d for narrow work, £280 11s 8d for putting, £32 1s 4d for rolley-driving, and £162 10s for shifting work.[74]

Piecework and the variability of conditions made it possible to argue at length over the rate and extent of the decline, but there can be no doubt that there was a decline. The owners showed an uncharacteristic reticence about the details because it was through detail, in a job paid in details, that the deterioration was happening. Only the very finest examples of gross earnings were quoted by owners. Only averages projected from *rates* of prices were used to estimate what could be earned, given constant employment and few fines. Thus the 1842 Royal Commission published the fortnightly budget of an Urpeth colliery family for 1841: there was no 'Micawberism' here amidst the mutton and butter and savings but, the family, with four male wage earners, was a carefully selected earning unit working a full fortnight without fines. The example was not typical and the industry must have known it. Similarly, the 1836 Report of the Poor Law Commissioners in its summary

of miners' earnings since 1816 made no allowance for short time
or fines.[75] The owners' published rates, for 1832 and 1844
respectively, showed a decline over the twelve years of about 4s
to 3s 8d score price for hewers, and 4s to 3s 6d per day for
putters.[76] The 1844 crisis was precipitated by cuts so large that
even the leading coalowner had to admit them to the government
as potentially damaging to the Queen's Peace.[77]

In 1797 Sir Frederic Eden's celebrated study of the 'Poor' had
compared the income of Newcastle pitmen as on a par with
Tyneside masons and joiners. Both crafts took about 15s per week.
In 1834, a reasonable assessment of hewers' earnings at 17s per
week, for those who were able to work all the days available, put
them just above '... persons employed as mere labourers in our
Manufactories [on Tyneside, who] are paid 14s or 15s per week,
in processes where no art is required'. Later, the union wryly
recalled Adam Smith's 1776 estimate of the pitman's 18s to 27s
per week, with employment 'as constant as he pleases'.[78]

At the same time as the Bond's clauses developed into instruments for greater exploitation, the Bond developed into an
instrument of greater control. The essence of the Bond had always
been to tie down an experienced labour force which was, intermittently, in short supply. This restriction on mobility later out-
raged Gladstonian Liberals who looked back upon an eighteenth-
century Bond as virtually feudal. They reproached it as a bill of
serfdom which chained the collier to his master and retrieved him
when he fled. When the Bond was formally ended in 1872, Glad-
stonians of all classes saw it as the sweeping away of an evil relic.
This was not an accurate representation. It misread the function
of the eighteenth-century Bond, and it misunderstood how the
Bond's function changed in the nineteenth century.

The Bond was, after all, a bargain of sorts, and 'fleeing' pitmen
who were escorted back to their contract, although liable to imprisonment, were in a more spirited position than that of a serf. For
example, in December 1777 Sir John Delaval suffered the absconsion
of five men from Hartley colliery. Pitmen were in such high demand
in that year that this was a minor calamity. Delaval's cashier wrote:

> I am sorry to Say that the Colliers work but badly and that 4 or 5 have
> within few days gone off ... [he talks of] ... an enormous sum laid out
> on binding Colliers and building their House − therefor no Care should
> be Wonting to Make up and Overcome that Expence.

In January, cashier Oxley had to explain that he had 'got only 2 of the Colliers back who were absented ... The rest being we think set out to Scotland'; but by February 'we have the Mortification of hearing that there are young men almost weekly running either to Sea or London service', and inspite of higher pay in March, absconsions and retrievals – 'John Crooks is in pursute' – continued throughout the Spring.[79] In April all the Hartley men struck work and by June were threatening 'to pull down the office; Burn the corves; pull down the Ginns; and pull up the wagon ways'. Delaval had to settle but two months later he suffered further inroads on his labour, this time from the Lambtons at Washington on the Wear. The Coal Trade disapproved of competition and called upon the two owners to desist. The Lambtons refused, and on the morning of a second attempt to lure Hartley men to the Wear John Crooks had to gallop south to Newcastle and come to a deal with the Washington agent. This agreement was in the event ignored and Hartley lost nineteen men and two boys. It had not been a good year for Sir John Delaval. John Crooks wrote his employer a fair story of Coal Trade mutuality:

> ... it was possitiveley agreed by mutual concent, not to hire of Each others men above Two, & should it so happen, that these were not to have a sixpence more than the sum given by Each to their own people. Yet notwithstanding what had passed, the said Agent & Owners of the said Colliery, before many Hours Elapsed Hired Eleven of Hartley pitmen.[80]

Binding times could be times of competition for labour. Attempts were made to nullify the competition, at first without much success as in 1765 when a new, unfavourable, time was introduced and a testimonial system of changing employers was proposed. The testimonials were resisted as a *possible* life sentence with one employer, as in Scotland, and as against 'the ancient character of this Kingdom as being a free nation'.[81] During the Napoleonic Wars the employers, faced with a scarcity of labour, made determined efforts to regulate competition by basing the Bond on a Vend in workers. This time they were successful and the Bond began to change its function. As its 'bargain' became more standardised, so its controlling function became more prominent. The Bond came to be seen as a means for implementing 'blacklists' and getting rid of troublemakers. In 1826 John Wood was rummaging for 'unfit subjects to be bound' at Mount Moor colliery; in 1832 fifty men at North Hetton who had rendered themselves, in their own words, 'obnoxious to any of the numerous petty tyrants who lord it over [them]' were unbound to become 'ruined and expatriated'; in 1839 sixty-six men were imprisoned for the Chartist general strike under the Bond, and many more were victimised at the April bindings; and in the early 1840s one hears more and more of 'what is called the black list', 'the list of persons with whom the masters will not enter into a fresh engagement' 'so that the work may proceed pleasantly'.[82] Many black-listed men hailed from Poor Law Unions other than their present abode, and, once destitute, the local Guardians could expel them and their families from the parish. In April 1843 at Wingate, Monkhesledon, and Thornley, there were forty such groups of the migrant-destitute awaiting escort. As the Bond unhinged trouble-makers, the Poor Law pushed them out.[83]

At first, Bond and blacklist were used sporadically: after the United Colliers' Union in 1825–6; after the strikes of 1831–2; after the Chartist agitations in 1839–40. But after the NMA and the long strike of 1844, they were used systematically. The 1844 strike started as a dispute over short-time, reduced rates, and fines, but ended as a straight fight for trade unionism in the coalfield. The owners postulated a monthly rather than an annual Bond, and the mining community was only too aware of its implications. 'P.X.' told of the situation where 'a refusal or remonstrance to the most unjust demand was answered by the malicious, vindictive, threat of "Why, why, the binding's coming, thou'll be marked"'.[84]

A monthly Bond would tighten this sort of control twelve-fold. When the strike collapsed in August the owners had gained that control. In 1846 the Commissioner's report catalogued a victimised and frightened coalfield. The manager of Gosforth believed that 'The monthly hiring, by enabling us to get rid of bad characters as soon as they show themselves, will be some security to us.' Mr Taylor, for the industry, felt it was his duty to say 'the good workmen will not suffer from it ... only those who are mischievous and idle.' The Commissioner verified this great moral work, stating that 'It is working an improvement in the morals of the people, because they now see that they can be discharged for any misconduct.' Misconduct was a moral question and dissent meant immorality. The Hetton, Elemore, and Appleton colliery proprietors calibrated the propriety of 'their' families: 'We shall very likely have to discharge many before long, and they will be those who engaged in the strike.'[85] By the 1850s the Bond flushed the coalfield of its waste matter once a month, and held those who remained to a more disciplined, defined, and subordinate regime. The 1850s were hard times for the proselytising trade unionist. His ministry was invariably an intinerant one.[86]

The Bond changed its form as it changed its function. The 1703 Benwell bond is a simple, gainsharing contract.[87] Only hewers, 'Barrowmen', and their rates, are mentioned. Other matters are left to be decided as necessary:

> If any other Consideracon appear to be deserving either to Hewers or Barrowmen other than that already above menconed it is referred to ye Judmt. of ye viewer.

An Account of the Charge of working Coals etc in Houghton Colliery for 14 September to 6 October 1771 continued to emphasise the direct relation of work to payment:

To 292 Yards Boreing in the Coal at 3d per yard	£3 13s 0d
To Consideration for the drift Men working wett etc	2s 0d
To John Walker 3 weeks assisting the Overman at 8s	£1 4s 0d
To James Lacourt finding Candles, Nails, Oyle, repairing the Horseway & son $\frac{XX}{138}$ $\frac{corv}{19}$ at 3½d per	£2 0d 6d[88]

This is still clearly Journeyman Labour's bill on Mr Capital for work done, but it is noticeable that both payment and work have become more complex transactions. They have become, at length, formal bargaining matters.

In 1805, after nearly a decade of intensifying competition for labour, the northern owners decided to resist competitive bargaining. In the words of a Tyne viewer, 'the demands of the pitmen being so exorbitant, it was tho't preferable to submit to the inconvenience of loss of labour ... the unanimity of the Coal Owners ... will in the end prevail.[89] This decision implied ineluctable changes in the form of the Bond. It changed from a myriad of local hagglings into a more standardised cross-coalfield agreement. Binding money had once been the major enticement of scarce labour. In 1779, Sir John Delaval held his new bond in readiness to repulse Wear competition for his men:

As several of the Colliery Bonds in the River Wear Ends in the course
of the next month Tho' ours do not before the 3rd of Novr. I mean
to have a New Bond wrote out the first opportunity to be in readyness
least any shd. attempt to disturb us.[90]

In 1805 the owners' first collective action was to fix uniform
binding monies for all collieries. This was followed over the next
few years by efforts towards 'arranging some system of equating the
different wages' 'to approximate to an equalization of wages'.[91]
In 1830 standard putting rates were introduced. A synchronised
binding time was also introduced. As early as 1765, a local correspondent knew that this sort of standardised bargaining could
unify men as well as owners:

[this dispute is only] ... a Stalking Horse, in order to come at the Gold in
Hand, at the next Binding; and that all might be free at one Time of the
Year, when the Works, and Demand for Coals are at the Height ...[92]

The binding had always separated and shuffled men and owners,
but these moves towards standardisation and synchronisation col-
lectivised both parties into a clearer, and hardening, opposition.[93]

The Bond tended towards standardisation without achieving
it, but as mines became deeper and larger, and men and owners
vied more elaborately, the Bond became more complicated. The
Hetton and Elemore bond for 1829 was a nine page wad of 'Rates
and Prices ... terms conditions and stipulations ... Penalties and
forfeitures'. The Ouston bond for 1835 carried the usual conditions
but also reached into the village's social life, 'It being distinctly
understood and agreed that the Dwelling house provided ... form
part of the wages'. Families were allowed no 'Galloway, Ass, Gun
or Dog' and workers were made to agree 'that they will not become
members of any association by compliance ... [with which] ... they
can be prevented from the strict performance of this contract.'[94]

By the 1820s the Bond had become so long and complicated that
the men argued that the traditional way of reading it, aloud, once,
and in the open, was no longer fitting for the intricate legal and
technical document which it had become. George Johnson, viewer
at Willington, sought a way round local union cadres who were
sent to pick their way through his bonds' intricacies. Johnson was
advised to appeal over their heads:

If the Union men send their local committees only to hear the Bond
read, I shall most certainly adopt the plan, you propose, and not allow
it to be read untill the majority of the men are present.[95]

But the villages had need of their cadres, indeed, since 1811 the pitmen had been calling for professional legal advice to ensure understanding and fairness. In the nineteenth century, even the men's squiggly, idiosyncratic 'marks' had given way to an anonymous cross, merely the touch on the top of a quill as the viewer marked for them:

> ... they evidently repose much faith in the viewer, as scarcely one of the witnesses whom I examined could give any outline of the provisions of the agreement to which they had thus formally consented ...

Certainly, Henry Henderson, aged sixteen, had no idea: 'Signs the bond himself. Is read over to him in a crowd, but does not much mind what he signs to; thinks it is all right'.[96]

As the function of the Bond changed from a contract to a control, so its form changed from a bargain to a thing to be marked if you wanted work. The pitman with his bargain merged into the labourer with his wage. No matter how unequal respective parties had been, and for most of the time they had been, the Bond had once existed as an individual, negotiable contract for work performed, a pitman's lease. Attempts to standardise and synchronise the Bond during the war years had translated negotiation from individuals, and individual collieries, to the whole coalfield, and by the 1820s formal collective bargaining was apparent. At the same time, the Bond intensified its controlling and exploitative functions as an ever more complex undertaking. As the economic structure of the industry corroded within an expanding market, so the old pitmanship declined with it. With the introduction of the monthly Bond after 1844 the industry was effectively operating on a basis of free wage-labour with one month's notice. The pitmen sensed this deterioration in position and status. In 1831 they scorned comparison with wage labourers − 'we have been compared in point of wages, but not in point of labour'; they recalled what they chose to recall as their traditional status − 'The sun looks not upon any kind of labour that can in the least be compared to hewing and putting'; and they moved to defend an anachronism whereby 'The pitmen works by the bargain altogether; he works at so much per score, or so much per yard − he gets not a penny, but what is got at the greatest extremity.'[97]

5
The binding

The history of the binding is obscure until the 1790s when wartime competition for labour forced the owners to act, and, as so often happens in social history, crisis created its own record. Before this, the historian has only the occasional bond document and scattered evidences of separate bindings. It is therefore difficult not to agree with T. S. Ashton's comment that 'For the student of labour organization in the coal industry the eighteenth century belongs, indeed, to pre-history'.[1] There is some evidence of a labour shortage in the 1760s with intermittent high binding monies and owners' attempts to control the labour market; and there were labour shortages in the 1770s, although it is difficult to know whether the pitmen were able to exploit the situation.[2] For instance, Sir John Delaval had labour problems long before the previously cited incidents of 1778; in 1772 his viewer told him he had 'very troublesome work withe pitmen this Year ... some Collys. is giving six pund a man which makes them very fitt to sit with'. And in 1773 James Morgan and Michael Stoddart are evidence that Delaval's pitmen were enjoying some advantages of scarcity:

> Mr Water is inform'd that there is two of his Bound Keelmen, who have absented themselves from his Work ... that they are Sinking at Hartley, their Names is James Morgan & Michael Stoddart, he begs you will be so good as Immediately discharge them.

Two years later Sir John was suffering 'trouble with som of the men who run a way', and although these 'promised to behave themselves well for the time to come' we know that the Delavals had this problem at least until the end of the decade. An un-named memorandum made a typical comment: 'the men do not work half the quantity which they ought to do'.[3]

The Walker colliery bonds for the 1780s suggest a new stability in the labour market with binding money steady at a formal 1s

per man, and in 1789 the Tyne collieries were able to reduce prices
due to an excess of men over the Vend. William Thomas, viewer
at Denton colliery, reported that his allotted 22,000 chaldrons was

> ... so much below what was expected would have been Vended from
> this Colliery when the last Binding took place that more men were then
> Bound that the Quantity allowed will admit of being employed to allow
> them their usual wages of 2s. per day, orders were therefore given to
> reduce each man to 1s. 6d.[4]

The early 1790s are packed with labour troubles as seamen,
keelmen, and pitmen responded to the general and specific
demands of War on the North East's economy, the most specific
of which was the Royal Navy Impress. By November 1800 the ports
of Newcastle and Sunderland had lost 2,781 pressed men.[5]
Towards the end of the nineties the pitmen were clearly in a
favourable market position. At first, the owners had tried to hide
the situation. In 1797 Lord Delaval's agent was relieved to have
secured 'the necessary Complement, and at a less advance in
Wages, than might be expected, from the general appearance of
scarcity of Colliers', but in the following year competition from
rival collieries forced Johnson to add 5d. to score price, 'such
concessions as hurt my feelings much.'[6] The Delaval concerns
were around Seaton, to the north-east of Newcastle. As the labour
shortage became more apparent the main aim of Delaval's agents
was to keep their pitmen out of Newcastle which had become the
chief place of inter-colliery rivalry. In May 1800, when many of the
English labouring poor went hungry, the Delaval men were supplied
with corn to tide them over a lull in trade.[7] In the September only
twenty out of eighty Delaval men were bound at first, and the agent
found himself playing a watching and waiting game with the
Tyneside owners to the south, who in turn were watching and
waiting on the Wearside owners to the south of them:

> We have only bound 20, thirteen of them our own, & several from
> Murton & Blyth or farther ... Many of the collieries in Tyne have got
> but few bound & am afraid they may not have patience but break out,
> if they do! or are like to do it! We had better offer a Guinea for our
> own Men each ...[8]

In 1801 Mr Bryers was still trying to save Delaval's men from the
vulgarity of money. Scenes down on the Tyne were far from
modest, they had achieved national notoriety:

The pitmen at those places are hired for twelve months. A particular
time of the year in autumn, called the *binding time*, which continues
about a month, exhibits a succession of drunkenness and confusion
(to say nothing worse,) equally inconsistent with the interests of the
proprietors of mines, as to the peace of society. Public houses are
opened for the reception of the workmen of the respective collieries;
and should *recruiters* from other collieries make their appearance ...
violence too often follows ...[9]

By 1802 the Delaval pitmen were clearly learning their market
strength. At first they bargained cannily, and only twenty-five men
were bound in two days — 'the people came slowly & wished to
bargain either for the Boys or better Houses or such like trifles'.
This new confidence was difficult to sustain however and in the
end they were bound 'with some little promises to some of the first
rate men which are too trifling to mention'. The Delavals had given
four guineas binding money per man (four and a half guineas per
unmarried man), and although this is an immense sum compared
to previous years the pitmen could have had more than this had
they been aware of their true bargaining strength. Nearby Cowpen
colliery had in fact offered seven guineas but, as Lord Delaval's
land agent informed him,

Fortunate it was for us that at that time not more than 16 or 18 of our
men were unbound ... had we not been so far forward it is not easy
to say what would have been the consequence.[10]

By 1803 the situation had changed decisively. The pitmen were
now appraised of their strength and, in their reluctance to bind
for nearly a fortnight there was clearly some cohesion between
them. On Friday 30 September Forster announced the bond but
the men had already presented a petition and 'the general cry was
we must have all that is in the petition'. Forster went to Newcastle
the next day and found a similar situation there: no binding, and
the pitmen 'expect great things supposeing that there would be a
scarcety of men as realy is the case'. He rode back in the evening
and tried once more to bind his men but without success. On Sunday
2 October he was forced into granting improvements: improvements in the measure at which tubs were laid aside, improvements
in the width of the workings, improvements in wet work pay, and
2d. per yard extra for 'holeing' the boards. In spite of this only
three men and a boy condescended to be bound. Throughout the
following week Forster went 'amongst the Colliers' to argue, and

took with him the stentorian assistance of Messrs Bryers and
Brotherick. After a week of argument only three men had been
persuaded, 'the others being equally stif as on the former nights'.
On Saturday 8 October Forster returned to Newcastle where he
found 'nothing of consequence' and came back to find his own
men equally intransigent. On the Monday competitors finally
prised Forster into further improvements:

> ... a man from Hebron Colliery [Hebburn?] came amongst your
> Lordships workmen and was giving them every information about that
> Colliery also telling of the great earnings that was there, which inflam'd
> the peoples minds to a great hight.

At this, Forster immediately allowed a further 5d to score price,
4d to wall and headway yardage, £5 to £6 binding money and
'towards the evening they began to come forward but would not
still have bound had not Mr Bryers made them a present of a Little
hand money' of 10s to £2 10s according to the calibre of the man.
In 1803, in addition to large binding monies, hewing prices rose
by 6d per score on the Tyne and 7d per score on the Wear.[11]

In 1804 the 'Brotherhood' had appeared. On 30 September the
Hartley colliery bond was read and 'heard through very patiently
but none would come forward to bind'. For the first two weeks
of October an uneasy proprietorship waited for one of their number
to break rank, bind men, and begin the scramble for labour.
Moderate advances in score price and binding monies across the
coalfield were offered to the Brotherhood 'not more than an Eighth
part perhaps of what their petition amounted to', but the owners
dreaded not so much pitmen's eyes facing them across the table
as the first fast move of each others' purse-strings under it. Indeed,
Lord Delaval suggested binding first and asking questions afterwards but Bryers warned him of the consequences of such a deed:

> But as to this method of going into Newcastle to bind Men, As your
> Lordship recommended & as I thought then the only likely way to break
> their combination of Brothering, would be a most difficult business,
> for it is a fact that if we had begun to bind 20, 40, or 60 Men there,
> before five could have been agreed with, the whole of the agents would
> have been authorized by such example to do the best for their respective
> Collieries.[12]

On 18 October the scramble that everyone feared happened. After
two days of persuasion, Bryers believed he had talked the Delaval

men into being bound. However, Wear owners heard of Tyne binding monies of ten guineas, and immediately started mentioning twenty guineas, whereupon Bryers put up his money by £1 and, in a miasma of promises and rumours, the pitmen again refused to bind. At Cowpen colliery nearby, they refused a ten guinea binding. Bryers and the other agents sat in dread of a free labour market:

> We met Men & Viewers on the Road this morning & hear at Hadrick's Mill that Agents from Washington on the Wear had engaged several there this morning at 16 Guineas ... Mr Watkin says that for 20 years back such a binding has not happened.

Agent Thomas, on the same day at Denton, recorded even higher monies down on the Tyne:

> ... on Monday morning several of the Trade began to increase their binding money and to interfere with the Men of the neighbouring Collieries, and before Tuesday night the opposition became generally so violent that Twenty Guineas were given for a single Man.[13]

The binding monies of this spasm were massive. Thomas was thankful to get away with injuries to his purse of 1s 4d advances in two seams and a maximum binding money of 'seven Guineas to a young Man'. Delaval was less fortunate with injuries of twelve guineas per man and price advances, although his agent was pleased enough with that. He managed to bind on 24 October, but on the following day he recorded bindings of 'near thirty' at Plessey colliery and eighteen guineas at Cowpen, and even then 'Cowpen it is said has increased their Number but not so good workmen, & Plessey is many short of last year'.[14]

This 1804 binding brought the industry to its monopolistic senses. On 10 September 1805 it retaliated with cuts in binding monies, no advances on prices, a ban on competition between collieries, and a vend-allocation for pitmen as they had one for coal. Binding monies were standardised with a Tyne maximum of £3 3s for hewers who were householders, and £3 13s 6d for bachelor hewers, and £1 1s for bachelor drivers, and a maximum in the Wear and Blyth-Hartley areas of £5 5s for householder-hewers and £6 6s for bachelor hewers. It was agreed 'that each Principal write a letter to the Agent of each of their respective Collieries, on no account to exceed'. In addition, the binding was now to be a sober (and cheaper) affair. All men had to be bound at collieries and not public houses, all collieries were to bind simultaneously after a seven day moratorium, and 'no treat or drink shall be given, directly or indirectly, except the usual allowance of Liquor'. Moreover, 'no person whatsoever' was to 'be sent from one Colliery to another to tamper with or hire the Men of such other Collieries', and except for Wallsend, in order to 'put them upon a level with the adjoining Collieries', there was to be no increase in rates or prices. Extra treats, such as bread corn supplies, were to be stopped forthwith.[15]

The most punitive measure was the vending of labour. The basic plan was for an orderly enrolment of workers. The effective supply of labour would be manoeuvred so that its scarcity could not influence the market. Collieries were each allotted an annual base number of hewers (as they were each allotted an annual base measure of coals) calculated from their average hiring over the previous three years. From this average, to prevent the shortage from showing itself

> ... shall be deducted, one Man and Boy from every ten, in order that the new Collieries may be thereby supplied ... And that any surplus Men or Boys that shall remain after the new Collieries are supplied shall be under the direction of the Joint Committee of both Rivers.[16]

The Coal Trade Committee began a meticulous reorganisation of labour relations. They presided over the dissolution of a byzantine economy of peculiar arrangements, understandings, bargains, and customs:[17]

> Is Thos. Dixon, Underground Horsekeeper to have a Flannel Shirt and drawers? .. from the witness of the Colliery they had always been allowed a Shirt & Drawers.
>
> Is Mich. Chapman to have Grass for Cows and Galloways at £1 each?
>
> Thos. Craswell Hewer, first bound has got 8s. Earnest. Mr Robson says that extra Earnest was always given to the first Man bound.
>
> Mr John Ramsey says that it has been customary for many years at So. Moor to give the Bankmen & Overmen Binding Money and that he had bound the Men in question previous to the Resolutions of the meeting.
>
> Mr King says that it has always been his custom to pay 10/6 and 5/- to the first and second bound.
>
> Mr Bryers Ansd. the men at Hartley, Banksmen & Onsetters etc. were always paid the same as Hewers.

At Hartley Mr Bryers delivered Lord Delaval, and the Trade, of a successful binding. On 12 October 1805 the new regulated Bond was read, 'but those that were at Home (for many had gone to Newcastle etc.) seemed very shy & would scarcely take any liquor at your Lordship's expence'. The pitmen had massed at Newcastle and 'presented a petition according to custom, with a great many advances & demands'. But they were to find no bargaining in the city because the Trade 'have desired that no under viewer or other person concerned in hiring of pitmen from any Colliery, do shew themselves there or in the Neighbourhood thereof'.[18] For two weeks the pitmen either stood in vain at Newcastle, or tramped around the collieries to try and tempt a bargain, equally in vain. In the end it was the owners' solidarity at Cowpen which manoeuvred labour into a binding at Hartley. On 27 October Bryers reported to Delaval:

> Our Men were completely beat, they kept off with seeming indifference until about Six O'Clock on Friday Evening when we, as well as they, heard that Cowpen Owners had refused several & that they were coming to Hartley to be bound, which set them a going & very little difficulty was afterwards experienced.
>
> The Men kept up the good understanding amongst themselves to the very last & had several deputations at us on Friday still lowering in their Demands.

Bryers was jubilant. Although he had twenty-one hewers less than in the previous year, 'They are I think going to make a good year's work', and those previously 'guilty of much mischief & illnature, we shall be clear of them this year, as they are not nor will be bound again'. He was however more relieved than sensible about the situation. In November he was still scraping the labour market.[19]

In 1806 binding monies were again cut − this time to a guinea on the Tyne and two guineas on the Wear for householder-hewers. Again, the solidarity of the owners manoeuvred the men into binding. On 11 October at Denton:

> These conditions were refused on opening the bond and no Hewers were bound, but *the Trade refusing to make any alteration* which was discovered by the pitmen; the whole number wanted for this Colliery were bound on the above conditions this Evening.[20]

At collieries where there was a Brotherhood the pitmen decided to stick and play the same collective waiting game as the owners.

Thus did the men learn their best games from the owners. Bryers said it was confidently believed 'that many of the Hartley Pit-men would be very glad to bind were they not affraid', and he blamed 'certain combinators well known by the appellation Brotherhood under which the Men meet together and agree not to bind etc. unless their unreasonable demands be complied with'. By the beginning of November, with some men bound but the Brotherhood sticking out, the Trade had to relax its ban on competitive binding in order to accommodate all the collieries.[21]

By 1807 a general owners' fund had been set up with the 'power to provide for cases of hardship or emergency' for collieries facing organised resistance. The labour vending system was tightened in 1807, and colliery books checked for cheating in 1808. Monies and prices remained the same in both years, except for consecutive reductions for corvers, but a Committee was formed in 1807 with the express and crucial purpose of equalising rates throughout the coalfield:

> The situation of the Coal Trade being such as to give no reason to apprehend any difficulty in engaging the Workmen at the ensuing Binding, it appears to this Committee a proper opportunity for correcting certain abuses, and adjusting the Wages etc. of the different classes of Colliery Workmen, proportioning their Recompense to the nature and extent of their Labour ... If such an equalization of Wages shall appear proper it is recommended to make an accurate comparison of the earnings of the different classes of Workmen in every Colliery throughout the Trade.

The attempt made in 1809 to change the binding time from October to January[22] seems to have been successful because we find the Trade insisting again upon a January binding in 1810. The Brotherhood fought the 1810 Bond not only because of the January binding, but also because of its clauses on fines, short-time, and arbitration. For the men, this complex and encroaching Bond — a barrister had been used to draw it up — was clearly the last straw after five years of consecutive attack on their bargaining position. So successful had owners' tactics been that some collieries were back on 1s per man binding money and some had dropped it altogether.[23] A showdown was inevitable, and the Brotherhood counter-attacked through the October and November of 1810. Thirty-one collieries supported the 'stick', and it might have been the case that they subscribed to, and associated through,

a well organised formation, the 'Brotherly' Friendly Society.
But other collieries still had to be persuaded. The Brothers
'travers[ed] the country, not only individually, but in companies
sufficiently powerful to extort by fear'. The owners were entitled
to prosecute the pitmen for breaking their bonds, and they
fell about the leadership. One hundred and twenty were imprisoned
in Durham gaol and house of correction:

> The prisons were so much crowded that about 70 of the prisoners
> were on Wednesday last removed to the bishop's stables on the
> College Green.[24]

On 22 November the Coal Trade Committee retracted slightly,
and agreed upon an April binding instead of October or January.
In December Revd William Nesfield of Chester-le-Street inter-
vened and promised the Brotherhood proper negotiation if
they would only fulfil their bonds up to the January. Through
December 1810 and January 1811 magistrate Nesfield persevered
and had finally reached agreement by mid-January.[25] There
was little compromise over other issues, but the main solution
had been found in an April rather than a January binding.
On 16 January William Adey and George Ferry both of Jarrow
colliery, Jacob Bell from Rainton, and Richard Aisbitt from
Washington replied to the owners on behalf of thirty-one collieries acceding to an April binding. Their reasons for opposing
the January binding had not been only economic; there was
obviously a rich sense of place amongst men willing to go to
such lengths for a binding 'convenient not only to the removal
of their families but also to the commencement of the cultivation
of their Gardens ...'[26]

The Brotherhood was formed in the first wave of prosperity
brought by the War. At first the pitmen did not realise their
true market strength. By 1803 they were better informed and
trying to tilt the market accordingly. In 1804 we hear of a Brotherhood. Against the Jacobin scare of the 1790s, the Combination
Acts of 1799–1800, and the owners' sworn opposition, the
Brotherhood was cloaked in some of the 'Bend Sinister'[27] rig-
marole of the secret society and we know almost nothing about
it. Thomas Morrison, a hewer at Jarrow in 1810, knew the
Brotherhood but, incredibly, could not remember any of the
Brothers:

> Some of the pitmen were Brotherhood — a Society amongst some of the pitmen called Brothers — but does not belong to them himself nor can he recollect the names of any that do.[28]

But the pitmen were also a caste of workers with aspirations to a kind of guild. Aspects of the friendly society blended innocently with those of the secret society. On 24 October 1810 'the Bretheren' of the 'Colliers' Fund' founded their friendly society at Gateshead, and their rules and articles closely resembled the conventional 1810 *Articles Agreed to by Members of the Brotherly Society in Painshaw, New Winning, in the County of Durham.*[29] Both societies agreed to protect their members in hard times, pay them in good times, bury and elect each other when necessary, and generally organise themselves with the moral devotion of brothers' keepers. Some correspondence in the *Tyne Mercury* following the 1810–11 dispute suggests a significant Methodist and Jarrovian involvement in the Brotherhood, as its 'principal founders, supporters, and propagators', and certainly, the language of the Bretheren — 'a firm League, Covenant, and Agreement, to establish and confirm a sure, lasting, and loving Society' — smacks of the Methodist loving cup, but after that we are told nothing.[30]

If the Brotherhood stopped the owners having things entirely their own way in 1811, the varied nature of coalmining forced the industry to be less ambitious in its 1812 standardisation plans. In December 1811, the Coal Trade Committee on the subject resigned, 'having served for three years, and having in the course of the last, as well as the present year, made various unsuccessful attempts to establish certain general arrangements'. In March 1812 the new Committee reviewed its remit, but in less ambitious terms. They had already drawn up a comparative table of prices 'for different sorts of work', and hoped to arrange

> ... some system of equating the different wages so as to be beneficial to the Trade but are sorry to say that from the charges being so variously intermixed they are disappointed in their expectations. It is however recommended to the Trade to inspect the schedule of Prices made out from the several Colliery Bills to enable individuals to compare their own particular Hewing Putting etc. charges with others the better to enable the Trade to approximate to an equalization of wages.[31]

After the agreement of 1811 there appears to have been a period of peace. Compared with areas such as Lancashire or the West Riding, the government considered the North East to be stable.[32]

After 1815 there was a marked shift in the deliberations of the Coal Trade Committee away from vending men to vending coal.[33]

In 1814, there were still labour shortages and two Wear owners were warned as 'the principal parties exceeding the Numbers agreed to ... to preserve unanimity at the approaching Binding'.[34] In December 1815, Wear owners resolved to make 'a prudent reduction in the price of labour', and although Tyne and Wear were wracked with seamen's and keelmen's strikes in that year, the Wear pitmen waited for the expiry of their April bonds before they acted. The Rainton and Newbottle collieries were reported as centres 'of mischief and insubordination' through the April to June strike of Wear collieries. There were 'riots' (attempts to rescue prisoners from constables) at Newbottle, Ouston, and Murton (Lady Anne Pit), and efforts to spread the strike to the Tyne, but the struggle seems to have been unsuccessful.[35] This was hardly surprising. Owners estimated that one in twenty Tyne pitmen were unbound in April 1816 and such was the ensuing destitution, they resolved that 'each coal owner should endeavour to give employment to as many unbound men as he can with convenience'. In 1817 a government informer, admittedly not the most reliable source, could refer to the pitmen 'whose great privations have rendered them Desperate' as a ready source of trouble, and in 1818 Coal Trade suggestions that reductions should be made were dropped after consideration of their threat to public order.[36]

The April 1819 bindings on Tyne and Wear passed without comment or commotion. However, in September and October 1819 all the major Tyne and Wear occupational groups made wage demands which were complicated by a burst of working-class radical activity on both rivers.[37] Whilst there was agreement that 'The poor are certainly to be pitied ... their situation cannot be worse', pity was no antidote to fear. On 20 October the Mayor of Newcastle, anxious about £700,000 worth of shipping locked in the Tyne, told Lord Sidmouth that he had 'the most formidable set of Men to contend with, consisting of Sailors, Lightermen [keelmen], Pitmen, and I am sorry to add, of Radical Reformers ...' The crescendo came on 30 October when both 'Colliers & Seamen [were] demanding an advance of wages, and taking advantage of the general prevalent commotions'.[38] Nothing came of the pitmen's demands. The keelmen settled on 22 October; the seamen had sailed away, propitiously, on 3 September; the pitmen were left alone with their politics and their demands to fizzle out by late November, when it was reported that 'the Pitmen ... have broken up their classes, divided their fund, and the furniture in the private Room in which they held their Meetings'.[39]

The 1820 binding was accompanied by stricter controls. Owners were asked 'especially in the hiring of Strangers' to request 'a written recommendation from their last master'. This system had been tried in 1765 without success. There is no further reference to its success or otherwise after 1820, except for the coalfield blacklist which appeared from the late 1830s.[40]

In 1822 the owners conspired to abolish binding money except for the customary 1s 'hand' or 'earnest' money, and another Committee of five viewers was set up 'to revise the wages of all classes of workmen, the Hewers excepted'. The Trade had always found it difficult to standardise hewers' rates, given the variation and complexity of mining conditions, and of course the hewing elite was less easily replaced, and more easily provoked, than the other groups. 'Revision' meant reduction; in March, the Lambton and Londonderry concerns agreed on conjoint reductions. Buddle reported that:

> Smith, Mr Lambton's Viewer dined with me here to day – we have compared and regulated the wages of the different classes of our Workmen, and have agreed upon certain abatements to be made at the ensuing Binding ... We have not however ventured to meddle with the *Coal Hewers*, further than taking off the Bounty ... We think we can accomplish what we shall attempt without much difficulty ...

Buddle was correct; eleven days later, after a neighbouring colliery had left seventy unbound, he reported that 'their men ran upon us to seek employment, which alarmed our men so much, that they bound as fast as their names could be written'. For 1823 a minute from the General Meeting of Owners reminds that binding was still being organised within the framework of the Vend. Owners resolved 'that such Colls. as are desirous of parting with any number, or proportion of their bound Pitmen' must do so 'on condition of giving up a proportional quantity of their Vend'. For 1824 there is no minute, invariably the sign of an easy binding, and in the Londonderry collieries at least, 'The pitmen are working like a house on fire'.[41]

In 1825 there was another quiet binding but that year brought the 'Brotherhood' into the light with a declared membership of

four thousand hewers, a new name – 'the Colliers of the United
Association of Durham and Northumberland', and a classic statement of grievances – *A Voice from the Coal Mines*.[42] The
Brotherhood had had a flickering existence for the previous fifteen
years. Some sort of Tyne–Wear organisation existed throughout
the period. A South Shields magistrate wrote to the government
on 26 May 1816, on the eve of a meeting of Tyne pitmen. It had
become clear that elements of organisation were involved:

> There has been for a few days a Stoppage of the Pitmen on the Wear
> but I did not think it of Sufficient importance to trouble your Lordship
> till Yesterday I learnt a Deputation from them had been at a consider-
> able Colliery on the Tyne which was Quietly at Work but I understand
> it inflam'd the Workmen ...[43]

In 1819 it was thought that a strike could 'spread in a single day,
thro' the whole Trade, whenever the signal is given'.[44] This
would seem unlikely unless one makes some allowance for some
sort of organisation across the coalfield. And three years later,
in 1822, there is another telling reference to organisation when
Lambton–Londonderry joint reductions on the Wear were
presented as the signal for delegates to communicate:

> I dont know that the Tyne Pitmen have had any communication with
> the Wear Men, I cannot imagine that they have not, as usual, free
> intercourse by their Delegates and that if any stop at all takes place
> it will be general.[45]

The United Colliers had a long list of grievances. Apart from
the heaviest 'burdens under which they *heavily groan*' and which
we have already considered – fines, short-time, idle-time, and
new interpretations of the Bond – they also complained about
more tasks, and increased measures which compelled 'the workman
to perform more labour than that for which he is paid'. There were
further complaints about the safety lamp which enabled them to
be sent to more dangerous conditions; about money fines for
discipline (including the example of 10s 6d for cuffing the boys
even if 'ever so *unruly, impertinent*, or *lazy*'); and about 'the
insolent and contemptuous manner, in which we are generally
treated by the agents and men in office'.

Grievances were articulated in the billowing language of
'Humanity' and 'Reason' – 'The very Negroes ... enjoy more of
the pleasure of life'[46] – but in 1825 they seemed more ready for

talking than for doing. The union's points-scoring in debate with the Trade was consistent, yet, although there was the 'strongest possible inclination amongst them, to stop for an increase of wages', the prevailing slump meant that 'circumstances have not favoured their views'.[47]

Nevertheless, the pitmen made advances in the freer legal atmosphere of 1824–5. Buddle repeatedly used the word 'system' in his description of the union. He seemed to believe that the system had existed for some while; at Rainton, he talks of 'the first overt act of the Union' at a colliery where the men continued to call themselves 'Brothers'.[48] In October 1825 Buddle warned Londonderry that 'This Combination is gaining ground on a firm basis'; in February 1826 he warned fellow owners to take the union's 'great vigour' seriously, and in March even the resilient Lord Londonderry wrote to the government about commotions, riots, and the fact that 'The Union of the Pitmen is entirely established'.[49] And this established union was busy asking for more, as well as refusing to take less. Its membership was limited to the elite, the hewers. They continued the traditional benefit functions of the friendly society, and sought to control the binding and the transfer of labour, restrict output, negotiate rates and conditions, scrutinise the Bond with a solicitor, and associate under the discipline of a printed rule book.[50] The repeal of the Combination Acts in 1824 had brought the Brotherhood into the open. Angered by a Hetton strike in July 1825, Buddle could 'only wish that J Hume would change places with me for 6 months'. By November, with Jarrow strikes supported by combinators (plus £100.00 from Sunderland shipwrights), and Hetton emerging as the union headquarters, Buddle was an anxious onlooker, complaining that 'Our modern political economists & Northern *Feelosophers* little know the nature of the *Cattle* they were to let loose by the repeal of the Combination Laws'.[51]

In 1826 the owners announced a standard Bond 'which may be adopted by every Colliery in the Trade'. This was a serious attack on the competitive position of a uniquely skilled community in a (reluctantly) expanding industry. The Coal Trade pressed forward and, in late March and early April, there were strikes. Their effectiveness was uneven. The union could not talk the entire coalfield into solidarity and had to decide whether or not to stand out alone. Disagreement led to internal wranglings, and the two counties eventually shuffled into binding by the middle of April 1826.[52]

There were evidently unobtrusive bindings in 1827, 1828, 1829, and 1830. Trade *Minutes* are almost wholly given over to Parliamentary enquiries and Vend machinations. Moreover, the coalfield suffered from trade depression in these years. In 1828 Londonderry's new sally port of Seaham Harbour was opened with great fanfare, but his chief agent, beset as he was by banks, lawyers, and slump, thought the nation was staggering into 'a state of debility':

> There is no demand for any sort of activity, not even Coals, and God knows what is to be the end of it − the pitmen etc. are in a half-starving state, but submit with unexampled patience to the great deprivation which they are suffering.[53]

Trade was still depressed in 1830. The owners admitted to very low wages. Events in France, a new king, a general election, Reform agitation, rural disturbances left London waiting tensely for Northern trouble. In October the London press reported coalfield risings and slaughter and, although there was no truth in this, on 11 November Wellington reminded Londonderry, his former comrade in arms, of the more prosaic facts of civil life:

> I understand that the Coal owners upon the Tyne and the Wear propose to lower the Wages of the labourers in their Service this Month, and I have been already applied to for the Assistance of Troops to preserve the Lives and Properties of His Subjects.
>
> The interest of Debts is not paid and troops are not supported without Money and Money cannot be found to pay these demands without Taxes.[54]

Wellington's note was a large hint not to reduce wages in a Trade already under government scrutiny for monopolistic practices. Whatever Wellington intended or the Trade had intended, on 17 November the Joint Committee of the Coal Trade denied the government's information that they wanted reductions.[55]

The strikers of 1831−2 cited all the familiar union grievances, and others such as 'the clause which empowers their masters to turn them out of their houses the moment their time of hiring is up'. The arguments of Coal Trade apologists were also becoming familiar: the rights of property to do as it will with its own; market comparisons with other workers worse off than the pitmen; the traditional 'kindness and charity' of the owners, but their un-yielding chastisement when provoked; and the eternal impossibility of trade unionism:

> ... labour must always find its level, and that it is worse than visionary to attempt to raise the rate of wages when there is a superabundance of labourers in the market. As well might it be attempted to stem the flowing of the tide, or to arrest the progress of the winds.[56]

The owners always presented their case *post festum*, as if 'the turbulent and restless portion' of workers had already 'gained the ascendancy' and suddenly insisted upon a list of unreasonable demands. In contrast, the pitmen always presented a case of historical deterioration. Their demands could not be unreasonable because they were only the redressors. At the outset of the strike Revd Brandling reminded owners of the recent past:

> Many of your men have been here today − & by their account they have endured much hardship for some years − I certainly feel for them as I think I have heard you say − that they had endured all with much patience.[57]

At the beginning, the Coal Trade was intransigent:

> ... the Meeting was of opinion, that the only point which the trade ought to concede is, as to the length of the days Works of the Boys.[58]

This was a minor point. However, by June 1831 the union had led the pitmen to victory in most parts of the coalfield and had won its first organised strike. The Trade re-grouped and counter-attacked at the 1832 binding, and by September 1832 the men had been beaten down.

In March 1831 the union was openly preparing its offensive, 'one, or two, general meetings, and ... organizing their System of Committees, Delegates etc'. Hetton was generally regarded as the heart of the union. Thomas Hepburn, elected leader of the United Colliers, worked there with his cadre of union leaders. Hepburn was thirty-five years old. Having lost his father in a pit accident when he was a child, he had started work at Urpeth colliery in 1804 when he was eight. He had converted to the Primitive Methodists in 1822. The Cock public house in Newcastle accommodated the general and executive meetings of the union and served as delegate headquarters when necessary. The delegates no longer represented just hewers. Membership was now open to all (including 'boys' as half-members) under similar terms with similar objectives as in 1825.[59] On 28 March the Coal Trade Committee resolved not to hire men after 5 April unless under the old terms. Strictly speaking, the actions of both 1831 and 1832 were lock-outs, and both began after midnight of 5 April.[60]

Lord Londonderry was the weak link in the chain of owner opposition. Among owners, he could least afford a dispute; his Seaham enterprises had involved heavy borrowing and his papers reveal that he had serious cash problems. This was bad enough, but worse still, he did not trust his bank. He and Buddle believed that its stingy credit facility, only meeting wages, was a deliberate tactic by the banker and his friends, 'his lads', his 'Quaker friends', to buy their way cheaply into the Trade, over the bodies of bankrupts. The only way out of the impasse was for Londonderry to sell as much coal as he could without too much concern for owner solidarity or Vend allocations. This is what he did. To break the standstill Londonderry published a conciliatory pamphlet and met the hewers of his Durham collieries. At this stage both sides were otherwise gripped in the first climax of strength, the pitmen parading their case with zest before a grim and non-conciliatory ownership.[61] Londonderry's friendly overtures were met with gasps of disbelief by his colleagues in the Trade. On 9 May Londonderry asked Buddle to renege on the Tyne and to come to an agreement with the men. Buddle, viewer for his Lordship but also with his own reputation to consider, and Tyne investments of his own to protect, was acutely compromised by Londonderry's behaviour:

> I will endeavour to act upon your Lordship's instructions, with respect to the pitmen, as well as I can, but anything *underhand* is impossible – it would be known through the Trade of both Rivers, in a few hours, and we, one & all must strike our Collours. God avert such an issue, I shall never again be able to raise my head, after such a disgraceful defeat – it will be the death of me.[62]

It nearly was; in August, a disgraced and exhausted Buddle was to have a nervous breakdown. On 12 May Londonderry broke faith with the Trade and accepted union terms. His men were the first to bind. This action shocked the union almost as much as it shocked the Trade,[63] for Hepburn had sought a cross-coalfield agreement and Londonderry's unilateral settlement clearly threatened this.

But Londonderry's breach had opened a crack in the owners'

defences which ran and deepened much more quickly than the crack it had opened in the union's solidarity. As owners seethed at the settlement the union used it to support the campaign. On 18 May those pitmen who were back at work agreed to contribute one quarter of their wages to those still not working. Two days after the Londonderry bindings on 14 May, the second great Wear owner, Lord Lambton, started binding at his collieries. Buddle watched the Londonderry–Lambton settlements aghast. He believed Tyneside owners could never surrender like this saying that he himself was 'determined not to yield ... to the unreasonable demands of these ruffians. I will quit the Trade and emigrate to America rather than crouch to them'. Three days later (18 May) the third great Wear owner, the Hetton Coal Company, asked the Trade for leave to bind at the hewing prices of Lord Londonderry. On 20 May it did so: 'They got their Men bound at Hetton yesterday, by complying with their demands to the fullest extent'.[64]

With the three biggest concerns now out of the struggle, indirectly financing it against the other collieries, and producing coal, it was clearly only a matter of time before the rest admitted defeat. Their cause was now rotten from within. The big Wear collieries were selling without too much concern for the critical balances of the Vend and the smaller collieries could not afford to stand alone as sales and markets were lost. More than this, the union was now firmly wedged in the crack Londonderry had first made for it. Hepburn was calling strikes and making deals here and there as working pitmen were supporting striking pitmen to set owner against owner:

> The pitmen on the Tyne have laid off some of the Collieries this morning which had agreed with their Masters, and gone to work, because the Men had agreed for lower prices than the Union think they ought to accept. They have also compelled certain Coal-owners to discuss such petty agents as were obnoxious to them, & to hire all the ringleaders & Blackguards.[65]

In this atmosphere of impending victory, Buddle, as chief spokesman for the Trade and a hardliner against the union, was 'beset, hooted & hissed' wherever he went, but the menace of this was nothing to the shame of his association with Londonderry:

> I shall be very happy if your Lordship will explain your motives for yielding to the pitmens' terms, to the satisfaction of the Trade, as it has occasioned such a sensation ... as I never before witnessed.

Buddle was an intelligent and courteous viewer and correspondent for his Lordship, but with him there was no bowing and scraping. On 4 June Londonderry was directly informed of his viewer's contempt:

> I may, or I may not survive this storm, but if I do survive, I certainly will be very cautious, how I again, convict myself, in supporting the cause of those, who have not the moral courage, to support it themselves.[66]

On 13 June a disintegrating Coal Trade met to discuss the crisis, but many colliery representatives stayed away and, amongst those who did attend, there was no inclination to help those collieries still in dispute: 'they were likely to be left to their fate'. The victim collieries, alarmed and angered at such desertion, threatened to reintroduce binding monies and the astonishing sum of ten guineas was mentioned. On 18 June Buddle eyed a supine ownership. All Tyne and Wear except Tyne Main colliery had bound, and some like Callerton had paid two guineas binding money.[67]

It had been clear since the first week of June that the men had won a great victory. Buddle noted their elation, and their magnanimous treatment of himself:

> Pitmen have now found & established their power, and are devizing magnificent plans for their further agrandizement ... I am complimented for having fought them fairly, like a Man. I was chaired by force last Friday Eveng. at W. end and was obliged to abscond on the Sa. morning to avoid the honer of being drawn in grand procession from W. end to Newcastle ... I am now in favour again, without stepping out of my way to seek it.[68]

The manner of the control the pitmen wielded will be described in Part Three, but suffice to mention here that in June 1831 not only had they halted years of deterioration in pay and status, but they were also controlling production (maximum, 4s per man per day), controlling the labour market ('won't allow a Stranger who is not a regular-bred pitman to come amongst them on any account'), and seeking to extend their control of the pits by pressing for the removal of unpopular officials and embracing other workers – deputies, overmen, wastemen, sinkers, surface workers, craftsmen – within their ranks. In the summer of 1831 the pitmen were growing into a stature greater than that of redressors: practice was stumbling ahead of theory and, in the daily relations of work, they were beginning to test the claims of an owning class. In July, Buddle recorded that, in doing his rounds at Rainton and Pittington he found 'that the pitmen at both places, are completely masters of the Concerns'. On 14 July, and only two weeks before his breakdown, Buddle described how much, for him, normality had been dented, reality traduced, positions reversed:

> The Overman & their Deputies are entering the Union ... My nephew at Percy Main and his Under Viewer were compelled to go with the pitmen to carouse with them, in celebrating their Victory. What is to happen next it is impossible to guess.[69]

In fact, it was not so difficult to guess. The Coal Trade prepared to counter-attack at the next April binding. In January 1832 the Trade's Joint Committee resolved to 'circumvent the Colliers' Union' and set up an indemnity fund financed by a 2% tax on sales, and payable to 'any Coalowner [who] finds it necessary to adopt any Measure which is likely to cause his Colliery to be stopped work by the men'. Their flanks protected, on 10 March the Committee agreed not to bind any deputy, banksman, or 'keeker' (assessor of tubs and wages) in the union nor any unionists from another colliery, and to adhere strictly to the common clauses of a printed bond.[70]

While the Trade prepared for its offensive, the union sought to entrench its advances. This proved to be more difficult than they had imagined. At Hetton the winter of 1831–2 had seen perpetual wrangling, mainly over the classic issues of fines and the stowing of small coals, but also over deputies doing hewers' work, a gassy seam, and the negligence of the colliery surgeon. At Coxlodge and Kenton collieries the disputes were more serious. The introduction of immigrant leadminers from Weardale had provoked a strike. The local owners had embarked on this course knowing the Coal Trade would back them. They proceeded to evict. On 21 January 1832 the whole labour force was reported as homeless. By February, after two months of holding-out, the union was forced to accept the situation and allow the Coxlodge and Kenton men to seek work at other collieries.[71]

Hepburn and his delegates should have been warned by this because soon after the bonds were read in mid-March (only one third of collieries binding, and 'great bad humour amongst the Colliers') the owners decided to attack. With only half the collieries

bound by 14 April the Trade clearly had a struggle on its hands
anyway. They dropped their modest clause that deputies, keekers,
and banksmen should not be bound as members of the union, and
extended it to include union delegates (30 April), and all workers,
(5 May). On 12 May the Committee drew up an oath of fidelity
to apply to all bound men:

> I do not belong to the present Pitmen's Union, nor will I become a
> member of any Similar Association by a compliance with the fixed rules
> or regulations or occasional Resolutions which I can be prevented from
> the strict performance of any contract that I may enter into with my
> Employers.

On 30 May the Coal Trade resolved to break the union absolutely
and permanently: 'unanimous as to the necessity of adopting the
most efficacious measures to break the Union.[72]

Hepburn had decided to use the same strategy in 1832 as he had
in 1831: settling where they could, and using monies from working
members to support the actions at other collieries still in dispute.
In April the union was taxing its working membership at 5s in the £.
On 7 April the Trade Committee began to move against this
strategy. The earnings of working colliers were reduced to the
maximum of 3s per day, this was 1s per man per day less than the
Colliers had been restricting themselves since the previous summer.
On 1 June this policy was taken further when the Trade resolved
to pay-off working unionists who had not taken the 12 May oath,
evict them from their houses, and replace them with non-union
labour. On 16 June this eviction policy was made general, and on
23 June a memorandum was issued:

> Resolved, That the Rate of Work by all the Bound Collieries shall be
> the lowest Sum the Bonds will admit of, viz. 3s. per Day, until further
> Directions.
>
> Resolved, That it be recommended that those Collieries which remain
> unbound proceed without Delay to eject the Men from their Houses.

With its funds shrinking just as quickly as it members could be
evicted, in May the union was forced to increase its taxation of
working members from a quarter to a half. Major General
Bouverie, as officer commanding northern troops, feared for the
consequences:

> For Hetton Colliery alone I understand that between 8 and 900 Miners
> have been engaged to supply the Places of ejected Pitmen and as there

are few Pitmen without Families, this will give a tolerably accurate notion of the Numbers who are utterly and permanently thrown out of employment.[73]

Hetton had been identified as the union's chief redoubt. To overwhelm Hetton was to overwhelm the union. On the same day that the Hetton bond had been read and rejected – 'everything wrong the Delegates ungovernable' – its viewer had decided that 'a sweep must be made', 'As these Men's Movements will be wholly guided by those of Hetton'.[74] Two days after the reading, two weeks before the expiry of the old bindings, and over two months before it became general coalfield policy, Hetton decided to import non-union labour: 'Leadminers now determined upon'. On 10 April Hetton agreed to pay for Inspector Goodyear and seven Metropolitan police constables, and by 19 April Hetton alone was guarded by eight professional constables, forty special constables, sixty foot soldiers, and forty cavalry. On 21 April the Company began to evict. Twenty families, those of 'chiefly marked men', were turned into the street. The following night a bound pitman who had left the union was shot dead but this little local difficulty was not to thwart company policy: 'Turning out [was] determined to be carried on successfully at 20 to 30 per day'. On 24 April the Hetton pitmen, realising the turn in their employers' attitude, dropped all their price demands and agreed to settle for union recognition merely. There was no chance of this, given the identification of Hetton as prime target, with the Trade donating £2 per imported person in expenses and centrally directing imported labour there.[75] Through May and June immigrant workers moved into Hetton to replace the unionists: leadminers from the North Pennines, Swaledale, and Arkendale; others from Yorkshire, Lancashire, Derbyshire, Nottinghamshire, and North Wales. It seems that although the immigrants were said in many cases to be 'Capital good hewers', and did 'remarkably well', they lacked craft in the system of the pit and subsequently disappointed their patrons. The work depended upon cumulative skill and experience and this the immigrants patently did not possess. In May Matthias Dunn talked of the need for their encouragement, in June he was satisfied with their hewing, in July he was disappointed in their putting and driving, in August he was morose about the whole affair.[76]

Although Hetton remained the key battle, eviction was carried on throughout the coalfield:

> A large reinforcement of miners arrived at Hetton yesterday – Men from all parts of the Kingdom are flocking in, & 'eer long, a sufficient no. of strangers will arrive to supply all the Collieries that are in want of Men.

By June the army was in daily attendance at evictions; Dunn estimated that the Trade had installed 1200 non-unionists. On 12 June Brandling rejected a government suggestion that they should appeal to the men, refuted the notion that the dispute was over money, affirmed it was about the existence of trade unionism, and boasted that 250 North Welshmen had just been recruited without difficulty: the men 'can only be brought to understand their real interests by the Coal owners introducing new workmen, and shewing them that they can, if driven to it, do without their Services'.[77] The Coal Trade was showing signs of recovering some of its nerve. The 1831 defeat had shaken them, the March 1832 bonds had brought them back to the fight with tentative claims over who could and could not be in the union, and in May and June their confidence grew with every successful eviction, every batch of immigrants. This was a precarious confidence, quite impossible without the army.

At the end of June 1832 affairs appeared to turn again. The union had managed, on 18 June, to enrol forty-seven Wrexham men, 'Union men', brought in by the Trade the day before – 'they marched off in a body this Morning. This has given the Union great Confidence'. Moreover, those immigrants who were working were not profitable. On 28 July Buddle noted impatience, 'grumbling and snarling' in the Trade at the expense of blacklegging:

> Even Hetton, is making but poor work of it, with their large establishment of *raw levies* & I think Redhead is inclined if he could find a *loophole* to slip out of to break loose.

On 8 July General Bouverie reported to the Home Office that the pitmen were likely to win the struggle, and only his seven troops of cavalry and seven companies of infantry delayed their victory.[78]

It was at this point, between the end of June and late July 1832 that the union could have broken the stalemate. Hepburn had predicted the Trade's impending problems. At a mass meeting on

Boldon Fell on 26 May he had said he was confident of victory
as the costs of labour importation, indemnity funds, special
constables, Metropolitan police, and military, mounted. If the
union remained firm, rates and bills would do the rest. But a change
in tactics was also necessary. Union funds were diminishing daily
and there had been some complaining from working members.
The union could continue present tactics only if it lifted its own
imposed restriction on daily output and earnings. This would ease
the pressure on working members and release more funds for the
union, but it would also increase output and the stockpiling of
coals by the Trade. The higher the stockpiles, the longer the struggle
was likely to continue. On the other hand, the union could change
tactics dramatically and make 'a general stop immediately, in order
to bring the dispute with the Coal-owners to a speedy Crisis'. On
24 and 25 June the union delegates argued 'the expediency' of these
problems, and although some were 'of opinion that they will be
beaten by procrastination' it was agreed to continue the struggle
at half-cock for a further ten weeks. Events showed this decision
to be mistaken. After six weeks Hepburn decided to bring his
personal influence to bear and at a delegate meeting in Wallsend
on 8 August moved for a total and immediate strike, a last push.
Buddle saw the significance of this, 'If the majority should be for
the stop, I have no doubt a fortnight will settle the question for
20 years to come', but Hepburn's motion was not carried and,
logistically, the union was finished.[79]

Towards the end of July the cholera appeared. On 30 July cases
were reported in some colliery villages in Northumberland and
Durham; on 11 August there was 'havock all around'; and by
September 'Cholera is in almost all the villages to the South of
the Tyne'.[80] Union organisation staggered on through August
and September ('Hepburn and his colleagues ... indefatigueable
... to keep the spirit of the thing alive') although more drained
of its strength at some collieries than others. Hetton collapsed on
20 September. With 'Hebburn (sic) and the other leaders ... in
attendance' the agent and overmen were allowed

> ... to pick out as many and whom we please binding them under the
> declaration contained in the Bond against becoming members of any
> society acting against the free exercise of their working powers ...
> Notwithstanding great feeling prevails for some union of their own –
> which will I believe be carried on in spite of fate.[81]

There was a thinly attended meeting on Shadon's Hill on Christmas Day 1832. The meeting agreed to dissolve the union should the non-unionists not change their minds. On 16 February 1833, to the nervous amusement of a lately pulverised Coal Trade, the delegates disbanded:

> The only piece of intelligence of a lighter line which I have to com-
> municate is, that the *Cock Parliament* was dissolved yesterday, and
> the Union Army disbanded. *General Hepburn* has broken up his Staff
> & gone into *dignified* retirement to prepare his defence, against the
> Assizes where he is to be tried for a riot.[82]

The following decade was difficult and humiliating for the miners. In March 1833 the prices at which the immigrants had been hired were dropped − a tense moment and 'a knotty point' − but the pitmen were 'engaging ... with their Masters as fast as they can'. The surplus of imported men meant that 'the Masters cannot employ the numbers who are asking for work upon almost any terms'. The summer saw 'considerable distress' but the coalfield was 'perfectly peaceable', 'at even lower prices than they con-templated − as the pitmen are possie struck lest they should not get employment'.[83] The 1834 bindings were quiet: 'Nothing but their poverty ... prevents a general Strike'. In 1835 price reductions were considered and rejected; in 1836 they were considered, implemented by 10%, and accepted at the March bindings, although they were followed by a ripple of isolated strikes that winter.[84]

All the bindings from 1837−43 were quiet in spite of a strict labour vend which tried to keep wages at their lowest average. In 1837 serious labour shortages at the new collieries were masked by the labour vend − 'every Colliery in the Trade having their establishment of men fully employed'. In spite of this, the shortages do appear to have led to higher real earnings in 1837, a gain lost by 1839. On 3 March 1838 the viewers reminded the owners of the importance of not going over the 1832 agreed average of 30s per fortnight and

> ... not more than 6 men shall be employed at any Colliery from any
> other Colliery. And the Meeting wish the Committee to remonstrate
> with those Coalowners who are making extraordinary demands for
> Men, that the trade may not be inconvenienced and thrown into
> confusion.[85]

In 1841 all grades of workmen except hewers, no matter their colliery or conditions, were put on standard rates. In 1843, after Peel's reimposition of export duty and a fall in foreign markets, these rates were cut by ten per cent, and hewers' and putters' prices by 8%. Short-time meant that many men were only working a two or three day week for 9s or 10s: '... unless trade opens out so as to give the Pitmen better employment, nothing but starvation stares them in the face'.[86] Not even the best informed worker out of an economist's tract could be expected to stare starvation in the face and remain stoical.

During 1843 the National Miners' Association, founded in Wakefield the previous November, debouched out of bureaucratic beginnings to make its greatest strides in the North East. By the beginning of 1844 it had recruited nearly all the pitmen and boys, and Newcastle was its vanguard. The bonds were subsequently rejected, and on 5 April the most important coal dispute of the century began. Some form of union network had survived the events of 1832—3. The union had been banned by the new bonds, but its structures probably remained. In January and February 1834, Hepburn's renewed activity, with his former lieutenants Waddell, Pile, Atkinson and 'that slick headed, *ranting* Knave Charley Parkinson', had been reported like the rattling of old ghosts, but without anxiety.[87] In April 1834 pitmen had appeared in Owen's Grand National Consolidated Trade Union, and in July 1835 Hepburn and his cadre had agitated at Wallsend colliery in the aftermath of the explosion there which killed 102 on 18 June. Nothing seems to have been achieved, apart from the excitement and a brief strike at a couple of Tyne collieries the following month. Londonderry saw it as 'All Balderdash!!' Poverty was the owners' best defence.[88] After this failure Hepburn dropped out of sight to reappear again as a leading Chartist during 1838—9. The traditional view, set by Fynes, is that Hepburn was victimised from further work after the 1832 debacle. Fynes goes on to say that Hepburn then peddled tea around the villages before accepting work at Felling on the condition that he never again involved himself in trade union activity. Certainly, he does not figure in the NMA nor any other union activity after 1835. Hepburn worked at Felling until his retirement in 1859. He died five years later and was buried at Heworth.

The Chartist enlightenment of 1838—9 had no immediate effect on the terms of the hire. However, Chartism was crucial to the recruitment, theory, and practice of the National Miners' Association in the early 1840s. In 1844 the Trade refused at all times to negotiate, so much had the interpretation of the Bond changed, but the NMA's case is nevertheless interesting in the context of the hiring since 1800. The classic issues remained, but the new confidence of the union had articulated new demands as well as old grievances. The miners posed a six-month binding agreement from 5 April to 5 October. An October hiring would put them in a competitive bargaining position prior to the heavy winter coal demand, a position they had not occupied for thirty-five years. In earnings, they demanded weekly payments by weight; no payment in lieu; a proper pay-bill; compensation for all small coals rejected; payment for all coals hewed, and stone or 'splint' not to disqualify an otherwise full corve; 10s per week sick ('smart') money; medical attendance; and insurance for widows of 5s per week plus house and coals for the first year after bereavement. At work, hewers were not to do other men's work if there was no shortage of those men; boy trappers were to replace the recently introduced mechanical 'fly doors'; putters, drivers, and trappers, that is, the boys and lads, were not to work over ten hours a day; all workers under twenty-one were only to be hired under the Bond and not disciplined by it; and viewers were to be more discriminating in their use of gunpowder, for which allowances were to be paid to pitmen. In the management of collieries, some definition of a 'fair' days work and pay, in view of intermittent bouts of glut and idleness, was requested; there had to be either guaranteed work or guaranteed idle-time wages; and coal weights were to be tested by 'beam and scale' registered apparatus and open to government inspection, with all disagreements going to arbitration. Lastly, houses were no longer to be a part of earnings but instead be subject to a normal rent of £4 per year (the NMA obviously had eviction in mind here), and union members were not to be fined for absence from work if attending NMA delegate or public meetings.[90] This was the union's hope, but the events of 1844 were to show that they were to be disappointed.

6
Labourer?

The reformulation of the Bond as a contract of productive relations in the first half of the nineteenth century was not about some shedding of eighteenth-century 'pre-industrial' forms for nineteenth-century 'industrial' ones. Nor was the history of the binding during the period about the phoenix growth of trade unionism in the face of 'bad conditions'. Of course, it is possible to see features of both interpretations in what happened: the unprecedented economic growth of the coalfield, the sprouting of steam-engine houses and tall chimneys, the wittling away of the old annual Bond, and the tendency towards 'free' wage labour, are all features which can find a place in an imagery of 'industrialism' and trades unionism. However, such interpretations are more impressionistic than precise. One has to remember that although the old Bond was wittled away, what replaced it was aimed at a tighter regulation of labour on behalf of a property structure which, far from generating economic growth, actually resented it. Also, although the men undoubtedly regarded their condition and status as under attack, whether this was 'bad' depends upon what is meant by bad. The essential point must be that as former conditions and status deteriorated, the process of deterioration – closely supervised labour, standardised bonds, uniform rates of pay, and cross-coalfield negotiation – produced a new system which aided the development, in consciousness and practice, of trade unionism. The lines of coalowner victory ran closer and closer to the means of their defeat; the new attack on the pitmen produced practices and relations which enabled their defence. 'Bad' conditions can as little be seen as a 'cause', as trade unionism can be seen as a 'result': they can both be seen as a condition of each other in a critical struggle, within a given economic structure, between Capital and Labour for control.[1]

To summarise the argument: the pitmen could bargain their unique craft to gain market advantage in times of high demand for labour. This suggested itself, in spite of the formal obligations of the Bond, in the 1790s, and the propensity to use this sanction collectively grew from the early 1800s. The propensity, then, became self-conscious and would not go away even though from 1805 the coalowners tried to break its leverage in the collieries by systematising and intensifying the exploitation of the labour process. These moves only stimulated resistance. The friendly societies, the Brotherhood, the United Colliers, Hepburn's Union, and the National Miners' Association, all fought with increasing sophistication to limit Capital's regulation of the market and the labour process.

Such fundamental contests for the control of change in productive relations were accompanied by contests over social relations. Given the resistance the pitmen were being forced to make, it was important for them to retain, or create, a sense of their own legitimacy as 'regular-bred', of unique skill and inherited knowledge. Their right to bargain defined their patrimony. Their employers sought to deny them this right attempting to re-cast as *labourers*. To call the pitmen labourers had serious implications for the industry's productive and social relationships.

The idea of social interpretation, involving how people see themselves as well as how others try to see them, involves levels of prescription as well as description. The period of prosperity, 1797–1805, slowly diminishing thereafter to 1815, was later fixed by the mining community as the time from when the great deterioration began. Traditions can be made in two generations. As the contest became more intense, literate, recorded, and conceptual, it was necessary to have a perspective on it which was continuous with what went before – in other words it was necessary to have an historical past. The period 1797–1815, very roughly, as in the manner of these things, was invoked as the traditional time, the preceding order which had been upset by Trade demands 'ever since'. Thus, the pitmen were the redressors wanting nothing but their 'rights'; the owners were the speculators bankrupting the standing orders of perpetuity.[2] It is of course difficult to be sure that the pitmen were not accurate – it may be that the prosperity and degree of independence they enjoyed during the traditional period did indeed approximate to their position throughout the eighteenth century. But this is open to doubt; certainly, what evidence there is does not suggest it. Nevertheless, the whole tone of the pitmen's case throughout the first half of the nineteenth century is informed by a sense of *denouément*, which bore this factitious relationship to the past.

The invention of tradition needs symbols as well as histories. The binding time was not only an opportunity to renew contracts, it was also a holiday festival.[3] In his revelry, his showy independence, and his ultimate 'bargain', the pitman affirmed his social position which was not only set by the cash nexus. In the history of the binding it is noticeable, for instance, how both the Delaval and Londonderry concerns harboured an idea of 'our' pitmen. There are two observations to be made here. First, the idea of 'our' pitmen involved a sense of custom and stasis. They were Londonderry men, or Delaval men, and no one else's. As such, they were born to their labour, held it by custom, and enjoyed a notional right to it. This view of the job as a property, or a freehold, applied to positions of gain and status far beyond the lowly social world of the pitmen. Durham Cathedral had precentorships, its University had fellowships, Delaval had clerical livings, Londonderry had once held an army commission, which were seen in much the same terms. It can come as no surprise that, albeit in an understandably confused way, the pitmen tried to make a parallel case against market demands and labourer status. Secondly, the idea also involved a degree of loyalty between the master and 'his' men. This was an obligation which either side could, and did, come to see as broken, but in the early stages to some extent at least the pitmen reciprocated the idea.

At the Hartley bindings in September 1800 the first two men to bind, and who did so without negotiation, were men who were grateful: one Patterson, recently out of gaol for rioting, and another, Ralph Spooner, 'Son of an Old Woman your Lordship gives a weekly gift to, who willingly came forward through gratitude.'[4] The skills were always recognised: 'first rate men' were courted 'with some little promises', their calibre was exchanged in the giving of extra 'hand money' to clinch the bargain. In 1803 Delaval gave out hand moneys ranging from 10s to £2 10s. In times of labour shortage, all pitmen were courted irrespective of calibre — 'some Collys. is giving six pound a man which makes them very fitt to sit with'.[5] Drink was another symbol. At binding time its acceptance marked agreement:

> We read our Bond to the Workmen yesterday afternoon at Hartley but those were at Home ... seemed very shy & would scarcely take any Liquor at your Lordship's expence.

At the 1804 bindings Delaval spent £100 on drink and not all of it was the token stuff of agreement. In 1802 unwilling binders 'expect[ed] a few shillings given to them privately to drink', and in 1800, at one colliery, men were 'kept ... well supplied with Ale so long as they would drink it ... after which they got Hot Ale & Brandy for some time with an interest to keep them from Newcastle'.

In the early 1800s the drinking bouts at bindings in the northern coalfield were nationally famous, and it was still part of the expected style of things in 1820:

> Our pitman's Binding is to take place on Stdy, and as it is generally a drunken job I don't expect that we shall get much work out of them on Mondy & Tuesday.[6]

However, by the 1840s, binding time revels had been disciplined. In 1805, in order to curb rival 'treating' the Trade had banned binding at public houses and stipulated that 'no treat or drink shall be given directly or indirectly' although 'the usual allowance of Liquor' was still permissible. Alongside this, there had been moves to cut the paying of men from its drinking connections. Mr Nicholson of Shoreswood colliery dated this process from 1804–34:

> When I first entered into the coal business, it was the custom to pay the men in an ale-house. Their employers having all an interst in breweries, they had public-houses established in the collieries for that express purpose, and the men were all obliged to expend a certain sum of money every pay night.[7]

In 1842 tickets for free beer were given out on the one day of hire, quite unlike the days when 'they used to have any quantity of ale or beer given them', but there was no more bargaining and the drink custom, like the binding moneys, hand moneys, and other extras, had by then become perfunctory rather than celebratory.

The supply of grain was another symbol of peculiarity and prosperity banned in 1805.[8] Cheap grain seems to have been sold intermittently to the pitmen when necessary. In 1779 Delaval was selling meal to his men at 3d less than local shopkeepers, and 1781 unpaid corn bills show that he was in receipt of regular supplies.[9]

In April and May 1795 Tyne and Wear pitmen were in the van of popular agitations against the high bread prices and grain hoarding. On 7 May six pitmen-representatives were assured by Tyne magistrates that they would stop any grain hoarding which might have taken place — and this inspite of the fact that 'Grain is generally distributed to [pitmen] at a lower price than other labouring men'. It is from this year that corn allowances were regularly made to the mining community. At first this allowance was in barley, a cereal remembered by one pitmen as producing a bread 'as coarse and black as the coal':

> ... with regard to Barley the Labouring People in the Colliery District cannot bear the Idea of Barley Bread an attempt was made to introduce it in the year 95 by some Coal Owners but without Effect, as the Wkm. rioted and positively refused to use Barley even in mixture with other Grain exclaiming that their Owners wished to feed them like Swine.

Consequently, by 1800 'the Coal Owners are under the Necessity of supplying them with Rye at the Rate of 10s per Boll'.[10] It is as well to remember that pitmen won rye bread while northern agricultural workers had to make-do or starve. As George Culley wrote in 1800,

> Our poor people make their Bread altogether of 2 parts Barley & one of Pease unfortunately our Pease failed totally ... The Scots poor all eat out meal in Porrage. Hasty Pudding George Mennin can explain to you. But alas! our oats are all done, which I never knew before ... But last year God knows was a fatal one. However our poor have kept wonderfully quiet.[11]

There were other symbols. By the 1850s colliery celebrations at the owners' expense were likely to be morally educational. At best, they were little pageants of loyalty to the proprietorship. Earlier celebrations had been more celebratory of the pit in itself. They had been good days out, treats without homilies. When Simon Temple opened the Chapter Main colliery in 1810, a garlanded procession of eight full coal wagons preceded the festivities; when Hetton colliery was formally opened in 1822, workers' flags and bands paraded, men, women, and children jigged to 'The Bonny pit laddie', and the gentlemen owners 'partook of an excellent dinner at Livingston's' where 'some of the main coal were displayed at the windows'. At the Gosforth opening in 1829, there was a subterranean ball in the pit, a thousand feet underground.[12]

The community's response to the deterioration of these symbols was confused. They complained about 'the removal of many of our privileges', 'the insolent and contemptuous manner' in which they were addressed, they lamented life in 'the doleful hole' under 'a system so ruinous to us', but the substance of this sort of deterioration in human relationships was difficult to sift. Prices, fines, hours, measures, conditions, could all be seen; deep swirls in the consciousness of economic and social relations were much harder to perceive. The community's attitude to eviction showed this well. Most pit families lived in cottages supplied by the owners under their terms of contract in the Bond. In 1832 and 1844 hundreds of striking families were evicted. They had refused to renew their contracts, they could expect no more. And yet, what was a contract against a tradition? With factitious historical license the pitmen appealed to a 'reliance upon custom' 'from generation to generation': 'For centuries have they and their forefathers been the tenants of their habitations', and it was understood that, should they 'give "a fair days labour for a fair days wage"' then they would never lose their homes. This was woolly stuff, but how could a lawyer's contract cope with the conviction of people who believed, or said they believed, in the obligations of 'time immemorial'?

> The complaint of harsh eviction we found very general among the pitmen; but, from subsequent inquiries we had reason to doubt whether it was quite authentic. They all admitted the right of eviction, but they all thought that they might have been permitted to occupy their houses at least until new tenants came. The houses, they argued, were standing empty. It would have been a great convenience to the men to have been left a few days, and would have entailed no loss on the masters. The tone adopted in these complaints was, however, rather ad misericordiam, than anything like an assertion of rights ...[13]

Every eviction broke a strand in what was perceived to be an old, and in some ways honourable, relationship. To replace 'regular-bred' families with outsiders, other miners, farm workers, and Irish, and to tip them on the streets, was the action of wreckers. The owners, of course, had their own convictions. They answered with the laws of supply and demand tied to the twin pillars of want and deference in a society committed to the protection of its poor, from its poor, for its poor:

> To excessive Wages may be attributed many of the Vices which attach
> to the Character of a pitman. They give him *more than sufficient to
> provide the necessaries of life,* and from the want of *Prudence* the
> surplus is dissipated in riot and Intemperance.[14]

The pitmen faced up to those aspects of deterioration which
they could identify. In 1831 they insisted that all employees had
to be 'native of the county of Northumberland or Durham, and
brought up a Pitman'.[15] At the beginning of the century there
had been no need for this. The unique standing of the pitmen was
agreed by all observers; a few agricultural labourers may have sent
their sons to nearby collieries 'but, for the most part, the work
is carried on by regularly bred pitmen and their Families'. In a
sense, for such a self-conscious group, any comparison with other
workers was a disapprobation but, at least early comparisons were
favourable. In 1771 and 1797 estimates by Arthur Young and Sir
Frederic Eden put pitmen on a par with local journeymen and the
best paid 'manufacturers'. In 1776 Adam Smith twice quoted the
higher earning power of colliers over 'the most skillful artificers'
in support of his theories.[16] It has to be said that Young, Eden,
and Smith all chanced upon the coalfield during relatively
prosperous periods. It also has to be said that both Smith and Eden
referred to the pitmen as 'labourers'. However, Eden was simply
talking of 'labourers of all descriptions', by which he meant 'The
Poor'; and it was unlikely that Smith's ideal, analytical, ordered,
economy would heed local peculiarities of evidence. By 'skilled'
Smith meant apprenticed, usually in a town; by 'common labour'
he meant unapprenticed, usually in the country. During the 1810
dispute the *Newcastle Courant* stated that pitmen's earnings were
'far greater than those of any other class of mechanics'.[17]

In 1825, in reply to the United Colliers, the owners struck a
deft blow for reinterpretation-by-comparison. They claimed the
demands to be extravagant, comparing the miners earnings 'with
those of the robust agriculturalist, or sedentary weaver, and enquire
of the hewer whether he will change "Kavels"?' This comparison
hurt. The union deeply resented external comparison with weavers
or labourers; they wanted to be seen in the context of their own
history and the industrial changes which they had wrought. For
them, pitmen and mechanic stood together as signs of the times;
they '... reciprocally assist each other: once separate them, the
astonishing movements of mechanism must stand still, and its

glorious effects cease'.[18] But perceptions, and prescriptions, were changing. In 1812 Revd Hodgson of Felling had publicly questioned whether the pitmen's collective craft and knowledge could match the increasing dangers of their work. The safety movement gradually displaced pitmen's knowledge into viewers' and engineers' knowledge – properly constituted, certified and professional – and emphasised subordination, discipline, supervision, and management. During the 1831 dispute, Edward Smith, 'An Old Pitman', told Hepburn '... you are not Artists or Mechanics you have not generally served apprenticeships to other professions'; 'Philanthropos', a contending idealogue of the dispute, downgraded the pitmen even more, '... the wages of the pitmen, do, in point of fact considerably exceed those of the *ordinary* class of labourers'; and James Losh, a local capitalist and radical politician, prominent in the Coal Trade, answered to his own satisfaction the union's claim to be compared with mechanics: 'It is quite plain that the pitmen have good wages, and are in all respects better off than most labourers ...'[19]

By the 1840s there can be no doubt that official (State) categorisation at least, had fixed the pitmen as labourers. Sir James Walsham, Poor Law Commissioner for the area, and an expert in social categories for a system which operated by them, feared that pitmen's wages were dropping perilously close to those of the lowest class of Newcastle labourers. But Walsham had no doubt that labourers they must be. For the first time we hear of the dual class of 'agricultural and mining labourers'.[20] And if labourers were only entitled to a certain sort of social wage, so were they only entitled to a certain sort of comfort. The *Durham Chronicle* adjudged that the rosewood box of an evicted family, the Richardsons, was too good for them: 'It will be observed that mahogany is not good enough ... they must have rosewood'.[21]

The NMA in 1843 had enjoyed some legal success against the Thornley Coal Company, who, among other things, had imprisoned men for breaking their bonds. In law, the Bond retained the status of a contract technically binding both parties equally and it was here that the legal victories had been won. George Hunter, agent for Londonderry, recognised the risk of this. He pressed for the final act of reinterpretation of the Bond:

> From the conduct of these men ... it is quite evident we must have no more Bindings; they must be offered fair Prices, and if they like to work

at them − *do so* − but never again to allow them the power by any written Documents to haul you before the Magistrates whenever they please. My opinion is, that if the Coal Trade pursues this course, and makes the Pitman no more than a common Labourer, to be discharged for every Offence, we will soon crush the Union and have peace again.[22]

This, in fact, occurred. The 1844 dispute quickly jettisoned the nice points of prices, fines, and idle-time, to centre on the issue of the monthly Bond. The possibility of one month's termination of contract in a regulated labour market reduced the pitman to a 'common Labourer' contractually as well as socially. A general meeting of viewers in March 1844 recommended this course, and one month before the dispute started, the owners knew exactly what they intended to get from the union − submission. The monthly Bond lasted ten years, from 1844 to 1854.[23]

It is clear from the owners' decision of March 1844 that the pitmen's standing could not be redefined without concurrent changes in the manner of negotiation. The decade 1799−1809 had hurried-on collective negotiations. The move from individual, to colliery, to local, to coalfield bargaining between Brotherhood and Trade sharpened the perceptions of division. In 1765, when both sides had met in collective dispute, the owners had feared the outcome. They threatened the law but did not mean it, and promised a satisfactory compromise if only the men would go back to work 'as they are obliged by law to do'.[24] This flexible attitude hardened in the nineteenth century into stances which sought only to 'break the neck of this formidable combination' and refusals to negotiate at any stage on any point.[25] In 1826 the United Colliers heard a lot of abuse, but no negotiation. In 1831, in spite of a joint meeting of owners, delegates, and county justices on 11 April, it looked as if the same would happen until Londonderry broke rank and negotiated. There does seem to have been the semblance of paternalism between the Lord and the men of his 'ancient' pits at Rainton, Penshaw, and Pittington. In 1826 the Rainton men had expressed their faith in plain speaking with Londonderry, and in April 1831 it was he who first snubbed the magistrates as intermediaries and went ahead to make his own bargain in the May. Londonderry's language, a polite, distanced, conceit, signed 'you shall never be deceived in me', is interesting:

> If you will resume your Labours, I will at once give you the Thirty
> Shillings per Fortnight, and the Fines must be left to my honour and
> your Viewers' good sense ... There shall be no difficulty in the way
> of score work prices, only let me feel I deal with my own, and not with
> the Pitmen of other Collieries who can neither be attached to us nor
> our property.

Londonderry dealt with his own, and his own appreciated it so
much that two years later he was prevented from coming north
'as they are sure to get a hint of the intended reduction of Wages,
and will most likely be desirous of appealing to your Lordship'.[26]
The Londonderry and Lambton concerns were the biggest but they
were also family concerns. Being the first to negotiate they won the
loathing of a Trade of lessees and partners with a less direct sense
of involvement. Londonderry came to an agreement in 1831 for
other, more crushing reasons (bankers and lawyers) than his
paternalism, but it remains noteworthy that he squared the loathing
of his colleagues with the recovery of his lordly responsibilities
to his workers.[27]

In its drive for the monthly 'bonded' labourer, the 1844 dispute
was essentially about the destruction of what was perceived as a
battered tradition for what was prescribed, inaccurately, as a
market, but Londonderry, in his capacity as Lord Lieutenant of
Durham and leading owner, tried the paternalist ploy to break the
NMA:

> I was all day yesterday & the Day before with my men haranguing &
> demonstrating the folly and ruin to their union − It will be a great
> point if I can sever my men from the Union, & shew the example to
> the rest. You will observe those I have got to Work were Union Men
> − Three Pits are a good beginning.[28]

By July it was obvious that this ruse had not worked. He told the
Home Secretary of the inspirational and intimidatory effect of
union 'monster meetings' on his men and the end of their special
relationship with him:

> It now evidently appears to me that whatever influence individual Coal-
> owners may have over their own people so long as these assemblages
> & Meetings are permitted ... so long will the power of Mr Roberts &
> his leaders prevail.[29]

No matter how much the State's commissioners could regret the
intervention of trade unions and the demise of a moral economy

where 'Immemorial usages were considered almost tantamount to law'; and no matter how much 'mortification' owners could claim 'notwithstanding their long-continued efforts to cultivate a good understanding with their workpeople ... they were deserted, and lost all influence, from the moment that the delegates came among them'; and no matter what elaborate, romantic, mercenary, notions of paternalism were those of a Londonderry, the fact remains that throughout the ten months of dispute and impending dispute, from the first intimations of dissatisfaction in November 1843 to the surrender of the NMA in September 1844, the Coal Trade refused at all times to negotiate. Owners may have been mortified, but if so, why their 'silent contempt'?; and what kind of relationship did they want when men were forced to beg an audience, 'Once more we appeal ... can we obtain an interview? Tell us how and by what means?'; and what kind of relationship did they substitute for old 'paternalism' in the 1850s. – except a relationship of victimisation lists and Trade funds?

> It is agreed that a sum of about £50,000 shall be raised, as the first contribution towards a Fund for the support of Collieries the workmen of which may strike for an advance of wages; and also towards a Fund for obtaining labour from other districts or Counties, unconnected with this district.[30]

Ideologically, Labour's place in a proper productive relationship had been prepared by the 1820s. Malthus had made the first significant preparations with his model of a labouring poor petrified by its own instincts, and Nature's wish, within the ordained confines of supply and demand. There was precious little room in Malthus' social thesis for the positive intervention of the poor themselves. Similarly for the activities of trade unions. Popular Political Economy pronounced them a waste of time in the matter of wages. The working class were to be nullified by an educated acceptance of Nature's iron laws; when hard times came it was the market's inviolable operations which were the cause, not government or masters. As Harriet Martineau told Hepburn: 'combine against ill fortune instead of against the masters'.[31] In 1825 the Coal Trade had rejected not only the United Colliers' arguments but even the union's objective existence; one had to obey the market and that was that. In 1843 the *Newcastle Journal* modestly took it upon itself to lecture the NMA in the hard facts:

It would take a long time, however, to explain the laws which regulate
the rise and fall of wages, and at present we have not that time, or the
space necessary to spare... In the meantime, we cannot refrain from
expressing a general fact, that no combinations which have ever yet
been formed have been effectual in altering wages, either one way or
another. They depend entirely on different laws than the will of either
master or men. They depend on supply and demand.[32]

In a market whose major producers sought to 'vend' men as well
as coal, there was little that was 'natural' about the movements
of supply and demand. Rather, that reinterpretation of productive
relations which the mining community experienced as deterioration
was integral to the Coal Trade's exertions to maintain its economic
structure by regulating, standardising, and rendering pliable the
hiring of labour.

Royden Harrison has referred to the popular image of the coal
miner as the 'original and quintessential proletarian'.[33] However,
it is worthy of remark that this image originated more as a prescription of manipulability than as a description of militancy. 'Free
labour' under a monthly bond and the stricter supervision of the
labour process was an element of other plans in the 1850s for social
'colonisation', where the pitmen would do as they were told and
be versatile. Up to the 1840s, and into the 1850s, the pitmen did
not see themselves or their future in terms of a 'proletariat',
quintessential or otherwise. They had to associate, and battle,
within a space between two powerful dispositions. The first disposition was peculiar to the northern counties, and tended to favour
the *Bond* and *Bondager* system of hiring which operated on
Northumbrian farms and, in a modified way, in the lead-mining
dales. Here, legally binding contracts, low cash payments, and
close class control by employers, combined to produce good
social order, consisting mainly of hard, loyal work and rude
moral health.[34] It was common to compare these very desirable
features with the collective actions, cash nexus, and independent,
intemperate social mores of the pit community. The second
disposition was the coalowners' wish to enclose these undesirable
features and make the mining community more like Northumbrian
farm labourers or dales leadminers. Although their desire was to
break collective action, weaken the cash nexus, and control the
social mores, every move the owners made in that direction met
with an opposition which, although by no means successful, only

served to accentuate the undesirable features. The owners, given total control, no more desired a monthly bond or a company school house, than the pitmen did.[35] They hoped that the monthly bond and school house would enable their wider aim. In fact, it did not. Monthly bonds as a way of squeezing out 'troublemakers', and company schools as a way of indoctrinating children only carried the pit community further away from the ideal of Northumbrian labourers or Durham dales people. This study stops in the 1850s, in the middle of this process. The result is a certain confusion in language and terminology about described and prescribed changes in 'social character'. The northern coalfield was not seen as on its way to 'free labour'; nor was it seen, in honesty, as on its way to deference and dependence. Part Three of the volume will return to these processes.

Part One has studied changes at Work relevant to the generation of a new social character. It has been argued that by the 1850s a key restructuring of productive relations had taken place. There have been six areas of investigation. First, an unstable background of unprecedented economic growth and expansion of the labour force. Secondly, the gradual devaluation of the pitman's craft and autonomy, especially in the newer collieries, accompanied by a greatly heightened risk to life and limb in larger, deeper, and more dangerous mines, and the owners' imposition of more systematic modes of work. In response to the deterioration in their conditions and relations which this was thought to bring, the pitmen in turn sought to organise their labour around a policy of restricted output. Thirdly, the early nineteenth-century questioning of the pitmen's ability to perform their work safely and profitably – a tacit inquiry which flowered in the 1830s into a full critique of the temperament and valid knowledge of the whole community. From the late 1840s this critique drew the reply of more regulation, discipline, inspection, a formal subordination, and a 'practical' education. Fourthly, changes in the Bond from a bargain into an instrument for exploitation and control, a reinterpretation made necessary by the weakening structure of the northern owners' cartel, the Vend. Fifthly, consequent changes in modes of bargaining from local to coalfield negotiation, to no negotiation at all, which was attended by attempts to standardise agreements and polarise labour and capital. Lastly, the symbolic shifts in status, at once dramatised by an invented tradition of past order (1797–1815), and increasingly articulated in a vocabulary of Political Economy. By the 1830s, and much to his dismay, the true bred pitman was being called a common labourer.

The history of Work represents the shedding of a caste of pitmen in order to rehire from a market of labourers. It is a history easier to narrate than to quantify. Although Political Economy's universal concepts of 'labourer' and 'market' came to express the changes, it is obvious that they did not determine them. The concepts were applied over a history of crisis and response. Labour's experience of the process was both cumulative and immediate. Cumulatively, the 1832 defeat marked the beginning of the end for the true-bred pitman, and yet when Hepburn held immediate power in the summer of 1831 he was not to know this, nor were his successors to accept it in 1844.

Right up until the 1850s there were pitmen who hoped and worked for other things. As such it would not be sensible to try to assign relative 'weights' of significance to the six areas of investigation. One can identify the first expressions of new social character, and one can trace them to changes in work relations, but there can be no tidy list of lesser and greater determinants. The complexity and inter-relatedness of the process must stand.

Similarly, given Harrison's reference to the coal miner as 'archetypal proletarian', and the changes outlined above, it might be convenient to talk about the making of a working class. This is a much larger project, and in general and retrospective terms, it is acceptable, but for the purposes of this history, 'as-it-happened', the notion can be misleading. At the workplace, nineteenth-century developments were so uneven that the general phrase 'making of the working class', could be used to side-step history and neglect its actual convolutions. For the conditions and practices under which class made and re-made itself were also uneven. The relationships of class consciousness (rather than their mere expression)[36] across occupation, gender, place, and time, were more in the nature of a series of bruises rather than an open break.

In the North East, the mining community's first class-conscious response to the events engulfing them was in the imagery of a Radical-Chartist theory of labour value. Their greatest inspiration came from Chartism and this will be examined in Part Three. The concept of labour value was largely spread by trade unionists, many of whom were Primitive Methodist Christians with additional, religious notions of labour's dignity. In addition, the 1830s and 1840s saw efforts to reformulate the consciousness of coalfield women. This is a more indirect cultural history demanding different approaches. It is the cultural impact of Primitive Methodism, new concepts of womanhood, and the contribution of both to a new social character, which is the major theme of Part Two.

Part two

Culture

7
Methodism and social character

The Primitive Methodists alighted upon the pit villages, literally, from out of the hills. They were founded in Staffordshire in 1811 and reached Tyneside and County Durham from their Yorkshire circuits in 1820. By 1825 they were established in the coalfield, and by 1845 their role was already considered to be central to the life of the coalfield. They were hostile to the old life they found and passionate about the new life their religion offered. In the confrontations which occurred in the twenty-five years between 1820 and 1845, lie insights into the culture of the mining community.[1]

In 1846 Mr J Wales, underviewer for Lord Ravensworth at Killingworth and Burraton collieries, told the government commissioner of a great and recent change in social character:

> I have known this village all my life; the people are much improved, and bring up their children better; most of them attend some place of worship. Cockfighting, gambling, fighting etc. are nearly gone by. We have had four of the county police in the parish, and they have had a good effect in promoting better habits, in putting down card-playing and gambling in the public houses etc.[2]

Underviewer Wales went on to single out the village Methodists – Wesleyans, Primitives, and New Connexion – for particular praise in this record of regulation, propriety, and 'moral improvement'.

For the 1840s, Wales' comments were typical. Comments of this kind dominated the discussion of the colliery districts. William Morrison, doctor for the Countess of Durham's collieries, considered that the community was emerging from the greatest possible moral and intellectual darkness; George Hunter, underviewer for Lord Londonderry, thought that 'although there may be a little dog and cock fighting, there is nothing to compare with what there was formerly; John Harrison, viewer at Newbottle colliery, observed thankfully that 'there are few persons of an openly vicious character here now ... anything gross seldom occurs';[3] James Anderson, Home Missionary at Easington Lane, was glad to report that the drinking had declined; Dr Greenhow believed that the miners now washed more diligently than before.[4] A catalogue of vice – dog-fighting, cock-fighting, gambling, drinking, bowling, swearing, fighting, shamelessness, ignorance, and illiteracy – was observed to have fallen into recent and dramatic decline. Oswald Herbst heard '... it generally said, that a great improvement in many respects has taken place in the moral condition of the Miners during the last *twenty* years.'[5] There were other chronologies: since 'eight or ten years back', 'within the last ten years', 'of late years', 'in ten years', 'in the last fifteen years', 'fifteen or twenty years ago', 'twenty years ago', and at Hebburn both hewer and underviewer could agree that the improvement had first begun some thirty or forty years previous to 1846.[6]

Most commentators suggested the Methodists as the body responsible. In the words of Seymour Tremenheere, 'though still leaving much to be desired' the changes were 'greatly attributable to their exertions'.[7] Many owners, viewers, and vicars looked to schooling for future improvement, and some thought the sunday schools, or tighter colliery regulations, were equally important,[8] but the overwhelming consensus of consulted opinion praised the Methodist religious influence. The Church of England was hardly mentioned. George Elliot told of the 'great hold' the chapel had 'on the pit people', and although quick to point out that he was not a Methodist himself, the 'Methodists have done more to ameliorate the pitmen than the whole church put together'; John Reay specified 'the instrumentality of the Wesleyan Methodists'; John Buddle congratulated Methodism together with Temperance; the Haswell agent mooted the special ability of the Primitive Methodist lay-preachers; William Fordyce talked in terms of Methodism having 'neutralized' the traditions of colliery life; James Mather talked in terms of having civilised them. The correspondent to the *Gateshead Observer* perfectly caught the tone of the change, and its perception, when without contradiction he declared that,

> The day of darkness is beginning to pass away from the mining districts in the north. The Methodist preachers have been the great pioneers – preparing the way for the illumination of the people.[9]

Throughout the nineteenth century the pit itself was portrayed as a place of corruption: a training ground in 'deceit and evasion' in 1807, and a place where schoolboys went 'completely to wreck' in 1866.[10] There had always been moral concern, but the new colliery populations provoked a concentration of attention, effort, and fear over the pitman's moral condition. In 1844 the Bishop of Durham walked his cloisters under

> ... a painful sense of the insecurity, under which Durham and its vicinity, to the SE and SW are exposed ... The whole County from Durham to Hartlepool on the one hand, and to W. Auckland on the other is one vast excavation; teeming with a numerous and ignorant population.[11]

If the colliery districts had long been thought more disorderly than the agricultural districts, then the new colliery villages of the 1830s both compounded the disorder and deepened it into something approaching depravity. New excavations in the south and east of the coalfield not only brought new recruits to the industry, they also tempted families to move away from established pits. Whilst the established pits (for all their instinctive licence) did have some moral sanctions, the new pits encouraged higher levels of mobility, and mobility without sanction, it was argued, made these pits 'naturally the receptacles of the refuse of the old', manned as they were by '... the immediate importation of the scum, and off-scouring of a peculiar, mischievious and unlettered race'. For every expanding district, from Auckland in the south, to those collieries west of the City of Durham, to the new villages of the east Durham plain, the charge was the same: in an industry recruited from labourers 'the dross of society', the men of the new collieries were 'the wickedest set on the face of the earth'.[12]

These were the remarks of crisis. They were made as old meanings were breaking down and new meanings had yet to replace them. By the 1860s a lot of cultural effort had been put into recovering an order based on new meanings. The 1866 Select Committee reported as if substantial sections of the mining community had been recovered. It reported, in effect, not on one community but two. There was the 'better type' and the 'lower type' of family. The former was conceived as being by turns more prudent, educated, competent, industrious, and well conducted than the latter.[13] Much of this improvement was premised by an appropriate sexual division of labour between home and pit. The 1830s and 1840s lay in the middle of this process of cultural observation and change: in the 1842 Children's Employment Commission one can see the beginnings of the new observation, and hear the testimonies of change.[14] The Methodists saw themselves as cultural revolutionaries and established themselves in the years of crisis. However, they were not alone in their efforts. They operated within a context of 'moral improvement' generally. Before analysing the circumstances of their growth and the meaning of their cultural intervention, it is first necessary to account for the general circumstances in which they worked. This is the theme of Chapter Eight. It is divided into three parts. First, the pit village itself; secondly, local initiatives for order and regulation; and thirdly, State initiatives, which centred on the women of the village.

8
Moral improvement

The village

Part One dealt with the expansion of a coalfield and its workforce from the 1820s, but up to the 1860s mining families could only predominate at the parish level. Therefore, although there was diversity of settlement, especially on urban Tyneside and Wearside, the village is a true unit of study when talking about the northern coalfield.[1] Mining villages could range from places like New Cassop which in 1855 had a few cottages, retailers, and eight drinking houses, to Wingate, which in 1855 had 150 double cottages, 228 single cottages, six pubs, various shops, two policemen and a lock-up, a Primitive Methodist chapel, a Wesleyan chapel, and a station on the Hartlepool branch of the North Eastern Railway.[2] Within Hetton le Hole in 1850, there were various densities of mining families. Some zones had over 80% of householders' 'headed' by a miner; others had over 45% and a mingling with craftsmen 'headed' families; others had under 45% and a scattered collection of families involved in pit work, crafts, retailing, agriculture, and clothing and domestic goods manufacture. Nearby Hetton Lyons hamlet had its 'Quality Row' cottages for colliery officials and skilled metal workers.[3]

Although mining settlements were usually planted close to older agricultural villages and hamlets (New Cassop was one mile away from Old Cassop which had four farmhouses, some cottages and, Fordyce tells us, a good view of Durham City) and were *rural* communities where the settlement covered only a fraction of the area, their dominating physical image, the smoking colliery and its clanking railway, was uncompromisingly *industrial*. For example, in 1816 Hetton on the Hill in Pittington parish, was described by Surtees as 'a small village to the North East of Elemore', and, as

for Thornley in Kelloe parish, Surtees said nothing more of it
except who owned the estate.[4] In 1834 Thornley was 'three
farmsteads; and the village ... contains a public house, and the
shops of a blacksmith, and a cartwright and joiner'; some six
miles away, Murton contained only five farmsteads.[5] In 1831
sinking for coal began near to Hetton on the Hill; in 1834 a
successful sinking began at Thornley; in 1838 operations began
at Murton. By 1855 Hetton on the Hill was completely dominated
by its colliery neighbour at South Hetton and is not mentioned
in topographies; Murton's population had risen from ninety-eight
in 1831 to 1,387 in 1851; and Thornley, like the others, had
become a pit village whose 'old village' was insignificant besides
its 'modern village' of plant, railway, pit rows, pubs, shops, a
colliery school, Primitive and Wesleyan chapels, a Roman Catholic
chapel and school, and a library financed by the Thornley Coal
Company. In 1831 Thornley had had a population of fifty, by
1851 it had a population of 2,730.[6] For the people of the villages
the colliery defined the division of labour just as it defined the
geography and demography. Apart from domestic service, occasional agricultural labouring, and pauperism, there were few
work categories for women, and apart from farming and seafaring
most other occupations for men were in direct, or secondary
relationship, with coalmining.[7]

Criss-crossed as it was with roads, wagonways, and eventually
railways, the coalfield had one of the earliest and most developed
transport systems in the country. The villages were easily accessible,[8] and the mid-, east, and south Durham coalfield in particular sustained high levels of local immigration in the 1840s.[9]
Contemporary observers, especially those most concerned with
the correlation of morality with stability, assumed that economic
growth had increased the annual movement of population. This
was a reasonable deduction, but what evidence there is does not
positively support the theory. For the year 1805, one of great
demand for labour and only the beginning of attempts to regulate
it, annual mobility has been estimated at about one third. There
is evidence from Walker colliery between 1780 and 1795 to suggest
a similar level of annual movement well before this turbulent
period.[10] The mining population had proportionately more men
and young men, than the national average. It also had a proportionately younger population: there were more children under

the age of fourteen, more young adults (15−35) of both sexes, and fewer older (35 +) adults of both sexes.[11] Given the nature of the work available, and the newness of many of the enterprises, none of these demographic tendencies can be considered surprising. Northern mining families also tended to be larger than those of the other working groups in the area.[12]

With definite exceptions, the mining population appears to have been relatively healthier than the rest of the population. Given its relative youthfulness and, perhaps, fitness, nor can this be considered surprising. The annual mortality per 1000 of the Houghton-Chester district against the national average (1838−44), was lower for both sexes from 0−10 years, and then higher from 10−25 years; after that, Houghton-Chester males enjoyed a better average chance of living to 65 years than their fellow-countrymen. Durham miners also enjoyed a lower chance of death by disease than all English males and their non-mining counterparts in the county. As might have been expected, the Durham miner's chances of mortality by violence (roof falls, explosions, and miscellaneous, at work) were markedly higher than all English males, as was their chance of death by cholera and related diseases. The women of the village appear to have suffered worse than the national average from chances of death in the age groups 25−35 and 45−55. After age 55, their chances were markedly superior. The mining community, like the working class generally, suffered from appalling levels of infant mortality up to the age of five years.[13]

There was little officially-recorded pauperism in the villages.[14] The Old Poor Law was not considered to be over-burdened or abused, and the New Poor Law had a quiet beginning. The 1834 Report into the Poor Laws made it clear that there was no crushing pauperism in Northumberland and Durham. It gave three reasons for this: the sparseness of the Northumbrian 'peasantry'; the constant competitive demand for labour by the collieries; and the sudden expansion of coal, iron, and railway works in south Durham.[15] The North East in general did not suffer from the kind of mass cyclical and technological unemployment which afflicted other manufacturing regions. But to say that there was little pauperism was not to say that there was no poverty. The official registers of the new workhouses were not registers of need. Most of the coping with need, and primary poverty, and pauperism, and the threat of pauperism, was done by the women. When in the early 1840s the pitmen said that short-time and fines were impoverishing them, it seems that extensive family networks in the coalfield were able, minutely and intimately, to absorb that need which in other regions may have found its way into the daunting registers of the workhouse. That this was a woman's struggle may explain the silence; certainly, when in 1842 the Easington Union Board of Guardians decided not to appoint a salaried Superintendent it was because of 'the infrequency of applications from any able-bodied *male* paupers in this Union'.[16] Why the coalfield Boards were reluctant to admit women as paupers, and continued with out-relief in spite of Somerset House disapproval, and how poverty was coped with but not transformed into pauperism, is essentially to do with the status and condition of women and will be explained later. At least, the New Poor Law was not a public issue, although there were Chartist attempts to make it one. On New Years Day 1838 Joseph Raynor Stephens had stood in Newcastle and threatened war 'to the knife — to the death' if such 'an unjust, unconstitutional, and illegal parchment blot was carried in the pockets of the Poor Law Commissioners ...', but the cry of Ashton found no echo here.[17]

Local initiatives

The ruling class chose not to be near mining villages. A distaste for the pit mingled with ignorance about its workings. In 1786 the pit had been suggested to the Home Department as suitable body and soul punishment for the convict. There, the convict would be removed from view; the blackness would invite reflection on his soul, the labour would punish his body, and he would 'Sigh in Perpetual Darkness, and the whole length of [his] Slavery, will be One Mournful Alternative, of insinsibility and Labour.'[18] The pit remained a black mystery for outsiders. Going down it was a test of daring-do for professional travellers in the 1830s who wanted to give their readers some danger and excitement. William Chatto was dropped down the shaft on a rope without time to bless himself — 'Domine, salvum, me fac'. Revd Pearson shied away from the experience on grounds of his own cowardice and cleanliness. Local coalowners appointed their agents, and stayed away. Even that father of his people, Lord Londonderry, had to rely on his chief agent for an account of colliery conditions in order to prepare for debate with Ashley (who did know 'his' people) in 1842. As Leifchild reported in 1842, 'The arrival of the pitmen is the signal for the departure of the gentry'. As Tremenheere reported in 1846, the owner Charles Carr was the first resident gentleman 'at or near' the populous mining district of Seghill. Mining villages remained strange and secret places for all but a few.[19]

As gentry and owners neglected their ruling responsibilities, so did the clergy. In a century when State power was heavily dependent upon a clerical magistracy, Northumberland and Durham in general, and the mining villages in particular, were bereft of either the Anglican word or its flesh.[20] The pitmen were rarely to be seen near the Church of England, 'resigned' as they were 'to the care of the Methodists'. As John Buddle remarked:

> If the clergy were employed, *or would employ themselves* thus [keeping a close inspection of the pit villages] − it would add greatly to their usefulness and respectability, and to the support of the church. If the parochial clergy would so employ thenselves, zealously, we should not be so over run with Methodism, and all sorts of mongrel Sectarians and *Canters*.[21]

In 1859 one of the richest dioceses in Britain had to admit to the worst Church accommodation in the country and to 'Spiritual Destitution' in its own backyard. In 1882 the Archdeacon of Durham lamented the miners' 'prejudice against black coats' and the clergy's prejudice against black faces. The Church Congress was told that if '... a number of pitmen coming from a nightshift do not always look like men and bretheren [they] need not be afraid of the coal dust. It will wash off.'[22] Revd Broughton, of Washington, County Durham, had told the 1842 commissioner that he 'was not prepared to witness so much carelessness, irreligion, and immorality, having before [he] came here [having] lived in an agricultural district'.[23]

This kind of prejudice was easier to admit in 1882 than it had been forty years previously. The absence of a substantial middle-class and the neglectfulness of the Anglicans in a coalfield creaking and dislocating as it expanded were seen as facts conducive to terrible social breakdown. In an era when migration was presented as a moral condition,[24] the curate of Hetton le Hole worried about his lack of time to visit the 'distant parts of the parish', the Bishop of Durham fretted from afar about new pit villages 'little short of Heathenism' where 'there has never been so far as I can learn, any place of worship', and the National Society feared for the corrosion of those cords of religious deference and honest settlement by modern frictions. Spurred on by these threatening problems, the fear of Chartism, trade unionism, and Methodist rivalry, the National Society had made substantial efforts since the 1830s to put schools in the mining districts – twenty-six in the 1830s, sixty-four in the 1840s. These efforts however, were by no means sufficient to their self-appointed task.[25] The government commissioner surveyed a county

> Where formerly was not a single hut of a shepherd, the lofty steam engine chimneys of a colliery now send their volumes of smoke into the sky; and in the vicinity is a town called, as if by enchantment, into immediate existence.

The enchantment was all anarchy. Its people 'are never imbued with that respect for their employers, which long and permanent subordination naturally produces', the old sanctioning structures had been outflanked by a population growth and shift 'unaccompanied by adequate means to restrain, instruct, and guide'.[26]

However it was in the swelling cities that the threat was considered darkest, and where new structures for controlling the Poor had been initially conceived. Durham's first Chief Constable spent the 1840s calling on the county's 'friends of order' to supply more police 'to meet the addition to the population', these 'being of an unruly description ... by the extension of Coal & Iron Works etc'. But he never wavered in his conviction that Newcastle and Sunderland were the darker threats to order.[27] In 1842 William Anderson was generally supported in his view that although South Shields had three times more schools than twenty years ago 'yet the place is more wicked' than a colliery village – 'near a town like Shields the colliery boys will be vastly more immoral than in a distant district from the vice around them'.[28] Seven years later the question of class control was foremost in the town planning of Consett, a new iron-making settlement high on the Durham moors. The housing had to be solid, the wage-dealing open, the policemen professional. Eight day-schools and two churches were built under company supervision; the sects were considered zealous enough to look after themselves.[29]

The Sunday Schools had been conceived to meet the problems of city streets. Newcastle had its first sunday school in January

1785 and by June of that year five schools were operating upon those 'bred up in ignorance' who 'are always the most ungovernable'. By 1788 new schools for 700 children were teaching in North and South Shields 'under the auspices of a Gentleman from the Sunday Schools Association at London'. In 1816 the nonconformist Newcastle Sunday School Union was formed with thirty-six affiliated schools and three thousand scholars. In 1835 the Anglican Sunday School Association was founded.[30] From their inception the sunday schools were about the problem of order. The first Newcastle schools had been opened with a sermon from Revd Lushington in All Saints, parish church of the city's poorest area. It was from the crowded mysteries of All Saints' sloping lanes and shabby tenements that city disorder threatened an increasingly coherent, class-conscious, bourgeoisie who were settling in houses of fine taste in the upper parts of the city, away from the quayside and its tumult.[31] The 1816 Sunday School Union's first literature was Isaac Watts' rebukes to order, its first tract was by the Bishop of Durham on the 'moral disorders' of the Irish Poor, its first rules singled out the children of the towns as in need. Newcastle's Sunday School Teachers' Association (founded in 1835) listed its objectives and three out of four concerned city order: 'The town races and their drinking, gambling, and unruliness; the Harvest Hire of reapers, most revolting scenes of tumult'; the drink question and 'the revolting scenes of drunkeness which our streets exhibit on the Lord's Day.'[32] Other religious forces for civic order came out of the city. Some were the internal products of the sunday school structure: the Newcastle Bible Society, adjunct of the British and Foreign, was founded in 1809, and was led by Messrs Angas and Wawn, founding members of the Sunday School Union; the Newcastle Religious Tract Society, with twenty-eight officers and 220 subscribers in 1817, had many Sunday School zealots on its committee – Angas, Wawn, Fenwick, Pengilly, Brunting, Annandale; the Newcastle Adult School Society carried the sunday school impetus to 'the Instruction of the Uneducated Adult Poor'; the Wesleyan Methodists, largest single group in the Sunday School Union, founded their Lending Tract Society in 1823; Societies for the Promotion of Christian Knowledge worked in both Newcastle and Gateshead; the Bethel Union Society was founded in 1822, specifically for seamen.[33] In 1831, in addition to nine missions, Newcastle had four Bible Societies and seven tract societies, all founded since 1809 and all operating on sunday school principles that the ability to read, properly directed, would lead to a regenerated, reverent, and repentent student, nightly at home, and agog at the revelations of God and Nature: in the words of Gateshead's SPCK, 'led through Nature up to Nature's God'.[34]

The urban middle-class were clearly concerned for the moral regulation of the lower orders but it is difficult to comment on the success of their schemes. For the pit villages, standing at the missionary margin of civic order, it is even more difficult to follow a line from intention to effect. Revd Richard Donaldson of Morpeth was circumspect about the means of bringing the people to order, suggesting it could be 'partly done by those very useful institutions the tract societies which are actively labouring to undo the mischief. But this is an engine which works but very slowly & at best uncertainly'.[35] However, it is clear that as the pitmen were redefined in their work by the Trade from the early nineteenth century, they were also redefined as a social entity, by the cities, from about the same period, and that both processes of redefinition were connected. A growing market of mobile labourers was seen to threaten a settled society of orderly citizens. The process of achieving the 'market' invited conflict which, in turn, proved the threat; this proof of threat insinuated a disrespect which encouraged the moral judgement on them as mere 'labourers'. Revd Donaldson's 'engine' was essentially an engine of class sensibilities whose first and upward stoke came from city fears, and whose ultimate and downward stroke came from industrial processes. Thus the pitmen, always 'so different from the other classes of the labouring Poor', inherited a gathering reputation for 'moral darkness', 'a right to indulgence', 'drinking, gaming, fighting, quarrelling, swearing, and poaching' – the felt tumult of a 'self-willed people' whose many children were in 'want of proper control', who 'transmitted natural and accidental defects' which included lying and deception, whose own villages on pay-nights were 'scarcely habitable' for want of order.[36] In all of its range and ambiguity, the idea of 'Order' was pitted against them. The sunday school curriculum timetabled for an order of bells and inspections and silences in a beehive of rote and repetition; the Sunday School Union's reports from the mining villages are obsessed with the achievement of 'order and discipline' indoors over that which is 'Violent, rude, and ungovernable out of doors';

Revd Everett dedicated his book on a Methodist pitman to Mr John Reay, 'A Promotor of Religion, Sabbath Schools, and Civil Order'.[37]

For their part, the coalowners did not seem to have been particularly interested in establishing a close order over village life. Of course, one might not expect official records to be informative on subtle enterprises of this nature, if they existed, but from sketchy evidences the coalowners were characteristically penny-pinching and suspicious of any groups other than themselves seeking dominion over the pitmen. The Newcastle Sunday School Union had begged coalowners for money in 1818, urging them 'to recollect how much they owe to this society'. We do not know if any was granted; there was no recorded improvement in the finances of an organisation which in 1818 had administered the schooling of 11,000 children for £67 7s 1d. A lone Owenite in 1825 had spoken of preferential treatment for Wesleyans and Primitives in land allocation in colliery villages and, while it is true that the Methodists were not actively opposed by ruling cliques in the coalfield (as in some other regions), the charge could not have been true for long as the Primitives were roundly condemned for trade union involvement. Certainly, throughout the 1830s, the Primitive Methodist movement in the North East was worried about insolvency, but there is no evidence of any help from the Coal Trade. Indeed, the only note of direct, coal company involvement in religious missioning was very late and very slender: the hire of one preacher, William Gelley, to tour the villages in the 1860s.[38]

Company schools were rare until the late 1840s and 1850s,[39] although some schools had received small donations before those years. For instance, at Hetton and Easington Lane, the giant Hetton Coal Company patronised the national school (founded 1834, teaching 128 boys in 1840) with a paltry £21 per year, and the five sunday schools (Anglican, Wesleyan, Primitive, New Connexion, Independent – 600 pupils) with £12 per year to share between them. The curate of Earsdon parish in Northumberland had eleven thousand parishioners in an area producing £14,000 per year in coal royalties alone, and yet he could complain about his lack of facilities and personal poverty: £20 per year from his incumbency farm, £20 from the Duke of Northumberland, £40 from Lord Hastings, and barely £20 in fees.[40] The increasing stringency of the Bond and the appearance of colliery regulations tightened Capital's control at work, but apart from some small grants, an interest in police lock-ups,[41] one startling warning on Sabbath gambling, and a preference for other Methodist groups over the Primitives,[42] the coalowners seemed content to leave village morality to others.

Institutionally, the community had a relatively high provision of 'Schools and Places of Religious Worship'. Reports on 'nine principal Collieries in the County of Durham' in 1838, and four mining parishes in 1840, show a varying permutation of churches, chapels, meeting houses, schools and sunday schools in most villages.[43] All institutions were religious in tone, but the Methodists dominated. Hetton and Easington Lane (estimated total population, 5,887) had their Anglican church in 1832 and, by 1840 the average attendance was about 350. However, both the Wesleyans and Primitives had built their chapels in 1824, and by 1840 the Weslyans had an average attendance of 400 (133 members), and the Primitives an average attendance of 370 (150 members). In addition there were smaller groups of Methodist Independents, Methodist New Connexion, and Baptists. The Anglican sunday school had about 150 pupils but the Methodist groups had a combined total of about 600 pupils.

The teetotal movement in the North East was also closely intertwined with the Methodists, particularly the Primitives, although it received intermittent support from the Church of England and the Nonconformist groups. It grew fastest between 1835 and 1844 in artisan strongholds in the large towns and in the colliery districts. By 1838 it had an estimated membership of 11,574 but actual regeneration seems to have been first achieved by others: the problem was not so much reforming drunkards 'but the willingness of teetotalers to come together'. The moral imperatives were clear: when Revd Tindale visited it in the late 1830s, Thornley was

> ... a place notorious for drunkeness ... amongst both sexes; sunk and degraded as were the people of Thornley, they had not been favoured with the teetotal life boat till some time in last July.

Similarly, employers were reminded in 1840 of

> ... evidence of the happy change in the conduct of many in their employment — the indolent having become industrious, the careless trustworthy and attentive.[44]

The Methodist penetration was a fact which established authority had to live with, and, if there was acknowledgement of Methodist 'moral work' there was also creeping criticism of their potential as a working-class institution. Commissioner Mitchell acknowledged the sunday schools' work in reading and spelling with scholars, but blamed them for putting 'no ideas into their minds', while the Privy Council thought the sunday school

> ... an institution to which the serious minded will look with deepest interest. It is true that the instruction given at such schools must be very limited, and the teachers are often very little fitted, by their age and their habits of thought, to dig into the minds of others.[45]

The coalowners had made efforts 'to dig into the minds' when driven to it by more self-conscious working-class organisations, but their efforts had mostly failed. Colliery libraries and reading rooms had been founded after the defeat of Hepburn's union in 1832 and miners' Chartism in 1839, but they were sickly efforts massaged to life by company money. Cowpen library had only twenty subscribers, at Penshaw it was clear 'that pitmen were not the components of the reading society', Seghill's 600 volumes were 'entirely neglected' by 1846 — 'The strike knocked it all up' — and there were similar failures at Earsdon, Backworth, and other places. Tremenheere regretted the failure to achieve 'more sober and temperate habits of thought' after 1831, and Wallsend's nil response for a reading room was attributed to a taste for more convivial patterns of life. According to one commentator they found 'more amusement at bowling and at quoits, and gossiping together'.[46]

There had been similarly inspired efforts to construct an alternative system of saving. There appears to have been friendly society provision at most collieries in the coalfield. The Coal Trade recognised the potential of an independent working-class propensity to save during the 1831–2 strikes, and wished to control it in order to break unions. In spite of the stringent, almost Judaic, moral discipline of their benefit system, the mining community refused to surrender its rights of self-imposition and regarded the Trade's offer of money as 'a "take-in", intended as a fraud upon them'. The friendly society, with the chapel, represented the most successful form of self-imposed working-class organisation and moral sanction.[47] Early efforts at company schooling were equally distrusted. The pitmen saw 'lurking and hidden designs' in them, constant attendance was 'extremely objectionable', 'Boys must be flogged to school'.[48]

State initiatives and the women

Local sensibilities were joined during the period by national ones. Apart from the Poor Law Amendement Act, the State made its first significant penetration into the moral life of the pit villages with Lord Ashley's 1842 Mines Act. The Act became law on 10 August, and prohibited women from underground work, boys under ten years from colliery employment, and established a loose system of inspection. The provisions of the Act clearly reflected a compaigning metropolitan-bourgeois attitude towards working-class women and, in terms of the numbers involved, towards the bigger and more cost-sensitive problem of working-class children as well. Motivations were varied, but at the core lay a new sensibility of womanhood and motherhood and their proper refinements. The *Gateshead Observer* approvingly quoted a letter from the *Morning Chronicle* which supported the Act and the gentler rights of women from the harsher rights of labour:

> Is it among the rights of labour to blot out from that sex all form, and stamp, and character of womanhood ... to divest them of all knowledge of home, and all chance of womanly influence in the humble sphere of the poor peasant's hearth?[49]

This talk of a peasantry had a distinctive Tory-evangelical ring to it and, although one might expect such a discourse to defend hearth and home, its criticism of the 'rights of labour' was deceptive. The campaign for the 1842 Act was *not* about saving women from arduous manual labour; rather, it was about the regulation of mining communities which, by the early 1840s, were regarded as prime candidates for moral treatment. In fact, no women were employed in the northern coalfield. Some had been employed above ground in the late eighteenth century; and a few hundred were employed in sorting tasks, at 'bank', in the later nineteenth century; but none were employed in the early and mid-nineteenth century.[50] But this was not the point: the 1842 Act was careless of the fact that British 'womanhood' laboured in physically exhausting and unrewarding work, it simply wanted to organise pit village women as a means of educating pit village men in the lessons of morality and order. After all, thousands of the North East's girls and women laboured, for wages, in the most punishing jobs, and the Act did not apply to them, nor did it seek to. During the period there were female keel-loaders on the Tyne; female labourers to masons, bricklayers, and slaters − 'mounting high ladders and crawling over the tops of houses' − in Newcastle and Durham towns; and female workers in brickyards, nurseries, workshops, and 'the lower and dirtier departments of factories on the Tyne'.[51] Girls and women worked in the fields, when they were needed, at the most back-breaking tasks − reaping, hoeing and weeding, gathering. In Northumberland, the much vaunted Bondager system hired men, 'hinds', but included the hire of a female helper for the hind in the annual contract. This was one of the most rigorously controlling and poorly paid jobs of all British labour. The hind received a free cottage and garden, and was paid largely in kind. Out of £32 10s per year value of reward, only about £4 was in cash payment. The bondaged female received between 8d and 10d per day. Nor was this system a relic of some past age: it grew between 1790 and 1890 to include a quarter of all female agricultural labourers in Northumberland, a figure which represented one-eighth of all female agricultural labourers. The 1834 Poor Law Commission praised the system of behalf of the Poor; and farmers praised it on behalf of the land:

> Besides we have not only the man, but a *female worker* always at our call, which in my humble opinion, is the foundation of that *spirited* and well-conducted cultivation that everywhere prevails in these Borders ...[52]

All of this represented, in some sense, formally waged-labour, with either a written or verbal contract. It probably involved, excluding casual farm work, about 20% of all Northumberland and Durham females in the 1840s and 1850s.[53] For the women of the pit villages, the percentage was much lower. It is difficult to be sure of the first figure or how much lower than it the pit village figure was, because the census returns systematically underestimated the incidence of part-time waged-work in the home − a predominantly female category. Also, there were differences of opportunity for part-time waged-work between villages. In 1851 Hetton had fifty-six dressmakers, with their apprentices, working at home. Just how constant and formal this work was is not known but, in the same year, Monkwearmouth apparently had no such opportunities. In Hetton, apart from the dressmaking, domestic service was the only non-seasonal, waged opportunity for females and it tended to take them out of the village; in Monkwearmouth, only between 4% and 5% of the female population were in formally waged work; in Easington Poor Law Union, an area taking in many pit villages but other settlements as well, the figure was only about 2%.[54] All of these percentages are very likely underestimates, but it is clear that the pit village offered few opportunities for women to stay there and work for an employer.

Most girls and women then worked at home. This, together with ready opportunities for male employment from an early age, contributed to the high fertility of mining families. But this is not to suppose that female labour was not manual labour. It involved continuous physical work in support of the men and boys at the pit, and those who stayed at home. The gradual introduction of the two shift, then the three shift, system dispersed that work throughout the day and night. The colliery produced coal as much by the pounding of the 'pit wife's' 'poss' as by the nicking of the pitman's pick. The heaviest physical toil for females centred on the supply of fuel and water; it had to be loaded and lifted and carried, often substantial distances in the case of water, and it maintained that stream of baking, cooking, washing, cleaning, heating, and nursing of children that was the female product. Their labour was divided, with an ordered working week, ancilliary help from girls, widows, or other wives for particularly taxing jobs like laundry, and some economies of scale with mass baking sessions, cleaning days, and the like. If there was a lodger, some ritual of domestic service might be required. Within all this operated an informal economy of mutual exchanges and penny rewards – shopping trips, water carriage, taking breakfasts to the pit, child minding, home decoration, boot greasing, clothes 'dadding', midwifery, mutual support. Across all this, the married women carried the ultimate responsibility for the management of scarce resources: all of the evidence suggests it was they who controlled the budget, looked for savings, divided family labour, decided on need, watched for ill health. As one woman recalled for the early 1900s, 'Life seemed to be made up of turns', and it was mother who decided.[55]

There can be no doubt that the work of the pit village's women was as unremitting and skilled, and as organised around the colliery, as was that of the pitmen. However, unlike formal waged-labour for women, this informal labour was an area of concern as represented by the campaign for the 1842 Act. The aim of this Act was first, to mop up those five-thousand females in the country who worked in and around collieries, and get them in the home. Once in the home, the second aim was to encourage and foster other agencies to re-educate female mentalities in such a way as to make it a *proper* home. In this way, the women would recover their true natures and re-order their menfolk. As existing schooling was deemed unsuitable for moral improvement, and as the exemplary social classes stayed away from the villages, so the cosy hearth of the proper family home was prescribed against the disorderly attractions of the street:

> Thus that active benevolence of the higher ranks which induces them to visit the habitations of the working classes; to counsel, guide, and instruct them; to patronize their schools, and encourage their attempts at order, frugality, and amelioration, are here wholly deficient; and in no instance is this absence more lamentably felt than in the case of the female portion of the pitman's family. The females exercise, or are destined early to exercise, an unusual and unlimited influence over the miners; and nearly the whole of the arrangements and duties of upper-ground life are by common consent deputed to them.[56]

Of course, it was not enough that most pit village females were already in the house, as in the North East. This fact won an official approval which sometimes ran counter to other official descriptions of the women as poor housewives, but no matter what the present circumstances were, women would always fall short of the new ideal. 'Home! 'tis a magic sound! No word in the English language possesses such a charm ...', and the charm-makers had themselves to be charmed. Educational and evangelical notions of the proper home, and the woman's place in it, gathered influence from the 1830s. The first hint of interest in coalfield women along these lines appeared in 1829. Thereafter, Church and State, and Church operating through State as in Ashley's 1842 campaign, sought to deploy working-class women as their moral vanguard. By the 1850s and 1860s a Christian ethic of evil and good homes (slovenly and matronly wives), and a State sociology of rough and respectable families (ignorant and educated wives), was the most common representation of the pit village. Note this priest's advocacy of the collier coming home to 'the bosom of a cheerful and smiling fireside circle'.[57] The home is personified, and it is increasingly personified in female terms. The 1842 Report on the 'Sanitary Condition of the Labouring Population' placed an equal emphasis, as did Ashley in his Report of the same year, on the moral as well as the physical condition of the poor. The vice of the bad home, and the virtue of the good home, could be just as easily translated to descriptions of the bad and good wife: one was chaotic, promiscuous, unsettled, sensual, dirty, and unhealthy; the other was orderly, modest, stable, rational, clean, and well. And what was true of the wife in her home determined the family also. The problem was that 'the people themselves are inert ... they will not listen to any lectures ...' Before lecturing, the State would have to enable the means of a decent home in a healthy place. At least, this was Chadwick's emphasis. Others, like Tremenheere switched the correlation. Before enabling a decent home, the women would have to be lectured. But whichever way it was construed, woman-hood correlated with home-making to fulfil a uniquely appointed task. The woman was to be the 'father' of the man.[58]

This reformulation of women as model wives and mothers was as eagerly sought as the parallel reformulation of men as labourers. But it was not as eagerly contested. Ideas about the reformulation of women were the more powerful because they were directed at a group which was defined by gender, but 'properly' gendered by the behaviour and feelings of private persons. Whatever qualms the pitmen expressed about the threat to their true-bred 'manliness' carried by the new status of 'labourer', their resistance was collective because the threat was collective, and it was resisted through the tangible and measureable entities of hours, fines, conditions, and payment. Women, on the other hand, were collectively identified but singled out as private persons for the test of true and false womanhood. Put simply, whereas it was not objectively possible for the collier to decide of his own accord whether he was to be a true-bred pitman or a labourer, it was possible for the woman to decide of her own accord whether she was to be a true or false wife. The new, true, woman was cast in terms of what was natural and subjective, and her achievement of that status was private, in her feelings, in the 'bosom' of her family. She was encouraged to think about herself in this way,

while her husband — at the beck and call of market forces greater
than himself — was not. She was encouraged to be her own judge
and conscience, while her husband — systematised and disciplined
in a job which demanded it — was not. If the new womanhood
was to be contested, it was unlikely that the contest would be public
and collective, Rather, it was driven inside, behind the door, within
the feelings. Moreover, the idea of natural gender divisions could
be perceived by the mining community as something not in itself
undesirable: the national culture verified it, existing arrangements
in the pit village attested to it, new systems of pit work demanded
it, the male case for amelioration could be phrased as in accord
with it. After all, were not the most vivid wreckers of what was
'natural', the factory masters and coalowners, also the agents of
working-class deterioration? If Ashley stood against them, who
could stand against Ashley?

In this way one must see the reformulation of working-class
womanhood as *both* related to the regulation of men, and as a
separate matter with its own dynamic. Most men, radicals included,
found this difference impossible to detect. An early example comes
from the 1831 strike. Mr Scott took up his pen in defence of
Hepburn and the United Colliers and, in order to win sympathy
for the men, drew a poetic distinction between the male world outside the cottage and the female world inside it. In his call to 'ye
British females' he reminded them how collier mothers — were

> ... compelled to drag [their] infant, five or six years of age, from its
> bed ... give it a crust of brown bread and a little milk and water, and
> in the very cloud of night turn it from [their] door, half naked, whilst
> perhaps, the lightnings glared across the heavens, the hoarse thunder
> roared, and the 'pitiless pelting storm' descended upon its tender
> frame.[59]

If it was possible to frame such castings-out as heartless, one has
to note that they are portrayed as heartless for women. In this sense,
the rhetoric was from a male point of view: it was not the man
who cast the child out, nor was it the man who had to suffer the
night — the outside was his proper sphere as was the inside his
wife's. By 1849 the Chartist leader Thomas Cooper thought matters
had improved, but he continued to frame the improvement in male
terms of proper spheres. There had been moral improvement
because colliers' wives were now operating in their natural place
making better homes to make better men. Respectable families

were edging forward to become the majority, but Cooper's 'respectability' was measured as a male achievement of the intellect (literacy) and the will (teetotalism), based upon female functions in the home. In 1864, Thomas Doubleday, Secretary to the Coal Trade, refuted *The Times*' libellous and outdated remarks on the mining community in the same terms. Five years later, the visitor M. Simonin represented not just respectability, but citizenship, as a female-induced quality. Even if it took a Frenchman to say it, for the first time the men of the coalfield (if not the women) were citizens:

> It is in this country, above all others, that the dwellings of Colliers should be visited. The cottages in the best districts are ornamental, neat, in many instances detached, and even wide apart. The wife is at home, attentive and thrifty, making the husband's tea or the traditional pudding, and ready to do all that is required in the household. The furniture shines with a bright polish; order prevails everywhere; articles of luxury are seen, books, and a newspaper … It is not the house of a workman, it is rather that of a citizen.[60]

Home then, was the place where women were seen to fulfil their true and complementary natures. The pit, by contrast, unsexed them. The 1842 sub-commissioners were given clear instructions:

> In regard to female workers, you will inquire how far their employment during Childhood has prevented them from forming the domestic habits usually acquired by women in their station, and has rendered them less fit than those whose early years have not been spent in labour for performing the duties of wives and mothers.[61]

At first sight this would seem to have excused the women of the northern coalfield, none of whom were employed by the collieries, from charges of losing their sexuality. But it did not. The commissioners did not just produce a body of evidence; they produced a sexual ideology which came to apply to North-East women also. This was an ideology of physical and moral development where the male practices of the pit, and any contact with them, corrupted the natural sexuality of women. This was demonstrated in both simple and crude ways: of the difficulty of telling pitboys and pitgirls apart, 'but for the hair'; of belts and chains and harnesses strapping the body and 'passing underneath the legs'; of female maturation, hips and limbs; of infection and exhaustion. It was also demonstrated in more subtle matters of the mind. There was nakedness, and promiscuous opportunities − 'women … work by the side of naked men (daughters often do this beside their own fathers)'. There was degradation and brutality — 'associated as (these females are) with the lowest profligacy and grossest sensuality'. There was young and old, innocence and carnality, one gender (and sexuality) mixing with another, where the weaker would always succumb.[62] It was only a matter of time before the ideology of 1842 came up from underground and applied itself beyond work practices. In 1856 the pit was represented as a male culture whose location, dress, language and relationships were all a threat to women:

> The employment of females upon the 'pit banks and cinder tips' has long been pointed out as one degrading to the female character. The kind of attire rendered necessary by the masculine nature of the employment, and the blackness and dirt ... can scarcely fail to undermine their modesty and self-respect, while it is notorious that their association with the coarse description of men employed in that branch of labour, exposes them to every deteriorating influence of language, manners, and habits.[63]

If this was so, not everyone seemed to notice. The men and women of collieries employing females certainly did not. At Barnsley, boys and girls mixed as work-mates and friends, dressed or half-dressed, down the pit or in the street, with or without supervision. A solicitor clearly expected these people to be as shocked as he was:

> ... and I have seen them washing themselves naked much below the waist as I passed their doors, and whilst they are doing this they will be talking and chatting with any men who happen to be there with the utmost unconcern.

Similarly, a commissioner appears to have caused some amusement, if not embarrassment, by his own unease:

> Their sex was recognisable only by their breasts, and some little difficulty occasionally arose in pointing out to me which were girls and which were boys, and which caused a good deal of laughing and joking.[64]

In the North East, men and women washed openly and in one instance it was only when a London journalist came to call that the women had to cross the lane to change in what was the earth closet but what the journalist called the pantry.[65]

Nor does the mining community appear to have entertained

strong views on male dominance in the family. Like being clothed, this was a middle-class obsession and when the pitman showed no sign of it, he was called a coward or a fool. And if he did not strive to dominate the home, there is no evidence for early and mid-century that the public house was exclusively the man's domain either. On the fortnightly shopping excursions to Newcastle it was not considered improper for colliery women to smoke, drink, and be noisy, in city pubs – and in country pubs there were dances 'which would shock the delicacy of more refined society'. Girls would sit on boys' laps and, on the fiddler's call they had to kiss: 'Were a youth to neglect the performance of this established ceremony, his mistress would consider herself affronted'. The dancing was rowdy, perhaps drunken, and the courting, especially on the parents' part, indulgent. The traveller who passed a cart load of colliery women on their way home from market had to expect 'a shower of taunting coarse jokes'.[66]

In female affairs, the northern coalowners considered themselves acquitted by the 1842 Report, but this did not mean that they accepted its sexual ideology.[67] Londonderry told Buddle that he intended 'to cool down this humanity mania'. On 24 June he presented the Coal Trade petition and in the debate on the second reading of the bill on 14 July, with Lords Radnor and Wharncliffe, he criticised the hypocrisy and humbug of a bill which applied only to collieries and not to other arduous branches of female labour, which deprived needy women of a livelihood, and which interfered unwarrantably in the personal lives of blameless women. If the close mixing of sexes was immoral in collieries, why was it not immoral in overcrowded cottages also? This was plain speaking, some of it not without self interest, but it could not dampen the unctuous moralising of most Lords or those members of the other place. Although Londonderry was never a man afraid of swimming against the tide, he spoke incompetently and failed to find even a seconder for his motion. When he tried to compare the labour of pit women with that of Irish women digging potatoes in bare feet, the House laughed.[68] Nevertheless, most coalowners saw the bill as unnecessary as it was illogical. Who said colliery work unsexed women? Clearly Mr Dunn did not:

> The first [Wigan pit] that I went down was 85 fath, and I was not a little amused to find the Onsetter sported a pair of golden Ear rings, being a very fine figuring wench of 24 – in the following costume – *Shift*

of flannel, a pair of huge white flannel Trousers, a short bedgown and over all a smock sark of flannel – her head was bound by a Cotton round Cap, underneath which peeped as handsome a set of Curls as need be sported – The seam is 4 feet high and the putters principally Girls, being all furnished with Trousers and mostly jackets, I regretted much I had not a No. Country companion to share the joke. The Women of Whitehaven (from I suppose their petticoat dress) do not interest one half as much.[69]

John Buddle opposed the 1842 Act not so much on grounds of hypocrisy as on grounds of metropolitan presumptiousness. He was scathing about 'meddling, morbid *humanity mongers*' who have

... entirely over looked the *existing Laws* for the protection of the labouring *Infant* population – or to imagine how all the abuses complained of could possibly have escaped the notice and interference of the local Magistracy – the *Clergy*, and the Guardians of the poor!!![70]

In fact, the Guardians had lost much of their scope for regulating the villages. As Buddle wrote, the New Poor Law bureaucracy in London was arguing for a uniform system of relief based upon the new Union workhouses. This meant a diminution of that regulation which the vestries could once invest in out-relief. Designating 'sundries' and cash payments according to the known circumstances, prospects, and disposition of applicants, the vestries had been able to lay a heavy moral sanction over the village poor. Fearful of the consequences of losing this discretion, the Guardians fought to retain an intimate local power.[71] What had been designed to replace out-relief, the workhouse test, broke families and was accused of unsexing females on a far greater scale, and in a more vicious manner, than any pit. Evidence to the 1834 Poor Law Report contained warnings to this effect – 'no circumstances can justify the taking of Children from their legitimate Parents' – and the coalfield Guardians went on resisting the admission of their most numerous clients, widows with their children. Not that their resistance was purely principled, although some of it may have been. In an area where able-bodied male pauperism was almost unknown, the ideology of the 1834 Act did not fit the realities of pit village poverty. Workhouse relief was more expensive than out-relief and, in any case, impoverished widows were useful workers in the village economy. They took in lodgers, they laundered, they minded children, many of them were still mothers at home to their sons who worked at the pit. Family networks were the first to cope with primary poverty and kept it out of workhouse statistics.[72] If the Guardians resisted the New Poor Law, so did the local conservative press, and some gentrified groups, who rebuked the workhouse test as 'Unscriptural, UnChristian, and UnEnglish'.[73] So did the Chartists, in a different terminology, but still based on notions of what was 'natural'.[74] Faced with this contradiction in sexual ideology between New Poor Law and Ashley's Act, but unable to see the battle in other than male and class categories, the miners' unions could only snipe at the pretensions of a ruling-class womanhood, of which they knew little. Rich women were caricatured as in need of common sense rather than broken French, honest industry rather than new dancing shoes.[75]

In spite of its contradictions, the reformulation of the ideology and practice of working-class female sexuality went on unabated. The main agents were the coal companies. Village females were increasingly enclosed in the colliery's sexual division of labour. Females serviced the colliery's demand for male labour, and schooling serviced the male demand for female labour. Often the two demands clashed. It was difficult to keep girls on the school register:

> Of those who not having left have been away the majority consists of girls. Their mothers keep them away 'to help clean', 'nurse the baby', 'mind the house', 'go to the store' etc.[76]

The key principle of female schooling was to teach girls to be good wives and mothers. Although in the earlier part of the century views on the domesticity of coalfield women had differed – Mr Thomas thought them slovenly, the *Penny Magazine* thought them caring[77] – the official sexual ideology of the 1840s set a standard no one could reach. Ashley, and Tremenheere after him, presented dazzling instances of happy home-making. The 1842 evidences generally concurred that cleanliness was 'a predominant feature in the domestic economy of the female part of this community', but after this there would be only criticism. The women lacked 'economy and forethought' they had no method and were wasteful, they were indulgent, they needed to be re-directed having 'little or no opportunity of seeing anything but the homely work and cooking of the colliery village'.[78] And if schooling could not dispense the whole prescription, domestic service could complete a favourable circuit of class relations. The middle class would train the working-class female, she would train the working-class male, and he would relate more favourably to the middle class. Tremenheere suggested a joint enterprise of schooling and domestic service. 'Five respectable matrons of the working class' could be paid to take two girls each on day-release from school.[79] Alongside colliery labour, and schooling, and domestic service, and the battery of advice on the perfect home and the natural woman, there was also the reciprocity of personal sexual relationships, particularly in marriage. Colliers saw themselves as 'men' when they married, and they usually married when they became hewers.[80] Pit imperatives came to be male, home imperatives came to be female, and boys became men and girls became women when the two were joined to become one, in matrimony.

In 1867 the coalowner George Elliot stated his opposition to female labour in his pits, above or below ground. He admitted women worked just as laboriously in the fields and he agreed there were women who wanted pit work and had not duties at home, but he still opposed it: 'I do not know that I can give you very good reasons for not liking it, but I have a great dislike to it'. Of female field labour, he 'never knew that it was looked upon as ... derogatory until I read some accounts in the papers'. Elliot's decisive indecisiveness was hardly very masculine, but it was understandable. By the later century a great deal of male culture took its authority from a sharp, but contradictory, sexual division. The very language of talking about coal was gendered. Pits were given female names − 'Pitmen love the ladies' and regard 'the pits and their wives as the two main sources of ... comfort and well-being'. The earth itself was cast as a female much given to male attention:

> Durham being notably the greatest seat of the coal trade has perhaps been more bored and pierced by the instruments of the modern precious mineral diviner than any other place, and some of her hitherto virgin hills and valleys have had the peaceful quiet of long ages of tranquil fertility broken in upon by the clanking of huge engines, the snortings of the great iron horse, and the rattling of innumerable trucks and tubs.[81]

By the 1890s the common sense view of separate spheres was not likely to be contradicted by males at least. Looking back, the employment of women at pits had been 'revolting', 'painful', 'shocking', 'subversive', and 'almost unsexing' − although it is interesting to note that for coalmining, uncommonly for the period, female sexuality was not a universal condition. It did not apply to Indian women in British-owned mines.[82]

9
The rise of the
Primitive Methodists

From their foundation as a Wesleyan offshoot in 1811 the Primitive Methodists enjoyed almost continuous growth for the next hundred years. They started the century as a sect and ended it as a denomination. From the 1820s to the 1840s they retained most of the characteristics of a sect, in spite of clear trends towards denominationalism as represented by sunday schools and related activities. Although Primitive Methodist membership as a percentage of national population in 1851, and their attendance as a percentage of mining-district population, were both small − 0.51% and 5% respectively[1] − their influence went beyond formal membership. 'Members' were the hardcore of each 'class' and the group of classes which constituted a 'society', but members could be in the minority. In 1846 Murton Wesleyans made application to their 'circuit', a group of societies, to build a chapel. In presenting their case they outlined their strength: in addition to the eighteen full members, the trial members, and the sunday school scholars, the society had one hundred 'average number of hearers'.[2] Also, their strength could be heavily concentrated in certain places. By the 1870s they were the most important single religious group in the coalfield.[3] In the first half of the nineteenth century the Primitives made their most rapid progress nationally between 1827 and 1838, with an unparalleled average annual growth rate of 11.2% between 1833 and 1835.[4]

It is easier to report the facts of growth than to explain them. Religion has a cultural influence greater than the number of its adherents at any particular time. Religion and culture permeate each other to an extent that makes it difficult to evaluate where one stops and the other begins. The inclination has been to point out 'a general over-all correspondence' between religious growth and socio-cultural change and to leave it at that.[5] The aim here is to be more specific. Primitive preachers walked into a coalfield which, as we have seen, was already the object of structural and perceptual change. The task is now to establish how the most effective changers, the Primitive Methodists, fitted into this culture.

The Primitives were not the first Methodists in the mining villages. John Wesley had first strafed certain Durham and Northumberland villages in the 1740s, and these societies stand among the oldest in Methodism. In 1742 Wesley founded the Old Penshaw society and in 1743 preached at Pelton, Gateshead Fell, and South Biddick; he prized the souls of pitmen, and his journals take us into a sphere of the cultural which is as rare as it is difficult:

> A multitude of people [at Pelton] were gathered together from all the neighbouring towns, and (which I rejoiced at much more) from all the neighbouring pits. In riding home I observed a little village called Chowden, which they told me consisted of colliers only. I resolved to preach there as soon as possible; for these are sinners and need repentence. (1 March 1743)
>
> I found we were got into the very Kingswood of the North. Twenty or thirty wild children ran around us, as soon as we came, staring at us in amaze. They could not properly be said to be either clothed or naked. One of the largest (a girl about fifteen) had a piece of a ragged, dirty blanket some way hung about her, and a kind of cap on her head, of the same cloth and colour. My heart was exceedingly enlarged towards them ... (8 March 1743)[6]

This mid-Durham district retained an isolated Methodist presence until 1782 when it was connected into the new Sunderland circuit. This circuit was formed with 1,014 members, and took in traditional pit communities at Shiney Row and Penshaw (twenty-eight members), the Raintons (twenty-seven members), Lumley (fifteen members), Colliery Dykes (fifty-seven members), and North Biddick (fifty-two members), and stretched from Sunderland along the River Wear to Durham City, the area in between Wear and Tyne, and along the South Tyne as far west as Prudhoe. The Sunderland circuit cautiously added new societies piecemeal, occasionally enjoyed expansions (Old Penshaw 1806–7; Newbottle, Colliery Dykes, West Rainton 1808–9; Lumley 1820–1; Easington Lane 1828), and in 1836 was split into two circuits to absorb new developments in the coalfield. The newly designated Houghton le Spring Wesleyan Methodist circuit covered the mining area south and west of Sunderland, and began in September 1836 with a members-trialists role of 594, reaching a pre-1850 peak of

742 in March 1844.[7] When in 1839 we find both Wesleyans and Primitives coming together to finance the Sunderland Town Mission for the 'moral and Spiritual improvement' of the city, it must be remembered that the Primitives came as tyros to join a Wesleyan establishment which had been in the area for well over half a century.[8]

The first Primitive preachers, representing a Staffordshire sect barely nine years old but preaching a salvation self-consciously 'primitive', entered the North East from North Yorkshire in June 1820. The encountered little official opposition, although they were seen as seditious by some. The first society was founded at Ingleton, near Darlington, on 5 June 1820, and from there preachers preached, and tiny societies were formed, around Darlington in 1820, in Teesdale and Weardale the following summer, at Sunderland, North Shields, and Newcastle in the August, and in South Shields in December 1821.[9]

Their efforts had been renewed in 1821 in an attempt to ride a revivalist wave which had caught up Tyne and Wear Wesleyans in 1820. However, the Primitives did not enjoy revival before the wave of 1822 which first rose in Teesdale in the February and continued into Weardale and then into Wearside and Tyneside until early 1824, a revival which appears to have been shared by the Wesleyans.[10] The detail of this sequence of revivals is obscure but the Primitive preachers appear to have been able to exploit a situation in 1822 which they could not so well exploit in 1821. Responses to preaching could ebb and flow from place to place, and change in the same place over time, but they were explained in an idea of physical momentum where 'tears and groans' of the North Tyne could touch the South Tyne's 'mighty shaking amongst the dry bones'; a momentum simultaneously paced by extraordinary preaching, nightly meetings, and special services to attract pitmen coming from work where 'they dropped from their seats, and trembled like persons struck with paralitick strokes'.[11] Bolstered by their transformation from scattered societies to formal circuits, the North Shields, South Shields, and Sunderland Primitive circuits missioned their outlying collieries in the summer and autumn of 1823. Thomas Nelson undertook one of these missions. His labours were exhilarating; he was clearly both the rider and the ridden of a powerful psychic swell which swept him across twenty-five different places in thirty-seven days of field-preaching:

July 20 preached at ″ ″	North Shields camp meeting: many 'at liberty'. South Shields: many deeply distressed.
July 21 preached at	Waggoners' Row: three 'at liberty'.
July 22 preached at	Usworth: one new member, others listened attentively.
July 23 preached at	Hebburn: five new members.
July 24 preached at	South Shields: 'the word ran like fire among dry stuble'.

July 27 preached at
    ″   ″   ″
    ″   ″   ″
	South Shields: he thought he preached poorly.
	Templetown: issued new tickets to members.
	South Shields: 'many were powerfully wrought upon' and most of congregation 'at liberty'.

July 28 preached at	Monkton: local squire invites him out of the open into a barn, and 'I had a most powerful time indeed I believe I had not one dry thing about me, with sweating so much'.
July 29 preached at	Jarrow: suffering from a hoarse voice in the cold air.
July 30 preached at	Templetown: his voice is nearly gone.
July 31 preached at	South Shields: much crying and wailing.
August 1 preached at	East Boldon: a 'powerful time'.
August 3 preached at ″ ″ ″	Usworth: 'The rain came before I had done ...' Chester le St.: hoarseness prevents him from proper praying.
August 4 preached at	Chester le St.: young and old affected in a 'powerful time'.
August 5 preached at ″ ″ ″	Chester le St.: has previously been a difficult place but now shows encouraging signs. Low Flatts: voice still weak but wins four new members.
August 7 preached at	Ouston: to a large audience.
August 10 preached at ″ ″ ″	East Boldon: some affected, one 'at liberty'. Hebburn: large and powerful meeting.
August 12 preached at	Herrington: difficult place with no success.
August 13 preached at	Ayers Quay: difficult place with no success.
August 14 preached at	Bishopwearmouth: a large audience of hewers only.
August 15 preached at	Whitburn: broke previous 'hardness' to form a class of seven members.
August 17 preached at ″ ″	Hylton: a new class of five members. Hetton Houses: many in tears.

August 17 preached at Hetton Downs: much crying and praying, one 'at liberty'.

August 18 preached at Hylton: Nelson is ill, but 'some of the vilest characters in the place, are turning to Almighty God'.

August 19 preached at Philadelphia: many affected.

August 21 preached at East Rainton: good meeting — one man would have collapsed 'if he had not got hold of the door post ... His word is a hammer'.

August 22 preached at Cox Green: powerful meeting.

August 24 preached at Houghton le Spring: largest congregation ever saw there.
        ″   ″   ″ 'two miles from Houghton': largest open-air congregation he ever saw.
        ″   ″   ″ Shiney Row: to hundreds, many weeping.

August 25 preached at Sunderland: farewell sermon to 'thousands'.
        ″   ″   ″   ″ : Watchnight Service.

The Lord soon began to work powerfully so that both men and women were in distress until the Lord spoke peace to their souls. I cannot say how many professed to get into liberty, but the meeting continued until the next morning. Many were seized so as to be in apparent fits: but the Lord soon set them free.

On the same day that Nelson preached his farewell sermon his journal records that:

Last year at this time in Sunderland we had six in Society and one leader; but now we have 275 members, eleven leaders, and a very large chapel building ... What hath God wrought! Shall I say that this has been one of the best and most wonderful quarters I ever saw before?[12]

Nelson left but others took his place, and the colliery missioning appears to have retained its momentum throughout the year. By October there were as many members in the collieries as in Sunderland itself:

A very blessed and glorious work has gone on for some time in Sunderland and the neighbouring collieries. In Sunderland and Monk-wearmouth ... we have nearly 400 members. In Lord Steward's [Stewart's] and Squire Lambton's collieries we have near 400 more ... Indeed, the Lord and the poor colliers are doing wondrously. Our congregations are immensely large, and well behaved. It would do any of the lovers of Jesus good to see the dear colliers sometimes under the word ... Their hearty and zealous exertions in the cause of God would make almost any one love them. We have 5 preachers employed in this Circuit, and a blessed prospect.

It was from this first mission and its 'blessed prospect' that the Primitive Methodists established themselves in the North East as a movement dominated by pitmen and their families. In 1824 the Primitive Methodist Northern 'District' was formed out of the Hexham, Carlisle, North and South Shields, Newcastle and Sunderland circuits with twenty-one travelling preachers, sixty-one local preachers, and 3,632 members.[13]

Graph 1 **Memberships of Sunderland, Durham, North and South Shields Primitive Methodist circuits, 1823–45** (source: Primitive Methodist Magazine, 1824–50)

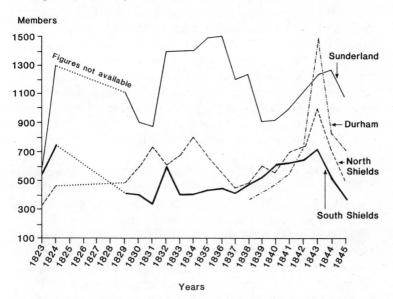

The mid- and late 1820s appear to have been years of stagnation in both the Shields and Sunderland circuits, with sharper falls between 1829 and 1831. The North Shields circuit however, appears to have held most of its revivalist gains, and even gone on to add to them between 1829 and 1831. The sullen mood of the county circuits was confirmed by Revd J. Petty's colliery tour in the summer of 1831. Judged against his own rigid aim of inciting village convulsions and putting converts 'at liberty', Petty's efforts were a failure. As we have seen, in these months the pitmen were on the verge of an unprecedented strike victory and do not appear to have been as mindful as Revd Petty of their future state. In July he preached at Easington, his 'mind much exercised through not seeing souls converted to God', in August at Middle Rainton with 'not much power', and at Houghton in 'a barren season'.[14]

Within four months this situation had changed dramatically. In October 1831, Sunderland contracted the first of a cholera epidemic which was to spread throughout the country. By December, it was in the pit villages of Tyne and Wear where it remained with 'havock all around' for nearly twelve months.[15] For the first six months of 1832 the coalfield sat expectant of disease and in the gripping immiseration of lock-out. Whereas Petty had preached at Hetton in July 1831 without response, between December 1831 and March 1832 the full and trial membership of the Hetton society rose from fifty-one to 278. Although cholera increased the whole circuit membership,[16] it is more instructive to see its impact in the villages. Cholera underwrote the preachers' words with a capricious, fetid, death. All of the societies experienced large increases in their membership between December 1831 and March 1832. The increases at Hetton and Pittington were explosive. The graph tentatively suggests that the larger the initial congregation, the more able it was to rouse its own revivalist momentum. The exceptions were Easington Lane, which with a large initial congregation of forty-nine was not quite able to double its numbers, and Pittington which with a small initial congregation of nine was able to increase its numbers over eight-fold.

If the increases were dramatic, then so were the subsequent decreases. The smaller societies, and Monkwearmouth, appear to have had more short-run success in retaining new members than those societies which enjoyed spectacular gains. The volatility of Hetton, major society in the circuit, major colliery in Hepburn's Union, is especially remarkable. To rise to nearly three hundred and back to under a hundred in twelve months was a statistical experience which could not have happened without cultural repercussions. The momentary nature of the response was under-lined by the Pittington membership which continued to fall throughout the last quarter of 1832 in spite of a late and 'very fatal' cholera outbreak there in November.[17]

Inferences about revival and atmosphere are tenuous. The more pertinent inference must have been to do with the connection of Primitive religiosity with the social world. More will be said later

Graph 2 **Full and trial membership of societies in the Sunderland Primitive Methodist circuit, March 1831–December 1832** (source: Accounts of Monies and Members, DCRO, M/DU 347)

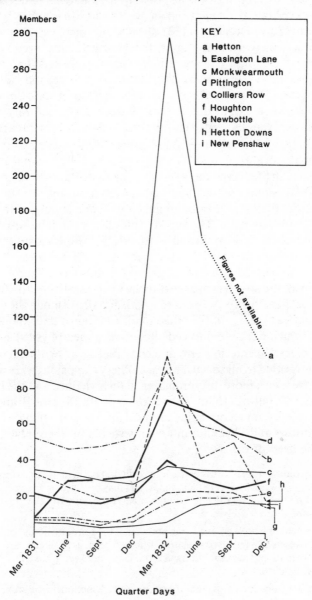

KEY
a Hetton
b Easington Lane
c Monkwearmouth
d Pittington
e Colliers Row
f Houghton
g Newbottle
h Hetton Downs
i New Penshaw

Members

Quarter Days

about the leading role of Primitive pitmen in the unions of 1831 –2 and 1844, however, when considering the relationship of Primitive Methodism to the mass of the population, the social issues of the strike do not seem to have been an overt factor. In graph 2, county figures for pre-December 1831 show slight increases and slight decreases; in Northumberland, the North Shields circuit grew (graph 1) although elsewhere it has been suggested that union successes in the summer of 1831 had created some indifference to revival.[18] Whatever the precise relationship in social matters there can be no doubt that in fear of death the community bent, momentarily and impulsively, to the fixed-will of the preachers.

Primitive Methodism was meticulous about secular duty and personal morality, but at its core it spoke wildly to what it saw as a 'soul' in life, perpetually on the brink of death. In Sunderland, passionate night and day visiting 'caused thousands to flock to the houses of prayer, bemoaning their sins, and crying to God for mercy'. In Newcastle 'The state of this place cannot be described ...', preachers were exhausted as 'Nearly all business is suspended but preaching and praying' to full meetings in villages where 'Cards have been banned, and fighting-cocks' heads cut off, and some of the worst characters are seeking the Lord ...'. In North Shields the preachers 'prayed ... eat and drank and slept among the dying and the dead'. Early in 1832 this circuit distributed three thousand tracts which darkly embraced cholera as a metaphysical sign.[19]

Cholera was intermittent, and construed as a 'sign' which was also a warning to all social classes. Colliery explosions were much more frequent, more discriminating in their victims, and the interpreting tract always followed the explosion. In 1812 the Brandling Main colliery at Felling exploded to kill ninety-two. Felling's forty-one widows and 133 children were instructed for themselves, and for the heed of others:

> The continuation of life is precarious to all; but particularly so to those who, as it were, carry it in their hands, and may be called upon to resign it in a moment, by the alteration of a current of air. But the greater hazard is in yourselves ...
>
> ... when we set too great a value upon men, the Lord, in mercy, often deprives us of a friend or a relative, who had been, as it were, a curtain between us and heaven, hiding us from God, and keeping us in thick, worldly darkness.
>
> ... there is no repentence, no forgiveness, no redemption, in the grave.[20]

The disaster tract always came from the outside. Within its puling moralism 'Do not cry, mammy – do not cry', and morbid lingerings over charred bodies – a style which found popular cultural form – there was a scalding injunction to convert.[21]

Given this weight of calamity and popular admonition, and the nature of Primitive appeal to death and guilt, one would expect a mass response from the bereaved community to the Primitive society.[22] The best example of a major disaster with available membership statistics, is the South Shields explosion in June 1839 where fifty-one were killed. Unfortunately this example has a serious gap: statistics exist up to March 1839, but do not reappear until June 1840. Nevertheless, whilst other societies had near stagnant or falling memberships over the fourteen intervening months, the memberships of those three societies nearer to the colliery (South Shields, Templetown and Jarrow) were increasing. The society nearest to the homes of the deceased, Templetown, increased most and doubled its membership. These trends are indicated on Graph 4. The following year the *Primitive Methodist Magazine* recorded the obituaries of four celebrated members killed in the explosion, Ben Gibson, Thomas Mould, Matthew Gibson, and Thomas Elstable. The funeral services were described as 'densely crowded'. The figures do suggest a local response to the June explosion, although it is as well to remember that the memberships of all the societies except one had begun to rise slightly up to March 1839.[23]

The circuits complained of difficulties from the end of the 1832 lock-out to the end of the decade. Victimisation and quickening economic development made for an unsettledness which disrupted membership patterns. Primitives had been widely implicated in the union: in March 1832 the Sunderland circuit resolved 'That Tuesday evening's service to given up to attend the Union Pray Meeting', but by September 'The Circuit be represented as sinking. The reason of which is the Collier's strike.' Next year, Sunderland reported 'great difficulties through the outward misunderstanding between the coalowners and their workmen'; Shields, 'great difficulties owing to the disturbances and movings in the collieries'; Newcastle, a fluctuating membership 'by reason of the unsettledness of the pitmen', and similar complaints followed for 1835, 1836, 1837, 1838 and 1839 with murmurs of internal strife exacerbating external problems.[24]

In spite of the early turbulence, the North and South Shields, and Sunderland circuits ended the decade with much the same numbers as they started it. The plateau Sunderland reached in 1832–4 was bemoaned, but hardly disastrous, and the circuit's falls in 1836 and 1838 were not due to membership decreases but a hiving-off of societies to form other circuits – Stockton in 1836 and Durham in 1838.[25] Indeed, the Sunderland circuit encompassed the heart of the Durham coalfield, and, measured with or without hivings-off, enjoyed steady growth and prosperity throughout the 1830s. In 1836, a 'Durham branch' was formed, taking in the city and seven colliery villages, with 173 members. By 1841, it had been made a circuit in 1838, had added fourteen new societies, and had won a membership of full and trial members of 584.[26]

At village level, that slender statistical evidence which does exist suggests a different growth pattern between Primitives and Wesleyans, and some greater volatility in Primitive over Wesleyan recruitment.[27] Graph 3 traces Primitive membership in three comparable pit villages from 1836 to 1841, and indicates some *pattern* of growth, with human potential for differences between societies. Haswell, Thornley, and Sherburn Hill were all new mining villages, commencing operations on 1831, 1834, and 1835 respectively. They lay within three or four miles of each other. Between 1831 and 1841 they all experienced dramatic increases in population: Haswell, 263–3,981; Thornley, 50–2,730; and Sherburn Hill, 337–1,946. In spite of this general comparability there were differences in the pattern of Primitive growth in each village. Clearly, the reasons for the differences were multifarious, and by no means all accessible to the historian. For instance, the rate of growth may simply have reflected the rate of incoming population. Equally, the rising fortunes of the Haswell society over the others from December 1839 to June 1840 could have been due – we cannot tell – to the settlement of a number of established Methodist families in the village. For Sherburn and Thornley the converse could have occurred. Individual societies with declining numbers could start their own remissioning programmes which could sometimes prove satisfactory – as with Lupton's efforts in and around South Shields in June 1838, and those of the Kelloe society from December to January 1843. On the other hand, such programmes could prove unsatisfactory – as with the Westgate

Graph 3   **Full and trial membership of Primitive Methodist Societies in three mining villages, 1836–41** (source: Account Book, DCRO, M/DU 25)

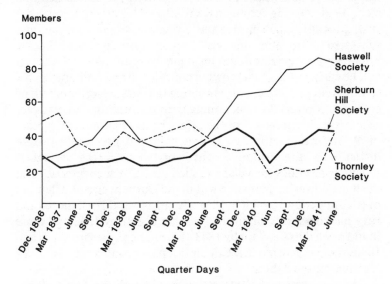

attempts in 1836: '... we were not sufficiently cautious in giving in the new converts. Some of these having no roots in themselves fell away ...' Lastly, one must be alert to the possibility of routine administrative changes in the historical record. Sometimes trial members were recorded and sometimes they were not. Did this mean there were no trialists or no recorded trialists, or did it mean that trialists were simply included in full membership figures? Is it possible to adequately compare societies and circuits with such differences in their record? Also, one has to watch for falls in membership in one circuit being the result of creations of new circuits out of the old – as with Sunderland's making of the Stockton and Durham circuits in 1836 and 1838. Similarly, some of the problems of 1833 may not have been solely due to the aftermath of the strike; in that year Conference instructed societies to omit children from membership lists.[28] Thus, while it is still possible to use Methodist membership statistics as a hand on the pulse of the emotions of the Poor, one must be wary of the more mundane historical and demographic factors which can affect the statistical picture of the relationship. Fleeting incidents of emotional significance to the village may have occurred which cannot be known today. Here, the historians is left with theory. Given the established relationship between revival and death in a coalfield offering serious risks to life and limb; and, given the strong identity of Primitive self-consciousness in a community subjected to fundamental revisions in its status, it is clear that the opportunities for emotional incidents were many.

The early 1840s saw a growing confidence and militancy in the coalfield circuits. A campaign in spring 1842 in the Northumberland collieries combined re-missioning with teetotalism and was very successful. The intensity of the campaign is illustrated in the case of West Cramlington, a village which had previously proved difficult for the Primitive cause. In twelve weeks of nightly salvation-meetings the village yielded up 102 new members.[29] But the most powerful campaign was in the Durham circuit. Cleft out of the Sunderland circuit in 1838 with just over three hundred and fifty members, this circuit had doubled itself by 1842 and more than doubled itself again by 1843. Throughout the late 1830s and 1840s they considered 'the Circuit in a prosperous state. By God's blessing on our labour'.[30]

These successes are interesting in view of the fact that the National Miners' Association, founded at Wakefield in November 1842, and brought to the North East union networks immediately after, was recruiting at precisely the same time. By early 1844 the NMA was established at every colliery and moved its headquarters from Yorkshire to Newcastle. The Durham Primitive circuit was enjoying large meetings right up to the beginning of the NMA's strike of April 1844.[31] Chartism also penetrated the colliery villages without any obvious inroads upon the Primitives. The circuit recoveries after the disruptions of the 1830s began in 1837, and although the increases were steady rather than strong up to 1841, the northern coalfield coincidentally stood as a Chartist stronghold from 1838 to 1840. In the detail of the villages this pattern is cautiously confirmed. Sherburn Hill, Haswell, Thornley, and Moorsley were all leading Chartist villages. Moorsley was first reached by Messrs Binns and Lawton of the Durham County Charter Association on 26 January 1839, and the other villages were systematically covered soon after. Chartist meetings continued at these places through the spring and summer of 1839 and their membership and financial support were among the best in the county.[32] The Sherburn Hill and Haswell Primitives, and the

Moorsley Wesleyans, enjoyed strong periods of growth from March to December 1839 – months of the most passionate Chartist commitment.[33] Sherburn Hill managed to enrol forty-five Chartists only two weeks after the first Chartist visit.[34] Thornley, on the other hand, was probably the most committed Chartist village, and its Primitives suffered a significant drop over the same period. However this negative correlation would look more convincing first, if the Thornley society had not begun its halting decline from March 1837, well before the Chartist penetration, and secondly, if it were not for the fact that many of the Thornley Primitives supported Chartism. On 9 March 1839 a meeting there added sixty new members to the eighty-strong Chartist branch, among their number '... a considerable number of Primitive Methodists ... several of whom came forward and enrolled themselves.' The following day saw the first of the Chartist sermons and collections in the Thornley and South Hetton Primitive chapels. The sermon was by George Binns for Revd J. R. Stephens:

> Great credit is due to the trustees of this [Thornley] chapel in so generously offering the use of the building. There is many a religious sinner who would have placed the chapel under lock and key, as a Radical Reformer approached. We trust the men of Thornley will know how to appreciate the liberality of the patriotic proprietors.[35]

One searches the records of Methodism in vain for more than a cursory recognition of the activities of 'secular' movements.[36] Miners' unionism and Chartism, on the other hand, echoed with the language and imagery of the Bible and neither movements recorded any significant opposition from the Primitives – in fact the situation was often the reverse. The community's ways of protest will be detailed in Part Three, but in so far as membership statistics alone are indicative, the way in which Primitive Methodism related to Chartist or trade-union ideology does not appear to have been a hindrance and may have been a help.[37] Given the fabulous other-worldliness of the Primitives, and given their renunciation of the secular and their distrust of rationalism this must stand for the moment as an enigma, an enigma in need of more subtle investigation into the rapport the sect could generate with the minds of men alive to the spiritual dimensions of the 'secular'. Lay-preacher Mr Turnbull, speaking at Swalwell Democratic Festival, revealed himself as such a man:

He had been censured by some of those who acted with him in religious
matters ... [but] ... Mr T. concluded, by affirming, that the earth, and
the fruit thereof, belonged not to a Northumberland or a Londonderry,
but to all God's children, the whole human race alike. (loud cheers)[38]

Certainly, the collapse of the strike in the Autumn of 1844 and
the poverty and victimisation which attended it brought serious
downturns in Primitive fortunes. All of the South Shields circuit
societies went into decline and accelerated decline from June 1844,
and in three places the decline was terminal. Durham sought
financial aid throughout the strike to carry a circuit whose members
could not even afford their penny tickets. In June the circuit had
to mortgage preachers' books into order to pay a part of preachers'
wages. The Darlington circuit was insolvent and could only afford
to pay its superintendent £4 11s 7¾d out of eleven guines owed
to pay its superintendent £4 11s 7¾d out of eleven guineas owed
become bodily ones:

> ... we have had many neglects but they have been accounted for; first
> the agitation and bad feeling that prevailed during the pit-man's strike
> and secondly the bodily indisposition of many of our local preachers
> occasioned we believe, in many instances, by their partial want of
> support during the strike and the excessive labours subsequently ...

> That the decrease of Members since March is owing, not to any
> negligence of Mismanagement of the superintendent but to the illness
> of our other two Travelling preachers together with the unsettled state
> of the collieries and consequent removals out of the Circuit of Members
> and local Preachers.[40]

The end of the strike and the razing of working-class forms which
followed it brought nothing so exotic as a rush to Primitive
emotionalism. The statistical excitement of the early 1840s was
doused as circuits declined and some societies closed. The recovery
was grudging, and as late as 1847 Durham still 'deeply deplore[d]
the low state of the Circuit, the want of influence in our religious
services'.[41]

The 1840s ended with difficulties, but in their first twenty-five
years the Primitives had matched and complemented social crises
with energy and will and had registered their presence. Chapels
and mahogany pews had been scarcer than the extemporaneous
fabric of long-rooms, living-rooms, converted cottages, and rooved
gable-ends, but after 1850 was the time of a chapel for every village
(or suburb), and an inflexible 'secular' involvement.[42]

Grah 4 **Full and trial membership of societies in the South Shields Primitive Methodist Circuit, 1837–48** (source: Lists of Members, 1832–41, Monies and Members, 1837–50, DCRO, M.SS/29, M.SS/23). For South Shields actual society membership add 100 members to graph figures.

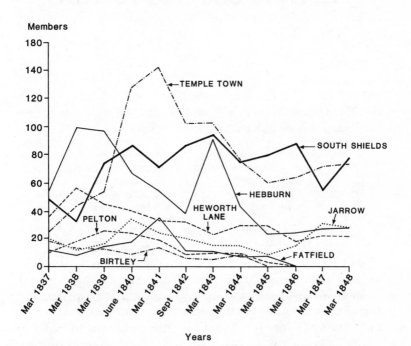

10
Conversions and revivals

In 1791 Thomas Curry, a Tyne keelman, sat expectantly in a Methodist service in Swalwell:

> No sooner was the text pronounced, 'Arise, shine, for thy light is come, and the glory of the Lord is risen upon thee', than he was filled with joy unspeakable ... To use his own simple language, 'his heart was like to jump out of his body'. For long after, whenever he mentioned this, his bursting heart found relief alone in a torrent of tears.

Now having 'meat to eat' which the world 'knew not of', Curry went on to compel his life, and his anxieties, to Jesus Christ. This kind of experience – Curry's 'joy unspeakable', his 'heart ... like to jump', his 'torrent of tears' – lay at the core of Methodism.[1]

John Wesley identified sure salvation as a felt experience of knowing God, a classic Pauline 'moment' and testimony. In the early years of Primitive Methodism, this experience of being 'at liberty' was usually preceded by mental and physical distress. Robert Young, a Northumberland pitman, was 'later powerfully saved' in 1822 after first being 'powerfully alarmed with the terrors of the Law'; Cuthbert Colling, a Weardale leadminer, heard Thomas Batty preach in 1823:

> Under his ministry he was brought into deep distress, and vehemently cried for mercy, so that his wife was afraid of his being mentally deranged. In six months he was brought into liberty under Mr Batty's teaching.

This 'liberty' was all heart and no mind. It could not be willed, or earned. It was not connected with status or morality. It was not necessarily the province of any organisation. It was transcendant and came by revelation: a lightning strike of God's grace, deep in the recesses of the individual. The Primitive could be a hearer, or a sunday school teacher, or a member, but not have liberty:

William Birkbeck of Pittington 'was noted for strict morality, but lived destitute of a change of heart' until ultimately receiving 'the pearl of great price' in 1851. Liberty could be won with other groups, or it could be found in private − 'I was drawn by the cords of love, and cannot state the particular time when I received the pardoning love of God, But I did receive it' − but its attainment, the swift flight of 'groan[s] being burdened' for that 'glorious sunshine of the presence and favour of the Almighty', was all.[2]

Making historical sense of this for the mining community between 1820 and 1850 is fraught with difficulty. There are general theories about conversions and revivals which have been tested and speculated upon in other works, but theories referring to, say, the West Riding of Yorkshire or the East Coast of the United States, will not necessarily apply here.[3] The specific nature of the historical enterprise denies direct comparison. In order to outline a theory which is faithful to its specific subject I shall consider a spectrum of ideas borrowed from other works but which nevertheless could suggest themselves as relevant to this work. It will be noticed that some ideas are more applicable than others but none of them can stand as a single, sufficient explanation for mass revival and conversion.

First, there is no question of revivalism in these years as stemming from capitalistic cabals.[4] The coalowners did not much try to encourage conversions in the hope that religiosity would raise their threshold of control. Methodism's record of moral improvement was praised by the Coal Trade and others in the 1840s but, moral improvement was not revivalism, the praise was not unqualified, the work was not fully understood, and the help given was minimal. Coal capitalism and the middle class remained interested in the problem of order, but whatever contributions Primitive Methodism may have made to its attainment, revivals pulsated too closely from and to the passions of the Poor to merit support. There are some areas which capitalism ignored, and revivalism received askant rather than interested attention.

Secondly, it would not be accurate to portray revivalism as streaming from the inspired words of the preachers into the simple mind of the crowd. This was the contemporary conservative view, a process which Robert Southey found 'disgusting',

> A powerful doctrine preached with passionate sincerity, with fervid zeal, and with vehement eloquence, produced a powerful effect on weak minds, ardent feelings, and disordered fancies.

There is some similarity with this position in the more recent idea which claims that the sweeping emotional doctrines of the preachers somehow 'fitted' the brutal existence of the Poor, an existence which had to find answer for a life of paradox and injustice.[5] The preachers could be a force for explanation, and what they had to say did at times clearly appeal, but the relatively high level of moral-institutional activity in the villages denied them the role as the only force for explanation. Moreover, there was a long-lived suspicion, particularly in the Wesleyan ministry, of any uncontrolled emotional display. Much of this stemmed from Wesley himself. Revivals such as those in 1822 and 1824 could burst upon the preachers in an unexpected way, and, although as experienced revivalists they sought to exploit them when they began, it was usually from one step behind. Sam Laister's preaching *Journal* recorded quite different responses from village to village before any momentum was achieved; Thomas Batty preached in Weardale for six months in the steps of five other preachers before revival suddenly came and 'the country was opening before us'; Revd Kendall referred to the slow, 'anthracite temperament' of the dalesmen, and Revd Dent witnessed the preachers as adjacent rather than central to the 1823 revival:

> There were many cases of prostration in connection with that great work. I have seen more than fifteen at one meeting, some of whom were sober-minded Christians, as humble as they were earnest. And what was very observable, there was nothing in the voice or manner of the preacher to account for such effects; no vociferation, no highly impassioned address. He stood as steadily, and talked as calmly, as I ever witnessed any one do ... having *in many instances, got to know substantially in his closet what was about to take place in the great congregation.* He did not take a falling down as a certain proof of the obtaining of entire sanctification; but ascribed much to physical causes – to nervous weakness. I do not recollect that there were *any* cases of the kind proved to be hypocritical mimicry. It was wonderful how some persons so affected were preserved from physical harm. I remember seeing men fall suddenly backwards on stone flags without being hurt, and on one occasion, in a dwelling-house, a man fell against the fire place, the fire burning at the time, without being injured.[6]

Revivals were big days, contingent and extraordinary. The preachers and their doctrines held only the theatrical centre; any revival theory which starts from the idea of Methodism's effect on the Poor is unbalanced because it underestimates the Poor's effect on Methodism and could not adequately account for the agonised 'hard places' and 'barren seasons' of the preachers' journals.

Thirdly, it is difficult to see the coalfield during these years as a new industrial 'frontier' manifesting psychic responses to unprecedented social experiences – a 'Burned-over district'.[7] Scorched perhaps, by raw new agitations of coal and rail feeding and attracting a growing population, but the coalfield was no frontier. The new villages were not remote, and their inhabitants tended to be local people from traditional mining areas, cognisant with the basic demands of pit-work. The new collieries tended to be more exploitative and troublesome it is true, yet the community had long known regular migrations, and apart from higher chances of death by disease and accident they enjoyed relatively good health. The region did not know the chronic technological and cyclical unemployment of other places, nor the mass induction of the workhouse. Neither could the coalfield be usefully described as an industrial district to compare with the new towns of Lancashire or the West Riding. Coal capitalism was old, its labour had long been by cash nexus (although the Bond was redefining its contractual status), the housing was not urban, and the work discipline of the factory simply did not and could not exist in the pit. The submissive element of conversion could have had its uses for the coalowner, but not of the type or scale as envisaged by Dr Ure's *Philosophy of Manufactures*. Coalowners were not like other manufacturers. Production remained more a leasing of their earth to the pitman's skill and experience and he was paid by what he 'won'. That 'inner compulsion' necessary for the factory operative was not an issue for the pitman.[8] Also, Primitive Methodism was more successful in the rural village than it was in the industrial town.[9] The revivals of 1822–4 began in the isolated leadmining and smallholding communities of the Pennine dales and gathered their own pace before spilling into Tyne and Wear basins and flooding out across railway plains into the villages. The notion of a 'Burned-over District' might carry points of contact for this study in the break-neck growth of the new villages, but the contacts are specific and not general. The coalfield was no black hole of Industrialism nor was it a frontier of the new society.

A fourth possibility derives from E. P. Thompson's startling application of the idea of a 'chiliasm of despair'. Thompson suggested an oscillating relationship between working-class political or 'temporal' aspirations, their defeat, and a reactive revivalism. Methodist growth up into the 1830s is postulated as a 'big-dipper' of political optimism and pessimism swinging across the conjunctures of class struggle. Thompson stiffened his theory by inserting an 'initial propensity' among the Poor to instability, an instability which could manifest itself in the village by 'any sombre or dramatic event'.[10] Broadly speaking, steep fluctuations of membership are typical for Methodism up to 1850, and are in fact inseparable from the movement's high growth rate over the long term. Matching this, any consideration of Thompson's theory for the coalfield must be done against a broad backdrop of steeply fluctuating and declining earnings in the 1830s and 1840s.[11] Methodist membership patterns in the coalfield from 1821 support parts of Thompson's theory: the first revival followed the Radical political failures of 1819–20, although whether there was any causal relationship has yet to be shown; membership was volatile for the whole period with room for independent climbs and falls at village-level; cholera certainly, and colliery explosion perhaps, were each followed by sudden responses to the prophecy, and the mining community (including leadminers) did experience high normal incidences of unnatural death by disease or accident. However, the theory is less convincing in its notion of an oscillation between temporal and spiritual ambition. Both Chartism and the National Miners' Association grew as the Primitives grew, and in the case of the NMA in 1844 and Hepburn's union in 1832, the Primitives fell as they fell. There is some evidence of a certain indifference rather than hostility to Methodism at the height of union-power in 1831, and the revivalist dimension of Primitive growth in the early 1840s admittedly followed the Chartist retreat and yet was coincident with trade-union advance. Moreover, in a fluid and moving society it is extremely difficult to identify causes of sudden growth among village groups. The reasons may have been 'sombre and dramatic event[s]' peculiar to a village, but they may equally have been more mundane. A new building or a famous preacher, the inability to afford class tickets, a sharp change in the population, or a subtle shift in its composition, could all have significantly affected membership.

The last idea is really a variant of previous themes and emphasises the psychoanalytical or psychological factor. Hazlitt named the Methodists 'religious invalids', Southey blamed guilt and sexual repression, and over eighty years ago William James in his famous *Varieties of Religious Experience* described nineteenth-century revivalism as the 'religion of chronic anxiety'. There are severe problems here because anxiety and relative deprivation could be shown to have existed in all historical contexts. Equally, some historians have pushed this approach beyond what they can reasonably know, but the weight of evidence demands that it be given some consideration.[12]

Conversions were undoubtedly brought on by the collective atmosphere of the crowd. During the 1823 revival, meeting rooms were so crowded that all furniture, even the lectern, was removed in order to pack people in:

> ... then some stalwart miner [leadminer] would come forward and stand with his back to the preacher, so that he – the preacher – might find support by resting his arms on the man's shoulders. There was competition for honour of fulfilling this office.

Coming from the crowd, physical emanation invited physical metaphors. 1824 preaching tours in the coalfield witnessed 'quickening', 'shaking', 'mighty', 'melting', 'powerful', times; converts 'fell before God' while the 'devil was roaring', the people 'crying out', and the 'Lord made bare his arm' as 'many wept and shook like leaves before the wind'.[13] Whilst the source of some revivals was inexplicable to the preachers, others were consciously and manipulatively planned. If a full revival was not possible, then services or camp-meetings could at least be expected to bear some conversions. When preacher Taylor referred to 'class leaders set[ting] their shoulders to the ark', or preacher Batty referred to the efforts of 'The noble spirited troops from Shotley Bridge and Newlands ... headed by their officers', both men were talking about existing members coming together in prayer or exhortation or song to swell the emotions, intensify the spiritual atmosphere, and somehow flood the normal sensibility of the unconverted. Everyone present would be aware that this was the explicit intention, that to be 'at liberty' was a desired state, that a sign of change was necessary, and that everyone prized it both for themselves and for others. Behind the intense emotional wall there would be an organisational hinterland of petty obligation and expectation.[14]

Apart from looking more closely at individual testimonies, it is difficult for the historian to make further comment. From their own stories the pre-converted were usually in a state of some anxiety. By definition, the experiences were psychological. It is clear that the emotions were being willingly manipulated in a way which often ended in abnormal, yet expected, behaviour. It is also clear that mass impulses towards emotional manipulation had a social pattern across wide areas over time, but could nevertheless, happen in one place at one time sometimes for obscure, sometimes for obvious, reasons. One might have expected impulses of this kind to have been current among intimate and interdependent communities, 'colonies of themselves [which] must be treated as such. Whatever direction you give to them it is retained'.[15] It is hard to know what more the historian can prudently say. Theories of sexual repression, or patrist guilt, or psychic frustration, are impossible to illustrate for the mass, and difficult historically to diagnose for the individual. Primitive Methodism was not the only working-class movement which knew and looked for emotional involvement, and the charge of 'disordered minds' would need, impossibly, to apply both to the masses, prompted by untutored instinct, and to trade-union and village leaders, who most certainly knew what they wanted, and why. The conversion phenomenon must be taken on its own terms and, after accounting for social interactions, cannot be reduced to any 'more real' levels of reality. There is no felicific calculus to be applied because at centre the experience lived only with its subject. It is a brave or foolhardy theory which tries to distinguish between genuine and ungenuine testimonies of spiritual experience.[16]

Later, conversion tears were frozen into myth. Wesley's weeping scenes with the Kingswood miners established a tradition. One of Wesley's biographers had him preaching to 'white lines on ... black faces ... tears running down ... sooty cheeks'; Nathaniel West wrote of 'large and silent tears rolling down ... black cheeks ... leaving the white streaks behind' during his coalfield tours in 1823; Owenite James Rigby, 'while painting the horror of the old system' at Bradford in 1838, said 'tears stole down many a cheek' as 'each seemed to feel his own case'. By the turn of the century, Liberal ideologues used working-class tears as proof of the individualistic moral conscience.[17] Above all, Methodism's veil of tears unfurls to the central fact of its early history: to what has been called the 'reactive dialectic' of the Methodist encounter.[18] The Primitive historian Kendall, writing in 1905 about the Midlands revivals of 1815, made interesting, if ambiguous, comment on this:

> Churches of long standing naturally made it their chief solicitude to keep their people from being 'drawn away and enticed' by the lawless [political] spirit abroad. They drew a cordon round the fold and tried to isolate their flock. But as yet our missionaries had no such necessary work to engage them. They themselves were outside the cordon, and any work they did must be carried on within the infected area.[19]

The preachers came to touch the quick of community life. In turn, the mining community shaped the style and substance of the Primitives. As men and women were the translators of religion and community, the exchange between them was not 'mechanical' and related, but 'organic' and instinctive. As such, clear perimeters between community and religion, and religion and community, across which the reactive exchange occurred, are not usually obvious. The exchange could operate at the casual level of vigorous female preaching from a vigorous female population; of using village bellmen to raise a congregation; of class-leaders who were also publicans; of classes held in pubs because they were too poor for hall-rent (and from which pubs they were expelled for making too much noise); of classes held in members' homes, allowing women a more central, if informal, administrative part; of classes held in colliery blacksmiths' shops (and from which they were expelled during a strike); of lay-preachers who possessed 'a good vocabulary into which [they] often threw the pitman's vernacular with effect'; or of lay-preachers who were attracted by chapel coffee and beef sandwiches.[20]

The exchange could operate at the deepest level of life and death. The Primitives' zeal for a righteous death found response in a community whose existing honour of death was profound, and whose funeral rituals were meticulous. Their direct attribution of God's hand in all things found response in a community some of whose beliefs could profer a magical technology of cause and effect. Theological bedizenment of signs and wonders found response in a popular literature of spiritual animations and correspondences, amply cross-referenced in Bible and Almanac. The Primitives' personal confrontation with the Devil found response in a community given to familiar intimacies with 'Old Nick' and 'Old Harry'. Joseph Spoor would muster a crowd and fill chapels with the declaration that he, personally, was 'to sell the devil up and leave him neither stick nor stool'; the incredible Thomas Bates 'used to have hand-to-hand encounters with the devil' at Hebburn colliery. In March 1824 Brother West was confronted at Stockton by a rival preacher 'who by his sentiments I took to be a millenarian'. The man infuriated West only when he dared to abuse the Devil, 'a work which Michael the archangel durst not attempt', and the Primitives sang him down.[21]

Missionaries and preachers rapidly learned the art of public spectacle. Often the preachers had to contend with the rival attractions of the flesh, and the huckstering methods of market and fair were incorporated into the religious repertoire. Joseph Spoor the keelman-preacher duelled with Billy Purvis the Newcastle showman for a crowd in Morpeth market place; Purvis lost and shouted at Spoor through his trumpet 'Ah war'n thou thinks thysel a clever fellow noo!' Thomas Batty's camp meetings were such 'that young men would say to their comrades, "Come let us away to Ranter Meeting and see them tumble down"'. Revd Hodgson Casson, a Wesleyan, 'whose personal and pulpit eccentricities were only exceeded by his devotion ... created a great sensation in the Gateshead Circuit' in the 1820s and 'Crowds were attracted by the notoriety'.[22] Extemporary preaching by a non-sacerdotal and working-class ministry (17s per week in Sunderland circuit, 1837) broke through the defences of dialect, registered the tone of an oral tradition, and met the taste for excitement and spectacle. Most exhortation and prayer was 'off the cuff' and lost to history. This description of a week-night service at Winlaton in the 1850s, from a Primitive who remembered, is a rare privilege:

> A score of voices of varying *timbre*, at the invitation of Matthew Pickering ... join in singing 'Thou Shepherd of Israel and mine', after which we are led to the Presence by simple heart-language. Jackey Parker prays with open eyes, fixed on the ceiling, and his wheezy voice, and his wrinkles become less prominent as he speaks of guidance and deliverance from his difficulties. William Armstrong, with the wooing note, gently and smilingly leads us from our doubts and fears. Then came the sonorous tones of George Spark, telling of perils manifold, but in the darkness of the mine there was still the gracious light; and how that voice rolled and swelled as he prayed that we might 'like Zachariah and Elizabeth' go 'hand in hand through Emmanuel's land, to fairer words on high'; then it broke as he told of those who had gone before. Robert Brooks, whose personality was unique, and whose seventy years sat lightly upon him, rejoiced that Jesus was the end

of the law. 'He has conquered for Brooks; oh, hallelujah'. ... Then Tommy Warren, the singer saint, took his part, he whose optimistic faith carried him through sorrows and over difficulties which would have paralysed less heroic souls. Ellison Clark, calm and judicial, and others less frequently heard, followed. Women were there, who came to keep their tryst and meet their Lord ... and young people were drawn and held by the mystic contagion.[23]

The popular melodies of the day were used indiscriminately and put to religious words.[24] Popular melodies from the body of the hall, the prowling rhetoric of the pulpit, the drama of conversion, the daring of Old Nick – a Methodist service was not unentertaining.

The entertainment and its missionary purpose was based, quite literally, on the living word. As words were the only resource a poor peoples' movement could possess in abundance, Primitive Methodism existed, above all else, as a voice. Hugh Bourne's original secession and expulsion from Wesleyanism had rested on his and his followers' insistence on speaking and singing as they pleased. Thereafter, the Primitives found themselves growing by free gospelism, conversation ministries, and no coherent polity or theology, at the same time as the Wesleyans found themselves stagnating in a pile of paper resolutions and reminders about orderly meetings, accredited pulpits, official hymnals, and monitored practices.[25] Much of the early opposition to popular Methodism came from people in high places who wanted the poor to keep their mouths shut and their heads bowed. Against this, the Primitives were looking up to an associational life whose vernacular spoke of independence and not dependence; whose extemporary litany of lay question and response, exhortation and prayer, echoed participation and not submission; whose crescendos of voice and music sang of a place for all and not a few; and whose testimonies of assurance by experience could only be expressed in words inadequate for, but unique to, that experience. No one else could know it, or say it, for them.

Across these voices lay a loose theology of Pauline Protestantism.[26] Out of Paul's personal experience had been built an intellectual system of Law, Fall, New Birth, Justification, Sanctification, Revelation, Perfection, Assurance, and Holiness. John Wesley had contributed and agonised over the personal and intellectual meaning of all this but in the midst of revival it is easy to see how minds less scrupulous than his could come to suspend the intellectual for the personal. Within moments, the struggling penitent could be represented as the incarnation of an entire Protestant tradition. How could a set of theological concepts compare with the living word of a direct experience of God?[27] Moments such as these validated the preachers' gospel. A good preacher was someone capable of conjuring up such moments; the preachers and their congregations knew this, and were bound to each other in the knowledge. This knowledge was experiential, but the speaking, if it could not always be rational, had to recognise its speaker. God's Word was epic, poetic, formal, spoken through mortal tongues, from Scripture. Preachers' and congregations' words were natural, vernacular, extemporary, spoken by themselves, largely by anecdote and refrain. Penitents' words were untutored and spoke out of the struggle within. Taken together, in the sequence of a service, these discourses brought God to the everyday and the everyday within sight of God.[28]

It is not surprising that women found their place with a movement which, in its early days at least, stressed the personal rather than the managed and depended for its premises on private homes. Wesleyanism had had its female preachers but in 1803 it had resolved that 'In general' women ought not 'be permitted to preach among us'. After Jabez Bunting took control, 'In general' became nearly always.[29] Primitive Methodism accepted female preachers until 1841. More than that, it had to defend both its female preachers and its female members who took part in revivals from those who would have women subordinate and silent (1 Timothy 2; 11–12: Corinthians 14; 34). Bourne's 1808 tract, 'Remarks on the Ministry of Women', asserted the scriptural right of women to be heard. Given the minor but famous role women were to have in the movement it is as well that he did. The first female itinerants (Ann Brownsword and Sarah Kirkland) received their wages in 1815.[30] Jane Ansdale, with her colleague Thomas Batty, were the greatest of the dales missioners in the early 1820s. In 1838, Sister Preston joined Sister Whiston as valued lay preachers in the Sunderland circuit, and in 1839 Sister Porteous was re-appointed to work with Brother Tindal as the second itinerant in the Durham circuit. In spite of her illness in the Spring of 1840, the circuit kept faith with her and continued to report its pleasure in her ministry.[31] This is not to suggest that Primitive Methodism espoused equality. In its theology it had to accept a basic spiritual egalitarianism because to deny that would be to deny its own revival

history. In its organisation women were allowed to speak as
itinerants, lay preachers, class leaders, exhorters, and sunday
school teachers, by a reasoning that was purely scriptural: they
could speak as Miriam or Deborah or Abigail spoke, but they could
not administer. The offices of steward, trustee, delegate, and
superintendant were barred. Even as itinerants they earned only
half wages.[32]

The reactive dialectic of Primitive Methodism with working-
class life was too licentious for some. Outside the home-based
activities of family prayer, moral instruction, preachers' lodging
and the accommodation of meetings, there were inevitable
criticisms of active female participation. Women activists were
cast as shrews, their husbands as cuckolds. Similarly, in an age
whose intellectual establishment viewed 'The Holy Scriptures
rightly understood' as not giving 'encouragement to Enthusiasm
or Superstition', Southey was condescendingly critical of a movement lacking discretion or intellect, Thomas Trotter attributed
religious enthusiasm to common drunkenness, and one 'lady in
the gallery pews' on hearing William Clowes the co-founder of
Primitivism pray in Newcastle in 1839, 'rose up, and, walking out,
exclaimed "O, what a mockery"'. The reviewer supposed 'she
had never before heard any one pray as if God were really present
in the congregation'. She obviously had not; one wonders what
her elegant soul would have made of the pitman John Grieves
who was given to 'perusing' Matthew Henry's *Commentary*
'with his handkerchief in his hand, wiping away the tears as they
rolled down his cheeks'.[33] In Weardale, the respectability of the
Wesleyans was compared with the 'din and disturbance' of the
Primitives. What could controlled and controlling temperaments
make of a class which heard 'through the medium of their passions'
and a movement which deliberately sited its meeting houses next
to the sinful, which gladly unhinged the emotions, which kept up
the ancient clamorous *lic wacce* round the bed of the dying, which
courted sexual innuendo with its late-night meetings, and which
was rowdy even in prayer?

> In prayer they work themselves into a complete phrenzy; sing at the
> stretch of their voices their hymns to some of the most popular tunes
> of the day ... and it does not matter whether he or she in the pulpit
> be preaching or praying, loud 'Amens' 'Praise God' 'I do believe'
> resound and ring throughout the building.[34]

Within the movement the obituary columns of the *Primitive Methodist Magazine* provide evidence about individual conversions. The source is limited. The obituaries are highly selective, only stalwarts (and the very young) figure, and most of the less constant of the fluctuating membership do not. The obituary column was a record of institutionally-defined piety rather than membership. Although the columns grew more elaborate and 'secular' as the century progressed, the model of piety remained intact: the moment of conversion, the manner of death, the degree of organisational involvement. It was important to identify the preacher. Whose ministry did the converted 'fall under', where, and how? How many 'changes of heart' and 'backslidings' were there before liberty was established? What kind of convert was produced? – and here the emphasis was usually upon the non-intellectual qualities: if a man, then it was common sense and 'plain truth'; if it was a woman then it was honest piety, 'An Israelite indeed, in whom is no guile'. Equally important was the manner of death. It was assumed that for the faithful, the closer they nudged death then the closer they nudged what was beyond.[35] Questioning could continue ('Is Jesus precious?') right up to the end. A raised arm, a muttered verse or text, an assurance of Jesus' presence, were the marks of a good death. There was relatively little in the *Magazine* on the members' secular lives. Sometimes not even occupation was recorded. There were traces of a social life when mention was made of the pre-converted state ('bold in the service of sin'), but much of the social record concerned organisational appointments in an ascending scale which started with sunday school teaching and ended with class leadership.

Most of the obituaries fixed the moment of conversion in the meeting room, chapel, or camp service. The preachers were listed: Casson, Suddards, Barnfoot, Nelson, Clowes, Batty, Oxtoby, Branwell and others – men in broad-brimmed hats, silk kerchief and workman's breeches, carrying umbrellas and a bundle of severe books – Wesley, Watts, Fletcher, Baxter.[36] Mary Porteous was sung to on her sick-bed by Branwell (1816); Mary Dent fell under 'the method and manner' of Clowes (1820); John Kirk was agonised by Oxtoby (1824); Spoor was tormented by the 'vivid and realistic imagery' of Casson (1827). We can occasionally see the preacher in the centre, sifting the wheat from the chaff – as the Wesleyan William Bramwell did at West Moor colliery in 1817:

... after a few had spoken of their Christian experience he said, 'I am just thinking, there are some penitents here' ... The first who rose was a stout young man who trembled exceedingly whilst he cried out, 'Oh do pray for me'. Shortly afterwards, Mr Bramwell requested all to kneel down; it seemed that every individual was engaged in earnest prayer. In a few minutes the young man was set at liberty ... Mr Bramwell prayed again and several more were made unhappy. Mr B then desired the people to sit down. We did so. In a little time, he again requested the remaining penitents to stand up; and this he repeated until there was not one left in unbelief.[37]

And the atmosphere complemented the preaching. The pitman George Clough attended the West Moor revival 'through curiosity and a love of fun' before seeing his friend fall and being prised open to 'distressing sorrow' himself (1830s); the pitman Robert Thompson was converted in a Haswell meeting which 'shook the place' (1851); William Wake fell in the charged atmosphere of a South Shields sail loft (1822); Hannah Race (c. 1824) would walk twenty miles for prizes of the sort won by John Maugham, a Hetton miner and Primitive interceder:

One backslider was awakened and cried for mercy, and after long and hard struggling found peace. On that occasion our dear brother manifested a zeal becoming his profession ... and when liberty was obtained shouted as one having found great spoil.[38]

Many obituaries reveal that Primitives came to the movement after involvement with other Methodist groups. It had been disaffected Wesleyans in North Shields and Newcastle who had first invited the movement's co-founder, William Clowes, to those places in 1821. Pitmen like George Fenton and Robert Fairley had previous Methodist New Connexion and Wesleyan involvement, Jane Smith had been with the Independent Methodists, and others, like the pitmen John Wall and John Clark, James Pyburn the Newbottle shoemaker and Sam Lowther of Percy Main colliery had had scriptural sunday school upbringings before settling with the Primitives. Wall was an ardent sunday schooler before 'he was led away by evil companions', and Clark could remember committing 'to memory several of Dr Watts' hymns for children' before conversion in adult life.[39] For people like these the scriptural reasoning of Primitive Methodism would have been already familiar. Connected with this was often some reference to the pressure of marriage on the man's religious consciousness.

The coalfitter and pitman John Tulip, not a man 'likely to enter upon the married state without serious reflection about his increased responsibilities', was converted three years after his marriage to the Primitive, Elizabeth Richardson.[40] Temperance was another antecedent. The Shieldsman William Waugh was converted in 1837 after taking the pledge: 'Having become sober, he soon became a thinking man. His reflections led him to mourn over the sins of his past life'; George McReeth, 'embracing total abstinence principles ... was restored to sober habits, which prepared the way for serious and religious thinking', and conversion followed in 1849.[41]

The death of loved ones invited introspection. The deaths of brothers, husbands, uncles, and children are also recorded as the grounds for conversion. The Houghton pitman Joseph Fletcher was converted after being 'called upon to follow in rapid succession the whole of his nine children'; the Shields seaman Michael Hutchinson was converted in 1837 after the drowning of his brother in the Gulf of Finland, the cabin boy having witnessed 'a wave lift him from the wreck when he was earnestly engaged in prayer'. Cholera and typhus made their mark: the pitman William Bruce 'saw the necessity of making his peace with God' during the 1832 outbreak, and we know that in this he was not alone.[42]

Although 'got separated' was a fairly common reference to the organisational involvement of stalwarts, the experience of moving from one village to another was rarely mentioned in any traumatic sense as a reason for conversion. There had always been the assumption of mobility in the coalfield. Members like John Sharp, a shoemaker who left Seaham for Hetton, were already members who would make it their business to meet their brothers and sisters on arrival. Moving might have meant a casual change of allegiance, as in the case of Ann Hutton who changed from Wesleyan to Primitive after shifting from Tudhoe to Shincliffe colliery, or Jane Corner who was converted in Darlington in 1831 after she 'got separated', but only two miners' obituaries vaguely identified conversion with moving.[43]

11
Discipline and morality

Those who were converted were saved only on condition. The 'saved' in Methodism were not an elect; when the Day of Judgement came, when 'the world cannot' and 'He will not' move to save, then the only test of grace was the sanctity of the soul. Preachers read that to loiter was to be 'guilty of the murder and damnation of all those souls whom thou dost neglect', and after conversion it was their duty to nurture and protect the souls of the converted. All worship gathered round this simple duty. Methodist services were called 'Means of Grace', and their calendar of worship, prayers, classes, camp meetings, love feasts, sunday schools and anniversaries all carried this theological significance.[1] The converted were saved primarily from this-world. To care for this-world, even an 'unwillingness to die ... doth actually impeach us of high treason against the Lord', and the saving of souls was 'a higher and nobler charity than relieving ... bodies'.[2] To be saved from this-world was to afford the delights of eternal life, everlasting rest, Zion City of God, in the next. This monumental promise, this guarantee of what was to come, represented a drive for a will of abstract, idealist, proportions. Revd Everett esteemed God's words as perfect, sure, right, pure and true:

> The law of the Lord is perfect, converting the soul: the testimony of the Lord is sure, making wise the simple; the statutes of the Lord are right, rejoicing the heart, the commandment of the Lord is pure, enlightening the eyes: the judgements of the Lord are true and righteous altogether, more to be desired than fine gold; sweeter also than the honey ...[3]

Behind the rhetoric lay absolute acceptance of Scripture as the criterion of truth, the arbiter of reason, and the proper articulation of all personal and social relations. For if experience of God was personal, the framework for understanding that experience most certainly was not. The Wesleyan Revd McAllum could tell his congregation that Jesus' promised legions of angels meant precisely 72,000 foot and 8760 horse, without question, as in Matthew 26; 53. Brother Wilson however, was prevented from preaching because his views on the reign of Christ and the New Dispensation were considered unscriptural and involved comment on 'the inefficiency of the Gospel'.[4] Experiences were free, but Scripture was sacred, and one had to accept this or be silenced.

In so far as scriptural theology articulated the shape and detail of human relations it can be said to have constituted an ideology.[5] It was, however, an ideology which did not seek to express or understand human relations in a way which connected them to their social conditions; on the contrary, the promise of a life-to-come glimpsed through the pages of a text that was Holy aggressively denied the importance of social conditions. Yet this is not to say that religious expression did not embody consciousness of self in society. Primitive Methodism grew during a period of social crisis. In general, no religious movement was more the product of social crisis, and yet no popular movement denied society more; no religious membership suffered harsher social conditions, and yet no membership denied the significance of those conditions more; no section of that membership was more conscious of social conflict than the pitmen, and yet no occupational group aligned themselves with Primitive Methodism more.

These points cannot be ignored, even if Primitive ideology tried to. The Primitive Methodists made their own subjectivity in a society of struggle, where violent death was never far away. As we do not know the heartlessness they perceived, so it is difficult to appreciate the 'heart' they generated. Primitive sentiments and practices were as structural and life-giving as they were ethereal and life-denying.

Denial of this-world rested upon ideological purity. From the beginning, the Primitive Methodists set themselves apart, as fugitives from the world. Their class tickets in 1811 were inscribed with Acts 28; 22 'for as concerning this sect, we know that everywhere it is spoken against', and the Connexion maintained both its cohesion and its apartness by a severe ideological discipline. The discipline came haltingly, and not just from the centre. A rough code of rules was drawn up in 1814, and in 1819 the first Primitive Conference took the authority to lay down the rule and guidelines of government. Bourne advocated more centralisation, but the associations were still fluid enough and lay representation was strong enough not to let him have his own way. He held on to the editorship of the *Magazine*, and his brother to the Book Room and press on the family farm at Bemersley, as consolation. In 1826 Conference finally brought circuits into line through financial controls, and, having regulated the administrative role of women in 1824, moved on to regulate children and teachers with rules for sunday schools in 1832. Even then, power and representation remained polycentric enough to warrant the opening statement that 'We do not say that at any place the people must be tied exactly to these rules; but still we do think they will be of great service'. It was not until 1849 that Primitive Methodism accepted strict central government: 176 pages of Minutes 'obligatory on the Connexion' addressed theological orthodoxy and the rules and procedures of discourse and funding. These General Consolidated Minutes, with their twenty-five page index and eight page glossary, provided for the function, solvency, conduct, thought, office and hierarchy of Primitive Methodism. They were written with one eye on the Wesleyan wrangling and break-up of that year, but their impetus lay in local practice and ideology. From the smallest sunday school child, to the most respected class leader, the movement looked for method and control over a wayward membership.[6]

From the beginning, the most important group to be disciplined were the preachers:

> That Bro. Garnett come on the Plan as A Preacher on Trial & that he be requested to preach a Trial Sermon & give an Account of the Doctrines he professes before the Committee the ensuing Qr. as prepatory to being approved ...

> That Bro. Hebbron & Dent wait upon Mr. Mowat as to whether he still maintains the heterodox opinion that the Punishment of the Wicked is not eternal and that they decide as to the propriety of Keeping his name on the plan as a preacher as they find.[7]

The entire loyal membership, the preachers in particular, experienced the movement and its ideology as a systematic epistemological and moral severance. For men like Hugh Bourne, wandering out of bleak moorland isolation and into struggle with the world beyond, the severance was sought. Many were familiar with the essential theology and scriptural fundamentalism, it was after all shared to varying degrees by all the religious bodies, but the

Primitives carried the tenets to breaking point and insisted upon separation. Men like Sam Lowther of Percy Main had the break forced upon them: on becoming a preacher in 1829 Sam was 'a public character' and 'had to pass through much persecution'. The weaker Methodists plagiarised Wesley (and were reprimanded for it), others relied upon verbatim hymns and texts. Revd Parker remembered a Methodist meeting in the 1840s when after the hymn 'We are marching through Emmanuel's ground' an old man prayed aloud above the gathering that they might all have a cottage in Van Diemen's Land. Parker asked who could fully explain 'these laws of mental association?' Of course he may have wished to emigrate. On the other hand it is possible that the old man confused the symbolism of Emmanuel with Van Diemen's land because he could not explain his religion as a set of intellectually coherent beliefs.[8]

The historical reality of the Methodist soul was manifest in the operation of the Methodist economy. It is possible to overestimate the sophistication of this economy in the years up to 1850, but we will concentrate on its patterns of discipline, its articulation of moral detail, and its administration of the individual.[9]

Above all, Methodism sought to constrain the temperament. The first mark of temperament was attendance and punctuality, and most routine business concerned these duties. The most frequent admonition was for preachers' neglect of the preaching 'plan', the commonest type of 'backsliding' was for members' non-attendance:

> That Bro. Finley's name stand on the plan without apts. in consequence of slackness in attending class & that Bro. Lister see him as soon as possible.

After attendance, patterns of discipline could run into many corners: the everyday-organisational − Brother Clougham failing to hold a leaders' meeting at New Durham; the higher-organisational − the Haswell society raising and spending money without permission; or the detailed-organisational, when 'Bro. Wilson, Butterwick, Coward, and Mason Compose[d] a Committee for making Rules which must be observed by those who sit in our Singing Pew.' Finance was close to the business of attendance. With average subscriptions at just over one penny per member per week, local societies were obliged to avoid penury by keeping their membership attendances as high as possible.[10]

Sometimes, as we have seen, it was necessary to check opinions – 'That Thos. Carr be requested to lay his political opinions aside' – but usually ideological purity was assumed to come from lengthy membership:

> A coal miner 6 years and half standing in society, 6 month ... an exhorter, 9 month ... a Preacher, 6 month ... an approved ... preacher, 18 month a Class leader ...

There were also, as one might expect, strict codes regarding proper conduct:

> 3. that he is considered to possess improving tallents is Pious and Generally useful ...
>
> 5. no smoker of tobacko is not imberrised in his circumstances has not made any ingagements relative to Marriage, has not been a traveling preacher.[11]

For the individual member, there are only hints at the consequences of a life struggle for control. The obituary columns record many 'lion to lamb' experiences. Men like the leadminer Joseph Featherstone whose 'sufferings were occasionally intense' though he was 'exceedingly affectionate, though the last trait was scarcely observable to any but those who were intimately acquainted with him ...' represent emotional surfaces and undercurrents common to many Primitives.[12] As, after Scripture, God knew all and saw all, then no detail was too small and no second was too short for a searching self-discipline. Once within Methodism, the member meticulously built the new soul, and its breadth and depth were angled by the form of the movement. The Methodist soul was articulated through the minutiae of self-surveillance across the smallest fraction of conscious time. The minutiae of detail and the fraction of time, in turn, dissolved into the space and timelessness of a soul that was *only detail* and forever *immediately* accountable. It may have been that mental rehearsals such as these were more available to women members. Detailed inner surveillance depended upon the individual's allotment of time. The mind had to seek permanent control over time in order to attain a moral unity of all time. In this unity the individual was answerable to God. As women were more able to allot their time, and as the surveillance of family morality was deemed to be their duty and their nature, it could have been that the female 'soul' was more placed to be reconstructed than the male. At any rate, in ideological terms at least, the newly formulated womanhood from the 1840s, morally defined and privately assessed, carried certain correspondences with the Methodist soul.[13]

Minutiae of moral detail and fraction of allotted time concentrated the individual. Around the individual stalked a brethren and a sisterhood who were all their brother's keepers. The Methodist economy sought to control every facet of a member's life:

> That Bro Jaques spoke unadvisedly to Br Charlton and recommends him to be more cautious for the future. That Br Charlton acted unadvisedly in circulating Br Jacques' observation and that he be recommended to be more cautious for the future. That John Whitfield is found guilty of circulating slanderous reports of Bro. Edgar.[14]

Demeanour was crucial to cross-checking morality. For instance it was not obligatory for Wesleyans or all Primitives to be temperate, but drinking in a public place took away a member's 'apartness' — that display of a serious temperament, that cultivated virtue which represented the movement as a whole — and hence the suspension of Brothers Lambert and Wanless for being seen in a pub in 1848. Given the mix of personal constraint and collective enthusiasm, and the scope for mistakes between morality and demeanour, circuits were plagued with scandal. Slander was built into the Methodist economy. Brother Craggs' three month suspension for 'writing scurrilous letter to the Superintendent & Spreading discord in the society' finds its echo in every circuit.[15] The drive for homogeneity among members exposed individuals in all their awkwardnesses, and it is hardly surprising, in an institution which was busy creating separate spheres for its women at the same time as it was erecting structures both intimate and overseeing, that some of these awkwardnesses concerned male and female relations. There were a stream of warnings:

> That Br Reed be recommended to resume his acquaintance with the young woman to whom he had promised Marriage and also to fulfill his promise at a suitable opportunity ...
>
> That Br Hardy be suspended till the quarter day he having married a woman not a member in society ...
>
> That Br Blackburn having expressed his sorrow for striking his wife, this meeting forgives him, and that Br Hopkinson informs him by note of this ...
>
> That Ralph Brown be expelled [from] Society in consequence of ill using & beating his wife.[16]

Much of the intimacy and oversight came through the class meeting. The class meeting had always been the main instrument of Methodism for it was here that members accounted for their souls and, with their punctual attendance and ticket subscriptions, sustained the institution. The entire Methodist bureaucracy of body and soul – circuit schedules, class lists, members' accounts, prechers' plans, leaders' minutes – emanated from the class meeting. The class meeting extolled a general discipline, and tabled that movement of forward and backward spiritual progression which isolated and pressured the individual.

The children were the most impersonally pressured. Children encountered the sunday school as a system run by extraordinary individuals of resource. The sunday school, in turn, encountered the children as initiates, as the many to be controlled by the few.[17] They were a mass, a mass to be ordered, disciplined, fragmented, and re-formed again as saved individual souls. Salvation for the child was perceived in the same manner as for adults. The most perfect Methodist child was 'but wise and stayed as a man', 'as serious as a woman of fifty', 'punctual in her attendance at school, grave before her class, walked in fear of God'. The Wallsend Wesleyans called a boy among them 'The Little Old Man' 'because of his stability, good sense, and sedative habits'. Isaac Watts' hymns, lined-out for the understanding that comes from repetition, resounded in every sunday school. Even above their teacher, their superintendent, and their betters, God saw every crease and wrinkle of a child's soul – 'Almighty God, thy piercing eye Strikes through the shades of night' – and beneath, quailed the vitality in which Satan dwelled. Watts' *Songs Divine and Moral for the use of children* pointed to evil in all that was not controlled:

> Why should I love my sport so well,
> > So constant at my play,
> And lose the thoughts of heaven and hell,
> > And then forget to pray.

The impetuous displacement of the pitman George Fenton

> ... sent down the pit at a very early age ... In this nursery of sin, he soon became an adept in evil ... and impetuously indulged in the low pleasures of the ale house, and the sabbath field sports ...

is to be compared with the positioned emplacement of Jane Lister

... naturally of a thoughtful, sober, turn of mind, retiring in her
manners, but cheerful in conversation, orderly in her movements,
and remarkably industrious ... obedient to her parents ... sparing
in words ...[18]

The sunday school gathered, sorted, surveyed, instructed,
punished, and flattered the children into its own system. Every
failure to achieve attendance, or response, or docility, resulted in
finer checks and more scrupulous efforts. The Houghton le Spring
Wesleyan Circuit opened William Street Sunday School in 1827
with a rough project of singing, prayers, and Bible study from
9.30 am to 12.00, 'the Scholars going out in rotation', and the
teachers attending to absentees. By 1839, the Circuit had a stricter
system. School management had been put in the hands of a general
committee before which all intending scholars had to appear; all
teachers had to be full members; only the superintendent minister
could inflict corporal punishment; book-buying had to be carefully
controlled. As well as school management, school discipline had
been diligently formulated: teachers were to avoid 'all levity or trifling with or before the children' and fines were listed for teacher-
absence; no child was to be admitted 'who is not clean and free
from all disease'; expulsion 'shall be done before the whole school
in order that the example may be a warning'; and 'Neither the art
of writing, or any other merely secular branch of Knowledge shall
be taught on the Sabbath'.[19] The Primitive sunday school rules
were only advisory, with hints on AGMs, Committees, Teachers'
Meetings, Treasurerships, and Secretaryships to start up an
organisation, but this did not imply any woolliness in how to
conduct it. The greater the numbers pressing upon it, the greater
the need for system. System would enable conduct, and proper
conduct was explained in ruthless detail. Much of this detail
addressed the teachers as much as it did the pupils. Both sides
clearly came from a culture unfamiliar with such systematic
matters. Teachers had to be loyal, prompt, stern, stationary,
temperate, distant, taciturn, reproving, and constitutional. In
addition, they had to make sure that all the children sang and
prayed in the proper manner, visit the absentees, count the books,
check the entry, and, last but not least, control the exit:

To deliver to the children, on the order being given, their hats and bon-
nets, previous to their dismissal; and see that they remain seated, silent,
and orderly, until directed to remove; and that they go out orderly.

Children had to 'come clean washed and combed', not bring sweets
or fruit, not remove books, not be absent, not curse, not swear,
not game, not quarrel, not lie, and not speak without permission.
Nor were they allowed to urinate more than once in a morning
and once in an afternoon, and not within the first hour, nor when
someone else wanted to. They were also encouraged to attend adult
worship.[20]

These prescriptions came in 1832. Between 1836 and 1843 the
Wesleyan Education Committee offered more precise and binding
rules. These were not just about organisation and conduct but
about statistical and categorised information too. Such a degree
of centralisation proved in the event counter-productive. In 1851
Monkwearmouth Wesleyan sabbath schools, pupils and teachers
together, broke away from the central body after being locked out
of their own (they thought) premises.[21] In fact, all sunday
schools, Anglican, Wesleyan or Primitive, appear to have encountered their children as a mass to be assimilated from the centre.
The Wesleyan and Primitive difference only appears to have
concerned the definition of that centre. For the Anglicans the
problem hardly arose.

Within a rota of prayers, paraphrasing, psalms, stories, addresses,
reading, the issue of books, and hymn-singing – the outer rota
of the 'floor' – wheeled the inner rota of the class. By bell and
whistle, clapped hands, and subtler adult gestures, the class sat
with the school, a part within a whole, pupils under teacher,
teachers under superintendent, and the whole surveyed itself across
the floor of the hall in a silence broken only on command. The
command would come from teachers, lowest in circuit officialdom,
but high in the eyes of children.[22] The teachers saw their charges
as a mass to be subjected and saved, but they necessarily appealed
to them as individuals. There can be no doubt that in class warm
and trusting friendships could be formed. Nor is there any reason
to suppose that the vigour and 'heart' Methodism generated was
lost in the teaching.[23] Even so, appeals to individuals could
themselves be impersonally practiced. Various prize systems were
introduced, many of them based upon attendance and Bible
knowledge. The prizes must have been valued, their price was high.
Memorising thirty-two verses per week over a year, who could deny
that Martha Holmes of Howden had earned her Bible?[24] The
results of all these labours were offered up in the Sunday School

Anniversary, one of the most important events in the Methodist calendar. Sitting-up before the congregation, attentive, quiet, clean, best-dressed, and remembering their lines, the children were in their place for all to survey and be proud of, the privilege of their Mothers and Fathers 'in Israel':

> The Scriptures and sacred pieces delivered by the children were highly appropriate, containing nothing to amuse, but everything to warn, edify, and instruct.[25]

In public, the Methodists found words to describe their educational achievements. Sunday schools were 'a benefit to the children with regard to their future civil relations to society', but this was only fashionable rhetoric.[26] The real reason for sunday schools lay in the movement's own ideological and organisational dynamic. It could do no other. Methodism insisted upon such a 'method' that it had to collide with all that was not controlled. Method began in the soul but showed itself in physical demeanour. Children were obviously ingenuous in both.

Moreover, the existing cultural life of the colliery community was seen as merely the gratification of the senses in drink and 'carnality', or the unleashing of uncontrolled gusto, in dancing and sport. Wesley could never appreciate the physicality of northern miners; he recorded their Sunday 'grand assembly ... to dance, fight, curse, and swear, and play at chuck, ball, spanfarthing, or whatever came next to hand'. The measured gesture of Methodism could not but be aghast at the arms and legs and feet of village customs. What many regarded as innocuous and sociable pastimes were railed against and eschewed by Methodists using the most extreme language. Thus Mary Cosens put away 'every contrary and carnal principle' and John Kirk his 'vicious passion' for drink, John Quilt was 'drawn from public houses', William Hindhaugh was no more 'addicted to cards and cocks', Cuthbert Colling was no more 'fond of athletic sports', or John Wall for 'drinking and throwing the ball ... his favourite exercises'. That Sunday was the only day possible for these recreations offended Methodism's Sabbatarian instincts and threatened the most important day in its institutional existence.[27] Other exercises may have been orderly in their own way but, it was seen as an order related to this world. The Chester le Street bandsman had to give up his dance music for chapel music, the Coxhoe sword-dance leader had to give up his swords to be converted into gulley knives to buy Bibles and hymn-books. Drinking was seen as the most common misdemeanour, for in drink people lost control of their souls through their bodies, as in this account of John Maugham's 1823 conversion:

> Drunkeness; a vice too common in these parts, and more especially among the coal miners, was, prior to his conversion, his besetting sin. To mingle with the motley crowd on the Saturday night at the ale bench ... and as it is natural to suppose, those seasons of riot and intoxication are generally signalized by quarrellings, fightings, and bloodshed; shrieks and howlings more dismal and terrifying than the war whoop of the Indian savages, frequently stun the ears of the astonished and peaceful traveller.[28]

The symbols of chapel vied with other symbols: in one cottage a picture of Wesley or a preachers' plan, in another Tom Sayers and 'The Manchester Chicken'.[29] The impetus to Teetotalism, like Sabbatarianism, always existed in the Methodist economy and the national conference registered its approval and recommendation of temperance societies as early as 1832. Local relations appear to have been warm and the Sunderland circuit was famous for its early adherence to the cause. In 1833 all of the circuit's preachers and most of its officials were teetotalers, and Hugh Bourne, who had never touched alcohol in his life and who considered Temperance to have joined him rather than the other way round, praised a Sunderland where 'the Lord owns the labours of the teetotaler' and a Durham Circuit where teetotalism 'was advocated in a religious way'.[30] Although temperance and other causes matched, in an oblique way, the ruling concern for working-class order, it is as well to recognise that its first impulse came from within the Methodist economy. As such, the Primitive position on drink could invite as much criticism from a Coal Trade connected to the drink trade and a coal ownership tied to drinking custom, as from their employees who valued its social and recreational significance.[31]

Control of the body indicated moral discipline, and moral discipline indicated the state of the soul. To lose control was an affront to the soul and an invitation to the vices of this-world. Was not the public house the home of criminality and destitution? Was not vice and hopelessness the ashen reality of this-world's pleasures? Primitive Methodist discipline and morality conjoined

in an intellectual cult of plainness. The plain man exhibited not
only his control, but also his existence in the world but not of the
world. Plainness began with the body:

> 4. That Bro. J. Clarke be advised to putt his white trousers off.
>
> 5. That Bro. Atkinson give the above advice.
>
> 6. That Bro. Brooks be requested to become more plain and grave in
> his attire.

It ended with the soul:

> His piety resembled the smooth, still flowing river, more than the
> shallow, noisy brook.[32]

Plainness became the intellectual mark of the Methodist working
man against the frippery of the sensuous and the arrogance of the
self-willed. The Sunday black suit marked out men who spent the
day in school, chapel, and class, and not in bed or in the field;
of men like William Willis who 'hurt [him]self very sore to get
scholarship', who was teetotal and had 'been tried by people but
have never broken through, and never intend'. Fifteen year old
Willis — whose exertions bear contrast with the Sunday over-
sleeping, games, and roving of seventeen year old William Hardy,
putter at Auckland — read the Bible, teetotal newspapers, and
English history. The Haswell pitman William Scott who was
'accustomed to sit reading' 'in a garret for hours together', and
his fellow hewer, Peter Mackenzie, 'imbibed the spirit and letter'
of hymn book and Bible. Men like these were too disciplined to
waver from plain scholarship.[33] Although 'The library, the house
of God, and the bookseller's shop were places where you might
seek Brother Chapman' he was 'not quite so self-opinionated as
most self-taught men are'; Brother Simpson 'was remarkable for
sound sense, rather than subtle or comprehensive thought'; and
Brother Charlton, 'Though not a deep thinker, nor given to
abstract or speculative inquiries ... had a mind of great activity
... [when] ... Dealing with facts which could not be gainsaid'.[34]
There was a revolutionary capacity in Methodists like these,
disciplined, controlled, and dealing with facts which could not be
gainsaid.

12
Preacher vanguard

P.S. I conceive the worst feature in the whole matter, to be that religious fanaticism which prevails among the Pitmen, they are embued with it to a great degree; the delegates are chiefly Ranter Preachers, who have acquired a considerable fluency and even in some cases considerable proficiency in public speaking. The Great Mass are successively ignorant and therefore became the ready tools of these designing individuals – they [not clear] all their speeches with large quotations from scripture which they pervert to achieve their ends; where the men have gone to work and made agreements with their employers, the delegates have been regularly chaired in the same stile as an M.P. and of course long speeches are delivered by them – giving inflated accounts of the Victory they have obtained over their oppressors, and that they were only able to achieve by the support and decrees of Providence – such Doctrines inculcated among an ignorant mob may lead to fearful and fatal consequences.

In the two great unions which led the miners from the 1820s the Primitive Methodist preachers played the leading part. According to Seymour Tremenheere this 'fact is notorious, and was adverted to by every one connected with the principal collieries'. It was a 'testimony' which he 'found unvaried at each colliery'.[1]

Coalowners and officials from every part of the coalfield acknowledged the unique strength of Primitive leadership. Tremenheere underlined the union's vanguard role: 'No argument had any chance of obtaining access to their minds, except those suggested to them by their own periodical, or by the delegates who addressed them'; and the delegates – 'leading men ... able to express themselves' – were invariably the preachers. T. J. Taylor, a coalowner, had argued with them:

Generally the men professing to be Methodists and Ranters are the spokesmen on these occasions, and the most difficult to deal with. These men may be superior men to the rest in intelligence and generally show great skill, and cunning, and circumvention.

The *Durham Chronicle* had heard their oratory:

> ... the turbulent and restless portion of them have gained ascendancy
> ... over the mild and timid ... whom they constantly harrass to attend
> almost daily meetings of the men belonging to each colliery, and listen
> to the wild and frenzied declamations of the Ranter Preachers who,
> on these occasions, play the orator.[2]

As well as their energy, these 'turbulent and evil disposed'
'designing', 'educated people', brought to their union a missioner's
knowledge of uniting and pledging. National Miners' Association
delegate-preachers were frequent speakers at teetotal missions in
1843 and the chapels and societies were drummed into regular
union prayers. Union 'lecturers' were scheduled and disciplined
by preacher-'plans', sunday schoolrooms were used when publicans
refused, and all the emotional experience of Methodism was
offered up to the sustenance of a striking community:

> The men are wrought into a state of excitement by first holding prayer
> meetings ... [then villages combine] ... where after a repetition of the
> same excesses they are addressed by a lecturer who is a stranger to them.
> This new method of combining enthusiasm with the infusion of bad
> principles may still keep the men from work a little longer.[3]

The preachers turned strike issues into religious issues. Men
told Tremenheere that they had gone to union prayer meetings
'to get their faith strengthened', a local preacher told his
astounded employer 'that "according to his religion, he could
not go to work"'. Given their loyalty to the union and to an
omniscient God, the preachers had little ideological alternative
but to deliver the union into God's hands. God was invoked as
a redeemer of the pledge to the union and as a punisher of those
who broke it. This somehow validated the abuse of strike-breakers
and showed its iron in the absolution of the murder of Errington,
at Hetton:

> The three leading men in the strike were William Dawson, William
> Richardson, and John Nicholson; they were pitmen. They were
> Primitive Methodists and local preachers. They frequently assembled
> the people, from 100 to 400 together, on the roadside, and offered up
> prayers for the success of the strike, and also that the men who were
> brought from a distance, to work in a colliery, the 'black legs', as they
> called them, might be injured, either lamed or killed; and they rejoiced
> when any thing did happen to them.

[In 1832] The Ranter preachers are lauding this act – the murder was the instrument in the hands of the Almighty, to inflict this judgement on the miscreant who betrayed the Union.[4]

Next to God stood His Word. Suffering hunger and coercion, the coalfield was quick to recognise the struggles of His People. Indisputable Scriptural analogy – 'Everything that could be collected in the Bible about slavery and tyranny, such as Pharoah ordering bricks to be made without straw' – flowed through speeches to the union, and from the union back again into Primitivism itself. Revd Spoor spoke for the union in Mr Dobson's long room at Willington; a preacher who opposed the union was dragged from his pulpit at Wingate; other preachers who opposed were obliged to leave their congregations; the Wesleyan ministers who stood aside were jeered: 'the Ranters used their influence to disaffect our members'.[5] The local press may have found cause for hilarity in the spectacle of ignorant pitmen making a religious issue out of political economy,[6] but when the unions had been broken coalowners found revenge for the likes of Thomas Hepburn who had made Lord Londonderry bend the leg in prayer with him – 'he never entered upon the consideration of important matters ... without first praying to God'. On this occasion, 'the noble Marquis ... piously joined in the act of prayer' only because he had to, for through all correspondence between owner and agent trailed a personal contempt for working-class men who claimed to 'have' Knowledge. The preacher Charles Parkinson was characterised as a 'slick headed ranting Knave'. The tough bargaining of 'obnoxious' ranter preachers was seen to arise 'not always from taking the correct view of the nature of the disputes', but from self-satisfaction with their own superiority. Of course, the perpetual self-examination of the Methodist soul invited a self-absorption which others could call vanity, but the preachers' *religious* knowledge, which would not have embittered had it recognised class boundaries, now burst in as a political threat and was also adjudged to be false:

They are fond of becoming preachers, class leaders etc. themselves, and this opens the door to a vast deal of vanity and conceit; insomuch that I suspect there is more of a vain glory and hypocrisy, than any sounder feeling amongst such of them as have become attentive to matters of religion.[7]

When the strikes of 1831–2 and 1844 were defeated and the monthly Bond introduced, the union officials were the first to be victimised. Primitive Methodists constituted the majority of these men.[8]

It is not possible to draw the mind of the preacher-vanguard to an intellectual nicety. One must remember the eclectic nature of nineteenth-century working-class self-education, a process which grabbed at the elements of knowledge as they appeared. Thomas Burt chanced upon long words as he spoke them, at meetings, and learned them afterwards by chalk and slate. Men like George Young of Killingworth colliery, a teetotaler, Methodist, distributor of the *Northern Star*, trade unionist, and believer in 'Education', were not scholars after some pinnacle of intellectual coherence but men responding, through their lives, to critical events.[9] In this sense, learning was social, if piecemeal, and its instincts were practical. The preaching vanguard aspired not so much to a theory of society as to a social physics which put movement before consistency and success before explanation.

The Miners' Advocate, newspaper of the National Miners' Association, is the major formal source for the ideas of pit-politics during the first half of the nineteenth century. A typical radical newspaper of its day, the *Advocate* carried eloquent editorial and worthy educational items alongside plagiarised news snippets and correspondence with the membership. The anonymous 'editorial' of the newspaper came from the pen of the unions' national leadership and its editor William Daniells, a servant of the union who nevertheless held its key intellectual post. The organisation of the NMA will be covered in Part Three but at this point it has to be said that none of the national leadership, in terms of the union's charismatic speakers and writers, was a pitman.[10] Although working pitmen were well represented on the council resident in Newcastle, the tone and structure of the *Advocate* almost certainly over-emphasised the Radical-Chartist mentality of the union to the detriment of what was actually being said and felt in the villages.

A better indication of local response lies in the open-meeting. Between Februrary 1844 and April 1845 the *Advocate* reported eighty-nine major open meetings in the North East. Meetings could range from 'monsterations' on Newcastle Town Moor with thirty thousand regaled in the music and accoutrements of colliery unionism, to evening tours through a straggle of villages by pairs of union 'lecturers'. Speakers ranged from the magnificent Feargus O'Connor who came early and bellowed once, at a monsteration, in October 1843, to a man called Hebdin who spent August 1844 in the company of a local pitman on tour through the collieries of South Tyne. 1844–45 meetings were addressed by a total of fifty-six speakers. With the exception of William Daniells, the national figures were relatively infrequent speakers.[11] W.P. Roberts and William Beesley appeared at the early meetings, but once the union began to gather support and push inexorably towards a strike in the spring of 1844 then it was local faces who were stepping out of the crowd and on to the platform. Thirteen men were the most significant platform speakers with three or more recorded appearances: Mark Dent (Whitwell), Thomas Pratt (Castle Eden), George Charlton (South Shields), Robert Archer (South Hetton), John Tulip (South Hetton), Robert Henderson (West Moor), Joseph Fawcett (West Moor), Charles Revely (Wallsend), William Jobling (Walker), Edward Richardson (Derwent Ironworks), William Mitchell (Ouston), William Bird (East Cramlington), Martin Jude (Newcastle publican). Of these thirteen, the first five can be identified as Primitive Methodist lay preachers. Some of the others may have been. With other frequent Primitive speakers – Christopher Haswell, Charles Parkinson, Ben Embleton, Revd Joseph Spoor, William Bell – these men shared platforms with professional radicals such as Daniells, Roberts, and Beesley whose rationalist politics were far removed from the scriptural fundamentalism of the preachers.[12] Despite these political and religious differences one also finds common points of connection. This is a paradox which needs further explanation.

The NMA took the labour value of the coalminer as its first principle. 'What could be done without the coal-miners of Great Britain?' asked John Hall the General Secretary, and the union made it clear that without coal and the labour of its producers nothing could be done. Given their labour-value, the pitmen should make themselves 'a class worthy of being courted in their turn', and to do this the working-class must 'KNOW THYSELF' by 'the queenly power of reason'. Reason bestrode Knowledge and Freedom, but its application was not abstract. John Hall thought that the union's first step should be the formation of schools, reading rooms, and cooperative libraries.[13] These would enable

members to understand, explain, and see. The unions of both
decades published booklets in best 'Will Chip' style where union
members who 'saw' explained to those who did not. A dialogue
between 'Keeker', 'Justice', and '1st and 2nd Banksman' ends with
the '1st Banksman' crying 'I now see what I never saw before'.
'The goddess of reason', properly applied, would not only enable,
she would also create; because of her, 'the pure rivers of knowledge'
would 'burst forth and fertilize the moral desert', the working class
would cleanse itself from 'the stagnant pool of ignorance' and save
itself from 'the vortex of sensuality':

> The long dreary night of ignorance and error, of superstition and
> violence, of fraud and disunion is fast wearing away, and the bright
> refulgent sun of truth and knowledge, of peace and unity is appearing
> above the political horizon.[14]

A secular trinity of Reason, Knowledge, and Labour Value beamed
upon those pitmen who could spell words, read books, and perform
intellectual arguments. Given this, and given their 'moral' rather
than 'sensual' demeanour combined with a wariness of traditional
mores, it is clear that the NMA was an organisation open to the
preachers. John Hall insisted that 'only the provident portion' of
the pitmen could save their class, 'the other party would not give
an entries drinking for all the information that could be conveyed
to them'.[15] It seemed then that it was possible for the preachers
to approach the NMA's pinnacle of Reason by a similar route that
enabled them to approach Methodism's pinnacle of Salvation.
Through their trained voices, and in their seriousness as men apart
from the rest, Reason was as accessible as Jehovah.

Not that Jehovah figured much in the union's formal ideology;
He was more an ultimate intellectual proposition than a living
reality. The union's prize essay claimed that its work was to aid
the miners to improve Man, to fulfill the Grand Design, to glorify
God; an early editorial of the *Advocate* claimed dependence 'upon
a just God – public opinion – a good cause – and the united
and energetic exertion of the Miners'. God was 'long-stop' to the
cause; the NMA invoked Him as a last resort, without ontology.
Indeed, the union's reality was based upon its own efforts to
organise and unite, a rejection of mystery, and a knowledge of
theory and practice which looked to the time when men 'will
become omnipotent ... will have reduced all the elements of

creation to entire subjection ... in order to procure universal happiness'.[16]

The union's intellectuals threw themselves into this combat with a zest borne of self-discovery. The pitman's world had no connection with the middle class, radical or otherwise; the self-learning of the colliery village was wholly and immediately connected with working-class life.[17] This self-learning, secular or religious, was not the threadbare virtuous stuff of the city artisan – a democratic Lovett or a fastiduous Place, both in daily economic and intellectual nexus with a wider more power-ful world – it was rather the grand righteousness of the out-sider. NMA lecturers spoke confidently from within a tradition of previous unions ('I suppose you are one of the wits called delegates', 'I am sure, Tim, you have turned a fine orator'), and this tradition showed itself in a stiff, elaborate, enjoyment of the written word.[18] But they also spoke within the tradition of the chapel, what one coalowner was wont to call 'The *Canting Shop ... cunning*, mixed up with an abundance of Cant, and pure *Brass*'.[19] Throughout the continuous speaking and writing of the NMA both traditions worked together. The formal language of the *Miners' Advocate* could be 'union' or 'chapel', rationalist or religious, but it could not be any other. William Hamilton of Willington colliery called for justice in the language of Scripture:

> Shall I show you men stripped and wounded, and left half-dead; they may be seen in our cities, as well as in the highways between Jericho and Jerusalem – shall I show you the tears running down the cheeks of the orphans and widows – shall I call you to hear the cry of the hire kept back by fraud or violence ...?

'One of labour's meanest sons' called for unity in the language of the pulpit:

> Bitter tears have gushed from my eyes to think how we were wasting our energies ... Bretheren, I exhort you, in all earnestness, in the words of the apostle, 'That ye have brotherly love one towards another'.

A pitman from Walker called for freedom in the language of Reason:

> We believe that God created us to be free. He has given us a nature that is only in its element when it is free. We were born not to be slaves – we were born to be free .. we do not want to be masters as you charge us with – we want to be servants but not slaves.[20]

In all of this was not only the paradox that a radical newspaper published the Methodist voice and that a rationalist politics was strongly represented by religious preachers, but also that from the preachers' side, on one level they denied the validity of this-world and yet on another level supplied the voice for those most deeply involved in its struggles. The South Shields Primitive Methodist circuit lived through Chartism in 1839 and strike in 1844 without mention of either event. Formal Methodism continued to exhibit all of that condescension and quietism so beloved of its radical critics. W. Wawn, the Newcastle Wesleyan and sunday school organiser, pointed to the blessedness of the Poor; poverty was Christ's choice and God's blessing:

> He has preserved you from the delightful, silken, cords of pleasure, wealth, and honour, that binds down millions to everlasting destruction that he might attract your heart to himself.[21]

For their part, the national leadership of the NMA ignored the paradox of a rationalist politics and a religious representation, and suspended any inclination they may have had to criticise formal Methodism. In 1844 the NMA *Magazine* gently ridiculed the 'strange but impressive vulgar eloquence' of a Methodist sermon, but the sermon had been in Oxfordshire and they never attempted any sort of intellectual confrontation with the local preacher vanguard.[22]

The paradox however, was not lost upon others. Tremenheere reported that although the majority of victimised strike leaders were Methodists, at the same time it was to their credit 'that the improvement that has taken place within living memory ... is greatly attributable to their exertions'. From the 1820s owners and observers made the distinction between the 'higher' class of pitman and the 'lower' − 'long heads' and 'wrong heads'. How could it be that the union delegates, 'invariably' 'the most intelligent of that class of men', could lead a movement which was so obviously ridiculous?

> The owners of this colliery lent a house to the Primitive Methodists, for their religious meetings. At the time of the strike, one of the preachers preached in it in favour of the strike. Another of them took in the 'Northern Star', and regularly every week read it to a meeting of the men.
>
> I asked, during the strike, several of the leading local preachers, why they did not show the men that they were wrong, which as reasonable men themselves, they must know they were; but if they interfered at all, it was against us.[23]

A pamphlet of 1832 used Scripture to deny the leadership of the union stating that Christians and servants were always to be 'a yielding side',

> And when you *read the Scriptures* ... do not read so much (I find many do this) the threatenings of God against unjust and oppressive masters, as the duties of *servants*, and the blessing of those who are faithful and obedient.[24]

Such appeals did not have the intended effect of splitting the two traditions within the union. Local supporters of the Coal Trade, with their anonymous 'kind words' and 'open letters', sought to deflect the scriptural convictions of the preacher vanguard away from militancy and into quietism; the formal politics of the NMA, with its translucent Reason and over-bearing Knowledge, ignored the preachers' convictions. But both of these patterns failed to invade the trusted relationship Primitive Methodism had with the community, and the relationship the preachers had with themselves as men and 'souls' who had been revealed by their own interior need and effort. In combat, it was as difficult for the preachers to take up the neat politics of the *Advocate* as it was for them to submit to the quietist elements of religion. Both patterns were merely intellectual surfaces compared to the internal regenerative meaning that religion had come to have, a meaning recharged when the village found itself under attack and the preachers were once more cast as true shepherds of their flock. Within each social and personal crisis caused by confrontation between the Coal Trade and the miners, the thunder of the righteous was to be heard above the shrill appeals for quietism and the deep beneath the level statements of reason:

> That the labourer shall receive the first fruits of his labour.
>
> The labourer is worthy of his hire.
>
> Rob not the poor, because he is poor.
>
> Cursed is he that oppresseth the poor.
>
> He that oppresseth the poor, reproacheth his Maker.
>
> Whoso mocketh the poor reproacheth his Maker, and he that is glad at calamities shall not be unpunished.
>
> Gehazi took from the Syrian General, under false pretences, money which did not belong to him; for this he lost his health – his honour – his place – and his peace.

I will be a swift witness against the sorcerers, and against the adulterers
and against false swearers, and against those that oppress the hireling
in his wages, the widow, and the fatherless, and that turn aside
the stranger from his right, and fear not me, saith the Lord.[25]

At the beginning of the strike Robert Archer told a Black
Fell meeting that 'they were assured on the authority of God
that the servant had a right to be paid for his labour'; at the
end of the strike Ben Embleton took the chair in South Hetton
'and proved that the Union was founded on Scripture'. Chapter
and verse was quoted against all those who opposed the strike:
a local preacher was reminded to 'look into the word of God,
a work which he should have been well versed with' to save
himself from becoming like Gehazi, Achan, Judas, or a wolf
of the tribe of Benjamin; a Gateshead minister was reminded
the same; strike-breakers were appealed to on grounds of religious
brotherhood – 'your brethren have wept over you'; Christians
were appealed to on grounds of theology – 'Beware of striving
at gnats and swallowing camels'.[26]

In practical matters the preachers' paradox could be enrolled
for the cause. Their rhetorical skills, confidence, and moral
weight were all useful attributes. In the moral question of Drink
the preachers' teetotalism was shared neither by the national
leadership nor by the majority of their comrades. Yet it was
here, in close bargaining over the shifting minutiae of contract,
measure, and price, that the preachers carried an absolute superiority in their stand against something which had cheated generations of pitmen. The drink custom was one aspect of a supposed
'moral economy' cynically used by the owners both as a facade
to their actual imposition of new work relationships, and as
a straightforward method of exploitation. A drink at the owner's
expense could signify agreement. The owners desired contractual
agreement to each bond but not through the market relationship
of Capital and Labour, at least, not when that market favoured
Labour. Instead, they sought to nullify market forces by securing
local colliery agreements as rapidly as possible by the supply
of free drink. To take a drink suggested agreement; to take
a number of drinks added amity to agreement. In 1805 the
men had learnt that their collective refusal to take a drink was
crucial to their tactics:

... if binding them at a public house at Seaton Sluice could not be brought about − I fear an attempt now to bind them at the Colliery office will not be more successful, when the pitmen think themselves of so much more consequence than they did at that time.[27]

This was at binding time. A memorandum of 1824 gives a rare insight into the use of the drink-custom as a daily method of exploitation. Within the annual framework of the Bond the ever-changeful nature of mining necessitated constant revision of terms and prices. Buddle informed Londonderry that

When letting Bargains of Stone drifting, ridding Stones, cutting levels etc. to a Co. of pitmen; the Viewers, by *softening them* with a few shillings worth of ale, generally save a great deal more in money.

Moreover, drink was encouraged as a substitute for money, as symbolic of deeper work relationships across the whole mining economy:

When this happens [an example of horsekeepers being called out to attend sick animals underground] a small allowance of ale is given, as if it is but for half an hour, or an Hour that a person is employed in this way. If he is paid in money at all, it cannot be less than either a half or whole shift − 1/6 or 3/ − , but if rewarded by *Allowance (lowens)* a Tankard of ale satisfies him. This is the case with in-numerable jobs about collieries. If a Man has to put on his pit Cloths & go down the pit, for a job ever so trifling, if paid in money, he must have his shift, or half shift. But he will do the same job cheerfully for his *'lowens'* − a tankard of ale.[28]

This system could never apply to a teetotal Primitive. Also, as the industrial struggle intensified from the 1820s and the relations of master and men came under increasing scrutiny then the teetotaler found his opposition to 'traditional' mores rationally at one with the needs of his class. In this small way at least, the preachers' paradox was briefly resolved.

For individuals, the strains of paradox could be damaging. Robert Fairley and Ben Gibson were converted in 1829 and 1830 respectively, but their obituary columns record that in the strike of 1831−2 they lost their faith. Fairley 'was induced to take a prominent part' in the strike and 'his spiritual ardour was much diminished'; Gibson 'was shorn of his strength' through union involvement. It is not clear whether their religious convictions were sapped by connection with a rationalist union politics (as was the case with Thomas Hepburn),[29] or because their initial belief in the righteousness of the cause met with utter obliteration. Whatever the reason, it is clear that the union caused these men personal as well as public confrontations. Others suffered for holding too closely to their convictions. Made righteous by God, they were not to compromise with reality. Mark Dent, victimised since 1844, found himself hopeless in 1847 – plunged into 'a situation ... out of the reach of the oppression of the masters, and the low grovelling envy and black ingratitude of their men'. Ben Embleton, another victim of 1844, found himself close to destitution but faithful to, at least the language, of his religion:

> For the sake of Union principles I have borne your reproach; I am become a stranger unto my bretheren, an alien unto my mother's children, for the zeal of the Union hath eaten me up, and the reproaches of them that reproacheth the Union are fallen upon me! May every friend of humanity in the Miners' Association give me a helping hand, to help me out of the deep waters of want, and not suffer the flood of poverty to swallow me up.[30]

Methodist morality sought to change what it perceived as the existing 'way of life' of the mining community. We have seen that there were other forces which had the same boldness of aim and in their work for the 'moral improvement' of the lower orders they aspired to an intellectual and moral domination of areas of society which they considered disorderly or threatening.[31] Dominance was never achieved. Not only did class struggle throw up resilient forms of community defence – crowned by the powerful 'county unions' from the 1860s – but the outside moral improvers of the 1830s and 1840s failed to address extensive areas of village life. In the villages the moral, ontological, and intellectual areas were largely left to Methodist and Radical representation. The State legislated for women and children in 1842, but in its moral campaign it was largely let down. When it realised this, much later, it made its own efforts. Coal capitalism made only reluctant, small efforts, and with the exception of the Anglican National Society who built schools with dubious results from 1831, the local middle classes, gentry, and clergy tended to stay away. What efforts they did make were diffuse, and as distorted as they were prompted by city fears. Whilst moral improvement only partially penetrated the mining community, its most total success lay in binding the moral and class sense of its own busy and indignant practitioners. Uniting their *moral* perspective, which was involved, with their *class* knowledge, which was distanced, the drive for domination permitted a basic misunderstanding of what Methodism was doing. The Methodist soul and its public display won the movement early applause for its apparent pacification of the coalfield. Methodism's public demeanour was thought to correspond favourably with those prescriptions for moral improvement being made in higher places for passive over vigorous forms of working-class life. But observations rarely went beyond the cottage or chapel door. Inside its doors, Primitive Methodism was fusing with emergent class expression in a way which most startlingly revealed itself during strike actions, and which also revealed itself, and the tensions behind it, in the specific distaste the middle classes and others could show for Primitive 'emotionalism'. There was genuine dismay at the revelations of strikes or revivals because apart from their public manifestations, the rulers and improvers had very little knowledge of those areas of working-class consciousness which surfaced during them. Later, the Methodist role in moral improvement through revival was praised for producing respectable men and women, but the fact that revivals were contemporaneously disliked, and that those same men and women were victimised after strike into poverty, separation, and emigration, was not accounted for in late nineteenth-century chronicles of Respectability. This 'political' aspect of Methodist involvement was only acknowledged, inaccurately at that, in the working-class liberal-labour biographies of the day.

The dominant Lib-Lab moral power in the coalfield in the last quarter of the nineteenth century had its beginnings in the preacher-vanguards from the 1820s. The preachers emerged in crisis as the intellectuals of their class. The reception of the Primitive Methodist words and ideas was class mutated. Neither the printed rationalist opinions of the NMA, nor the distanced homilies of established religion could seriously challenge a Methodist consciousness so closely connected to the community. The points of connection are clear: the quality of Methodist appeal in a coalfield too often sickened by violent death; the self-manipulative revivalism of a people known for their physicality; the room for lay-involvement in the Methodist economy; the interaction of Methodist and class cultural forms; and the self-disciplining, self-respecting, self-educating, and self-absorbed elements of a growing, dislocated, redefined community increasingly forced to consider its own amelioration. Of course, the paradoxical logic of this-world and the next remained, but the making of class consciousness did not proffer a resolution of abstracts. Class consciousness was not an intellectual exercise in coherence. It was made and re-made in the face of immediate and practical problems.

The later power of the Northumberland and Durham county unions from the 1860s was carried by another kind of class-intellectual who sought continuity with his past. Methodism provided the obvious line of continuity because, unlike the Brotherhood, or the United Colliers, or Chartism, or the NMA, or any number of deceased formations, Methodism had survived to expand its numbers and influence. It remained where others had fallen and, although a different movement from fifty years before, its history was prized as a continuum − a rare enough commodity among working-class associations. Anglican homilies had never threatened it, it is hard to imagine what comfort a rationalist politics could have provided for mass burials. Primitive Methodism's relationship with radical trade unionism permitted an essential ambiguity. Ruling-class improvers took chapel morality at its face value and therefore misunderstood the movement's true status as a working-class association. Formations less closely connected than Primitive Methodism would not have maintained their position in the community; formations less ambiguous would scarcely have been allowed to. Such was the origin of the accredited resilience of the late nineteenth-century chapel. It was seen to represent the ethos of the pit village as an entity, as a pre-existing 'way of life' in continuity with its present. In this way an entire culture was said to reside in the presence and history of the Methodist moral intervention.

Part three
Protest

13
Direct action

> I argued the point with him at great length stating as the groundwork
> of my argument that if he sent me home without money for the pay,
> no argument which it would be in my power to urge with our people
> wd. convince them that the Bank was not *actually broken*: and that
> by 3 o'clock in the afternoon he might expect to be beset by 500 or
> 600 of the pitmen. For a long time he stared out, saying this wd. be
> a less evil than having money to find for the Notes tomorrow, and that
> he shd. tell the pitmen, that it was yr. lordship who owed them their
> Wages and not the Bank, and that they must look to yr. lordship for
> pay etc. etc. At length I prevailed with him.[1]

The banker was white-faced and his wife was crying. The viewer
prevailed because of the pitmen. His argument was the pitmen's
reputation for protest which directly confronted the objects of their
opposition, men and their property. If they were not paid, the
pitmen would 'beset' the banker for an explanation.

The district had known direct action of this kind long enough
for it to have become a traditional form of protest by the time of
Buddle's prevailing over the bank in 1825. Part Three will first
establish the characteristics of direct action and show how it was
more than a form of protest; it was a technique of social change
which was not only understood, but reciprocated, by those in
authority. It will then consider the political and trade union
experiences of the mining community during the first half of the
nineteenth century with a view to showing how and why the
community gradually gave up direct techniques.[2]

On 25 October 1731, Richard and William Crofton, Thomas
and John Bailey, Richard Oyston, William Davison and about one
hundred other pitmen assembled at Newbottle colliery and

> Armed with staves forceably enter'd into the said Engine House broke
> several lead Pipes by which the Engine was hindred from working &
> kept forceable Possession of ye said Engine House for a Night & a day

and then gave Publick Notice to these Informants that if the Engine was repaired or set to work before they had brought their Masters to their Terms they wou'd pull it down to the Ground and Murder the said Informants ... that these Informants made several Attempts to repair ye said Engine but were constantly disturb'd by ye said Pittmen, so that the Engine continued unwrought for the space of three weeks. And the Steward of the Rt. Hon. the Earle of Scarborough was Obliged to Submit to the unreasonable Demands of the said Pittmen, Otherwise the Colliery wou'd have inevitably been drowned and lost.

A week later another gang of pitmen, 'armed with Clubbs & Staves', went to Moaborn Smith's in Murton 'and did great Damage' to his

... fire engine ... and to his pump Work & Coal Shafts ... and threatened to take away his Coals ... destroy his Fire Engine and did break open his Granary ... & carried away thirty Coal Corves ... & burn & destroy the same.

At the same time, a few miles away, Anthony Laverick with seventy others had marched on Henry Lambton's pit at Bowes Biddick

... and then & there with force and violence threw ye Roller down the Engine Shaft ... and also severall pieces of Timber ... lying there and also a Grindstone and other things to ... stop the said Engine from Working or drawing Water.

On the following day, 3 November, the overman and engineer covered the shaft mouth 'with strong boards firmly nailed down to prevent any further damage', but on 4 November Laverick and his men were back with reinforcements from Murton. They broke into the locked engine-room and

... with force bruised the Waste pipe together and knocked it aside, pulled down the lead pipe call'd the feeding pipe and broke of the Cock there of and broke a hole in the boyler Topp and Curs'd and swore they would pull down the Engine while others of them were endeavouring to pull up the Scaffolding over the ... Engine Pitt ... and to damage the Engine shaft and pumps ...

Engine, coal corves, and timber were set alight and the gang moved north to the house of Mr Harrison, staithman at Fatfield, and there, 'Armed with staves' they forced an entry. After they had 'Drunk and Wasted Several quantities of his Ale and Wine & eat & Carried away his victuals, and ... Several pair of Shoes, Silk Handkerchiefs ... a Hatt and Perriwig', they went on to the home of another staithman, Samuel Anderson, and did further damage.

On 11 November we hear of gangs moving from colliery to colliery on the upper Tyne calling on the men there to come out. On the twelfth two delegates from each colliery agreed to meet the owners at Ravensworth Castle, where they assembled on the fifteenth. This intended negotiation was disastrous: the delegates grouped in such a manner that the Riot Act was read, and after this, Tyne-Wear allegiances of pitmen appear to have been promised for combined direct action on 17 November. At 11.00 am on that day a body

> Composed of Tyne Water & Wear Water Men to ye Number of Near One Thousand ... proceeded from Chester with a design to throw down all Ginns & Corves wherever they found them Standing & to resist in Case of opposition, and that this design came from the Wear Water Men who said they would do the work ...

The pitmen were barred by military force at Urpeth. No account exists concerning the aftermath.[3]

The evidence for this account is not disinterested, yet it is clear that the bearing of the protest involved a controlled crescendo of violence against men and property. In their direct threat to capital investment, their calculated closure of production and halting of distribution, and their candid intimidation of individuals, these actions of 1731 are characteristic of coalfield protest in the eighteenth and early nineteenth centuries. The actions could be across the entire coalfield, or limited to a certain asset. In 1754, one Valentine MacCartney threatened to drown Nicholas Lambton's mines. In 1765, amidst a protracted and disciplined dispute, men of six Wear collieries 'resolved ... to destroy all the Engines, Ginns etc. belonging to all the Collieries on that River', and on both rivers they 'burnt and otherwise destroyed the utensils of many coal pits, set fire to the coals both above and below ground, and broke up the coalways'. In 1778, the men of Sir John Delaval's pits 'threatened to pull down the office; Burn the corves; pull down the Ginns, and pull up the wagon ways', and in 1789, men from Tyne collieries did, with precision, 'commit divers acts of violence to the machinery &c':

> ... he saw one William Ford ... take the Rope from off the Wheel of the Engine used for Drawing the Coals ... & put the same over the pulley wheel belonging to the said Engine ... by which great Damage was done ...
>
> ... Wm. Coxon of Carville ... [who] ... in fixing a clog of wood on the said Engine ... by which means this same Engine ... was very much damaged ...

... but the said Rioters not being satisfied with such mischief did cut down the legs of such Engine ... for the purpose of pulling down the wheels ...

As late as 1829, John Buddle could testify to a Lord's Select Committee on the real possibility, if he cut wages any further, of the 'destruction' of the mines, 'with all the machinery and the valuable stock vested in them'.[4] Direct action not only confronted the means of production but also the product itself. The marching gang could call out workers in other collieries, destroy, scatter or confiscate the coal at bank, or prevent its transportation to market. In 1765 the *Newcastle Journal* criticised a loose force of pitmen ready to call out, and keep out, workers from other collieries; in 1771 Tyneside gangs moved 'from Colliery to Colliery to put a stop to all work, they are at present at the Collierys on the Sunderland River'; in 1793 Walker colliery was prevented from working by a hail of coals thrown by men assembled at 'the underside of the Heap' and aimed at 'every person near the Shaft'; whilst in 1800, much to the alarm of the local agent, a 'great number' of pitmen from Cowpen and carpenters from Blyth

... have passed through this place this morning with Bludgeons in their Hands, supposed for Hartley to raise the Men there & have on their way taken Mr Wright's Carpenters with them and endeavoured to lay off the Wagon men ... & how far they may do mischief on their return we do not know ...[5]

The wagon men were an important group to lay off if the owners were not to rely on coal reserves to enable their resistance. The pitman's economy could not withstand a long encounter; his action had to be short, sharp, and effective. The 1765 dispute saw the overturning of 'Waggons laden with Coals' and 'mischief to the Waggon ways' throughout the coalfield. The following year Joseph Blacklock and twenty-two others were prosecuted for 'Obstructing Seven Coal Waggons' and 'throwing Wasting Scattering and destroying' coals at Lamesley and Whickham; in 1775 Robert Beverley and others were prosecuted for:

Riotously forceing compelling and obliging divers persons employed in loading and conveying Coals in Waggons ... & preventing such persons from loosing their Horses from the said Waggons for the space of eight Hours and upwards and for breaking and destroying such Waggons and consuming the Coals therein.

At other times, the capacity for direct action ranged to threats to burn ships at the quayside.[6]

In spite of the authorities' tendency to exaggerate reports, either out of panic or for their own advantage, there can be no doubt that wrecking the production and distribution of coals intimidated opposing interests and that it was intended to do so. Buddle had warned his banker about being 'beset', Robert Beverley and others were prosecuted for 'violently besetting' and thus 'greatly terrifying and disturbing the said George Wilson and his Family'. This experience was not pleasant and it was not sought. Viewers and under-managers were very conscious of the pitmen's capacity for action. They faced intimidation from below and had responsibility to above. Potentially troublesome situations could be met by selling the community cheap meal as in times of dearth, or by making idle-time payments during natural or Vended interruptions to normal working. In 1800, when cheap meal was distributed throughout the coalfield Houghton pitmen even took their employers to court over irregularities in its controlled price. The men won, and a local newspaper was not slow to exploit the victory. The matter showed that it was always best for the pitmen to lay their complaints before the magistrates and that 'assembling in a riotous manner ... can only add to their grievances'. In March 1789 Denton colliery's vend was cut to 22,000 chaldrons and its viewer estimated that this would cut average earnings from 2s to 1s 6d per day. He knew that his colliery was now under threat, and that prudence was his best course. Pitmen from collieries below the Tyne bridge

> ... assembled ... in great numbers and laid in all the Collieries on the North Side of the River below Bridge at several of which they did considerable damage. Being informed that they had reached Newcastle and were proposing to continue up the North side of the River to the collieries above Bridge it was thot prudent to lay in our Pits, preferring the payment of £8.14.6p day to Men and Lads for lying Idle ... to the hazard of incurring much greater Injury to the Colliery by acting in opposition to the intentions of so dangerous a combination.[7]

The next day the viewer had not seen the below-bridge gang but still feared their rumour, and thought it wise to 'discontinue our workings this day likewise'. The day after, the *Newcastle Courant* printed two Acts of Parliament concerning the felonious destruction of collieries. Three days later the men of the viewer's own colliery 'assembled and laid in all the pits' without difficulty. An offer was immediately made by the owners but ignored until the 20 March by which time 'a large Body' had moved to lay in pits to the west of Denton, but with 'no other injury'.

The Denton viewer's recognition of the threat, and his attempt to circumvent its course, testifies to the pitmen's known capacity for retribution. The mining villages' social cohesion and distance from authority clearly made them a potent force. This reputation was well attested both locally and nationally. The army took careful note; the War Office had long known miners' capacity to cow local authority by roving intimidation. Pitmen were commonly charged with possessing a wilful temperament, or picking on weaker trades, or simply being ignorant and gullible.[8]

The keelmen and seamen also enjoyed deserved reputations for direct action.[9] For the keelmen, stoppage and 'riot' were almost synonymous deeds. In April 1768 the Newcastle keelmen stopped work and hired a solicitor to fight their case. The city authorities however, knew the likely outcome of stoppage:

... if these men remain quiet, their lying Idle will not be of much Damage, but it is scarce to be expected that they will long remain without work or without Mischief ... a few days will determine Peace or War with 'em.

Three years later again the city was poised between peace or war:

... no Riots have yet happened here, but it can scarce be supposed that such a Number of Men can remain long idle without breaking the peace.

'War with 'em' would mean the men's direct confrontation with the means of production. In the keelmen's case, the river would be the target and their action aimed at immobilising its commerce by blockading it with their keels.[10] Similarly, they resented any arrest of their number and at times made their release a condition of settlement. The river was also the scene of conflict between the seamen and shipowners. Here, the seamen's technique was to hinder the sailing of vessels whose owners had not come to terms:

... the sailors is stoping all the ships that gos into shields & sunderland and will not lett them go out to any other port untill matters is mad up.

In 1787, hundreds of Tyne mariners

... did unlawfully and Riotously assemble and gather together in divers Boats on the River Tyne with an Intent unlawfully ... to obstruct and

> hinder every Ship or Vessell there on the River Tyne ... from going
> ... out of the Harbour ... unless the Master or Owner of every such
> ship ... should by Notes in writing ... promise to pay every Mariner
> ... wages at the rate of five Guineas per Voyage.[11]

On 16 January 1816, the *Tyne Mercury* reported in full one argument between shipowner and strikers taken from the evidence of William Coppin at Newcastle Sessions, who with his brother was trying to break the seamen's embargo. After a mid-river duel the deck was invaded and the vessel seized:

> At this time the boats with seamen were plying on the river, and one
> of them, with Dale in it, came alongside.
>
> *Dale:* Where are you going with the ship?
>
> *Coppin:* You have no business with that.
>
> *Dale:* You have a good berth, and had better not leave it − I am
> determined she shall not go to sea.
>
> *Coppin:* I have no hands on board [meaning seamen] and will go.
> [By this time the ship 'Joseph' is surrounded by seamen in boats.]
>
> *Dale:* We are coming to board the ship.
>
> *Coppin:* I will mark the first man who comes on board.
>
> *Dale:* We can play at that game as well as you; that is the worst word
> you have said this day.

The seamen appear to have had a fine theatrical sense in times of dispute. In 1768 they took their case to the streets and marched with flag and drum 'and threatened Destruction wherever They came'. This was not plunder however, more collective bargaining by disciplined 'riot'. 'The men are proceeding with flags displayed and Drums beating to the great Terror of the Country':

> Notwithstanding the Presence of the Detachment at Sunderland, the
> Sailors marched in a Body thro' the Town by beat of Drum, abstaining
> however from committing any Violence ...[12]

Pitmen, keelmen, and seamen were all considered to have a 'Disposition' for action. After disturbances at Hexham in 1761 the Duke of Northumberland admitted to not having 'been informed of any further particulars', but nevertheless felt free to comment that 'from the riotous disposition of the Colliers and Keelmen in that part of the Country I fear greater mischiefs ...'. Sunderland's 'Principal Inhabitants', unlike the Duke, lived close to the scene of greater mischiefs. In 1785 a petition of magistrates, leading merchants, and shipowners complained that

> ... they have ... much to dread from the turbulent spirit of the Sea-
> men, Keelmen, and Labourers belonging to the said Town and Port
> and particularly the former who have lately assembled in large
> Bodies, demanding exhorbitant Wages, Threatening, and doing much
> Mischief ...

If Sunderland's leading citizens feared trouble from within, they
also feared it from without:

> That another description of Men called Pitmen who work in the
> Collieries adjacent to the said Town, from their number and habits
> of Life discontents frequently arise, which call for the interposition
> of the Civil Power aided by a Military Force.

Their request was for a permanent barracks of soldiers.[13] In
1793, after a sequence of actions by all three groups, the Mayor
of Newcastle asked for a barracks of horse because of the 'turbulent
Disposition' of the seamen and the 'tumultuous spirit' of the pitmen.[14] Connected in their work, and lack of it, by a commercial
interdependence, it was joint action which most frightened local
authorities. In June 1740 the Sheriff of Durham began to panic
when he heard that Stockton bread rioters had called on the pitmen
for reinforcements, and in the same month the Mayor of Newcastle, faced by a bread riot of pitmen, feared for its consequences
upon the keelmen, who, 'Wanting Work will be too Apt to Joyn
those Rioters, which will make a most formidable Body not to be
restrained by any Civil Authority'. The prospect of united action
remained distasteful for both civil and military authorities well
into the 1830s:

> If the Pit men continue refractory they will be awkward persons to deal
> with, one pit man being equal to 3 weavers at the least, and should the
> discontent spread to the Keelmen & Sailors it may become very serious
> and the force at present in Newcastle would be very soon harrassed
> to death.[15]

The disposition for joint action was encouraged by joint issues.
Coal was such an issue, but here their respective actions tended
to be in serial order. More spontaneous action was provoked by
the periodically high price of wheat where pitmen, keelmen, seamen
and other labouring, craft, and smallholding groups could act
together, bound by their mutual dependence as petty consumers
on bread as a staple food.[16]

1740 saw high prices nationally but they had been preceded on

Tyneside by a hard winter which had stopped the Coal Trade. After over a hundred years of price stability, prices of rye and oats increased by up to 100% in six months. In early June crowd actions forced large reductions in wheat prices at Durham, Sunderland, Stockton, and Carlisle. In Newcastle the mood was uglier. There, the Corporation was sympathetic to corn export, indeed the mayor, Fenwick and his brother the MP were themselves corn merchants. On 9 June the city 'mob' was embodied and on 10 June a counter-veiling, irregular militia was raised, with promises from Alderman Ridley that a fixed price of 7s per boll would be imposed on corn factors.[17] The promise was not kept and on 19 June the pitmen, keelmen, and town 'poor', with assistance from Wearside pitmen and their families, stormed the granaries, seized a rye-laden vessel, and proceeded to sell the grain to themselves at the promised price. The mayor had to admit that the pitmen were 'manifestly too strong for the Magistrates'. On the following day the action continued in Newcastle, and substantial direct actions took place in Sunderland; on 23 June the principal inhabitants there petitioned for troops. In Newcastle the militia and gentle persuasion seem to have broken the crowd's momentum, but either on the 25th or early morning of 26 June, the 'Colliers, Wagoners, Smiths, and other common workmen' caught the militia off-guard and re-entered the city, taking *de facto* control. Frenzied negotiations between the mayor, corn factors, and the crowd followed, but a panic shooting affray between a remnant of the militia and the crowd resulted in a frontal attack on the Guild Hall and the ransacking of the town court and chambers: 'the most outragious Riot that ever happen'd in this Town':

> Stones flew in among us from without thro' the Windows like Canon Shot ... at length the Mob broke in upon us ... They Spared our lives indeed but Oblig'd us to quit the place Then fell to plundering and destroying all about them.[18]

That evening the army clattered in from Alnwick, scattered the crowd, made forty arrests, and stayed for a month. The August Assizes inflicted seven years transportation on William Kid 'for feloniously taking Money belonging to the Mayor and Burgesses', and six others 'for being concerned in the late Riot'. All the thirty-three others, except one, were held until the next Assizes when they were discharged.[19]

In the spring and autumn of 1795 there were other serious examples of crowd action. Again, the poor responded to a national dearth with an 'illegal and temporary regulation of the market'. On 25 April Stockton and Durham acted, on 27 April Darlington, and on 30 April Chester le Street market was regulated by 'colliers and other workmen bordering on the River Wear'. A week later Tyne pitmen laid in pits and factories, drew the Light Dragoons, and on 7 May negotiated at Byker with magistrates, constables, and army over the hoarding of supplies by factors. Although Newcastle city authorities had already been hoarding since January under government instructions, when in July and August, along with County Durham magistrates, they asked if they could detain vessels loaded with corn for export, the government refused. In October a thousand Weardale leadminers gathered at Wolsingham 'for the purpose, they said, of regulating the market'; and at Newcastle on 10 November

> ... a number of workmen employed in this neighbourhood assembled in this town, and in the several markets seized the different articles of provision, which they in the presence of the town's officers sold out to poor and labouring people at reduced prices. The butter intended to be conveyed to the hucksters they retailed at 8d. per 1b; the wheat then in the market at 12s. per boll (the ordinary price in former years); – and after obtaining a knowledge of the dispositions of the forestallers of potatoes, they sold them publicly at 5s. a load (the usual price, but one third less than they have lately been retailed at) and immense quantities were disposed of at that rate.[20]

Food was the most common but not the only issue for joint action. In 1757 the government sought to make up for the loss of regular soldiers to the Seven Years War by raising county militias. The Act of 1757 laid down that each county's quota was to be filled by a ballot of all eligible males. Although the Act allowed for (expensive) substitutions, its requirement of compulsory service was met with rioting. The Northumberland Militia was first raised in January 1760 and the following year, as stipulated in the Act, amended lists to include newly eligible eighteen year-olds were to be presented to Deputy Lord Lieutenants. Early February presentations faced serious disturbances in County Durham: in Durham City hundreds assembled 'whereby the Inhabitants are put in bodily fear'. On 28 February the East Chester magistrates were stopped in their duty at Gateshead by being forced

to surrender their ballot-lists to a large crowd. A broadsheet
declared that 'it is a thing that none of us will submit to, to be
ballotted after this manner ...'. On 2 March lists were seized and
destroyed at Morpeth and on the following day at Whittingham.[21]
By now much of Northumberland's labouring population seem
to have been on the move, determined to resist the Act. Indeed,
a sermon preached to Morpeth nonconformists after the March
events obliquely suggests that the rural poor may not have been
alone in this.[22] The Deputy Lieutenants for the County resolved
to stand firm at the Hexham presentation of lists on 9 March. Six
companies of the North Yorkshire Militia were called to the
town where they formed a scarlet and green square before the
Sessions Hall against a large crowd of husbandmen, small farmers,
labourers, pitmen, weavers, tailors, shoemakers, domestics, and
moor-wallers.[23] The lists were taken and the Lieutenants heard
some petitioning but would not desist from their duty. After being
under arms for four hours – two hours 'wth. their Bayonets
touching the Brests of the Mob and the Mob great part of that
Time braving them with their Clubs flourishing about Heads' –
an attack was made on the Militia's left line. An ensign was shot,
the line broke, and the magistrates 'gave the Command to Fire
which was well observed':

> The Grenadiers fired but once, which cleared our front, and in a minutes
> time there was scarce a man left but the dead and wounded. As soon
> as ever the smoke of the first fire had cleared away, and I saw that the
> resistance had ceased, I ran up and down the line to make the men give
> over firing.[24]

One minute of fire into a dense crowd at short range had to take
its toll. Estimates of the dead have ranged from twenty to 120 but
with many staggering away wounded into ditches and churches,
it was not possible to know. The Riot Act had been read twice
and the affair was so serious that the Secretary of State decided
to put it in the King's hands on the morning of 13 March. As late
as 1794 the North Yorkshire were still nicknamed 'The Hexham
Butchers'.[25]

14
Street drama

The actions of 1740 and 1761 were without doubt great 'risings of the people', but the way in which an action could become a 'riot' was not just a matter of legal definition.[1] It was also an uncertain matter of crowd, target, and magistrates whose business was the King's peace. Crowd actions were dynamic; what they were, and what they became, moved across a spectrum of popular thrust and establishment parry which changed from moment to moment. The eventual outcome depended on direct acts and relationships: a magistrate who was afraid of the crowd could, by his own alarm, turn an action into a 'riot', both legally and actually; a crowd intent on its objective could do the same, no matter how sage the authorities might be in their response. In this sense, although there were patterns and even rituals of direct action, each action needs to be understood on its own merits. Moreover, these patterns – the march, the public display of grievance, the style of violence – constituted techniques of social agency which were a familiar part of the wider culture.

The possession of colours and bands to march and celebrate was common for those labouring groups with a strong sense of their own identity. In 1763 the Delaval brothers led three hundred of their workmen to celebrate the King's birthday, 'and the Rear [was] brought up by a great number of working Colliers, all in their Best Dress ... who marched four abreast, with Colours flying carried before them, and a genteel Band of Music ...' In 1822 Hetton colliery was opened by 'the Newbottle band of music, attended by about one thousand workmen, with flags flying and cockades in their hats, marching in regular order'.[2] The Seamen's Association concluded their 1801 annual general meeting in Shields by going 'in procession to the church, attended by their colours', the keelmen marched annually through Newcastle to music 'accompanied by their wives, daughters & c', as did the cordwainers in celebration of their patron saint St Crispin. In 1767, at the laying of Hexham bridge foundation stone Sir William Blackett led gentlemen, freeholders and workmen – 'a Pair of Colours being carried before them, Drums beating, Music playing, attended by the Company of Butchers with Marrow bones and Clevers ... followed by the Company of Free Masons'; twelve years later Newcastle Corporation gave dinner for workmen on their new bridge, 'to which they proceeded with music and colours flying'. South Shields' 'sure, lasting, and loving' Friendly Society laid it down in article twelve that bretheren should march at the funeral of bretheren 'in proper order according to Seniority'.[3]

Public display had other uses a good deal less stately. For 'national' events or local elections, local authorities would throw public parties which appeared to lack only decorum. Sunderland in 1741 celebrated Admiral Vernon's naval victories: 'The Night was usher'd in with drinking loyal Healths, while the Drums beat, Musick play'd, Bells ring and Guns fir'd; the People round the bone-fires were treated with Liquor and Money thrown among them. About Eleven the Gentlemen paraded ... with Drums and Musick'.[4] As in all patriotic expressions of this kind, there may have been scores at home to settle as much as there were enemies abroad to vanquish. Certainly, working groups in the town would use its narrow streets and its standing 'public' to shame individuals who had offended them. The hapless Newcastle undertaker William Scott was seized by joiners' apprentices at Pilgrim Street gate one April evening in 1768 and then 'by force' was 'hoisted upon a stang and carried shoulder height thro' the streets till at last they came to the Side, where he was rescued by some of his friends'. The *stang*, and *riding* it, takes its place with ducking stools, rough music, whirligigs, and pillories as a direct form of popular sanction against those who had bruised community mores. A long pole to which the offender was strapped by his shoulders and dragged, the stang seems to have been most favoured by the seamen, although it was sometimes used by the keelmen. In 1783 Sunderland tars returned to port to seek out those who had informed on them to the press gangs: the informers were mounted on a stang 'and carried through the principal streets, exposed to the insults and assaults of an enraged populace, the women in particular bedaubing them plentifully with dirt etc'. Tyne seamen who refused to join the strikes of 1792 and 1815 were similarly humiliated by this 'cruel and brutal practice'[5] − although it must be said that the stang, like the entire action, was done with a precision and discipline which impressed the authorities. There were also other, incidental, forms of public humiliation − like stripping, nose pulling, jostling and jeering, and, as with His Majesty's press in 1792, the seamen 'compelled them, with their jackets turned inside out, to march out of the town'.[6]

In 1792 and 1815 all striking seamen were roll-called daily and subjected to a control which included those who had degraded the action as well as those who had not joined it:

[1792] ... yesterday three of the Sailors who had not been quite punctual at their Meetings were stripped Naked and made to walk in that situation up the street of South Shields and around the market place.

[1815] ... and some of the Men so assembled took Tar and paint and put the same upon the Face of a certain Man ... And then the said Man ... was put upon a Pole and carried to different parts of the Town and then to ... Jane Forsyth's Field and he was there punished by knocking him down.[7]

When street drama was employed against property or authority we see its techniques most vividly. Here the display not only proclaimed feelings and the threat of action, it also embodied them. Marching through the district the commotion retained a fine sense of discriminating riot. There was the sight of physical force in numbers, but the essential aim was moral persuasion by means of an overbearing display of self confidence. Violence against persons, if not property, was mainly suggestive. In 1740, after storming the granaries, the Newcastle crowd, 'elated with this Success' proceeded 'in Triumph about the streets ... huzzaing and blowing horns ... well armed with Cudgels'. The pitmen's later capture of the city and release of its prisoners saw them march 'in great Order through the Town with Bagpipes playing Drum beating and Dirty clothes fixed upon Sticks by way of Colours flying'. In 1768 it was the turn of the seamen:

On Saturday the 3rd Inst. about 4 or 500 Sailors at Tinmouth [Tynemouth], joined by great Numbers from Sunderland, assembled in a tumultuous manner, with Flags and Drums, to the great Terror of the Inhabitants ... upon the Pretence of demanding an Advance of Wages ... On the Day following a Body of Sailors, to the Number of 400 at least, marched up to Newcastle with a Flag, and a Boatswain and His Whistle, to call to Order and threatened Destruction.

The seamen, in turn, were 'awed from proceeding to Violence and by Persuasions' by the suggestive presence of soldiers drawn up on the Sandhill. The seamen waited until morning when they went to Sunderland, 'where They did great Damage by extorting Meat, Drink, and Money from many People by Violence'. Meanwhile, the Newcastle soldiers had been ordered to Sunderland in pursuit, but the seamen, 'their Number being augmented by other Sailors at Sunderland ... returned to Shields, where they did great Damage to the Shipping and threatened to do more that Evening'. Thereupon they returned to Sunderland for a final blast of defiance:

> Notwithstanding the Presence of the Detachment at Sunderland, the Sailors marched in a Body thro' the Town by beat of Drum, abstaining however from committing any Violence, and after They were without the Town They dispersed.[8]

This action frightened the authorities all the way down the line to the Secretary of War's office in London. Lord Barrington was moved to make enquiries about stationing a permanent force in the area. In his original request for assistance the Mayor of Newcastle drew specific attention to the accoutrements of intimidation – 'the men are proceeding with Flags displayed and Drums beating to the great Terror of the Country' – and in general the magistracy were alert to the ferment of the march.[9] Magistrates' letters to the Home Department did not lack detail in matters of symbolism. A crowd on the march was there to intimidate and deter by an overwhelming impression of pullulating plebeian activity, and flags, banners, and mottoes were central to that impression. In 1819 North Shields justices permitted a Peterloo protest meeting by the Political Protestants only 'upon a pledge being given ... that everything should be conducted in the most regular and peaceable manner – that no Music or Banners and no Sticks or Staves ... no appearances of marching or arraying themselves in any manner', and were relieved that the meeting eventually took place without the plangency of threat. Newcastle magistrates were less prudent: the Town Moor Peterloo protest paraded beneath an overarching forest of catchword and symbol – black banner with a red border *We mourn the massacred at Manchester*, gold letters on a blue flag *Rachel weeping for her children*, and others. That each side recognised the role of street drama is shown both by the authorities' sensitivity to it and the Radicals' efforts to play down its meaning.

The radical editorials of the *Tyne Mercury* perorated on the horrors of Peterloo for seven consecutive weeks but at the same time tried to deny any offending sting from a demonstration which, if without sting, had no meaning:

> ... there are banners at it, but they bear for their inscriptions 'Justice', 'Annual Parliaments' &c. 'Order, Order', 'Liberty or Death', and such like expressions, the last of which is, or was, universally to be found in the song books, among toasts and sentiments, and on soldiers' caps, and is as common a phrase as 'God Save the King' or 'Rule Britannia'; there is marching, but one witness says that he has seen that used by benefit societies; there are sticks, but two or three witnesses deny that there are any clubs, or any thing but what is commonly employed by a countryman ...[10]

The threat of action was always present and the imagery of the crowd declared it: the secret bravado of smugglers or poachers; the speared loaf, drum, dirty-clothes banner and other insignia of bread-rioters; the horns of Highland crofters or Welsh 'Scotch Cattle'; the invisible intimidatory presence of a Ludd, or Swing, or lesser correspondent; the symbolic chest of Lewsyn yr Heliwr; the effigy-burning and abuse of the high, mighty, and notorious:[11]

> ... it is almost an honourable distinction to be marked out for insult & outrage by an infuriated & infatuated populace ... I do not lay claim to any such distinction, from any personal violence that has been offered me; & am well satisfied that the compliment has extended no further than burning me in effigy within sight of my castle-gates, with threats ... of demolishing my castle windows. I hastily wish your lordship had experienced no stronger tokens of the sovereign will & pleasure of their Majesties the people.

> Nothing of material importance has occurred in our concerns — but I was tried, condemned, and hanged in Effigy, at Rainton on Thursday.[12]

It was out of this whimsical world of symbols that the crowd developed their initial styles of class loyalty. The broad culture of street drama ran to the depths of the early labour movement as a form of internalised, self-induced, drama — something which the Methodists matched and copied. Buddle passed 800 pitmen parading 'with music & Colours' and insisting *Nail your Colours to the Mast, Death or Liberty* for Owen's Grand National in 1834, but this insistence, and its dramatic posture, did not stop on the

Shields Road. In the year of Tolpuddle it continued in the secret initiations of colliery cells, at night, in the villages, and continued into the debates on the strategy and public representation of Chartism:

> The ceremony is performed in private, and one of these Vagabonds is wrapped in a White Sheet, and the other in a Black Cloak during the inauguration – with open Bible, naked Sword, lighted Candles etc. Nothing but their poverty ... prevents a general Strike.
>
> They were all moral-force men, and all physical-force men. (Cheers). What did they mean by moral force? Did it mean that they denounced all violent measures? ... There could not be an exhibition of moral force without physical force. It was an act of self defence ... and, unless the legislature should convince them that a petition was the merest farce in the world, they were all physical-force men – (Cheers) – not for the purpose of destroying life and property, but of convincing the oppressors of the people that they would suffer no longer in silence. (Cheers) ...[13]

If the Poor practiced one form of street drama, then authority practiced another. As well as gentlemanly drums and flags for national events and local elections, the State used the law as a controlling ideology through the awesome spectacle of Assize and gallows.[14] The surge of eighteenth-century capital statutes, most of them related to property, included the Coal Trade with statutes in 1736, 1769, and 1800 for the protection of collieries against arson, sabotage, and destruction.[15] When this ideological force broke down, the black cap majesty of the Law was replaced by the red coat terror of the army. Except in times of war, regular and militia forces were not big enough to dominate the country. Thus, from its inception (or re-inception) as the most important coercive instrument at the beginning of the eighteenth century, to its demise around the middle of the nineteenth, the army relied more upon the show of force than its actual use. Like the marching crowd, their's was mostly a reserved violence, as at Kersall Moor, Manchester, in May 1839:

> One wing of the 10th came by a morning train yesterday; the other by an evening train, which made everybody suppose two regiments had arrived. We made also a great show on the 23rd, and it is generally thought we had then 3000 men under arms: we had not 1000.
>
> But I lay down as an axiom, and our first, greatest principle, that the queen's troops must not be overthrown anywhere, because the effect in the three kingdoms would be fearful.
>
> ... the *prestige* of mastery is with them ...[16]

The prestige of mastery could not be dented; the army dressed and manoeuvred to make the State strong, itself brave, and others afraid. The right uniform and a horse could in an instant, turn the look of a pimply youth into a hard horse-soldier. An 1821 Radical tract recognised the prestige of soldier-red for the labourer and sought to mock it. The Volunteers represented more a colourful display of loyalty than a military force and therein lay their attraction:

> The coarsest manufacture than can be made of wool, dyed of a brick-dust colour, goes down with him, because it is in imitation of scarlet or crimson cloth ... these fine allurements ... have drawn in and been the *destruction* of more men in reality, than all the killing eyes and bewitching voices of women ever *slew* in jest. Today the *swineherd* puts on his red coat, and believes everybody in earnest that calls him gentleman; and two days after, *Serjeant Kite gives him a swinging rap with his cane* for holding his musket an inch higher than he should do ...
>
>> It's but for yen and twenty days,
>> The Foulks's een aw'll dazzle, –
>> Prood, swagg'ring i' my fine reed claes:
>> Odds heft'. my pit claes – dist thou hear?
>> Are waurse o' wear.[17]

And it was not only the soldiers themselves who saw the value of this swagger:

> The people, it must be owned, in the simplicity of their hearts, gape with admiration at the passing spectacle ... and feel themselves awestruck with the grandeur of the cavalcade which would trample them in the dirt ... Politicians, observing this effect of finery and parade on the minds of the unthinking, take care to dress up the idol ...[18]

However, the army had to deal with matters when the calvalcade failed. The defeat of even a single sergeant and his men could upset that controlling poise which was meant to exist between rich and poor, army and crowd. During the North-East labour disputes of 1792–3 cavalry were used to 'frighten the Pitmen in a Return to their Duty', and fright depended upon the impression of mastery: 'you will as far as possible avoid exposing yourself ... to any hazard of an ineffectual attempt'. The authorities ultimately relied upon the show of terror to a 'turbulent' people:

> ... notwithstanding the discreet and lenient use which the Civil Magistrate hath in all instances made of that [military] Force, Experience hath shown that the powers delegated to him by the Legislative would on every occasion be defeated if it was not for the terror of a Military Aid ...[19]

These same magistrates and merchants had needed the services
of a Militia against the seamen only two years before − 'their
numbers had so increased that the drums of the North Yorks Militia
beat to arms ... the regiment paraded the streets ... the mob dispersed'[20] − but the 'terror' of soldiers who had no prestige could
easily collapse into mockery and then riot. The North Yorks had
been reduced to shooting at Hexham in 1761. The Newcastle riot
of 1740 had been encouraged by ridicule − 'the white stocking
regiment' − heaped upon a city militia hastily assembled to deter
the mob. When regulars finally arrived at five o'clock in the afternoon, this same mob responded quite differently in the face of
those who looked as if they would act as soldiers under discipline:

> ... when they were come near St Nicholas Church, word was brought
> that the Rioters in number about a thousand were coming up the Side
> with great Fury most of them armed, Capt. Sowle upon this order'd
> his men to halt, and immediately load their Musquets & fix their
> Bayonets, which was done in the face of the Rioters, and had a great
> effect, for they were now convinced that the Soldiers had power to fire
> upon them, which they before imagined cou'd not be done, since the
> Affair of Capt. Porteous at Edinburgh. This circumstance, and the
> appearance of the Soldiers drawn up in Order ... struck such a Damp
> upon the Spirits of the Rioters, that they fled with the utmost
> precipitation ...[21]

15
Reciprocal elements

Regular soldiers deterred, but magistrates were not always in a position to use them. There were usually very few troops available in the area, the means of calling them out was cumbersome, and the army did not relish the job.[1] As well as their expense and bad reputation there was a constitutional suspicion of regulars going back to at least 1688; Blackstone decreed that '[our laws] know no such state as that of a perpetual standing soldier', the condition emanated from 'temporary excresences bred out of the distemper of the state'.[2]

The regular army was small, unpopular, unenthusiastic, and untrained for domestic combat; irregular forces were all these things and worse: the militia lacked discipline and morale, they tended to be under-strength, they had no prestige of mastery. John Dryden thought them only capable of the destruction of roast beef, and only quick 'to be Drunk, the Business of the Day'.[3] In 1793 James Rudman complained to the Home Secretary that, threatened by a general strike in Coal, the North East had insufficient troops, and a militia four-fifths of whom were useless; Thomas Sanderson complained that Sunderland had thirty soldiers against a thousand keelmen 'exclusive of their Wives and Daughters'; Charles Brandling complained that the militia had made no impression whatsoever on the seamen, and marines were needed to take their place.[4]

Local magistrates did not have constant means of coercive aid and were hemmed in by a confused legal position on their right to use it. The 1714 Riot Act (1 GeoI c.5) had tried to clear up common law confusion on the difference between an illegal assembly and a riot, but magistrates remained unsure. The Riot Act could not always be properly read or heard, the army was not trusted, and the point at which the force of arms was lawful was unclear.

Magistrates and soldiers remained liable to prosecution for forced dispersal (as after the Wilkes Riots, 1763–8) *and* for negligent dispersal (as after the Gordon Riots, 1780).[5]

In May 1740 the Sheriff of Durham, facing county bread-riots, was wrapped around with all these problems. He and his magistrates had no military force and were uncertain of their legal powers to use one. At Stockton

> ... severall persons were taken up but lett go again upon promises of being quiet, but I rather believe the Gentlemen were in no condition to force them away. I presume my friend Hodsworth so near a new Election wou'd not be overforward to think of soldiers.

Troops were ordered from Berwick, but by the second wave of crowd actions in June, Sheriff Williamson was forced to raise the *posse comitatus*. His magistrates were ordered to 'command all persons from fifteen to sixty to attend me at Sedgefield ... in order to march to Stockton'. Williamson was in a quandary. Thinking aloud to the Bishop of Durham he rehearsed his strategy: if faced by a mob he would read the Riot Act, take prisoners if there was no subsequent dispersal, and, should there be resistance, condescend 'to a general battle'. If there was no mob by the time of his arrival, 'I know nothing but to march back again'. This in itself was a problem because Williamson could not afford to pay and feed his men on stand-by duty, and a dismissed posse might be difficult to raise again. The Sheriff resolved that his best plan would be to persuade the merchants against exporting their corn.[6] In fact, no strategy was required because there was no confrontation – a common experience for late-coming forces. Arriving with his posse at Sedgefield, 'Mr Hedworth and Mr Bowes [local magistrates] insisted on it, that when I came there, their Power ceased; and that if necessity required it, I was to give the orders for firing'. Williamson disagreed replying 'that the Justices were the proper Persons, for in Obedience to their Warrant I had raised the County; and that I was to be commanded by them'. A legal huddle followed where Williamson could not be advised by his lawyer. This does not appear to have calmed his nerves, and, eager nevertheless to show his valour, the Sheriff of Durham opted for discretion:

> ... relating to the giving orders to fire he [the lawyer] exprest thus that it was too delicate a Part for him to determine ... but he told me by

word of mouth twice, that if he was in my Case, he would not give orders to fire ... I would willingly have done what was right, but the Thoughts of Shedding Blood, and being tried for it, to me, I own, was terrible.

I said to let you see I will go as far as any of you, if you Mr Bowes, Mr Hedworth, and the other Justices, will sign such an order, I will joyn with you in it, but I will not do it alone, and thus we parted'.[7]

It was this weakness of authority which, by default, gave the crowd in action some standing. If coercion was cumbersome, if magistrates were dubious about their exact role as coercers, if the crowd felt its actions to be legitimate and its techniques typical, then it is clear that in the precarious and contingent drama of the street, the Poor could meet their rulers in a situation which admitted reciprocity. Indeed, crowd actions as a method of social agency were sometimes connived at by the rulers themselves. The 1710 Sacheverell riots in London were encouraged by Anglican clergymen; crowd action and popular pricing was occasionally enacted in the presence of local magistrates; the city 'mob' could be raised for political, or religious pressure. Wesley was no stranger to this, saying once that the Newcastle mob 'have commonly some humanity left', and Barnard Castle's squirearchy even provided their mob-captain with a gold-laced hat and sword: 'thus equipped ... paraded the streets ... sounding a horn, call[ing] the people together at his pleasure'.[8] The Wearside mob seems to have served General Lambton's political interest. In 1761 his defeated election opponent mused that 'A greater number would have appeared at the Poll but that General Lambton or his Friends had sent for the Pittmen of Lambton which occasioned such a Riot that no business could be carried on ...' In 1819 'Radical Jack' Lambton himself led keelmen to smash a loyalist address, and two years later local Tories regretted how easily Sunderland Whigs could use their network to raise a crowd:

The fact is, that the 'Running Fitters' – the link in the chain between the Fitters, and their Keelmen & Coasters – are the real *moving political pivots*, of *Mobility* in Sunderld.
On all publick occasions, the fitter has nothing to do, but to give his running Fitter a hint, what side he wishes his men, alias his mob, to take; and the said Running Fitter, can (by *certain strings*, of which he has the complete management) *work* them as well, as a Show-man, manages his Puppets. The *Lambtonians* are tolerably expert at this kind of acting ...

Once the Whig crowd was raised, other fitters were their target. What was a 'riot' to a Tory fitter was mere politics to a Whig fitter.[9]

Of course, factional puppetry of this sort was dangerous play for men who ultimately believed in the due processes of their own rule. At the centre of the crowd's reciprocity with their rulers was the coercive weakness of those rulers. If the crowd's action had a standing and needed to be negotiated, it was generally because authority had no other recourse. In 1820 the landowners of Knaresdale were plagued by poaching leadminers: their authority was *ad hoc*; they were reluctant to use troops, special constables had failed, local men would not join a posse, the leadminers had no deference for property when it claimed game birds, the lead companies were not willing or able to exert pressure, the moorland terrain was difficult. In the end it was necessary to negotiate:

> ... after that the Gentlemen in the neighbourhood of Alston, got the Business settled between Mr B. & the Poachers, by their agreeing to dispose of their Dogs & Guns & Shoot no more on his liberties − I am inform'd that it cost Mr B. £200 Pounds before he got it settled.[10]

Both of the North-East's major crowd actions of the eighteenth-century had been preceded by negotiations between magistrates and crowd. In 1761 the Hexham crowd had presented petitions before the militia were attacked and the shooting started. In 1740 Newcastle magistrates had bargained frantically when it became clear that a hastily raised militia could not handle the situation: 'we therefore Could have recourse only to Persuasions and Arguments with the Chief of them to disperse and return to their Work. But all in vain till the Merchants proposed to sell on the next Market Day' 'at the price it actually cost them & they produced the Invoices of the several parcels to confirm the Truth of the same'. Later, after the first attack on the Guild Hall, Alderman Ridley went beyond reciprocity by coaxing the people to the quay-side and begging them to unload a ship of its corn − 'some seem'd to be satisfied with this but in ten minutes they withdrew one after another and left him almost alone in the ship, they had indeed more tempting Game in View'. After the Guild Hall had been looted, the crowd 'safely conducted the Magistrates to their own houses in a kind of Mock Triumph, Mr R. seeing now the true Design of the People ... They were not to be brought to Reason'.[11]

What one historian has called the 'probing confrontations'[12] of crowd action always included negotiation. A marching gang did not dismiss negotiation, it invited it. In 1765 the coalowners 'earnestly recommend[ed]' and 'used all possible means of persuasion' to prevail with the pitmen. And it was prudent that they did; during 'the greatest Riots and Outrages' the nearest regulars were stationed at York. In 1768, marching seamen were blocked by troops in Newcastle, 'and after some discourse with them by the magistrates' returned to Shields. Again, it was prudent that they did; ten days later the War Office rejected the idea of a permanent military force in the city. In 1786, the keelmen dispersed after 'the timely interposition of the Right Worshipful the Mayor, and other Gentlemen concerned'.[13] If reciprocity rarely spilled over into actual sympathy, the predictability of direct action was at least accepted. Courts appear to have been lenient on pitmen guilty of sabotage, riot, obstruction, and assault; popular pricing for bread was one thing, but popular pricing for butter was 'inexcusable' as 'butter is not a necessary of life to the poor'. On the other side, trusted magistrates or solicitors might be asked to arbitrate or advise by pitmen, seamen or keelmen, and even as the authorities felt their control to be slipping, as in January 1793, the seamen still insisted upon their loyalty 'under a constitution which we admire and venerate'.[14]

The predictability of action, and how to cope with it, was inextricably connected to how the Poor were regarded as a whole. Control was not just a question of the Riot Act, or soldiers, or negotiation, but involved a complex, total relationship with the lower orders. There was a sense in which those in authority, up to a point, fully expected a degree of turbulence from people whom they saw as originally lazy or shiftless needing the discipline of poverty to make them work, whose minds were 'unletter'd and untutor'd', whose temperaments were 'like spoiled children'.[15] In 1819 the Duke of Northumberland, reporting a fracas in a North Shield pub, was anxious to know whether it had been political, or just 'one of those casual disorders which are of such frequent occurrence ... on the Evening of Saturday'.[16] The difference mattered a great deal to Northumberland's expectation of the Poor, its reciprocal implications for him, and hence his capacity to rule and act like a Duke. Similarly, keelmen could harass passers-by, intimidate men still working, and steal bread and vegetables, all

in a single afternoon – but the *Tyne Mercury* could still praise
them for acting so well. Seamen could forcibly detain ships and
create serious hold-ups but, a coalowner's agent could still see
them as 'Arbitrary poor fellows'. As late as 1844 Lord Lieutenant
Londonderry could still refer to Durham as 'a County who must
always be subject more or less to the Freaks and Bustings out of
a great mining population'.[17]

Londonderry expected nothing less from pitmen he liked to call
his own. Why then should he expect more from a swinish multitude
whose very swinishness made his rule such a duty? In 1761 most of
Northumberland's tenantry appear to have been in rebellion against
the Militia Acts. Sir Lancelot Allgood of Nunwick House, near
Hexham, went with the county magistracy to Newcastle leaving
his wife Jane at home. On the day of the Hexham massacre, Lady
Allgood's tenants escorted her from her home 'telling me it was
for my own safety that they were coming to burn the House'.[18]
Taking her through a wood they stopped at a gate. Here, she turned
and confronted them. Her account of the confrontation is a
remarkable expression of the psychology of the gentry as an
eighteenth-century ruling class. Lady Allgood was probably afraid,
perhaps nearly hysterical, but she could not surrender herself to
fear of a folk she saw as inferior and whose behaviour she saw
as pathetic. Her contempt sharpened her duty. Even in a situation
where her authority was challenged to the hilt, she was still able
to retain the appearance of authority, and show the flag:

I stopt & asked what was the matter I was not affraid if they were all
surrounding me I knew God would protect me & he was all sufficient
let who wou'd be against me & just came by at the time half a hund[d]
– like so many thieves & dogs whip'd to their Kennel I lectured them
most stoutly told them they deserved what they met with wou'd not
take my advice who had told them what they must expect for I had
sent up the day before to let them know their assembling themselves
in that manner wou'd be deemed Rebellion & must be treated as rebels
& if any of our Tenants or whoever they were that lived upon any part
of our estate went with the rebellion even they nor none belonging to
them should have habitation here again & this morning I have sent to
tell them if they don't behave themselves quietly & decently as loyal
subjects ought to do in a christian Country they shall have a regiment
of Soldiers to drive them like a flock of sheep to Slaughter & teach them
what it is to go to fight because they won't learn to fight like a parcell
of wild Irish as they are. I have sent a message to R-- of Smalesmouth
that in regard to his father & Mother I wou'd indulge him if he wou'd

make publick submission to the Gentlemen [JPs] when he was sober
for what he had said & done when he was drunk if not I had witnesses
enough to hang him at the next Assizes & Robson of Shittlington a
lying good for nothing fellow came cringeing & fawning to beg I wou'd
not be angry he cou'd not help it they forced him when I knew all the
time he was a ring leader ...

[she told them to return to their work]

... they went as quietly by here as cou'd be said they only wanted to
right themselves I told them that was nothing but rank rebellion & as
such they should be treated. Mrs Reed and her family ... was here for
about an hour & we both agree'd leaveing the Country was giveing the
people too much encouragement for their wickedness & leave no check
upon them ... I am in no sort of apprehension for any bullies & threats
I tell them their Curses are blessings to me but redoubled curses upon
their own heads God knows everything they say think or do tis dareing
him not me & they may depend upon it they'll meet with their doom
his hand is not slackened he can make pharoahs of them now as he
did in defence of the Children of Israel pray make com^ts & best thanks
to the Gentlemen Officers & Common Men of the Militia for proveing
themselves freeborn English Men & doing their duty so properly & if
ever shou'd be in my power to serve any of them the meanest of them
may depend upon it my com^ts attend all the Gentlemen who I con-
gratulate upon haveing that true spirit of liberty to dare putting the
laws of their Country in execution tho bullied & Hectored.

During these few critical days Lady Allgood's performance constituted an illusion of authority. Soon after the incident she tried
to defend her house, but she knew that her real authority existed
beyond rusty guns:

[their son] came yesterday to defend me as he said but I told him he
looked so frighted I rather thought he meant I was to defend him.
Jack Baty has got four of my father's old Blunderbusses out he says
he knows the good they have done they are as rusty as if they had been
taken out of the river I survey'd all their warlike accoutrements last
night & laughed most immoderately they put me so much in mind of
Falstaff's company ... Mr Beaumont staid all night part of our body
guard tonight is Will Coulson of Simonburn and Joe Corven I told
Beaumont I wou'd appoint him Capt. of the guard tonight his bulk
will best suit Falstaff's.

... a child might take every man of them ... I find my threatening a
regiment of Horse has terrified them out of their senses the a^ccts of
their simplicity makes me laugh to think that a woman as I am without
arms or any offensive weapon should subdue a whole country ... here
all was peace & serenity only we laughed at the simple amazement of
the poor creatures & our own armaments'.[19]

The threat of cavalry, and the shootings at Hexham, were reminders of whose was the ultimate power, but it is clear that Lady Allgood's continuing authority was woven through a thousand threads of personal relationship which together made up a social system. Her self-confidence as a ruler existed first through her perception of the ruled as 'poor creatures'. In so far as they were poor creatures, they needed her; in so far as they needed her, their independent actions were pathetic; and in so far as their's were pathetic, her's were just. Of course, the pitmen, keelmen, and seamen were a different proposition from the tenantry. Yet even for them the psychology of rule in eighteenth-century England depended upon its successful and minute practice. Social relationships carried the controls of bearing and distance. If the mob was not deterred, then there were always the troops to call on. The strategy of the troops was only a more awesome manifestation of the psychology of that bearing and distance: the mob, 'poor creatures' as they might be, could only go so far and no more; the rulers, bound to some reciprocity as they might be, would only let the mob go so far and no more.

Later, when considered by a radically politicised middle-class, the reciprocal elements were seen with a new understanding:

> A mob they [the ruling class] know, and would always have them dispersed by the military, as soon as two or three are gathered together; but the people, as a part of the constitution, they could never discover.

The 'people', in this context, were those tradesmen and professional people who clothed booted, and worked for the gentry. It was their intelligence which was insulted by an aristocratic bearing and distance which by 1821 they found no longer tolerable:

> ... if there be any body in the neighbourhood very low indeed, so low, as to be removed from all possibility of clashing with his importance, such a one he will make a companion, and shew him most marvellous marks of humility and condescension. ... Indeed, for the sake of obtaining a little popularity, he will notice cottagers and poor children at play, and make extremely free with clowns, jockeys, grooms, huntsmen, ... But keep your distance, ye little squires, parsons, and professional men, who make saucy pretensions to knowledge or ingenuity.

This radical middle-class understanding became less radical at the point where the 'mob', the 'very low', became the poor as a whole. The author noted the elements of reciprocity – the relationship between haughtiness and swinishness – and castigated them as the same evil:

> He is abjectly servile to his superiors, insolent and neglectful to the middle ranks, and free and easy to the humble sons of poverty, who will bear a volley of oaths whenever he thinks proper to discharge them, and who, if spit upon, will not spit again, because they are this workmen or tenants.[20]

From the French Revolutionary Wars in the 1790s one can see a distinct change in the climate of authority between rulers and ruled: the oaths and the spitting increased; the humble acceptance did not.

16
A changing climate

The war period and just after it was a watershed in social relations. A number of serious industrial disputes with pitmen, keelmen, and seamen, a mounting fear from above of politicisation from below, and a series of repressive Acts by central government to curb both political and industrial association, all combined to irreversibly change the climate of relations between rulers and ruled.[1]

We have seen how the pitmen were reformulated as workers by an industrial process which began, effectively, in 1804, and how they were beginning to be redefined as a social-moral entity, at about the same time. Having come through the formative Bond struggles of 1804–10, and the various post-war difficulties, in 1820 the pitmen entered upon two decades of unprecedented coalfield expansion and conflict. Encompassing all this was general fear of that disorder brought by urban-manufacturing systems to their districts. The Newcastle printer, Eneas Mackenzie, warned in 1827 of threats to designated authority; the people now

> ... move in crowds; and hence, when they suffer any temporary distress or deprivation, they easily receive the impulse given by bustling or designing individuals, and readily become infatuated by·the acts of theological or political demagogues.

Happily, the writer could report that Tyneside was not yet a manufacturing district and that urban chaos had been avoided, a state attributable to 'the wise moderation of the magistracy, who permit the utmost freedom of discussion, and resist the acts of weak and designing alarmists'.[2]

Mackenzie's commendation of the good sense of magistrates was quickened by his fear of alarmists within the bench's own camp. The rash of industrial actions in the early 1790s brought some alarm, the saving grace was that the actions appear to have occurred without 'politics'. Tyne seamen were out and about in November 1792, a prelude to the wider seamen-pitmen-keelmen-shipwrights' disputes of 1793, but Christopher Blackett could report from Newcastle that 'No Seditious Handbills have been circulated here; nor have I heard of any Pamphlets of such a Tendency'. Given the absence of any firm contrary evidence, Blackett's judgement seems to have been correct for 1792, and for the remainder of the war years.

It was not until 1819 that a fear of political consciousness, wedded to industrial dispute, gripped the minds of the magistracy. In 1817 Whitehall expected disturbances at Shields, Newcastle, and Sunderland mainly because they were ports, and pitmen, keelmen, and seamen had been (and would be) happy to indulge expectations since the seamen's action in October 1814, – yet in 1818 a government secret committee did not include the North East in its schedule of dangerous (by which it meant, political) places.[3] The events of 'Peterloo' on 16 August 1819 prompted the resurgence of Newcastle and Gateshead's 'Political Protestants', a resurgence made more fearful by the direct actions of Tyne keelmen during September and October. On 11 October an estimated 30,000 Tyneside Radicals, including iron-workers and seamen, marched onto Newcastle's Town Moor to cheer invective against the upholders of 'Old Corruption' – tax 'vampires', war-mongers, and usurpers of liberty – who had forfeited their right to rule:

> We may compare the borough mongers to cow keepers, and surely they are bad cow keepers, for they not only bring us home leaner and fewer, but they sabre us without mercy.[4]

Three days after this there was a serious quayside clash of keelmen and marines, where one keelman was shot. Although there is no direct evidence that the keelmen were ever politicised, from the first apparent confluence of their action with the Political Protestants' resurgence, local magistrates feared for the worst. The worst was and continued to be for a long time afterwards, a simultaneous action of pitmen, keelmen, and seamen, led by Radicals who 'appeared amongst them'. On 2 October Castle Ward magistrates called for a crushing military force, and on the day after the Town Moor demonstration Chester Ward magistrates told the Lord Lieutenant that they could not guarantee civil order.[5] After the keelmen's affray two days later, the rest of October saw magistrates, mayors, and Lords Lieutenant writing letters of unprecedented desperation. On 20 October, the Mayor of Newcastle reminded Sidmouth that the keelmen had £700,000 worth of shipping caught in the Tyne, easy prey for 'Sailors, Lightermen, Pitmen, and I am sorry to add ... Radical Reformers'. On 24 October, the Duke of Northumberland wrote that all magistrates fear the seamen and clamour for marines. The next day magistrate Thorp reported political and military training of 'the labouring ranks' and his letter was followed two days later, by another from a Gateshead ironmaster calling for the spiking of port cannon. On the same day the government was told by magistrate Riddell that his colleagues were able but, living under 'A considerable degree of alarm ... as our population is very great, and a part of it ripe for mischief'. On 29th and 30th Sidmouth was informed from Newcastle and Sunderland that the pitmen, seamen, and others were ready to rise, and on 2 November the 'others' were named to include Wearside's 'manufactury classes' who 'would I fear come forward if any commotion should take place'. Virtually all of these reports stressed the need for heavy military assistance, requests which were sealed with approval by the Duke of Northumberland's 30 October instruction to his county magistracy to enrol as many special constables as possible and, 'where the nature of the Population requires it, an Armed Association'. Amidst so much consternation it may be added that the keelmen were not changing their feelings about the reciprocal elements of protest as quickly as were the authorities. On the day after one of their number was shot on 14 October, the keelmen went to the magistrates to demand a warrant for the arrest of the marine officer who gave the order to fire.[6]

By November the keelmen were back to work, but by now the magistracy's fear of political infiltration had become self-sustaining. They seem to have lost their powers of discrimination. The pitmen became the new objects of fear. On 10 November magistrate Clark had to admit there were no signs of trouble, yet was convinced that 'in case of extremity', whatever that might be, 'no reliance can be placed on a very large proportion of the Pitmen'. On 15 November, his colleague Thorp at Ryton went close to defining this extremity by reporting pitmen's plans to take middle-class hostages, 'particularly the ladies, to attend with them, in order to secure themselves against the attack of soldiers'. It was the senior magistrate, Archibald Reed, Mayor of Newcastle, who most clearly reflected the changing climate of relations. In the month betwen 11 November and 10 December he sent five letters to Sidmouth which described the pitmen as proto-revolutionaries: first they were 'ripe for mischief', then they were 'rapidly arming', 'as bad as possible', in possession of gunpowder, and fully armed. Reed's accounts were short on facts and long on fear; from 20 November Whitehall was noticeably circumspect about his objectivity and must have felt justified in this on receipt of his 10 December missive containing four affidavits from informers, astonishingly presented without qualification as to their veracity. Magistrates like Reed and Thorp succeeded in creating their own field of nervous force. Lord Lambton criticised Reed's scaremongering at higher levels but Major General John Byng of Northern Forces supported Reed by saying that Lambton (in London) was not in a position to know the facts (Byng wrote from army HQ in Pontefract). On the other hand, Major General Barnard, in Newcastle, was suspicious of the city's magistrates. He thought it was his 'duty to make an immediate report' to Sidmouth 'lest an exaggerated statement might reach your ears'. Nevertheless, the whole area was so tense that it was impossible for Thorp to leave his house for one night without rumours – he lived near the radical iron-village of Winlaton. Of course, it would be wrong to identify Thorp and Reed as merely magistrates in a panic. There *was* political penetration of some sort and on 18–19 December thirty-eight North Durham magistrates met to discuss the possibility of armed Radicalism.[7]

Whatever the practical situation, the autumn of 1819 represented a critical break in the attitudes of North-East authorities to protest. A nervous sensitivity to what was deemed 'political' hardened ruling-class attitudes to the Poor, reinforced their feelings about the degraded culture and low status of the Poor, particularly the pitmen, and ultimately destroyed what reciprocal elements remained in their attitude to popular protest. Political consciousness, by their definition, seemed to deny reciprocity and forfeit negotiation: what compromise could there be with politicised men who not only quarrelled with your behaviour but even rejected your social position? This was class politics and although changes

in sensibility of this kind do not happen overnight one can perceive
in the conduct of later disputes a fear and intransigency which was
not there before.[8] The pitmen's strikes of 1831–32 and 1844
were fought to the death with the magistrates standing back, and
when the unrest was considered purely 'political', as with collier
Chartism in 1838–40, the response was appropriately immoderate:

> ... all of them armed, and at any time they might choose to come to
> this town ... What would be the consequences of their visit here? every
> house would be pillaged and even human life sacrificed to the shrine
> of ambition, by those idle vagabonds ...
>
> ... [they are defenceless] from an attack of the Pitmen in our Vicinity
> who might continue in the undisturbed power of committing every
> imaginable Outrage & Violence on Persons & Property in this City for
> several Hours before it would be possible to obtain Relief.[9]

Before the political fear of 1819 it had been mainly seamen's actions
which had probed the confidence of authority. Their 1793 protest
against the Impress Service involved daily marching and speech-
making in defiance of Newcastle magistrates' wishes, and at Shields
the seamen would 'not allow any of their body to go to jail'. After
the war when the withdrawal of military and naval presence
coincided with the demobilisation of North Eastern tars, the
seamen's 1815 action was hurriedly met with calls for massive
military forces. Magistrate Green wanted cavalry and 'about 200
infantry', Mayor Cramlington wanted nine hundred, magistrate
Fairles, witness 'During the last thirty-five years ... [to] ... disgrace-
ful tumults on the River', wanted a river police. When the seamen
repeated their action the following year, local and central government immediately buckled their belt – five hundred special
constables, regular troops on standby, two Royal Navy sloops
cruising off Tynemouth. In 1818, even the faintest glimmer of
trouble was enough to have Newcastle's Mayor Forster complaining that the area had 'only two weak troops of Horse'.[10] This
jittery decay of confidence was not inconsequential for the pitmen.
Their 1810 dispute involved eventual negotiation but not before
163 had been arrested by the Royal Carmarthen and Forfar Militias
backed by the 4th Dragoons. Scattered colliery actions in North
Durham in 1816 met with a refusal to negotiate and the rapid arrest
and imprisonment of Rainton and Newbottle leaders. As a sign
of the changing climate the *Newcastle Chronicle* thought it
lamentable 'that these men have not yet learned that it is not by

tumult and riot that such an object can be accomplished and that such proceedings only bring misery and ruin upon themselves'.[11]

Ideally, magistrates would have preferred disputing workmen to submit to their judgement. If this was not done and 'tumult and riot' was the resort then, in spite of the magistracy's military weakness, tumult did at least have its own predictability: the game had been played before. What confounded local authority was the disciplined action of poor people who held back from tumult. From the 1790s disciplined mass action became more common, and with it the magistrates' capacity to control became more questioned. The 1765 strike of all Tyne pitmen did eventually open out into sabotage and violence, but at one point both the magistrates and owners were at a loss as to how to deal with it. They had the right to imprison men who had broken their bonds, but as well as a little legal difficulty over exactly when the 1764 bonds expired, there was the greater strategic difficulty of imprisonment. It was

> ... very well, where two or three or a dozen men desert their Service, and has been many times properly executed with good Effect, but where there is a general Combination of all the Pitmen to the Number of 4000, how can this measure take Effect? ... [the House of Correction] does not carry with it the least Appearance of Terror so as to induce the remaining part of so large a Number to submit.

In 1800 the authorities faced a variation on the same problem. At a time when pitmen were in short supply and coal was in high demand, Lord Delaval's Cowpen men refused to work. Imprisoned men could not win coal and effective examples could not be made of men who, at that point, had not rioted:

> ... your Pitmen do neither molest nor threaten any one, but obstinately refuse to go to work. I need not inform your Lordship that under these circumstances they cannot properly be said to be Riotous.[12]

These are only glimpses of a problem which was to become general by the 1830s. It was in their different responses to these early changes which brought local magistrates into conflict with owners during the war years. The owners were intent on tipping the balance of reciprocity in industrial relations their way. The magistrates were not so intent, but their declining self-confidence and growing propensity for panic did not aid their case.

In November 1792 Tyne seamen demanded a rise in voyage-money from £2 10s to 4 guineas. According to the Navy, the seamen seized the river in the traditional manner, and with calmness and civility allowed to sea only those ships which had negotiated the rise. From the magistrates' first attempt to conciliate through the mediation of Capt. Leakey of HMS Racehorse, an aboard ship meeting which failed, they incurred abusive criticism from the shipowners. Thomas Powditch, North Shields shipowner, complained directly to the Prime Minister about magisterial 'supineness' —

> [the owners'] ... experience of near thirty years had convinced them that no reliance could be placed on the magistrates of the River Tyne for the Protection of their property or on County Magistrates for the Protection of either Persons or property.

Powditch ended in a way which was to become characteristic of correspondents, by looking over his shoulder at a 'country cover'd with Thousands of Pitmen, Keelmen, Waggonmen, & other labouring men, Hardy fellows ...' His view was corroborated from an unexpected quarter five days later. Rowland Burdon MP looked uneasily at places like South Shields — fourteen thousand labouring inhabitants, growing, without a magistrate — and claimed acts of violence had already occurred. Yet 'the Magistrates do not think the time yet come to show themselves ... [they] are either diffident of their power, or unwilling to exert it'. Another shipowner, on the other hand, said there had been no violence but still condemned County magistrates for irresolution after their general meeting on the eighth.[13] In spite of such criticism (sent to the highest quarters), and heavy local pressure to intervene against the seamen, the magistrates beavered away and on 13 November won the seamen's agreement to submit to their umpirage. However, on the fourteenth the owners refused terms. Undeterred, the magistrates strove to make the old system work, and five days later managed to effect a settlement. The army acknowledged the split between magistrates and owners and, unfairly, criticised both groups equally for a failure which had resulted in the need to call in troops. The Navy restricted its criticism to the owners who they claimed had not helped the civil power. The Member of Parliament, once he involved himself in negotiations, made amends for his earlier remarks by praising the magistrates' role in the unprecedentedly difficult situation of aggressive shipowners and disciplined seamen:

> There has been thro' the whole of this affair, a degree of system &
> order unknown in former riots, so much so, as to make the Part the
> Magistrates had to act, embarrassing and difficult.[14]

During the 1793 disputes this time it was the coalowners
who pushed the Mayor of Newcastle to ask for a permanent
barracks of horse and pressed the courts to inflict heavy sentences.
The Mayor complied, but magistrates Fenwick and Bigges'
ability to negotiate and settle lost, in the Coal Trade's eyes,
'a fair opportunity ... of making a very necessary example for the
benefit of the Trade ... Alas! The Arm of Justice in this Country
is Nerveless'.[15]

The remaining war years were relatively quiet from the point
of view of civil order. In 1810, magistrate Nesfield negotiated a
settlement in the collieries. However, in 1815 it was the shipowners
who again returned to the offensive, once more going over
magistrates' heads and applying directly to Admiralty and Home
Department for military intervention – 'the step originates with
the Committee alone'.[16] In 1816 Sunderland magistrates were
reported for their lethargy by those 'having some property at
stake',[17] but it was not until 1819 that the view of the magistrates
(at the prospect of political infiltration) finally coalesced with the
demands of property-owners (in dispute with their employees).
At least, the magistracy's revulsion had attracted sufficient
'Military of one sort or other' to use, should their courage be great
enough. In 1819, with the magistrates at last alongside them, it
was left for owners to criticise owners:

> I understand the Men alledge that their employers load the keels with
> more than the usual quantity of 8 Chaldrons (which overquantities the
> Coal Owners give to the Ship Owners instead of reducing the Price and
> only pay the same wages; this is not a time my Lord for Masters to
> do any thing that looks like oppressing their labourers).[18]

The rapid change in protest relations after 1815 was prodded
by political fear, but accelerated by the receding presence of
military force. The war had brought the embodiment of the Militia
and the expansion of fencible and regular forces, continually in
movement across the country, as well as the raising of new irregular
forces – the Volunteer Corps and Armed Associations of 1794–
95, the supplementary Militia in 1796, and the Local Militia in
1808. At any one time local authorities seemed able to call out

a considerable show of force, as at the King's birthday celebrations in 1804 when Newcastle Corporation mustered 8000 uniformed men from a twenty mile radius. Most of these men were irregulars of varying regularity: the Derwent, Gateshead, Sunderland, Usworth, Chester, Hexham, Newcastle, and North and South Shields Volunteers, the Staffs and Fifeshire Militia, the Newcastle and Wallsend Rifle Corps, and the Usworth, Durham, Gibside, and Axwell Cavalry. Only the 7th Dragoon Guards were regulars, and they manoeuvered in the centre.[19] There are occasional examples of ready access to war-time forces in times of industrial dispute – against pitmen in 1800 (Delaval Volunteers) and 1810 (Dragoon Guards, Welsh and Scots Militias), fishermen and seamen in 1806 (Royal Scotch Greys), and seamen in 1814 and 1815 (Royal Marines, Yeomanry Cavalry). The additional threat of the Royal Navy's Impress Service was seen by some as another deterrent. Apart from a short hiatus in 1802–03 the Impress continued active service in the North East from 1793 to 1815. When contending with the major labouring groups, including tradesmen, early in 1793, Joseph Bulmer of South Shields hoped for the press to round up the leaders, and Thomas Sanderson of Sunderland thought the 'Gov. ought to make a sweep among them':

> I am well convinced that a smart Impress among the Keelmen – 300 of them can well be spared – will restore us to peace, but I would *not for the world* that this hint should fall from your lips, so as to find its way by any means to the North.[20]

The following months saw the 'most desperate contest', on ship and off, between the press and seamen, but the Service continued to press. In April, 250 North Shields men were taken and detained aboard armed ships until the regulating officers selected forty of them. By December relations with the seamen had deteriorated so much that the Mayor of Newcastle had to persuade the Impress Officer to stand off.[21] The Newcastle Impress was dismantled for the Amiens peace of 1802–03 but resumed operations with a 'hot press' in 1803. The flow of men from the North East was heavy. Under the manpower levies of 1795 Newcastle and Sunderland together were second only to London. In 1809 the Service played a major part in restoring order after the Tyne keelmen's dispute of that year, and the Admiralty ordered a second 'hot press' the following year. In 1811, when Newcastle was suffering 'many outrages ... in the streets ... chiefly by sailors and ships' carpenters' it was recalled that

> The streets of North Shields were lately infested in the same manner, but a few visits from the impress officers had the effect of restoring good order, and we understand that a good many prime seamen were by that means obtained for the navy.[22]

After the war only the regulars and the Yeomanry remained for serious duty. The regulars were thinly spread, down to 64,000 in 1820 after a wartime peak of 237,000; in August 1819 the whole North Eastern area had only two troops of Dragoon Guards at its disposal.[23] The propertied part-timers of the Yeomanry had disgraced themselves at Peterloo and were 'not men'.[24] Northumberland and Durham had thirteen troops of Yeomanry in 1816, but even during the 1819 scare the Lord Lieutenant of Durham was warning his magistrates against its use at the same time as Mayor Reed of Newcastle was having difficulty in finding volunteers for its service. The aura of incompetence which surrounded the Yeomanry prevailed. In 1830 John Buddle explained to Londonderry that they were a 'laughing Stock':

> I have frequently seen the military called out, in our Pitmen & Keelmen's *sticks* – both Yeomanry and regular Cavalry. The former, were generally, a laughing Stock, to the mob, while the latter were always feared & respected ... A painted Staff, with G R upon it, is more awful, in the hand of a Special Constable, than a Sabre in the hand of the same individual, as a Yeomanry Man.[25]

Given the paucity of regulars and the unreliability of irregulars, authority's response to the mounting challenge after 1815 was strangely scrappy. There were faltering steps towards a regular police, but they were not an effective national force until the second half of the century. Newcastle, Sunderland, and South Shields had small regular police forces in the 1830s, but in spite of (post-strike) 1833 resolutions from magistrates and coalowners for a proper police, encouraged by government hopes for a capitalist-financed regional force, it was not until 1839 that a County force was recruited.[26] Durham's force had only eighty-one officers; nevertheless, it was highly unpopular among rate-payers. In 1841 memorials from 196 townships prayed 'for the dismissal of the Constabulary or for their withdrawal from the rural Districts and relieving them from being taxed for their future support'. The magistrates, whose was the final responsibility, voted against this by a majority of twelve, but when their Lord Lieutenant tried to augment the force after the 1844 pitmen's strike they met him 'with violent opposition'.[27] The piecemeal muster of special constables featured as a response to civil disturbance but the regular army remained the only serious aid to the civil authority from the end of the war to the 1850s. The hardening post-war attitude to protest, the fading of reciprocity, and the unwillingness to form an adequate civil force, meant nothing short of dependence upon the army. The army's nerve was never in doubt, but its presence was provocative and its tactics were resented in an increasingly embattled coalfield.

17
Political Protestants, United Colliers, women

Although the fear of popular politics swayed ruling sensibilities (and reports) in 1819, there is enough evidence to reveal some sort of Radical penetration. The first significant Radical stirrings were in July from 'mostly low Tradesmen ... discussing their rights as they call it'.[1] Soon after Peterloo, radical 'Reading Societies' and Manchester emissaries appeared in Sunderland among those 'chiefly of the lowest description', the South Tyne iron villages of Winlaton, Swalwell, and Blaydon quickly showed their political colours, and seamen and other sections of 'the working classes of the community' were reported at the Newcastle demonstration on 11 October.[2] The local leaders were that classic blend of artisans, workers, and miscellaneous intellectuals: Layton, a schoolmaster; Douglas, 'an Atheistical or Deistical Shoemaker'; Drummond, 'an apple seller in the streets'; Turnbull, a master joiner; Hogarth, a watchmaker; Ramsey, a Wallsend pitman; the Hodgson brothers, weaver and ironman.[3] The pitmen were never the committed revolutionaries of some magistrates' imaginations, but the spectrum of evidence is enough to persuade that in the autumn of 1819 the mining community received its first political education.

In early October, a 'system' of political classes was reported on the Wear, and Tyne colliery representatives were in conference with the Radicals.[4] This was Revd Thorp's information, but his judgement could be less reliable than that of John Buddle. According to him, the Hodgson brothers were effective in the collieries, and the pitmen

> ... went home full of enthusiasm and burnt their Backy, but did not disclose the resolutions of the meeting. It is clear however that their heads are quite full of the 'grand meeting' at Newcastle: and as it is reported that Hunt is to be there, I fully expect that they will lay the pits idle, to go to the meeting, which will occasion the loss of two days work at least.

I don't know what all you clever fellows in London are about, not to send Wooler and his Black Dwarf to the D..l. it is he, who is doing all the mischief amongst us. Hitherto *we* have fought our Cocks, drunk our *yell* & chewed our *Backy* quietly. and on a pay night amused ourselves with a 'canny bit on a fight, nobit to ken whee was the best hewer'. But now we read the Black Dwarf, damn the *Greatins*, burn our *Backy*, and talk of *'puttin aw t'reets'*. Why don't you send Wooler to Botany-bay & melt his types into pewter spoons?

Hunt did not attend the grand meeting on the eleventh but contingents of pitmen did. That they took time off work to attend to politics is complicated by the fact that the Durham pitmen's favourite fair, the Houghton Feast, was held on the ninth, and that usually involved some holiday. At Hebburn, one consequence of the meeting was that the pitmen asked for increased prices to compensate them for despotic taxation.[5] For the rest of October classes were reported as forming in the North Durham and Tyne collieries, with centres at Penshaw and Hebburn. At Mount Moor colliery on Gateshead Fell 'all the Pitmen except 5 have joined the Radicals'; at Heaton colliery classes doubled in a few days and 'one Rick Wilson' was reported to be training them in 'the exercise of the Pike' with a stick 'as to be used both against Cavalry and Infantry'; at Penshaw the pitmen read and executed the rule-book of the Political Protestants:

> The Colliers here meet every evening in the Fields ... They ... frighten everybody into complete subjection, by what they call 'marking'. If the Landlord of a public House says, or does anything real, or imaginary, to offend them, he is *marked*, and no one will enter his house again, until he makes his peace with them & the same thing with Shop keepers & Tradesmen of every description. Hence we have the 'Shoemaker of the People' − the 'Taylor to the People' etc.[6]

From this late-October peak, November was quiet − Buddle thought the crisis was over − and the December reports clearly reflected the respective states of confidence of the reporter: the pitmen were either secretive, or sullen, but they were not demonstrative. Apart from some demand for higher wages, politicisation brought no industrial action, and by January 1820 the tide had turned.[7]

Unless the impact of the Six Acts late in 1819 was greater than previous repressive legislation, it is hard to know what to make of this climax and recession unless one sees it in revivalist terms.

Certainly in their prohibition of large meetings, duties on news-papers, and extended powers to magistrates to search and arrest, the Acts must have had a silencing effect, but enthusiasm appears to have been waning before December and it could be that the contemporaneous Methodist encounter described in Part Two is relevant here. Both the sudden prescience of the political inspiration, and the unexpected speed of colliery recruitment, 'with the rapidity of lightning', suggest parallel experiences:

> Until within these few weeks, our Colliers ... never troubled their heads with politics. But within a very short period, their very nature in this respect seems to have been completely changed.[8]

The Political Protestants grouped in classes of twenty to learn. A new class leader was elected monthly and subscriptions were one penny per week. The class existed to pursue practical politics, but its essential duty was to 'read or cause to be read interesting extracts from papers and other political publications' because 'We sincerely believe that political ignorance has been the principle cause of all our unparrallell'd misery and degradation'. Recommended works were Major Cartwright's *Bill of Rights*, Wade's *Black Book*, Bentham's *Reform Catechism*, Cobbett 'On gold', Sherwin's *Political Register*, and Wooler's *Black Dwarf*. The *Black Dwarf* was everywhere and was everywhere spoken against. One zealot went so far as to propose the withdrawal of licences from 'every Ale House, Spirits Shop, Eating House' which took it. It was 'received with avidity', was sold to 'murderous effect' and was said 'to be found in the Hat Crown of almost every pitman you meet'.[9] How the community received the shining reason of Radical politics it is difficult to tell. The pitmen and their families left no record of this education. Those who observed them saw only sedition and misinformation where the class leader contrived only to 'dispel their supposed prejudices'. Classes in sedition were represented as political scrimmages crouched round their leaders, where 'conversation is carried on in a low tone' to 'prevent disclosures' to cupped-hand-to-ear magistrates. The pitmen's capacity for learning was described in a way which only reflected the prevailing prejudices of the Trade itself. The pitmen's ignorant belief in universal suffrage was, they said, a belief 'That we shall all suffer together'; the pitmen's greedy belief in state reform was, they said, a belief 'that their wages for 160 days out of 260 working days ... goes to pay Taxes ... They extend their views of *reform* to every subject'.[10] Little can be learned from these fleeting observations. More important than their intellectual instruction was the Political Protestants' stress on the need for self-control. The movement put itself into the hands of the class leader who was to discipline the political activity of his members: if a member 'does not reform, he is to be expelled, as unworthy of associating with the true hearted friends of the people'. The very act of associating, by rules, to learn, was a controlled form of protest which Mackenzie said 'rendered them sober and thoughtful'.[11] At the Newcastle demonstration, Hodgson the ironman, after an astonishing peroration on English Law, Taxation, Socrates, and United States of America, finished on the politics of Order. Order assayed the people and challenged an enemy who could only recognise a mob: 'If you wish them to drink vinegar at your expense gentlemen, go home when you leave this place, and do not let them say you were guilty of the slightest disorder or irregularity'. And 'vinegar' was swallowed: the classes marched away, no stragglers were left behind, the Shields seamen refused their ale, drank water, and proved their mettle. The government was notified that 'A most formidable Meeting passed off without Tumult, but the order and organization of such a Body was more frightful, as to the future, than Violence'.[12]

The first open declaration of a formal miners' union came in 1825. As we have seen, a *Brotherhood* had existed since 1804, and although it had fought trade union actions particularly, and with some success in 1810, it had only publicly admitted to a friendly society role. This was due to its position in law. The basis of all English law rested on the idea of a contracting property-owning society. As such, the law was inherently hostile to all combinations of workers, a hostility shown in the forty or so eighteenth-century statutes against combination in specific trades, and in the predilection of judges to view all combinations as criminal conspiracies. Breach of contract was another common charge, and although pitmen's actions could be timed with the ending of their contract, the Bond, the Combination Acts of 1799 and 1800 comprehensively banned all combinations whatever their timing or objective. Yet the government was not inclined to bring prosecutions. It had hoped that a comprehensive banning, and summary justice, would be bait enough to tempt employers to prosecute. But employers were not inclined to bring prosecutions either. They feared the expense, the reprisals, the rivalry of other employers, and looked back to government: the government feared the burden, the partiality of such a role, and the grotesque inversion that impartiality would bring should they be asked to prosecute combinations of employers. Thus the pitmen, clearly in association during the twenty-five years the Acts were on the statute book, were not prosecuted. There were other ways in which the Coal Trade could deal with Brotherhoods, and they were in hand. The repeal of the Acts in 1824–5 (5 Geo IV, c95, 6 Geo IV c129, s. 1) greatly encouraged workers' combinations to come into the open, even if the Act of 1825 only permitted their liberty to associate and little else. Certainly, actions in pursuit of combinatory objectives were generally unlawful, a hard fact which trade unions were to learn in the courts over the next fifty years. Nevertheless, repeal in 1824–5 appeared to clarify the situation and a dissembled combination within a reticulate Brotherhood emerged in 1825 as the United Association of Colliers on the Rivers Tyne and Wear with a preamble to their rule book which listed the Acts since 1793 which had made their insurance and combinatory practices lawful. The new Association began on the Tyne in March, had a delegate structure by July, and seems to have entrenched itself on both rivers by October. Hetton colliery assumed leadership and graced itself with a purpose-built union hall the following year.[13]

The United Colliers were a union of hewers postulating a political economy on the side of those who created value. Rejecting the traditional techniques of direct action, their first objective was to counter Coal Trade encroachments and to achieve some systematic control over their conditions of work. Over the whole body sat the General Committee of elected representatives from each colliery, meeting monthly at the Cock Inn in Newcastle and appointed for one year. Below them sat colliery sub-committees, elected from the membership and meeting every fortnight, whose job it was to collect subscriptions (4½d per fortnight), to regulate membership (hewers only, with normal friendly society actuarial safeguards), and to review rules and policy. The Association observed usual friendly society functions and sought to regulate the commodity market by restricting coal output (no more than 4s 6d per man for an eight hour day, surplus to be surrendered to the union). It also monitored the labour market by the issue of transfer certificates to migrating members and by insisting that all bindings be approved by an appointed solicitor.[14] Although members were barred from 'speaking against the King or his government' during union business, the United Colliers' apologetics were prompted by a political reason. Reason was 'the gift of God to man', but God's gift annulled God's mysteries: 'In proportion as this benevolent doctrine [Christianity] is received and acted upon by mankind, will vice, oppression, extortion, and every evil be diminished'. Men had to act to avoid their own degradation. Restriction of coal output and control of labour input would check competition, 'an infamous system' under which they laboured, whilst their own discipline would 'avoid uproar and confusion' and give the owners the opportunity to restructure the industry.[15] The United Colliers spoke as men who knew their own value within a political economy of capital and labour. They organised and reasoned after a blend of friendly society prudence and Radical enlightenment.[16] Buddle referred to the 'long heads' and 'wrong heads' amongst them: the former wished to build the union and restrict output and so distend a change, the latter were 'for trying their strength at the ensuing binding'. The latter had their way at the 1826 binding after a more uniform Bond had been introduced, and the Trade tried to victimise local leaders. The response was uneven, the strike was defeated, and the United Colliers refrained from combat although Hetton remained the leading colliery. In 1829 Thomas Hepburn, Charles Parkinson, and the brothers Robert and Christopher Haswell − all leaders in 1831 − were working side by side there as hewers.[17]

The structures of the Association were reported to be hardening again in March 1831. It is likely that they had remained intact since the mid-1820s and were now preparing themselves for united action against the 1831 Bond. There is some difficulty here because although their organisation remained, the 'United Colliers' title appears to have been dropped for the 'Friendly Society' title in June 1831 as most of the coalfield friendly societies were incorporated.[18] For the next eighteen months the organisation was popularly referred to as either the 'Pitmen's Union' or 'Hepburn's Union'.

Part One traced the chronology of 1831−32; Part Two explained the role of the preacher vanguard. There can be no doubt that Hepburn and the delegates wielded unprecedented power. The membership was now bigger, including all colliery workers who were natives of the coalfield, and not just the hewers. Moreover, in spite of arguments within the union over the conduct of the action, Hepburn's eventual tactic of support for those branches which had not settled from those which had, within an overall strategy of restricted output, represented a revolutionary change in coalfield protest. The 1831–2 contests were seen by later generations of trade unionists as the beginning of their history and the end of their pre-history. By will-power and persuasion the delegates held the Union together. They recognised the central fact that a relapse into traditional methods of direct action against an ownership which despised their existence, a magistracy no longer so given to reciprocity, and an armed force primed by a government in crisis would be instantly crushed. Moreover, they recognised that to be crushed would bury any hopes of stemming the deterioration in work and status which they had experienced for over twenty years.

The personal sway of the delegates was known to be crucial. At the beginning, Buddle had greedily looked for dissension between leaders and led; near the end, he had to admit that 'Hepburn and his colleagues are indefatigueable ... to keep the spirit of the thing alive'. In April 1831 the Trade admitted to the spirit 'which binds them together', and only in January 1833 could they pronounce that 'Hepburn & his brother delegates' can no longer 'keep up the esprit de Corps'.[19] Delegates were libelled and ridiculed in the press for

> ... unsettling men's minds by their preposterous and nonsensical doctrines, teaching them to consider their masters as ruthless tyrants, unreasonable and unjust task-masters, slave drivers & c., and designate honest labour to be worse than negro slavery, Egyptian bondage & c., and decent servitude, unworthy degradation, abject dependence, slavish submission & c., and put the unmeaning (in their case) words of liberty! independence! & c. into their mouths.

> ... Deputies Hepburn, Arkle, Atkinson, and others of them ... having 'the gift of the gab' find it much easier to speechify about 'natural rights' than to dig coal; and much more profitable to have the fingering of the Union Funds than to be simply in the receipt of wages produced by honest industry.[20]

From the beginning of the dispute in April 1831, to Londonderry's collapse in the May and its domino-effect on the Trade, to near total victory in June leading to control throughout the summer, Hepburn's delegates assumed an increasing power. As the union swelled with colliery carpenters, smiths, wagoners, and enginemen during April and May so did its ambition mount. There was April talk of bringing 'all classes of labourers into it ... even the Farmer's servants', and May talk 'of fixing a maximum price on Corn, Butchers Meat etc., And ... to raise the Wages of their Women who work in the Fields'. By the end of May, delegates were in the fields fixing milk prices with farmers and meat prices with butchers; in June they were negotiating with retailers. The June victory even inclined the 'petty-officer group', overmen, deputies, wastemen and sinkers, into union ranks. Buddle weakly joked that he saw 'nothing left for the Viewers & Agents but to do the same'. Restriction meant that the men at the coal-face, and not the viewers, determined production: this was seen as the seat of power. The pitmen 'found & established their power', working 'steadily at their own rate'.[21] But more than this fundamental inversion of authority, the union sought to pervade at every level. Under weekly instructions from the delegates the men tried to determine the number and nature of the work-force, the appointment of managers, the appropriate kind of work for the old and infirm, and the contractual conditions of the Bond.[22]

The union strove for control under the wary eye of the army. Apart from the recruitment of special constables, some little-used Yeomanry, and the importation of a squad of Metropolitan police into Hetton, the problem of order lay with Major General Sir Henry Bouverie. When the threat of disorder was greatest, in the spring of 1832, Bouverie commanded a force which he considered unequal to the task.[23]

At first Bouverie had been persuaded by the owners to force the opening of key collieries. He did this at Lumley on 7 April 1831, but a counter-attack by unionists three weeks later, accompanied by incessant demands from the owners to force more collieries, led the Major General to reappraise the situation. On 8 and 22 May, having realised the Trade had put him in a position he did not want, Bouverie refused their requests to force more collieries, and told them he would not protect non-working collieries, a 'Rule which I have laid down ... [because it is] ... absolutely necessary to draw a line somewhere'.[24] Reluctant to be drawn into the battlefield of Capital and Labour the line Bouverie opted to draw was the traditional one of upholding law and order by the soldier's 'prestige of mastery'. If Bouverie saw Capital's battle with Labour as distasteful, he saw the magistrates' pursuit of law and order as artless. In May 1832, obliged to protect blacklegs and uphold order while hired ruffians turned families out of colliery houses, the magistrates slid into fights with the community. At Friars Goose, on the Tyne, after first being repulsed by fist fighting, the constables returned to a gun battle where they were defeated for a second time, their carbines were broken and thrown into the river, and their number scattered: the 'pitmen fought gallantly and charged the 1st Division of Constables – overthrew & disarmed them'. Only the arrival of cavalry, and forty-one arrests, saved the day. Bouverie knew the courage of his adversaries and the delicacy of his mastery. He rebuked the magistrates for their incompetence: they must never again act

> ... in a loose and desultory manner without Consent or Communication, [or] the result must inevitably be that the Constables will be overcome and discouraged, the new hands will be frightened away, and the engagement of others rendered unprofitable, and the troops being always called for after the thing is over, will in a very short time become the laughing stock of the Country ...[25]

For their part, the magistrates began with the intention of fulfilling their traditional role and suggested to both sides that they might arbitrate. Mayor Reed of Newcastle was not very sanguine about the chances of this for, as he told Colonel Sir Henry Rofs, 'so far from the Coal Owners being anxious to come to an immediate accomodation with their Workmen the very reverse is the case' – they hoped a shortage would raise coal prices. Reed also suspected that as long as magistrates and army held the ring the owners could look forward to higher prices and a sound thrashing of the union; he was consequently anxious 'to throw those Gentlemen upon their own resources'.[26] On 7 April Northumberland magistrates made their offer of arbitration. This embarrassed the owners. Keen for the fight, they feared arbitration would be seen as 'cribling' to the union; on the other hand, a refusal to negotiate would be bad for their public image. On 11 April owners, delegates, and magistrates met to talk, but on the following day delegates and owners met without inviting the third party. The magistrates withdrew as arbitrators and reverted to law and order. It seems from this juncture that most of the *active* magistrates were men

with interests in the Trade. Bouverie particularly disliked this
feature of the civil power, and after the disputes were over and
the union was beaten, a government report strongly urged the
appointment of stipendiary magistrates in the coal districts for 'as
the majority of magistrates in this District being themselves Owners
or interested in Collieries – their Decisions and proceedings were
often liable to misrepresentation'.[27]

The senior courts took a harsh anti-union view from the outset.
Sentences at the Durham Assizes in 1831 and 1832 were heavy.[28]
At the trial of the pitman William Jobling, accomplice in the
murder of the elderly magistrate and shipowner, Nicholas Fairles,
Mr Justice Parke took the opportunity to say that the deed 'might
be directly attributed to those combinations ... [which must] ...
one day or other, be put down':

> I am afraid this is one of the melancholy consequences of that combi-
> nation amongst workmen which has prevailed in this country for so
> long a time ... To that cause I attribute that want of moral principle
> which could induce you to stand by and assist a person in inflicting
> a mortal blow on that Magistrate ...[29]

Parke was no doubt stiffened in his animus by the Home Secretary's
letter to all magistrates in the North East two weeks before.
Melbourne reminded them to be vigilant against violent, unjust,
seditious, tumultuous, and inflammatory trade union actions, and
in so doing affirmed where the government's sympathy would lie.
Parke, 'after placing the awful emblem of justice on his head',
sentenced Jobling to be hung, covered in pitch, encased in iron
stirrups and bars, and then re-hung in chains at the scene of the
crime. On 3 August 1832, flanked by fifty cavalry, eight Hussars,
and fifty foot, Jobling's coffin-carriage trundled from its Durham
City scaffold through the colliery district to the Shields turnpike
at Jarrow Slake. There, his head thrown back and his face covered
in a white sheet, Jobling's body was raised to swing in the river
wind 'as a warning to all others'.[30]

The owners welcomed the conflict. Although always capable
of internal disunity, the Trade saw the union as an external threat
which could bear no compromise. Once they had recovered from
Londonderry's May 1831 desertion and the pitmen's subsequent
victory, they resolved to break the union utterly. In January 1832
they began a fighting-fund, in March they decided not to bind
anyone who was a member of the union, in May they embarked

upon the mass evictions and blacklegging.[31] If the army could be persuaded to go beyond their duty, then so much the better. On 27 May 1832 Bouverie told the Home Office that magistrates, whom by now he saw as synonymous with owners, were trying to alarm him with stories of the pitmen's capacity for insurrection. Bouverie admitted he had yet to see such acts — 'nor do I believe that they seriously entertain any such notion' — but as the army beheld the owners' intransigence then they grew more and more uncomfortable.[32] On 12 June the leading coalowner and magistrate, Robert Brandling, summarily dismissed Bouverie's suggestion that the owners should negotiate, and clearly stated that it must be a fight to the finish. After this Bouverie could be in no doubt, and five days later he despondently viewed the prospect of pitmen's defeat by starvation in a region where lives and property were defended only by 'almost military occupation'.[33]

Hepburn's first strike statement was an exhortation to

... keep good order, and every man to take care of and protect his neighbour and prevent injury being done to any one. He would allow no person to be stripped, as had been threatened to strangers coming amongst them; and should any transgress the order, or occasion any breach of the peace, he would himself represent such person to the magistrate, and get the delinquent punished; as it was only by good order and a peaceable demeanour they could hope to obtain the approbation of the magistracy and the good will of the community at large. A cart with ale, he observed, had been brought on the ground; the object of the proprietor was well known, it was to make money; but he hoped none of his bretheren would taste it, or encourage him; let him go elsewhere and sell his ale ...

It will be asked, how are pitmen to better their condition? the answer is, by union and fidelity one man to another.[34]

These words were not protocol, they were strategy. They may be compared to a coalowner's view that without troops to frighten them, the pitmen may 'do as they please'. It is clear that if Bouverie worried about the forms of prestige and mastery of a previous era, the union looked to new forms of (its own) prestige and mastery. William Scott, and the delegates themselves, gave notice of the demise of reciprocity and the new elements of protest:

... satisfy the public that you are not that idle, disorderly, demi savage crew, which your oppressors wish to represent you ... Be, therefore doubly guarded in your conduct by night and by day, at home and

abroad. To transport or hang a few of you would feast the savage eyes
and hearts of your enemies ...

But I would counsel you, to a man, to be doubly guarded against that
individual amongst your own body who proposes to offer violence or
injury ... let PEACE and ORDER be your motto ... for on this alone
depends your ultimate victory ... Many efforts may probably be made
by your enemies to entrap some of you into a breach of the peace, and,
after so entrapping you, they will then have what you have not hitherto
given them viz. a shadow of an excuse for calling out the soldiers ...
to overawe you by calling out many of your sons and brothers, armed
with a gun and bayonet, to frighten you ...

To accomplish their own sinister purposes, they have employed every
means, every stratagem, in their power, but hitherto in vain − viz.
hiring the Press to circulate statements which the least boy that enters
the Coal Mine can contradict − threatening to starve us! − swearing
in Special Constables to intimidate us! − calling up the Yeomanry
Cavalry and bringing troops, both horse and foot, from various parts
of the Kingdom, and also some Naval force − In some cases the Riot
Act has been threatened to be read amongst us, when peaceably
assembled to discuss our grievances! All this has been done with a view
to intimidate us, and, we believe, to excite us to a breach of the peace;
but, thank God, hitherto without any effect, or indeed any prospect
of accomplishing their wicked purposes.[35]

These were not the words of the politically innocent. On the
contrary, they were calculated efforts to politicise perspectives.
Hepburn and his delegates sought to take actions off the streets
and frame them in a context of political economy, to give the
membership an understanding of their whole oppression, to
forfeit the traditional impulse to act directly, and replace it
with a reasoning organisation which carried out its own policy:
'Knowledge is Power'. Scott reiterated the ideology of the Political
Protestants and the United Colliers − the feudal slavery of
the Bond, the liberty of Reason, the value of Labour, and the
dignity of Englishness. Hepburn called for a reading, thinking, and political community with a library in every village;
he challenged the silent owners to debate where 'he would beat
them at all points'. The delegates praised the Northern Political
Union, defended their personal morality, and denied smears
that they were 'wild and frenzied' preachers − far from this,
the preachers had 'by their character ... made use of this influence
to repress the forward from acts of violence'. Delegates Arkle
and Edgar made the case:

They were at first described as a few wild and visionary enthusiasts; and afterwards as a lawless banditti of ignorant savage barbarians ... But did their opponents know that the more any society of men are persecuted, the firmer becomes their bond of union? Let them examine history, religious and civil, and the proofs would be found ...

The Delegates, though they had been reviled, had been acknowledged to display intelligence as well as intellect. They were valiant in their cause − not with zeal without knowledge, but with zeal governed by knowledge.[36]

In the early stages, when the Trade sent two emissaries to the Cock to meet the General Committee and dissuade them from negotiating through the magistrates, they

... found the Delegates assembled, to the amt. of about 200 all seated, at tables so contrived as to bring them all into one large room. Hebburn [sic] was chairman, & Dixon (of Cowpen) was secretary − Pen, Ink, and Paper was placed at the corners of all the tables. When Hunter & Forster were introduced by a Backworth delegate, Hebburn was on his legs speaking. After reprimanding the delegate, for having introduced 'the Viewers' so unceremoniously without first duly announcing them, & stating the object of their visit − they were asked, what they came there for?[37]

Hepburn's etiquette of the educated was not for all. He was never such a complete master of the collieries as he was of the Cock Inn. His first call for discipline was hardly made when there were direct attacks on Netherton, Bedlington, and Jesmond collieries. Pit-head gear was smashed and burning hay was thrown after it down the shaft. The men struck at midnight, 'spoke not a word − nothing was heard but the trampling of feet'. In May 1831, with the Wear owners out of the contest and the dismayed Tyne owners beginning tentative evictions, viewers and agents were subjected to the traditional intimidations − burning effigies, rough music, harassment on the roads, attacks on their homes:

A system of terror and annoyance ... against the Viewers & Agents of all the Colls. which have not complied ... Men assemble in the night dressed in Women's clothes, fire guns and pistols, break their Windows, destroy their Gardens etc. etc.[38]

In June and July harassment continued against those owners who were pressing convictions at the Assizes, and at South Moor six arrested men were rescued from the constables. Nevertheless, the first round of struggle passed with general surprise at the system and order of the pitmen. In their collective strength, by the rule book, they had 'surpassed all previous expectations'.[39]

Apart from a mass attack on the working Waldridge colliery in December 1831, an attack which was not missed as an opportunity to spite the union − ('Where were these reasonable, restraining ... unionists upon this occasion?') − Hepburn managed to control affairs through to the next binding in April 1832. By then it was obvious that the owners intended to destroy the union. Bouverie saw that the spring policy of eviction and blacklegging could only provoke violence and grieved at the prospect. He prayed that the men would now see the folly of their ways.[40]

The avalanche of violence Bouverie predicted broke quickly in April with a 5 am attack on South Shields colliery, the daring rescue of those arrested, and the murder of the blackleg, Errington, at Hetton − a shooting which it may have been that Hepburn had some forewarning about and had strived to prevent.[41] In May there were pitched battles and mass arrests at Friars Goose (Tyne Main colliery), in June the magistrate Fairles was murdered, and in July the pitman Cuthbert Skipsey was shot dead by a policeman during a repulsed attack on Chirton High pit.[42] As evictions mounted and blacklegs arrived from all over the country, the invitation to localised, direct actions increased. As they increased then so did the provocative presence of army and police. Hepburn's control fell like sand through his fingers. Privately, the owners understood the delegates' dilemma:

> They prefer Boldon Fell, as being out of the immediate neighbourhood of any Colliery − to keep the men out of the way of doing mischief as much as possible ... For Genl. Hepburn, like the Duke of York, can lead his Men into the field, but cannot answer for bringing them off again'.[43]

By August, the union's control of its members had completely broken down, and the cholera had arrived. Hepburn's union was effectively finished.

The owners had slain the beast but some of them learned from its activities. They set about forming their own friendly societies where the pitmen surrendered control in exchange for the owners' payment of one-sixth contributions. These were not successful as abandonment of the union was a precondition of membership.[44] Others appreciated the shift in protest the union had represented.

Major General Bouverie, if not Viscount Melbourne or Mr Justice Parke, had learned that unions were not about violence or direct action; the Radical, Mackenzie, saluted the preacher vanguard in 1834 for 'exciting the men to union, perseverance, and order'; the coal viewer Henry Morton told the commissioner in 1842 that 'It is much to their credit that, during the great strike ... scarcely a solitary instance of the destruction of colliery machinery occurred'; and, such are the refractions of history, the mid-Victorian minister Walters could later praise the men of 1831 as creatures of his sunday schools.[45]

Women were involved in the union's business but not in a manner which Revd Walters or other later commentators saw as fit to mention. They emerge in the latter stages as intimidators of those men who went to work. At South Shields, crowds of men and women gathered daily to make blacklegs run the gauntlet; at Benwell, gangs of women − 'Amazonian assailants', according to the *Newcastle Journal* − harassed working miners; at Friars Goose, women ran with the men against evictors and special constables.[46] For these women, and for generations of women before them who participated in and sometimes led direct actions, the new formulations of 'womanhood' from the 1830s onward represented something other than their 'natural' state.[47] Elizabeth Parkin attacked swinging a stone in a stocking, and the woman at Wideopen who assaulted the Welshman Davies with a poker hit him so hard that he knew nothing more until he awoke bleeding, on a slag heap a quarter of a mile away. Maria Carr was evicted from her home still sitting in her chair, cheering on the protesting crowd with a bailiff's hat in her fist.[48]

In spite of their daring − some would choose to say, criminality − women such as these were only extras in the union's struggle. Their deeds were marginal, and only occurred to the extent that Hepburn and the delegates lost their influence. Seen from the union's point of view these acts of limited and direct violence were relics of a technique of protest which should have had its day. However, to say this is not to say that women were incidental figures in the history of coalfield protest. The union was a male organisation; that women were not central to its activities is hardly surprising. Instead, women had their own sites of struggle and protest − poverty and housing in particular − which, although more intensive during periods of lock-out and eviction cannot be

solely measured in terms of lock-out and eviction. A history of
these sites demands from the historian another set of themes and
a different chronological sense. It also demands a conscious urge
to recover female experiences subsumed in the chapters of other
histories − of the Poor Law, of housing, of public health. The
new and recovered themes would focus on the lives of women as
the prime bearers of family need and as the major administrators
of the domestic economy. Trade union brotherhoods, conditions
of mining, bonds, fines, accidents, and status would be replaced
by more emphatically female categories of experience: women's
box clubs, mutuality, family, poor relief, sanitation, overcrowding,
widowhood, and personal morality. Similarly, the key chronological references would be different. 1804, 1810−11, 1819,
1831−2, 1844, are dates for male protest in ways that they are not
for female protest. The New Poor Law from 1834, or Ashley's
Act of 1842, or schooling initiatives from the late 1840s, or various
dates from the 1880s when new water supplies or houses were built,
would loom larger. One might even have to expect another kind
of chronology: the public, collective struggles of men lend themselves to set pieces and crucial dates; the more private and personal
struggles of women do not. Such a history would look so different
that what can be attempted here is only a mapping of the ground.

The New Poor Law came as a particular problem for the women
of the coalfield. The 1834 Poor Law Amendment Act (4&5 Will.IV,
c.76) sought to remove poor relief as a factor in the determination
of wage levels by limiting relief to the workhouse, and by making
the workhouse regime 'less eligible' for those who elected to be
there than the conditions of life for the lowest paid labourer outside its doors. By doing this it was hoped that the New Poor Law
would benefit the nation by clearing the labour markets for the
untrammelled operation of supply and demand − 'labour' would
be encouraged to work, and work at the market price. As women,
and widows especially, were the major recipients of poor relief
in the coalfield, this ideology and practice bore directly upon them.
Their predicament within the Poor Law paralleled the pitmen's
predicament within the coal industry: both were subjected to
pressures to expose them to market forces.[49]

In fact, the northern Poor Law Unions understood from the
outset that the less eligibility principle was inappropriate for the
coalfield. Numbers of able-bodied male paupers was miniscule.

In 1844 for instance, Chester le Street and Easington Unions had no paupers in that category; their major recipients were 113 widows and 285 children, and sixty-six widows and 114 children respectively, and these people were all supported, in their homes, by out-relief payments. Relief expenditure in the coalfield was low, and the Unions wanted to keep it that way.[50] Poverty, it seems, fluctuated for families, and was largely absorbed by the women operating through dense kinship networks. To distend that poverty which was not absorbed, or only partly absorbed, into pauperism, by limiting relief to the workhouse would be as expensive as it was stupid. In 1838, twenty-five Houghton Guardians protested to the Commissioners in London

> ... that from the Working Class in this Mining District being so inter-married and related to each other, those who may need parochial relief can be and have been kept considerably cheaper and better by giving them Weekly relief and allowing them to remain with their friends, than could possibly be done by keeping them in the Workhouse.[51]

The sixty-nine year old widow living in a Thornley Coal Company cottage in 1845 received 1s 6d per week out-relief. The non-resident widow living in a colliery cottage with a coal allowance and 'personal help from friends and neighbours', received 2s per week. From the point of view of the local Guardians it was absurd to have to argue with the Commissioners whether these widows – a socially useful group in the villages – should or should not be helped.[52] Although some wives lived a casual relationship with the Poor Law, being 'deserted' by their husbands from Mondays to Fridays, receiving indoor assistance accordingly, the local Guardians were fully aware that some of this desertion was only a pretence and were not worried by it. They insisted that widows and children were their major category, that widows were poor but not idle, that colliery accidents had often been the cause of their widowhood and that there was no pretence in that, and that out-relief was convenient, cheap, and sensible.[53]

The women's first struggle then, after the struggle with poverty itself, was with the Poor Law Commissioners. The Commissioners' ideology was unyielding but the 1834 Act had left local Guardians with discretionary powers which they largely chose to use. These powers were wide in the case of the non-able-bodied, and even existed for the able-bodied. In the decade between 1842 and 1852 the Commissioners tried to constrain discretion in the latter case, and in the north their efforts were specifically applied to the mining districts. The 1834 Report, with little evidence, had warned how parish relief had aided the pitmen in their recent dispute; relief had acted, it was claimed, as a 'branch bank to the Pitmen's Union'.[54] This view persisted. Of all labouring groups, the miners and their taste for trade unionism had to be discouraged. Outdoor Labour Test Orders in 1842 and Outdoor Relief Prohibition Orders in 1844 were deployed against the pit villages. In February 1844, two months before the beginning of the strike, Assistant Commissioner Hawley instructed the Guardians responsible for Wylam colliery in Northumberland that miners' Restriction policies had forfeited their right to relief even when it had been the owners who had temporarily closed the colliery and caused the destitution. When the strike began, families in the Easington Union arranged to be 'deserted' by husbands and fathers 'with the intention of throwing their wives and families on their respective townships'. Out-relief was refused under the Outdoor Labour Test Order; the women would have to enter the workhouse – 'many of the women left the board room threatening to take their children to the overseer at night'.[55] In 1852 the Commissioners' third attempt to limit local discretion came with the General Outdoor Relief Regulation Order. This Order, number 27182/52, urged Guardians to refuse all out relief to the able-bodied except in the most exceptional and stringently regulated cases. The Easington Guardians responded by threatening their resignation. The Sunderland Guardians saw it as a slur on their integrity, and warned that they would continue to go their own way. From the correspondence it is clear that able-bodied poverty was a regular, if short-lived, experience in the pit villages for which any system other than out-relief was wholly inappropriate.[56] The Guardians were the ones in a position to quarrel, resign, or refuse. It was not they who were poor, or who suffered the policy, however formulated. If the women's struggle was indirect it was nonetheless real.

The women's second struggle was similar, and this was with the coalowners. Local Guardians wanted to keep to an out-relief system because it was cheap. The northern area in general had a high percentage of working-class residents and low-rated property. If the Guardians tussled with the Poor Law Commissioners over policy, they also tussled with local companies over rate assessment.

This was true in the coalfield in spite of the fact that there, poor relief expenses were falling as working populations grew.[57] Coalowners acted, it would appear knowingly, to keep rate assessments for their properties lower than what they should have been. Monkwearmouth overseers had a serious rates litigation with Monkwearmouth colliery in 1835–6. In 1836, Sir John Walsham, Assistant Commissioner for the region, lamented the £30,000 paid annually in rates: he imagined, given the great coal wealth of the district, a figure 'quintuple that amount might be nearer the mark'.[58] Underrating appears to have been going on since before the New Poor Law. In 1829 John Buddle briefed Lord Londonderry for the forthcoming Parliamentary inquiry into the Coal Trade. From points one to eight Buddle outlined their case, but on point nine he demurred. Short-time was

> ... a delicate point to notice, as the Collieries do not maintain their own poor. They only pay with the Lands according their Rental for the time being, and when they cease to work, they leave the Lands burthen with the whole load of paupers they have created. I therefore submit that your Lordship should not touch upon this point.[59]

None of these policy and rating matters were resolved during the period of this study. It was the case, and it continued to be the case for the rest of the century, that apart from tiny amounts of out-relief, as well as the owners' maintenance of widows in company cottages – although not usually their original cottages – the mining community cared for itself in sickness and in death. The friendly societies, small and large, registered and unregistered, were the agents of this in the first half of the century and female societies appear to have been common.[60] Their distinctive role in relationship to the men's societies, other than the obvious degree of autonomy and control they conferred on women, is not clear. The Women's Box Society at the 'Sign of the Hawk, Gateshead', or the Friendly Society of Women in Easington Lane, were typical in that they shared similar objectives, rules, and customs as the male societies. Actuarial safeguards were primary, as was organisational discipline, and women members were obliged to submit to the majority, drink at funerals, not swear, fight, gamble, speak out of turn, 'bear a bastard', or bring children to meetings 'except such as suck at the breast'. Some female societies had male treasurers, and others, such as the teetotal Female Rechabites urged the same moral imperatives, with a female nomenclature, as the male versions.[61] Whatever the form and objectives of their association, coalfield women looked to each other and not to a careless patronage or a begrudging poor relief for their insurance.[62] Later, when pitmen's organisations achieved stability and solvency it may have been that women's efforts were rendered more marginal. The Hartley Relief Fund was set up in 1862 to administer help to the 116 widows and 274 children left destitute by the death of 204 men and boys in a colliery accident. The Fund was plainly necessary, and it seems to have been properly administered, but female claimants were only assessed through a male line of what their male relatives did, or who they were: 'the case of the Widow of the late John Manderson ... the first to volunteer to enter the Shaft ... took as loop as he stood week day clothes on'.[63] The same was true of the benefit role of the Northumberland and Durham Permanent Relief Fund, set up by the miners after Hartley, and the Durham Miners' Association from the 1870s. Between 1862 and 1880 the Relief Fund dealt with 65,000 disablement claims; in 1892, with assets of £142,495, it looked after 1,008 widows, 1,269 children, and the 950 permanently disabled. Most of this was miners' money. The coalowners had contributed between 5% and 10%; since 1875, the royalty owners had contributed £11. In addition to this astonishing act of collective insurance, the Durham Miners' Association had paid out £194,000 in sick and death benefits between 1881 and 1890, exclusively miners' money for other pitmen and their dependents.[64] The Aged Miners' Homes Scheme was soon to follow to save the old from poor relief. The effect of such vastly impressive association, alongside the work of the national friendly societies, if it saved women from the Poor Law must have also been to save them from their own insurance practices. Apart from the women's friendly societies, the houses they had to administer, and the informal networks of family and street, the history of women's struggle with poverty is the history of dependency, of the muteness, loss, or neglect of female protest, and its channelling into dominantly male forms, alongside the broader class-struggle.

Most colliery housing was company housing. Houses were provided free or at low rents. By 1914 many coalowners wanted to be free of the responsibility and expense, but this was not so in our period. At first, the coalowners were the most convenient providers; later, housing became seen as a means of colonisation and control. For the nineteenth century, if pit families had problems with their housing, their quarrel was directly with the owners.[65] However, the housing problem was never central to trade union activities until late century; the main brunt of it fell on the women.

Colliery houses were overcrowded and lacked adequate sanitation. Most families lived in two roomed cottages built in rows and squares. One observer in 1849 discounted the 'attic' or loft space as constituting a separate room and reckoned in consequence that half the mining population lived effectively in one room.[66] As pit families were larger than average (mean household size, Hetton 1851, 4.8 persons) and there were very few decent alternatives to company housing, the problem was acute. Families lived cheek by jowl inside and outside their homes. If the men struggled, publicly, with coal, the women struggled, privately, with water. Drainage was poor, usually an open channel between rows, and easily blocked; privies, where they existed, were shared with other families and were often unhygienically situated; waste was thrown onto open ashpits and dung hills close to the houses. Of course, there were exceptions to this, but the low standards prevailing can be seen in the fact that the new rows at Kelloe and South Hetton in 1842 were considered an improvement on the old because they were built on sloping ground. When it rained, 'filth of all kinds' was washed away.[67] In most villages fresh water had to be carried, and it was not always clean. Along with the ceaseless loading and shovelling of coal, essential to the warmth and health of the family, the carriage of water from standpipe or well was a laborious female job. At Ludworth in 1892 it was a two-mile walk. Many houses were jerry-built. They suffered from smoking chimneys and damp walls, a foul combination.[68]

Local government did not have the power to deal effectively with these housing problems until the 1890s. In the 1850s the relationship between bad housing and epidemic was locally recognised, not least because of cholera outbreaks in 1831–2, 1849, and 1853, but it was left to *ad hoc* representation – Guardians', or ratepayers' petitions, or letters from concerned individuals – to agitate the case. It was not until the 1890s that local authorities, through their medical officers backed by the central statute, attended seriously to the problems of water supply, its purification, the removal of refuse and sewage, and the improvement of housing stock. In 1892 Durham County Council sanitary committee declared the coalfield's housing problems as urgent. By 1907 Chester le Street Rural District believed it had made inroads on sanitation having built fifty-five miles of sewers, but overcrowding remained critical.[69]

Until the 1850s poor housing was not a local public issue. There is little evidence of female protest. Inside the house, dealing with practical matters of nutrition and health, their struggle was private and indirect. When women were asked their views, their first questioners were not politicians or landlords but journalists, and their answers were not the 'opinion' of organised bodies but the moans and complaints of individuals. And they had a lot of moans to make. Joseph Cowen's *Newcastle Weekly Chronicle*, a Liberal-Radical newspaper with strong coalfield sympathies, took up the issue in 1872. For two years the *Chronicle* orchestrated a campaign to improve the material conditions of the pit villages. When the journalist-traveller arrived in the village of the week the men were often away − at work, in bed, or elsewhere; the women were left alone and had their chance to speak. Their protest found its way, *sotto voce*, into the literary and political conventions of Liberal journalism. It may have found its way, again through male channels and by methods as yet unknown, into the Newcastle Co-operative Society's 1884 decision to make home loans available to miners and their families. But it is only by reading 'between' the accounts, as it were, that the sites and expressions of women's protest become apparent.

Water was the most pressing problem. The cry for water was 'the cry from every home'. At Backworth the girls at the village pump complained, '"Wetter disn't often come ... in when it dis it's nivvor fit te use, it's sic filthy stuff"'; Broomhill had just suffered scarlatina and 'the women folks are in a great state of excitement, and, taking us for an inspector, they pour into our ear loud complaints of the badness of the drainage'. The village well (or street oven) was the place where women made common cause:

> Have met occasionally the female orators of the community, to hold parley on things in general. Not much is said by them in the matter of women's rights; the subject of the 'higher education of women' hardly engages their attention; they have a much more immediate subject of interest in the affairs of the village.[70]

Another subject was jerry-building and overcrowding. At Acomb, women said that families were sleeping three beds to a room. The journalist fretted on how this sort of thing involved 'a lowering of the tone which ought to be carefully kept high in all matters relating to the sexes', but the women had more practical matters in mind. At Thornley they showed him the best they could do with their houses so that he should not be deceived:

> [wallpaper] ... is apt to drag and droop against permanently wet walls, however thick the paste may have been. Still, what with flaring wall paper, arsenical green paint, bright whitening, and brighter black lead, together with a plentiful sprinkling of not very wholesome looking sand, there is in many of the cottages a superficial look of cosiness.

At Fourstones, the skirting of cottage floors was coloured in chalk 'spicy designs' and 'flowery devices'.[71]

Twenty years later the *North Eastern Daily Gazette* mounted another campaign. The series was called 'The Homes of the Pitmen' but it was the women who talked. The reporting was generally of the 'one good dame assured me ...' variety. At Kelloe, women showed him the blocked sewage and middens; at Charrington women pointed to the leaking roofs; at Easington Lane a women asked 'How can we or our bairns be healthy?' with impure water; at Moorsley a woman revealed the pillows she put between sleeping children and a wet wall; at Ludworth the 'woman of the house called her garret a "shackrack"'.[72]

The journalists were glad to write these words down; they were not so quick to take their speakers seriously. Seriousness was the journalist's job; the women had just cause, but their other job was to be feminine. It was hard to see them as workers and to see their complaints as labour complaints. There were too many asides in the reports on the women's hard appearance – 'the haggard women beset my companion as we pass, and pray to be removed into better houses' – and throughout, women were being looked-through, beyond their garb, at the feminine ideal beneath:

> The women are hard at work to-day; but one can guess by the aid of fancy that many of them would look stunning on Sundays ...
>
> A stranger who did not understand how matters stood would be astonished, in walking through the streets of a working-class quarter between nine and ten o'clock in the morning, to find two thirds of the women unwashed and uncombed, with their clothes pinned ... He would mistake them for squalid, dirty people, which they are not ...[73]

Even when it might be seen 'how matters stood' – that women were part of 'labour' too – there remained an air of parody, of pleasure in the analogy rather than a systematic way of seeing:

> [women] ... work as hard in their houses as their sooty companions do in the pit; and, so far as we could learn, their hewing, putting, shoving, and washing is neither limited in hours nor paid at either the old rate or the new rate.[74]

Poverty and housing were sites of struggle which invited such an attitude. After all, nearly all the written protest was done by men against other men, whether Poor Law Guardians or sympathetic journalists. However, the later 1830s and 1840s saw forms of protest which involved women in more explicit and constructive ways where they found their own tongue. Chartism, and the union which followed Hepburn's, the National Miners' Association, appear to have galvanised women into a less dependent awareness. That this awareness was lost or neglected in the later nineteenth century is a matter only recently recognised.[75]

18
Chartists and the National Miners' Association

The pitmen's immediate response after 1832 was day-time quiescence and some night-time sabotage. There was an inconsequential wave of isolated strikes against price reductions in 1836. The vending of labour continued. The Northern Political Union was revived under Chartist headings in June 1838, but the pitmen stood back. An NPU rally on Christmas Day 1838 toasted 'The Pitmen of the Tyne and Wear'; Hepburn, who was a key figure in the NPU throughout 1839, had to apologise from the platform for their lack of involvement.[1]

The first significant Chartist penetration of the pit villages was made by the Durham County Charter Association, founded in Sunderland in November 1838. At their quarterly meeting in Mr Hill's Coffee House on 7 March 1839, delegates from ten collieries were warmly welcomed: since January there had been seventy-four Chartist meetings in colliery districts.[2] NPU and DCCA activity began in November 1838 and continued through the spring with mass meetings in Newcastle and Durham at Whit, but it was not until the national excitements in July that they bore action. As the Chartist leaders met in Convention and Parliament considered the national petition, local Chartist speakers were receiving rapturous applause in the villages and strikes broke sporadically across the two counties. On 9 July pitmen in the Easington area commandeered wagons of the Durham and Sunderland Railway and rode in triumph to swell the ranks of the Chartist rally on Sunderland Town Moor. William Redhead of Thornley declared that the pitmen were 'the bees who made the honey', and in the euphoria James Williams and George Binns of the DCCA presented themselves as the pitmen's political leaders.[3]

Around Newcastle, the NPU had created a crescendo of Chartist activity from early in July 1839, sparked by the Birmingham riots and arrests on 4 July, and led by nightly meetings on the Forth from 8 to 17 July — eleven days of intense politicisation. Serious fights with city police on 20 July were followed by orders from the Home Secretary 'to repress and put down ... unlawful meetings', and a wave of arrests in August. Newcastle's Convention delegates Dr Taylor and Julian Harney had already been arrested at Birmingham and Bedlington, on 5 and 8 July. Williams and Binns were taken quietly in Sunderland on 22 July.[4]

All of this pressure looked to London, where the Convention had returned from Birmingham, for resolution. The House of Commons had rejected the national petition on 12 July and a thinned and tormented Convention (only thirty members) narrowly declared on 17 July for a 'sacred holiday' of the working classes to bring down the government. This general strike was planned to last three days from 12 August, but the intervening weeks found the Convention wavering in its resolve. Bronterre O'Brien came out against the plan on 22 July; Feargus O'Connor was sceptical, then hostile; national reports were not encouraging. Some time just before 19 July, Newcastle Chartists had sent out a warning from the Convention against partial strikes and in favour of 'universality of action'. On 5 August the Convention council called on the movement not to strike. As London wavered amidst internal splits, resignations, and arrests, the NPU and DCCA backed the strike. Only the pitmen followed it, they had been stocking up for the contest since July. On 12 and 13 August Northumberland and Durham saw a splutter of strikes in hard-core Chartist collieries, led by Seghill and Thornley, but

> ... their stopping in this neighbourhood or continuing to work, will hinge upon the intelligence the newspapers bring tomorrow — as to the extent of the Strike in the South. If it appears that the strike has not taken place to a considerable extent in the manufacturing districts — the pitmen will I think go to work again on Thursday ...[5]

On 14 August, 'as other Classes of Workmen had not come forward', the DCCA called Durham back. The Northumberland collieries around Bedlington stayed out longer, but they were back four days later, and by 24 August arrests under the Bond had been made, and pikes confiscated or handed-in.[6]

This was by no means the end of Chartism in the coalfield for, the movement was to exist in other guises through the 1840s. However the high summer of 1839 was the beginning of the end of that brand of tumescent politics which called for class revolution without class unity. In December 1839, three months after the dissolution of the National Convention, the NPU District Convention reported on an organisation badly damaged by failure, arrests, and the withdrawal of public house licenses from meeting places. The pitmen were not mentioned alongside the builders, shoemakers, coachmakers and twenty other trades who were listed as supporters. December and January saw secret talk of armed rising (Frost's insurrectionists had entered Newport on 4 November; he was charged with treason on 14 December) but nothing came of it. Chartist speakers continued to tour the pit villages but in June 1840 the government was pleased to be able to withdraw troops and marines from the area, and in July the Tyne was reported as talkative, but free of meetings.[7]

The magistrates had looked on as Chartism had penetrated the collieries during the winter and spring of 1839. They were uneasy, yet took no steps. It was only after the call for a general strike, as sporadic strikes snapped around their heels, that the magistrates took positive action. On 18 July Lord John Russell informed them that it was 'of great importance that the Pitmen ... should not ... be led to join the Meetings of the Chartists' and on the two succeeding days Sunderland and Durham City asked for troops.[8] As the mining community prepared for 12 August, the magistrates recruited hundreds of special constables and the Home Office authorised their equipment of cutlass and pistol. General Napier, in command of Northern Forces, took the pitmen very seriously. Ideally, he wanted his troops concentrated in three blocks – one at Manchester to watch the 'manufacturers', one at Newcastle to watch the colliers, and one in Yorkshire to watch the other two.[9] Nevertheless, while the army waited, confident about its ability to handle a fight, the authorities based their tactics on the knowledge that although 'in all the Collieries the Chartists are numerous ... taking the Miners collectively, there is a considerable Proportion of them disposed to be quiet'. The pitmen would be overawed by the presence of soldiers and a 'snatch' of individual ringleaders. Whenever it was enacted, this plan seemed to work. Cowpen square, defended as a fort, was rushed by the 98th Regiment in full skirmishing order. Magistrates, police, and dragoons toured the villages as an intimidatory and assuring exercise. Thomas Burt's earliest memory was of a cavalry trot

through Whitley village − 'a spectacle ... unusual ... [and] likely
to impress the young imagination'. On 14 August Matthew Ridley
'proceeded with a Troop of Dragoons to Seghill in order to intimidate the refractory' and arrest four men. On 15 August Seghill
was partially back to work. At Gosforth, the commital of men
to the House of Correction 'had the effect of inducing the Gosforth
pitmen to resume their labour ... I do not apprehend now any
general outburst of a violent nature'.[10] Nor was there; given the
executive weakness of the Convention, once the pitmen struck for
a political end, there was nothing more they could do but retreat.
Chartism could muster great numbers; the problem was always
what to do with the numbers once the protest had been made. The
owners recognised this and kept out of the struggle. In this way
they isolated 'politics' at the level of its own rhetoric and gave
its practitioners no immediate reason for making political and
industrial connections. Owners threw out the suggestion that they
should employ their own special constables because what they

> ... dread more than the Chartists, is lest this excitement, which is at
> present purely political & of which the men are beginning to tire, should
> by the interference of the masters be diverted into discontent against
> themselves ... they think and with reason that a Pitman's strike for
> wages is a far more serious & unanimous affair than a strike for
> Chartism.[11]

At the NPU Christmas Day rally in 1838, Dr Taylor, delegate
to the Convention, had called on the 'Men of Northumberland
and Durham, and you men of Winlaton who in 1819 so nobly
did your duty' to hear him.[12] Chartism in the North East stood
squarely in the historical and intellectual traditions of 1815−20.
The year 1819 symbolised what might be achieved when people
were so moved. Movement was essentially a rational process
against 'a system ... which has no other foundation than error,
robbery, and fraud'. According to the zetetic principle, Chartism
would apply the force of learning and association, men would
come to Knowledge and Reason, Old Corruption would shift,
and Democracy would operate. From Newcastle, the *Northern
Liberator* insisted on the 'Moral and Religious Obligation to Study
Politics', that only at their peril did the people remain 'ignorant
of the principles of political relationship'; from Sunderland, the
DCCA urged self-instruction by classes 'especially' in 'the history
of our own country, discussing its great events philosophically,

not as mere matters of fact, but noting their bearing on our present state'. The best 'means of gaining our object is to spread and diffuse knowledge', and Chartists should 'take up these Questions like Men, and calmly and rationally discuss their truth or falsehood'.[13]

The enemies of the people remained the aristocracy. Politically of course, 'THE THING' was opposed to the rights of men. But more than this, its life in the social structure was presented as worthless. The aristocracy contributed nothing to the wealth of society and yet took the greater part of that wealth. In an economic *debauche*, made possible by illegal encroachment on the property and privileges of the people, the 'perfumed Lordlings' had driven the country to want and ruin: the loss of eight million acres of common land in seventy years; the game laws and the persecution of those 'manly Sports and Recreations which were once the Health and Pride of Englishmen'; from 1776, crashing taxation through bad laws, wars, and debts; the repressions of 1819 and 1832; and the insolence of 1839 – rejecting the petition 'as if ... mere children'. In an apt description of landed power, James Williams called for the aristocracy to be swept 'from the face of the earth as cumberers of the ground'.[14]

The economic dimension posed tantalising questions for North East Chartism regarding its attitude to the middle classes. Radicalism had developed its theory since 1815–20. It continued to configure political democracy with a split view of society's productive and unproductive classes in the style of Wade's *Gorgon* or the later Owenite *Crisis*, but since 1832 it had to account for the middle classes as a political force. The split view of productive and unproductive classes offered a chance for a middle and working-class economic detente as co-producers of the nation's real wealth and 'necessary articles':

> I ask the middle classes of Sunderland, will they support the man who supports the people, and will the people support both? The object we are contending for is not the robbery of a faction – it is not the robbery of a few, or the robbery of the many ... it is the assertion of a principle that all men are equal ...
>
> Tell me not that property ... is in mortar, bricks & stones. No; all property is in your blood, bones, and sinews – in a poor man's life, wife, and children ... [and] ... when that property is infringed upon, in order to aggrandize an idle and profligate aristocracy, I say we are not preserving peace if we allow protection to property.[15]

In the NPU's *Address to Middle Classes of North of England* the appeal was made precisely on the possibility of detente. However, the productive-unproductive view of society was not without class ambivalence for with it went a strong belief in the labour theory of value. This theory criticised the absurdity of the aristocracy and, on the same grounds, the absurdity of the 'middleman'. The middle classes were questioned not only about their apparent reticence in support of the political cause – 'Gentlemen, We address you in the language of Brotherhood probably for the last Time' – but also about their economic relationship. If Radicalism had once harboured some hope in middle-class politics, Chartism mixed its political disappointments with an economic theory which sought to explain the middle-class reticence. Their wealth was seen as in political nexus with a corrupt aristocratic State. In so far as State laws protected and enhanced the property of the rich but not the labour of the poor, the middle classes had to decide with whom they would work – through State, or 'People'? On their decision hung their role: parasites or producers? George Binns told a Chartist meeting of his conversation with a North Shields shop-keeper. He had told the hapless shopkeeper to supply credit during the forthcoming general strike, and when the response had been unenthusiastic he had bullied him into support by threatening his property:

> But I showed him that the best way to get 20s. in the pound for every debt, was for him to act with and stand by the people ... there would be little security for his coffee, tea, sugar, bacon, or bread ... when six millions ... were driven to the dreadful alternative of force ...
>
> ... There is not a Star that shines upon the breast of a lordling, there is not a coat upon the back of a middleman – not a parson wears a lawn sleeve, but is indebted for it to your industry.
> Their grandeur emanates from your industry; and if the loom were shut up tomorrow ... and each labourer were to demand the Charter before he cut it down [the golden harvest] – and if every department of industry were stopped at its source – I ask, how these middlemen would shrink into the littleness of their nature, when they saw all their wealth & grandeur in society was a humbug ...'[16]

A 'sacred holiday' would test the theory. As 12 August approached the tone got sharper. The NPU pamphlet *General Strike*, sold in Newcastle for a ½d, referred to 'Money-mongers' as well as lord-lings, and made it clear that the working classes could expect to be on their own: 'For seven years we reposed with confidence on the Justice and Patriotism of the Middle Classes', but now 'your labour is your own, you can do with it what you please':

> ... the Lesson now about to be taught to the idle and impudent consumers will have the speedy Effect of admitting those Men into the Constitution without whom the Waters of England would be without a Ship and her Lands would be a solitary and noiseless Desert.

If there were elements in this ideology which bore obliquely on the pitmen – a deteriorating status, the 'taxation' of fines and price cuts, a middleman class of agents and viewers, the political tonality of 1819 and 1832 – it was the theory of labour value which best grouped these elements, and expressed them. Williams, Binns, and the Convention delegate Robert Knox spent months in the coalfield articulating the theory with a Cobbett-like instinct for the concrete:

> [Queen Adelaide, widow of William IV, lived on £100,000 p.a.] ... What would it do? I will tell you. If there are 2000 persons in the town of Hetton, that sum would give a little fortune of £50 to every man, woman, and child, in the town every year ... Another woman, called Victoria, receives five times the amount of the other ... Throw the two queens and the young one's mother together, and their united beggings would support the half of the population of the county of Durham in their present condition ... Now allow me to pop the question. Where do these titled beggars get this money? What rights can they show for it? Did they earn it by any labour either of their head or hands? In good sooth most of them are of no use to themselves or any body else, and not fit to produce sixpence worth of that wealth which they squander so lavishly ... Who is it that produces all this wealth? It is the working men – the men who labour with their hands – who produce all that is eatable, drinkable, or wearable, or that affords shelter for all.[17]

This argument from labour by hand and head moved to hands alone in the final strike call – possibly a dangerous argument from Williams the bookseller and Binns the bourgeois, but Hepburn had said he would vote for Dr Taylor's election to the Convention whether he were doctor or blacksmith, and pit-Chartism shared his disinclination to quibble. William Redhead had come up from the pit to join the fight believing that when the contest was on, his duty was plain. Why had the miners come?

> Whoy, to struggle for liberty. Are we to hev liberty? We must hev it ... This is a movement for you! ... I was up to my knees when the news came ... I did not expect to hear such an electrified speech from Mr Duncan. What do I see? I see the bees who make the honey.

> When the bees come out of their hives, then the grey headed drones
> go in and get the honey. (loud laughter) They get it out of your employ-
> ment, but we will not let them have it any more as they have done.
> Let them go to themselves – It is the duty of every shopocrat and every
> publican's duty to join this glorious cause, and let every man have a
> voice in making the laws. We have got down to this monsteration, and
> if you want a lift, our friends are ready to give you a lift ... Let us be
> continually on the look out, and when we get news from any place,
> let us be up and at it.[18]

With the theory and tactic of labour value went the attendant tactic
of controlling the retail trade by exclusive dealing. This plan was
especially suited to the pit villages and was forwarded by those
Female Political Unions founded in the coalfield in 1839.

The first move appears to have come from the women workers
at Cookson's Plate Glass factory in Newcastle. In November 1838
they disputed the sacking of Mr Thomason, an employee of
Cookson's and a secretary of the NPU. The next month these
women were raising subscriptions for the 'national rent'; on
Christmas Day Julian Harney came to praise the ladies of the NPU;
and on 3 January 1839 the Newcastle Female Political Union was
founded.[19] From this point, over the next six months, the pit
villages became centres of female Chartism: Northumberland
styled its branches Female Political Unions, Durham styled them
Female Radical, or Charter, Associations. Seghill, and Bedlington
FPUs were founded in February, New Durham and Broomside in
March, Thornley in May, Quarrington, Kelloe, Coxhoe, Easington
Lane, Haswell and Sunderland in May and June 1839.[20] These
were only the recorded societies – usually founded and graced
with a guest male speaker:

> The other evening he [James Williams] visited a colliery village where
> he never before could get an audience of 12 persons, and he was met
> by the whole population, men and women. Thirty-eight men and twelve
> women enrolled ... and since that fifty had joined, which he believed
> included the whole population.

Chartist speakers were always claiming whole populations, such
was their strategy of overwhelming numbers, but, given the rush
to the colours, the popularity of female 'events' in the region, and
the broad spread of female societies, it seems likely that there were
other, smaller societies not recorded. Women (and children) seem
to have stood with the men from the start – at Bedlington, 'Every

man, woman, and child ... marched out ... 7 or 800 people ... in one dense moving mass' – but the formation of female societies was new, a genuine watershed in the history of women's politics.[21]

Their politics was not gender politics. It was class politics where women asserted their duty to be involved. The Newcastle FPU cited low wages, deteriorating work, the naval impress, poverty, the Poor Law, and class oppression among their grievances. They explicitly rejected the new formulations of womanhood as a hypocrisy which sought to bar them from their men and from the reality of all their lives:

> We have been told that the province of woman is her home, and that the field of politics should be left to men; this we deny; the nature of things renders it impossible, and the conduct of those who give the advice is at variance with the principles they attest. Is it not true that the interests of our fathers, husbands, and brothers, ought to be ours? If they are oppressed and impoverished, do we not share those evils with them? ... We have read the records of the past, and our hearts have responded to the historians' praise of those women, who struggled against tyranny and urged their countrymen to be free or die.[22]

Sometimes, those records of the past could go very far back. In Elizabeth Mallet's speech from the chair to 320 women of the Thornley Association, we hear a woman who knew her Old Testament heroines – women who in their heroism were far removed from domestic duties, stating

> ... that her husband had served in the army and was ready to lead or follow. She, too, had learned what pistols were made for, and she would say to her husband in the language of Ruth 'whither thou goest I will go', even if it were to the mouth of the cannon. (loud cheers) Mrs G Smith said, that from the earliest dawn of reason, her soul and affections were with the cause of freedom ...[23]

The cause of freedom could carry many duties. Women were adept at translating Chartist thinking into social life. Soirees, teas, festivals, processions and regalia were their gift to the movement. On 5 February 1839 there was a DCCA Festival at Bishopwearmouth for pitmen and their wives; on 11 June South Shields hosted a 'Female Democratic Tea'; on 23 July bedecked Chartist children marched through an embattled Newcastle; in December there was a tea for Harney at Winlaton in 'The Highlander' where the women were strongly represented. Amidst the speeches and toasts (for the People, for Harney, for Frost and other patriots), there was singing

(Harney sang 'When this old cap was new'), and dancing (to 'the patriotic band'), and green and crimson wall hangings, and portraits, and supper. The final toast was from George Julian himself: three times three for 'the health and happiness of the cannie lasses of Winlaton', and an air, 'The Lasses O'. Radical teas such as this replaced the old, gentlemanly, political dinners; teas 'enabled a man not to come himself alone, but to bring his family with him' – a little mark of good manners which many pit villages would hardly recognise.[24] Party moods however, invited party favourites. Henry Vincent was popular with the female radicals of the south-west. In the coalfield and the lead-mining dales it was the young London republican Harney who was known to the women. He tended to speak directly to them. In Alston, Harney 'looked to the women of the North' to 'propel onward the men of the North', and James Ayr followed him to insist 'that the females were, if possible, still greater victims than the men to the present damnable state of society'. Harney's gifts from women included a plaid, a scarf, and hot cakes.[25]

It is perhaps necessary to qualify the meaning of this female involvement. There is no doubt that the women were not valued by the men as much as they might have been. After all, there is no recorded example of men bearing gifts for female guest speakers. The Charter itself did not demand female suffrage, although more on tactical grounds than principle. Male attitudes could be seen as condescending: 300 men, we are told, filled Newcastle Music Hall in January 1838 to make politics; this assemblage was 'gladdened with the presence of some very pretty ladies' who were duly toasted – 'Our country women – our mothers, our wives, and our daughters; they never shall be slaves, nor insulted by Poor Law Despots – Tune, Home! Sweet Home!' When troops wheeled against a Sunderland Town Moor rally the first cries came from women on the *outskirts* of the crowd, crowds whose female numbers the *Newcastle Journal* refused to count. Stephens' famous war cry, 'For children and wife, war to the knife', echoed by Harney at Alston, was *for* women and not by them.[26] Nevertheless, from reports, written by men it is true, female Chartists did not seem to have found this tone offensive. And they were far from passive in their collaboration. The men might have done most of the talking, but they had their lessons to learn too:

On Wednesday last Mr Reaves of Sunderland visited this place (New Durham) to get up a meeting in support of the Charter. A room having been obtained, Mr Reaves proceeded to the spot about the time announced for the meeting, but to his surprise, instead of finding a room full of men (who had not had time to get so early, just having left work) every part of the large room, window seats and all, was occupied by the canny women of this place. This was an agreeable surprise ... and whether he would or not, there was nothing left him but to address the women, for they got him into the room, locked the door, and set him upon a chair, declaring that he should not leave until he had formed a female association. This was done, and the next morning half a dozen of these patriotic women were running about the town with a pastepan and bills, calling another meeting for Saturday next.[27]

Three weeks after their formation, the Newcastle FPU had met to implement a system of exclusive dealing. This was to be the leading-edge of their politics and it meant sharp engagement with the world outside the movement. First, they agreed to solicit retailers to contribute to the 'national rent', and second they agreed not to deal with retailers who opposed them. They resolved that '... a shopkeeper who will not admit the claim of their fathers, husbands, and brothers is an enemy to their rights and interests and ought not to be supported'.[28] Exclusive dealing was the consumer's theoretical complement to the producer's labour value. The 'national holiday', or general strike, would buckle and bring down the State in a mass demonstration of the power of labour value; exclusive dealing – ranging in sophistication from the woman's basket to O'Connor's Land and Labour Bank – would build up a new fabric by a continuous demonstration of the people's consuming power, a power to accumulate and administer its own capital.[29] Through the spring and summer of 1839 exclusive dealing and rent-collecting emerged as a widespread intimidatory force. Shops were visited, monies were collected, deals were made, and names were taken, usually by the men, with care and system. Once the people knew their friends, the women shopped accordingly. Ben Embleton was often asked 'by the people in the outbranches for the names'; when he went to Sacriston he had to make do with eggs 'as the butcher of that village happened to be an intolerant'. In June, the Fatfield branch met with a senior Newcastle Chartist to plan their dealing.[30] Although the strategy had been used before in the coalfield, in 1819 and 1832, news of it fades after the events in July and August. There is talk of Chartist shops and even a Chartist Cooperative Joint Stock Bank in October 1839,[31] but it is not until the National Miners' Association in 1842–3 that we hear again of organised dealing in the pit villages. It was then called 'unionism' and it clearly inflected union strategies to the site of female power. The dealing was no longer exclusive; it was negotiated by price:

> The women are forming a Union to bring down the prices of Butchers' meat, Milch, Butter, Potatoes etc. This I think a capital burlesque on the Pitmen's Union ... the Women certainly will not be able to carry their point ... at the Maximum price of 4½d p. 1 lb [meat] at which they have fixed it.[32]

When the strike came 'shopocrats' were pressed to accept negotiated prices and extensive credit on the grounds that as the primary and true producers of shopkeepers' 'secondary' wealth, pit families deserved their support. Grocers were warned, and, when the strike was over, some grocers published ingratiating advertisements saying how much they had helped. Later, possibly in 1845, one thousand women assembled at Thornley with music and banners. Mrs Winter of Kelloe chaired, and explained their objectives. Thornley and Kelloe had been female Chartist centres and there was continuity too in the fair price of beef:

> Three gills of milk ... should be sold for a penny; beef for 4½d a pound; butter, 8d; ... It was further decided, that if any housewife should pay higher prices than the 'scale' she should instantly be reduced to the unadorned simplicity of Mother Eve ...[33]

It could be that what we see here is a Radical strategy, particularly female in its operation, and at least thirty years old in the 1850s, which formed a tradition upon which the Cooperative Wholesale Society was founded in the 1860s and 1870s. The CWS was always pilloried by its opponents as a 'petticoat' organisation, and there is evidence of continued female pressure especially, against butchers. Urpeth colliery Cooperative Butchery was set up in 1872 after just such pressure. The power of this tradition may explain the remarkably rapid growth of the CWS in Northumberland and Durham.[34]

Whatever the manner of female Chartism as a support and complement to the movement, men dominated its political discourse. Here, labour-value theory was presented not only as an economic fact, or as a way of accumulating working-class capital, or the human dignity which went with it; it was also presented as the means to political revolution. Dr Taylor

> ... hoped they would carry out their objects by peacable means ... There was at this moment one body that would gain a bloodless victory — he meant the colliers. (Hear, hear) If these but struck work for one month London would be one ruin. Let them refuse to 'howk' coals either here or in the North, and very soon the Aristocracy would neither have victuals or a fire to cook them.[35]

In a wry piece of political journalism published on the day of the Newcastle riot, the *Northern Liberator* both guarded and hailed, assured and threatened, the revolution:

> [Chartist] meetings are conducted with all the regularity of a piece of mechanism; their proceedings are not characterized by that violence that springs from want bordering on destitution ... The County of Durham is making very little noise; the Riot Act is never read; the torch of the incendiary is unlighted; the bleating of the sheep may be heard; the cattle on a thousand hills ruffling the midnight silence, there is no watchdog barking at the approach of midnight depradators; the man of property may have a bolt upon his door, but he is safe without it; the heavy tramping policeman may be in the streets when the world is sleeping and the sun is set, but he walks alone and he walks in peace. But mistake not this general calm; the spirit of freedom is progressing; the work of organization is going on. Against the present corruption, *numbers, honesty, talent, courage*, and *skill* are leagued, and none can doubt the issue of the contest.[36]

Chartism was in deadly moral earnest. Just as Hepburn had called and continued to call for a discipline nourished by moral cohesion, Chartism preached that moral declension was political declension. Politics was posed against the pettier forms of traditional violence in the *Northern Liberator* for 20 July 1839.

> Twelve months ago colliers met at the cock pit, or delighted in a dog fight; now, they read the *Liberator* and *Star*; the cock pit is lost sight of in the intensity of political feeling and determination.

When the NPU had organised a counter-demonstration to Victoria's coronation festivities in June 1838, infantry and dragoons had harassed the periphery of the meeting. Feargus O'Connor, who had been speaking, protested that this provocation had deliberately sought a conflict in order to inflict a defeat: 'Supposing one unadvised or intoxicated man ... had commenced a collision, where would that collision end?'

Did these tinselled troops yonder think by parading before him their
cannon, their sabres, and their bayonets, to unnerve him or shake his
resolution? If they did, they had mistaken their man. He thanked them
for their support ... They had proved to the world that as peaceable
men are always determined, so also determined men were always the
most peaceable.[37]

Political involvement eschewed the traditions of direct action.
In another way it embodied them. General strike theory was in
fact a call to direct action which muddled the theory at the point
of action. Some Chartist theorists like Harney not only advocated
a 'show of strength', but were also willing to use that strength in
a blow against state power. The Convention, and through it the
people, would defend themselves from the State's inevitable attack
and in this way the people's defence would turn into the people's
attack. Others like O'Connor blurred their theory at the point of
the blow: if moral force failed, physical force 'like an electrical
shock' would 'effect what the other had failed to accomplish'.
Harney had called for war, if necessary, and James Ayr had
warned that 'if a hand was lifted' against the Convention, Newcastle would be another Bristol and 'he should have an eye for
an eye, a tooth for a tooth, blood for blood'. Alexander Somer-
ville's dissuasive *Warnings to the People on Street Warfare* was
sold on the streets of Newcastle for a penny in May 1839.[38]

Between Harney's 'ARM! ARM!! ARM!!!' at one end of the
strategic spectrum and the fluid gradations across to moral force
at the other, the movement initially rested its theory on the hope
that the language and presence of physical force would somehow
of itself enact the change. This was a political version of that
reserved violence of the direct action tradition. Thus in Alston,
Dr Taylor could boast, without foundation, that 700 men in
Winlaton armed with rifles were ready to support them; thus,
Thomas Devyr's claims (made forty-three years later) of 60,000
pikes, thirteen inch shells, five inch grenades, and sixty-five armed
districts ready to follow Frost; thus, the fierce language of Edward
Charlton's advocacy of Chartism based on 'God's Holy Word'
at the Groat Market Chapel in Newcastle; thus, their solicitor's
warning that had Williams and Binns 'wished to appeal to brute
force, they could have brought down 20,000 miners in three hours
notice'; thus, the NPU's ludicrous overestimate of miners' strikes
on the day of the petition − 25,000 men with another 7,000

following; thus, Chartism's running battle with the press over coverage and numbers – 'an outcry ... not only for refusing to report the trash which they vomit forth at their meetings, but also for misrepresenting ... the number, intelligence, determination, and love of order of the persons assembled on such occasions'.[39] The very language of Chartism was insurgent; words were revolutionary forces. The England of Chartist speakers was a bold country where every errand boy was contemptuous of death. What chance then for the 'bludgeon policemen' or 'musket soldiery' against this sort of people? North-East Chartism was, if not an armed force, at least a force with access to arms. Later, this was attested as an accepted fact.[40] The salient point is not so much that Chartism's claims and propositions were, or were not, 'true', more that at critical moments the spirit of the claims appears to have deluded the movement itself. Both Williams and Binns fudged the issue of armed insurrection at the crucial point of the manner of its execution. Their listeners were left high and dry with only a rhetoric of inference and suggestion:

> If you are not prepared to support him [Convention delegate Robert Knox] by all means, you must quickly be prepared for it ('we are prepared') – This country is on the verge of a mighty crisis. We are living in excited times, and we know not what a day or an hour may bring forth. The first signal of insurrection on the part of the country may be a flame which will wrap England in light. (George Binns)

> ... you must prepare yourselves for the worst ... Why the gentleman who sits on his four-footed stool, who, I suppose, is dubbed Sir Oracle, told me today that this is a recommendation to arm. I care not what it is, or what the consequences may be to me as an individual. I know it is my duty to tell of these things. It is your duty to act up to them at once. I have one word more ...' (James Williams)[41]

These words certainly frightened some magistrates, and possibly the army,[42] but when the day was named and Chartist collieries moved to the political hilt, some of them armed with pikes as at Thornley and Bedlington, they were defeated by muddled theory, confused strategy, and the unmistakable reality of the troops and arrests they had suffered seven years before.[43] The pitmen's political commitment to the Chartist theory of labour value had been demonstrated. It was their misfortune that the theory had been used more to adjourn the realities of power and protest than to explore ways of confronting them. One of their leaders, Robert

Lowery had been presented with a Winlaton pike — 'a formidable weapon ... to strike and thrust with'. He said that his wife took it for 'a proper-use'; for breaking up round coals in the cellar.[44]

The debate was resumed on 7 November 1842 with the foundation at the Griffin Inn, Wakefield, of the National Miners' Association.[45] By August 1843 the NMA had 20,000 members; by January 1844 it had an estimated 50–80,000 members from all coalfields, a growing fund, its own newspaper, and forty professional 'lecturers' in the field. Northumberland and Durham had nearly total adult membership, and by 1844 Newcastle was the Association's headquarters.[46] Grouped around its newspaper, the *Miners' Advocate*, the NMA was a political trade union.[47] By creating a national organisation of coal, lead, and ironstone miners of all grades, its leaders hoped to make an effective weapon for the theory of labour value. From its origins, Chartists were at the union's intellectual centre.

The first traces of revived unionism in the coalfield are a letter from George Binns in the *Northern Star* of 15 January 1842 calling on two counties' delegates to attend a meeting in Chester le Street on 22 January 1842, and an advertistement in the same issue 'by order of the Thornley Colliery Union' calling for a meeting 'to adopt measures for resistance'. From the summer of 1842 to the summer of 1843 Chartist speakers from within and outside the region were active in the coalfield with O'Connor's *Northern Star* in support. Two months after the Wakefield foundation, David Swallow, the Yorkshire miner, Chartist, and first General Secretary of the Association, came to speak at Scaffold Hill near Newcastle. After this he was taken round the coalfield by Ben Embleton,[48] and in March 1843 Embleton again presented Swallow to 20,000 pitmen at Scaffold Hill for the formal inauguration of the Association. Swallow was followed by P.M. Brophy, a professional Chartist lecturer, who delivered a pungent class analysis of the nation's difficulties and was warmly applauded. In May 1843 the Association chose Newcastle as the venue for its annual conference, and in the July 120 Northumberland and Durham delegates assembled at the Black Swan in the city.[49]

The Chartist connection was soon challenged. In view of the falterings and collapse in 1839, the disastrous attempts of O'Connor and others to exploit as Chartist causes the Plug Plot Riots of 1842–3, and the independent tradition of unionism in the coalfield, the Association's intimacy with Chartism at the higher levels met with opposition. At the March 1843 rally on Scaffold Hill, Ben Pyle, previously one of Hepburn's cadre, and William Cloughan, the Scottish leader, had both pointed to the dangers of overt political involvement. Ben Watson criticised Chairman Pyle for implying that Chartism was destructive: they were not opposed to property, only that working men should receive so little for their property which was their labour. Pyle accepted this, but warned them again

> ... not to split upon politics, or they would never be firmly organized. They must use moral force and then they would be safe and powerful. (Cries of 'We know all that, but you said the Chartists were destructive').

In July, the Elswick branch came into the open with its *Address to Union*, which repeated Pyle and Cloughan's warning and launched an attack on William Beesley, an ex-chairmaker from Accrington turned professional Chartist and union organiser. Beesley had an irascible temperament and the Elswick men feared that although 'he may accomplish his own ends' to 'induce them to a premature strike ... the Union might be severed to atoms thereby'. Undeterred, Beesley continued to press for Chartism and in the same month secured a law fund, persuading the delegates to employ W. P. Roberts, a Chartist solicitor from Bath, relative of John Frost, and friend of Feargus O'Connor, as their attorney. Roberts joined the Association as 'Solicitor General' in August 1843, with Beesley as his clerk.[50]

Roberts' subsequent successes and his acid wit only served to increase the strain with the non-Chartist lobby. Trouble came to a head in February 1844 when Elswick again criticised the political connection, adding that Roberts had contravened the constitution, drawn up at the May 1843 conference, by his encouragement of partial strikes at single collieries. Their pamphlet was put in every copy of the *Miners' Advocate* with the connivance of the Executive Council. Roberts answered immediately, calling on the Durham delegates for a vote of confidence, which he received. The *Northern Star* then pitched in with a startling attack on the Executive Council: 'too idle to work, and too poor to live without labour', they were , the *Star* said, in league with the owners. The Council, who with the exception fo the Association's president, John

Hall an ex-flax dresser from South Shields, was comprised of pitmen or ex-pitmen, gave its reply on 1 March appealing to local knowledge of their record and experience. The next day, Roberts repeated the *Star*'s charge at a mass meeting on Shadon's Hill, spicing it with tales of council's drunken evenings with coalowners. A second reply followed on 6 March. The Council re-asserted its virility: 'time will tell *who* is sold to the masters, and who will give the masters battle when the struggle comes'.[51]

Those arguments were taken to the national conference at Glasgow in April 1844. Although the conference succeeded in patching up the quarrel it also decided to let Northumberland and Durham go it alone with a strike to begin that month. The question of a national strike had been raised and deferred at the Newcastle and Manchester conferences of September 1843 and January 1844, but at Glasgow, the northern delegate committee, after being defeated on the issue of a national strike, won their appeal for a two-county contest. Strategically, this was a nonsense. It was contrary to the spirit of the Association, it ignored the existence of large coal stocks, and did not accord with the lessons of labour value. However, the northern delegates, still smarting from the 10% and 8% reductions of the 1842 Bond and confident of their independent strength and value, asked only that their brother counties should keep blacklegs out of the fray. It could be that the arguments over Chartism had provoked their militancy. The delegate committee of eight included two members of the Executive Council, John Hall and John Stokoe, as well as three Primitive Methodist lay-preachers, Messrs Haswell, Tulip and Embleton. Roberts, along with Martin Jude the Treasurer, had argued against a strike.[52] The pitmen of Northumberland and Durham went into the hardest contest in their history with their leadership at odds with itself, and a theory which remained untried. This was a situation which the local press was not slow to exploit:

> We need no better proof of the movement being in connexion with Chartism, than the fact of its being promoted by such men as Beasley [sic], Daniels [sic], Roberts, Byrne and the whole tribe of Chartist orators ... and conspirators in this district.
>
> We respect the honest miner ... but we tell him that a change so desirable will never be so consummated on the plan laid down by the Chartists in politics and infidels in religion, in whom he now blindly reposes confidence.[53]

The original argument with Chartism had been tactical. When it became personal it had got out of hand. Although the official Chartist connection had been rebuffed by the exclusion of O'Connor from the Manchester conference and the rejection of a Chartist handbill at Glasgow, the chief national posts in the Association remained staffed by committed Chartists. On the Executive Committee sat William Daniells, editor of the *Advocate*, a Scots ex-carpet weaver; W.P. Roberts a solicitor; William Beesley; John Hall, General Secretary; and Martin Jude, treasurer, a Newcastle publican and ex-collier. Although the *Advocate* was unstamped and constrained in its coverage of political news, it nevertheless presented the struggle in the context of political economy under the classic calls to reason, discipline, and labour value.

The Newcastle conference of May 1843 had drawn up the constitution. Apart from the recruitment of union lecturers at 18s to 21s per week, and a national dimension with its conferences and executive, the organisation was similar to that pioneered by the United Colliers and Hepburn. Each colliery formed a branch which elected delegates, took subscriptions, reasoned policy, operated by the rule-book, and restricted out-put. The funds were subject to much speculation in their day, but it is likely that reports were exaggerated. When it struck, the Association was unable to afford regular payments and only three were made, adding up to 7½d per man. The main break with tradition was that this was a fighting union. It had no benefit function, its subscriptions were low (6d to join, 1d membership card, 1d per week), and it was open to all miners 'to equalize and diminish the hours of labour and to obtain the highest possible amount of wages'.[54]

It was at branch level that organisational discipline was fought and won, and it was understood at the outset that the conduct of the strike lay in the hands of the local delegates. Their ceaseless platform meetings and 'inflammatory harangues' maintained discipline. It was the 'Delegates with their local Committees ... [who] ... may best succeed in Keeping the men who are off work in a state of delusion, & in inducing those who have resumed work to discontinue their labour'. Londonderry's early hope that the platform could be legally banned was rejected by the Home Office.[55] Whereas eighteenth-century pitmen had demonstrated as a short, hostile intimidation of specific persons and property, by 1844 the demonstration was more about publicising the discipline and dignity of 'Labour' over a long drawn-out contest with 'Capital': 'In order to convince the Inhabitants that there are not such a "GREAT NUMBER" of Miners left the Union A PROCESSION will take place', and seventy-two colliery branches listened to their delegates in the pouring rain beneath their banners on Newcastle Town Moor. Meetings such as this where the speeches 'sunk deep into my very soul' were 'Mighty incidents' to the pit boy Ned Rymer.[56]

The first call was always to order. Roberts brought all his great eloquence to this call. Speaking of the troops stationed in the coalfield, he cleverly inverted the miners' frustration into that of the soldiers':

> Their's had been no ordinary trial of patience: they were told that their sabres should be *fleshed* − blood red and black − that they should 'have a shot' at living men − real colliers − with an occasional splash through a colliery 'town' − scouring the cuddies − frightening the children − and drunk (after the victory) through the night ... How miserably have they been deceived: − not a *skirmish* − not a row − no 'pitchforking the natives'. Up and down − and down and up again − over the bridge and back − looking at the water − gazing at the omnibus − journeying to the farrier's forge − pulling up a horse's foot and letting it fall − drunk, sober, or fuddled − walking, riding, or eating beef − they breath and move − a glorious and honourable demonstration of the power, the might, and the majesty of THE PITMEN'S UNION.[57]

Order was a deduction of Reason. The *Advocate* taught reason at every opportunity. Headed 'Knowledge is Power', it educated the membership in everything from the irrationality of swearing to the economic history of property, from the bourgeois misunderstanding of crime to the twin evils of society, competition and over-production − 'HYDRA HEADED MONSTERS'.[58] The pitmen seem to have been able pupils. The vicar, the Chief Constable, and the Lord Lieutenant all testified to their order, with no cases of direct action against plant or property.[59] This should have been clear before the strike. It was a changed pitman indeed who went to the soldiers' barracks to dissuade them from their duty, or who scoffed the owners' threats and bribes:

> He has threatened to starve us into compliance. He has likewise promised to give us 6 half Barrels of ale, which we have refused determined not to be won over by such like insinuations.[60]

The case for order was greatly helped by the Law Fund and Roberts' appointment. Roberts engaged the owners at close quarters, over individual colliery disputes, in front of magistrates. In the autumn and winter of 1843−4 the court rooms rang with his invective against the anomalies and absurdities of the Bond. Acquitted on a legal technicality after taking the case to a higher court, Roberts' victory for the Thornley men in January 1844 made him a hero. It also seemed to prove the case for reason and order.[61]

An ideology of labour value informed the whole strategy. The essence of the action, a withdrawal of labour preceded by a policy of restricted output, rested on the premise that without labour and its product there was no value. Once labour was withdrawn, all one could do was wait. To be tempted into other forms of action was destructive and unnecessary. By Restriction and labour-withdrawal the commodity would become scarce, the Vend policy of overproduction of cheap coal would end, and the 'middleman' who filched the surplus value would wither. There was enough in the operations of the Coal Trade visible to pitmen which could encourage them to see the industry in this way. Even the Trade's own accountancy procedures privileged the hewers as the real producers: hewers constituted 'getting' costs, all other grades of worker were classed as 'oncosts'. For over twenty years popular socialist political economy had been offering models of exploitation based on labour value theory which could, in part, be made to fit the Trade. Coal, like land, was a natural factor with relatively simple measures of in-put and out-put: the earth was leased, labour hired, men went down, coal came up, profits were made. More-over, coal dominated the region, physically and imaginatively; it did not involve, at the face at least, complex systems of labour division or machinery; in a steadily rising market with no real rivals it did not seem to need special marketing; it did not seem to require a growing managerial class because it retained the impressions of paternalism and labour autonomy, with contracts. Yet it was rife with rents and revenues (royalties which in the 1850s exceeded gross profits) and was accumulating capital at unprecedented rates. All this as the pitmen's prices and conditions deteriorated. It was therefore feasible to see the appropriation of surplus value not as endogenous to the structure of property and class relations − a structure under pressure from other capitals − but as an exogenous process now acting unreasonably in its levels of exploitation. The Vend itself was construed exogenously, as a greedy force battening on the industry to distort, and quite improperly to destroy, that industry's existence as an economy where all could claim their fair share. After all, even the coalowners had defended the Vend from parliamentary criticism on similar grounds. The greed had to be stopped; the owners had to be shown that labour had its claims too and a strike to demonstrate the power of labour value would do just that.[62]

The extraction of surplus value was seen then, in the classic, Radical fashion as an exogenous tax. The filching and fattening was seen in the most literal way. Branch presidents and secretaries worked out the exact amount for their collieries and sent them to the *Advocate*. Thomas Pratt, for Castle Eden colliery:

Main seam hewing prices 1842: 9/6 per score 21 tubs at 7¼ cwt. tub.
     "   "   "   "   1843: 8/5 per score 21 tubs at 7½ cwt. tub.
  − Equivalent to 1s 4¾d. per score reduction 1842−43.
      "   " £26 17s 4¾d. per fortnight.
      "   " *£698 12s. 3½d. per year*
Reductions on putting 1842−43 equivalent to *£166 16s 8d.*
Reductions on narrow work 1842−43 equivalent to *£68 18s 0d.*
Total Reductions in the main seam 1842−43, *£934 6s 11½d.*

I heard that a certain Noble Marquis, some years ago, declared that the whole of his collieries, for the last four years, had not brought him in as much as would buy him a pair of boots. And he is one of the most extensive coalowners in England, or in the world. Most of his understrappers are 'gentlemen' to whom, if you approach, it must be hat in hand. He had unshipped several of them, but not before they had 'feathered their nests well'.[63]

John Buddle's death just before this letter had been followed by news of his £150,000 will. He had been chief viewer to a 'Noble Marquis'. The agents and viewers, a growing managerial-professional class, 'cribbed' the men's money 'in the shape of fines'. Making themselves rich, 'they had scarcely thrown aside the pick when they obtained their carriage'. This was sharp comment, based upon what the pitmen could see. What they could not see − that coal made fewer personal fortunes for its masters than iron, steel, or cotton, and far fewer fortunes than finance − they could not know. Of what they could see, it mattered little that the number of viewers who moved from pick to carriage was small. A poor boy like George Elliot, a Penshaw pit lad aged nine in 1824, might be a consultant, head viewer, leaseholder, and partner by 1843 (and owner of Penshaw by the 1860s), but he was an exception. The pitmen's real point reflected the rise of the viewers as an elite. We have already noted how the ownership recruited largely from within its own, dynastic ranks. The viewers played an indispensable role in the investment plans of the partnerships and the more entrepreneurially-minded among them enjoyed unrivalled opportunities to make early, and informed, assessments of risk and profit. With every accretion to their status – as engineers, knowledge-brokers, managers, partners – the viewers distanced themselves from a work force with whom they were in daily contact. With every new investment the pitmen were reminded of labour's decline amidst so much capital. Educated by labour value as the true source of the capital on which all that status depended, they sought not expropriation but redress. They wanted fairness. They asked for balance.[64]

It was here that the argument from labour value, founded on a distinction between productive and unproductive classes, began to warp. The pitmen were never previously in doubt about whom their opponents were, and certainly the thrust of their 1842–4 agitation remained directed at 'owners' and 'masters'. However, the leadership, speaking through the *Advocate*, gradually reformulated this simple view, accepting that though the pitmen were productive through their labour (i.e. their property), the owners were also productive through their capital which was their property. The Association existed to redress the balance of one form of property, Capital, over the other, Labour. Both forms had their place and both now had their representative defenders: the Vend, which kept coal scarce and rewarded Capital; and the NMA, which by Restriction sought to make coal scarcer still and reward Labour. Deteriorations in work and status were understood accordingly as a failure of balance; redress was a natural quid pro quo:

> The last four years we know full well, our wages have come down,
> As far as 25%, five shillings in the pound;
> The cause of this we do not know, but we feel the effect,
> We're meanly fed and poorly clad, and treated with disrespect.
>
> Our masters say we might have earn'd, more money the last year
> But live and let our Neighbour live, this is the course we steer;

Had we not restricted ourselves that each might have a share,
One-fourth of us would paupers been to live on Workhouse fare.

I wonder how the masters can find so much fault with men,
For joining in a Union themselves for to defend;
These twenty seven years or more they've had their monthly Vend,
For to keep up the price of Coals, which they to market send.[65]

If Labour's money had been legitimately earned as members
of the productive classes, then so had Capital's; if both sides were
suffering deterioration then the fault lay with the 'middleman-
agent'. It had been suggested that

... the Miners' Union was established to set the men against the masters,
we deny this *in toto*, and we wish to give it the most unqualified
contradiction.

We are not so ignorant as to believe that he who sinks his capital should
not be remunerated ... But while we admit this, we claim the same
protection for our capital, namely, our labour.[66]

Both sides would gain from a restriction of out-put, based on the
Vend model, awarding just wages to Labour and proper profits
to Capital. It was even suggested that there were owners 'who know
nothing about the fines taken from their men', and that owners
and men should be on guard against 'a disposition on the part of
some of the Owners to break up the Vends altogether, and sell
what they can'.

We have not been kindly treated by your agents ... all the kindness we
court is to have an interview with our real employers.

Ask what it is that has reduced your profits and our labour? We say
over-production and competition. When we worked less hours we were
better paid ... your profits were greater.

We unite to reduce the hours of labour, to call into employ the
unemployed, and ultimately to make the product of our labour scarce
in the market, and thus give an advance of profit to the employer and
better wages to the workmen.[67]

No matter how naive the union's case might have been in the
matter of class relations, in terms of the industry's economic
performance their demands were not unreasonable. In spite of all
the wasteful over-capacity of the Vend the British coal industry,
with the northern coalfield in the van, was managing to hold down
prices during a crucial period of national economic development.
Throughout the eighteenth century to 1815 coal prices rose less

quickly than prices in general, but from 1815 to 1830 coal prices fell by only 21% against a 37% fall in general price levels – a noteworthy achievement in an industry suffering inherent problems of diminishing returns and rising marginal costs.[68] Of course, the overall strategy of the Vend was to retain price stability in order to ensure market share and regular demand. Demand does seem to have been fairly inelastic over a range of prices, a range which the Vend could not go above and which it existed to prevent renegades from going below.[69] But demand inelasticity assumed a regular supply. It only took small cuts in supply to raise London prices, and it was this supply which the union, imitating the regulations of Vend, sought to regulate on its own behalf through Restriction. And if the pitmen could influence the market, they could also put pressure on the owners. The productivity of the northern coalfield was the highest in Britain. Capital in-put per man in the UK coalfield doubled between 1816 and 1866. In the early century, the northern hewer, cutting coal at about 4.3 tons per shift or 1,160 tons per year, was producing at twice the rate of Scottish or Black Country hewers. Between 1800 and 1830 northern levels of output per man-year were always between about fifty and seventy tons in excess of the national average. Between 1830 and 1840 the excess grew to a massive 105 tons: 343 tons against 238.[70] Figures such as these were not available to the pitmen, but they instinctively grasped that their demands were possible without ruination:

> It may be very well to say that if the price of coals rises, so much will not be bought. But we know what we are about, we know that coals must be had. This country could no more go without coals than without meat.[71]

This was a 'labourist' political economy posed mainly against the market. The Capital–Labour division was assumed, but its current 'Tyranny' was a malfunction. The malfunction would only be corrected by Labour realising its true predicament and forcing its solution upon blocked minds and narrow interests for the good of all. Labour had lost its property just as men had lost their political rights. In the same way Labour would re-claim its property in the name of precedent, natural justice, and its own productive value. To win the strike would mean economic franchise, to lose it would mean dispossession. Just as Chartism swerved from constitutional libertarianism to social revolution and back again

as the best way to win the political franchise, so did the Association
sway between the constitutional rights of all property (including
Labour), and social revolution as the best way to win an economic
franchise. In this case, from the *Miners' Advocate* of 13 July 1844,
social revolution was posited as a solution to the problem of why
are men inevitably hypocrites. The link between political economy
and total human worth reveals an Owenite strain:

> ... society is based on a wrong foundation, and from its very consti-
> tution – from its arrangements into the classes of capitalists and
> labourers – from the unprincipled competition of the former, and the
> unhappy dependence of the latter, truth and goodness exist in our
> vocabulary to cloak selfishness and malignity.

For a union so politicised, the Association propagated a class
view of the economy which was strangely benign on the matter
of class as a political and social formation. Even if their union's
interpretation of class and economy was inadequate, the miners
nevertheless received an education in political economy whose
deficiencies in class analysis would be made up in the course of
the strike.[72]

The owners were implacably opposed to the union. They were
united in their opposition at the beginning, and at the end, and
refused throughout the five months of struggle to negotiate on any
point.[73] The pit community, they said, was well-paid, fed, and
housed compared to other labourers. The problem was that
coalfield population exceeded the demand for its labour in a
depressed market; it needed positive checks on reproduction. Here,
the owners' imagery of labour was the opposite of that from labour
value. Far from being the dynamic maker of value and surplus
value, labour – at least 'population' – was a dependent entity,
living only by a ratio of (its) numbers to (their) capital assets. This
neo-Malthusianism was in fact more a quarrel with women than
with men. The careless indulgence of wives was matched by the
good pay of their husbands.[74] The two went hand in hand: callow
girls met headstrong pitboys on high wages 'at the earliest age which
nature allowed and passion prompted', and the result was early
marriage and large families.[75] Just as 1812 was the year when
Revd Hodgson questioned the experience and craft of pitmanship,
so it was the year when Dr Baillie questioned the experience and
craft of nursing children – 'too long left to the management of
the lowest of the sex' who 'follow implicitly the example and

transmitted custom of their great-grandmothers'.[76] The inca-
pacity of working-class mothers to prepare their daughters stems
from this time. Coalfield babies kept coming, and they kept
coming to adolescent mothers who scarcely knew 'which end of
the baby to take hold of':[77]

> ... the unbridled freedom prevalent in the pitmen's houses, in the female
> part of their youthful population. So long as heads of families are
> receiving high wages girls cannot be prevailed upon to go out into
> service, or if they do, will commonly return home within three or four
> months. The result of habits like these might be anticipated *a priori*.

> The pit-population of the Tyne and Wear affords an example more
> complete than any other, of the principle of population operating in
> full vigour − in the absence of external influence, and (hitherto) of
> internal checks.[78]

The Poor Law Commission in 1834 heard many evidences of how
relief and prosperity eroded restraint − 'illicit intercourse has, in
almost all cases, orginated with the females' − and in its bastardy
clauses, the New Poor Law discouraged out-relief or putative
payments for single mothers. This was strictly applied in the
Sunderland and Hexham Poor Law Unions.[79] Unbridled female
carnality or low marital age were hardly matters the NMA could
negotiate on, and, ready with their plans and legitimated by the
State in their arguments, the coalowners set about the destruction
of the union.

With the support of the Home Office the coalowners began a
May policy of selective eviction, beginning in each village with the
president and secretary of the NMA branch.[80] As cottages were
emptied of families and furniture, workers were brought in from
other coalfields and from the Londonderry estates in Ulster. Chief
Constable Wemyss knew that these measures were intended to
'bring matters to a crisis'.[81] As Lord Lieutenant of County
Durham, Londonderry was responsible for law and order. He had
coveted the post and had been grateful to Peel when he got it, but
as the leading coalowner he also had to look to his business
interests. At the commencement of hostilities he had to be called
from Paris by letters from the Chief Constable, Hindhaugh his
viewer, and the magistrates.[82] The Londonderry concerns had
high stockpiles of coal. The strike meant that this stock, which
'in the late state of the Trade it had become difficult to say how
it was to be got rid of' could now be sold 'at excellent prices',

'converting the Old Heaps into Money'. Nathaniel Hindhaugh
made his employer's civil and commercial duties plain:

> As Lord Lieutenant and head of the Magistracy, your lordship will
> maintain the peace of the County; but as a Coal Owner your interest
> is directly opposed to any communication with your Pitmen having
> for its object the immediate resumption of their labour. They are
> perfectly quiet, and it is for us to let them remain so while their services
> are not wanted.

On 24 April, Hindhaugh had informed him that 'a cessation of
the Strike in less than three Weeks would be positively injurious
to your Lordship's Interest', and Londonderry followed his
advice.[83] After a convenient wait of five weeks, and with an
elaborate flourish, Londonderry resumed his duties as a Lord
Lieutenant of impeccable paternalist credentials:

> I was all day yesterday & the Day before with my men haranguing &
> demonstrating the folly & ruin to them of their union ... It will be a
> great point if I can sever my men from the Union ...

> I had a long meeting of the men employed in my Collieries to Day.
> They were very civil & seemed deeply weighed down by their position.
> On several little points of Detail they made Grievances but the greatest
> one of all is the Bond, now continued to a Monthly instead of a 12
> Months Agreement.

Now eager to settle for civil as well as for commercial reasons (by
14 June the strike was 'very disagreeable' to his concerns),
Londonderry immediately took this major grievance to the Trade.
His fellow-owners however were intent on the monthly binding
for this point above all others reduced the pitman to a labourer,
freed the labour market, and secured control:

> The real objection which the Men have to the Month's Hiring is, that
> it gives the Power to the Coal Owners to discharge any man for ill
> behaviour on a Month's Notice. *It is considered by the Trade at large
> that such a Power ought to be possessed by the Owners.*[84]

The Lord Lieutenant continued, unsuccessfully, to press the Trade
for a settlement. By 4 July the strike was doing 'incalculable'
damage to his business and local clergymen, shocked at the owners'
'one sided view of the subject', were pressing for a settlement. As
a consolation, the extent of Londonderry's failure could always
be presented as the extent of his good sense and paternalism:

No arguments would induce them to make a move towards the Pitmen. In vain I urged in my opinion the propriety after 10 weeks resistance of endeavouring to open a Door to negotiate on the Bond ... In vain I pressed that clauses might be introduced in the Yearly agreement to compel the men to do the stipulated work in respect of the Bond. In vain I entreated the Experiment might be tried when my men declared their only object now was to be sure of their Houses & Home for a year. It was all to no purpose. I had to make my choice under these circumstances of standing by the Trade or leaving them, and although I think them quite wrong I could not under the present position of affairs do otherwise than adhere entering my protest & my reasons on the Records of the Trade.[85]

The magistrates' first and only instinct was to call for more troops and police. Durham JPs could not 'for a moment consider [themselves] secure from violent riot'. Troops from the 37th Regiment and 89th Hussars were called in. Except through Londonderry's independent offices with 'his' men, the magistracy made no attempt to arbitrate. The Chief Constable had a force of eighty officers; a number he considered inadequate. The only reason why the coalfield was not swarming with more uniforms was the Home Office's refusal to supply Metropolitan police, requested by the Coal Trade Committee and a group of Durham magistrates who went over the heads of the Lord Lieutenant and the main body of magistrates. Incensed by this, Londonderry forced all county magistrates to reconsider, and reject by fifteen to ten, the request. But the magistrates were also reluctant to fund additional County police, a decision in which they were opposed by Londonderry, now at odds with all parties. The following month, the Lord Lieutenant bowed to the collapse of his peculiar notions of paternalism.[86] In the event, the magistrates' only recourse was to enlist special constables. These were recruited with difficulty and without conviction. In areas 'where the population is nearly all of one class' special constables were 'a force upon which very little reliance can be placed'. The pitmen's self-discipline in fact excused the specials from the test, but had it come there would have been no doubt about the result. Owners thought the specials were unable 'to act by themselves'; magistrates thought them 'quite inefficient from their fear of the Unionists'; the pitman Joseph Peel thought he was worthy of firmer opponents as he rescued his brother from their grasp: 'Before my brother shall be taken out of Bigge's Main, the Soldiers will be to fetch, and then

they will find some difficulty before they get him'. The Chief
Constable said of his confidence in his specials, 'I have none, they
have none in themselves, neither have the owners, nor the men
who are disposed to work'. In despair, some Durham collieries
hired police squads at their own expense.[87]

With oversight over the entire situation the government showed
its Peelite intelligence. The Prime Minister himself had refuted
early panic responses to the Miners' Association; it had remained
within the law and as long as it did so there was nothing he would
do. Sir James Graham, the Home Secretary, was sure of the need
to 'break the neck of this formidable combination', but with the
day to day matter of order on his mind he advised magistrates to
show the 'utmost patience and forbearance', and the army to show
discretion. In view of the army's traditional role, the Home Office's
advice to Lieutenant General Sir Thomas Arbuthnot was a sign
of changing times:

> ... it will be very inexpedient to bring up a Military Force within sight
> of the Meeting (which might have the effect of exciting and irritating
> the people assembled, as if done for the purpose of overawing) ...
> [troops] ... should rather be stationed at a convenient and safe
> distance.[88]

The strike opened with a meeting on Shadon's Hill on 8 April
1844. Most of the men and boys of the two counties appear to have
attended. They marched in by branches behind bands and gathered
on the natural amphitheatre of the hill. The *Advocate* for 20 April
1844 was 'glad to see that the meeting was honoured and cheered
by the presence of a great number of the "fair sex"'. The voice
of Primitive Methodism opened the proceedings. Mark Dent took
the chair: 'we will abide by our Association – we will stand
together till we obtain our rights – we are determined to be free!'
Dent was followed by three other delegates, each of them
Primitives. George Charlton moved the first resolution, that it was
their 'lawful and inherent right' to obtain a proper price for their
labour. This was seconded by Robert Archer, that this right was
supported by men's and God's laws. John Tulip moved the second
resolution, as 'the bees who produced the honey' they would not
sign the Bond, and he was seconded by William Jobling who called
for unity and lawfulness, 'liberty or death'. The third resolution
was moved by Edward Richardson, that they should support the
alternative Bond, as compiled by Mr Roberts, and Thomas Pratt

seconded with a summary of their grievances: long hours, intense work, low boys' wages, poor ventilation, and dangerous underground innovations such as canvas doors and Shetland ponies. Joseph Beeston moved the fourth resolution for order and negotiation, and William Daniells, editor of the *Advocate*, congratulated the men on their peaceful conduct to date. The last resolution came from William Mitchell who called upon the government to withdraw the export duty on coal and prayed that the 'iron arm of oppression will soon be broken'. The Chartist Robert Byrne then called for peace to 'masters, blacklegs, blue legs, or any other legs', and others joined in the joke. George Charlton envisaged the masters stripped and sweaty filling coal tubs before they could appreciate labour value, Mark Dent said he had once heard of a master who tried to hew and had '*blushed* his hands'. The meeting ended with criticism of Joseph Pease, the Darlington Quaker and financier, for his anti-union stance with support for slave-owner compensation, and with preacher Dent's benediction that in the battle between Labour and Capital 'RIGHT WILL OVERCOME MIGHT'.[89]

The primary battle was by labour, with labour, to control itself. Northumberland and Tyneside seem to have been fairly solid, but the newer mid-Durham collieries contained minorities of workers who continued to work after 8 April. The days immediately following the Shadon Hill meeting saw the effective intimidation of these men, and some women, from filling wagons at the pit-head. South Hetton was completely stopped on 8 April, Thornley, Pittington, Rainton, Penshaw, and North Hetton on the following day. Haswell, Kelloe, and South Wingate closed on the 10 April, and by 12 April Castle Eden, Trimdon, Evenwood, Coxhoe, Cassop, Ludworth, Murton, Monkwearmouth, and Edmondsley had closed their gates. 'In short the Pit District is now in the hands & at the mercy of the Pitmen'.[90] Intimidation quickened the efforts to recruit special constables. County Durham had completed its recruitment by early May and Northumberland by late May, although the magistrates of both counties were never happy about the quantity nor the quality.[91]

Intimidatory tactics, used first on local men who continued working, and extended later to blacklegs coming in from outside the area, were disciplined and selective. The community reapplied the techniques of direct action within a larger strategy of political economy. Intimidation is a sort of violence, but physical hurt was rare: the object was to frighten or to humiliate. Going to and from work blacklegs had to pass by the contempt of an entire community: 'the people don't attempt to injure ... but they get Tin Pans & every Tin Vessell they can lay their hands on, to make a noise, and annoy the people on the way Home':

> On their coming to bank at 12 o'clock they found a large crowd assembled, who assailed them with loud shouts and threats, the sound of a trumpet, and other noises, and the men were bustled by the crowd, but eventually succeeded by the assistance of the viewer, in reaching home without sustaining any serious injury. Hunter, one of the wastemen spoke to being pushed on and off the road, until he was landed in the hedge by Atkinson and Richardson: and another of the wastemen deposed to Grant having a tin trumpet and shoving him from behind, and to Vasey attempting to trip up his heels.

Sometimes the 'hissing and groaning', bustling and 'clapping their hands' was spiced by stones and buckshot. Coal-filling was stoned at bank; William Stoves at Castle Eden sat till 9.30 pm in his pit clothes as the crowd stoned his home; at Thornley shotguns were fired outside cottage doors.[92] Rough music played in the day and 'Rebecca' played at night. Wallsend, Thornley, Fawdon, and Monkwearmouth were all visited by her 'daughters' who inflicted abuse and harassment. Thomas Johnson, engineman at Castle Eden, was told by 'the Mother of so Numourous a famely' that if he was 'inclined to live a little longer' he 'Must Join the Union as Soun as Posable and Be As a Man in the Land of Freadem'; the fillers at North Hetton were told by 'Swing' to do their duty or 'take your fate like the dog and the Bull'.[93] It could have been that 'Rebecca's' night visits were the work of real women. Women re-assumed their traditional role in the intimidation. They were present in all the crowd actions, and seemed the 'more reckless', 'worse than the men'. They were 'generally put in the front, when ever a tumult is to take place', and their particular role was the humiliation of men who dared not, or would not, hit back. At South Wingate

> ... a rattle was sent round the village and a number of women assembled had proceeded to the pit heap ... and began to take away the men's shovels. A body of men followed the women, and incited them on to attack the men at work, by different exclamations and encouragements ... A body of women took hold of one of the men named Young, and were forcing him towards the pond, and beginning to strip his clothes off ...

At Byker, blacklegs had to scamper under a hail of offal from fishwives.[94]

Intimidation was well coordinated as a system both within and between the villages. At Kelloe on 10 April a crowd marched out behind their delegate with their banner at the head and met the men and women of Cassop who were arrayed the same. The force then went on to East Hetton colliery to throw stones at coal-fillers and police. The *Newcastle Courant* testified to the high level of coordination between villages. It was so high that even individuals moving from one colliery to work at another faced intimidation on leaving as well as on arriving. John Shipton's removal cart was surrounded at Coundon, rattling tea trays scared the horses, stones were thrown, the road was blocked, the contents of a chamber pot were tipped over his helper. Within the villages, Thomas Wood, viewer of Thornley, testified to a 'very violent & well organized ... continual system of terror'. 'Sentinels' were posted to watch for incomers and when sighted the alarm was called:

> The cry of 'all out' is not used for a meeting. The men are then summoned by a rattle sent round the place, with an intimation that a meeting is to be held at such and such a place and that all men are requested immediately to attend. The cry of 'all out' is only raised when there is to be a tumultuous meeting.

The police were usually the cause for alarm. Although there was a remarkable degree of respect for regular policemen arrests unaided by soldiers were always at the constable's own peril: 'He said if I did not relinquish my hold he would knock my bloody brains out'.[95]

The village could impose its own rough-handed control on fragments of workers who would not strike; Burdon told the government in June that 'The system of intimidation is nearly universal'. Small squads of constabulary were quite unable to defend strike-breakers from crowds numbering hundreds. However, the May decision to evict delegates from their homes and force the opening of selected collieries, aided by concentrations of police and troops, followed by the Trade's June announcement that it would not negotiate, proved to be more than the community could handle.[96] As strikers were evicted and 'strangers' installed, the cases of riot, assault, and intimidation increased. The *Newcastle Journal* did not help matters by extensive reportage of the influx, and inaccurate, gratuitous comment on how easily new men could master the pitmens' skills.[97] By 12 June the situation in the major Durham collieries was as follows:

	Men hewing	Men having left NMA	Families evicted
Lambton's collieries	141	18	107
Hetton colliery	148	52	174
S. Hetton and Murton	178	126	69
Londonderry's collieries	282	78	176[98]

Fearful lest their general control would collapse in a random scatter of small riots and arrests, the NMA responded by convivial demonstrations of strength. The first evictions at Tanfield were treated in a festival atmosphere as the evicted were each celebrated as victors. The place was carefully chosen as 'an outside and thinly populated portion of the Colliery district ... for the purpose of awing and intimidating the orderly and well-disposed portion.[99] Rallies like this were stepped up through late June and July. The NMA moved new professional lecturers into the field and these joined with local Primitives in highly enthusiastic union 'prayer-meetings' from village to village. As late as 29 July only 1,467 men had left the union; disconsolate at the news of Roberts' re-appointment, Londonderry commented that 'This does not look like giving in. I am almost fearful of bringing over more Irishmen'.[100]

The union's defiance belied terrible suffering. By 11 May even the hostile *Newcastle Journal* had to admit to 'the greatest distress' prevailing, with some too weak to leave their beds. Starvation was reported by Mr Hawley, Assistant Commissioner, and in June an eighteen-year-old miner at Elswick colliery died from malnutrition:

> Multitudes of them resort to the sea shore living & sleeping amongst the rocks, where they exist on refuse fish, and any other eatable matter they can collect; many of them are provided with Guns, and the small birds which they procure by this means have for some time contributed to afford them the means of subsistence; and begging is extensively resorted to.[101]

In the second and third weeks of August the move back to the collieries began. The Bond was signed on the terms and conditions offered previous to 5 April. To stem the flood, the NMA called for an orderly and negotiated return. Some of the militant collieries retrenched and redeclared the battle, but by 10 August with over 6000 hewers already at work there were more men than jobs.

The *Advocate* asked the Trade to employ local men, being of a higher moral character than the 'mean crouching slaves' who had replaced them. The Executive Council, beaten into an owners' market and no longer in control of labour, thought they 'must in future, proceed with more caution'. The National Conference, meeting at Wakefield in November, changed direction. It denounced strikes as acrimonious, internecine, painful; it talked of a 'new light', of action through public opinion, parliament, and its own circumspection.[102]

Some hard-core branches like Cramlington and Thornley agitated on. In December the militants called on the two counties to 'shake off our apathy'; in January 1845 they lectured in the moonlight because the pubs were closed to them. But there was no mitigation: the monthly Bond would very soon secure their unemployment, the community needed to work almost on any terms that would feed it. In February the Oldham strike fund received not a single northern contribution, in April W. P. Roberts could only muster a small crowd at Thornley, in March 1846 the former president of the NMA was driven from Haswell after trying to raise money for the Lancashire strike.[103] An era of trade unionism had ended.

Conclusion

The National Miners' Association had injected a theory of political economy into a trade dispute. From the Brotherhood's efforts at controlled bargaining early in the century, through the political penetrations of 1819, the emergence of the United Colliers in 1825, Hepburn's strategies of 1831–2, and the Chartist enlightenment of 1838–40, the pit villages had assimilated a theory and practice of trade unionism.

From inside the villages this new consciousness of 'community' grew reactively and tensely with traditional, direct, modes of protest. The sense of labour-value reacted with an older sense of the true-bred pitman and the national importance of coal; the calls to order demonstrated the tension of a union control which was in fact precarious; the women remained adept at older methods of direct action; they showed some collective realisation of their new position as the disenfranchised, as dealers, and as bearers of family need; and they were articulate, when consulted, about housing, Poor Law, and sanitary arrangements — even if they exerted little pressure here as an independent body.

From outside the villages there were parallel developments. After 1819 the reciprocity of direct action, the cohesive role of the magistracy, and the coercive weakness of government were diminishing factors. Labour and Capital, already moving apart by financial and structural changes in the industry, were more and more left to their own devices. The magistracy increasingly evacuated the middle ground and relied upon army and police to keep the peace. The dissolution of reciprocity and cohesion lessened the usefulness of direct action as a technique of protest. By 1839 Chartist agitators had recognised the political implications of these developments, and charged the magistracy with the responsibility born of their own neglect: '... the magistrates, the dispensers of law, the redressors of grievances in the constitution, as it is called – it is to them we look – at their feet we will lay all the acts of blood that may take place ..."[1]

The NMA had met the new situation with a theory and an action to accompany it. The 1844 strike represented a climax of new developments, a coalescence of a political-economic view of labour and its orderly and united withdrawal as a form of social protest, even, it was hoped, as a technique of social change. The idea of a strike was premised by the idea of labour value. NMA policy tried to unite 'Labour' and 'Capital' as common property interests against the market. Capital's refusal to talk, let alone unite, made unorganised labour the union's most besetting problem. In truth, this had always been so. The monthly Bond, signed after the collapse of the strike, made the organisation of labour more difficult still. The union rumbled on at local level until the end of the decade. In 1849 and 1851 there were strikes at the leading union collieries, Seaton Delaval, Marley Hill, Hetton, and Lord Durham's pits, over the same issues, and with the same results as in 1844 – eviction, blacklegging, victimisation, defeat. Some sort of union network was still operating in 1854, but as a nationally co-ordinated movement, the union had been waning since 1847.[2] From the Coal Trade's point of view, the Vend was cracked so badly in 1844 that it never recovered. There were attempts, in 1845 and 1847–51, first to amalgamate all collieries into one company, and then to re-regulate production according to particular markets. Meetings were held, prospectuses were printed, committees were formed, in 1851 even an agreement was reached, but it all came to nothing. Lord Londonderry had derided the schemes, he and Lord Durham had refused to co-operate, new railways carried other counties' coal into London at prodigious rates from 1850, and the venture fell. After 1845, coalowners in the North East competed with each other and with other coalfields in a virtually unfettered market.[3]

In the midst of defeat the Executive Council had appealed to young pitmen to 'Read ... Think for yourselves ... Associate ... Learn to speak in public.[4] These men were to be the next generation of trade unionists in the new era of county unionism from the 1860s. It was this generation which surrendered to the employers' market practices and, in their conciliation and sliding-scale schemes took the market as the standard by which Labour was to be remunerated. Concurrently, they toiled with no little success to regulate and protect the position of their members in that market. The industry experienced a massive growth in manpower, nationally there were half a million miners by 1873 and over a million by 1913. By then, hewers were back to artisan levels of pay if not artisan levels of status. If Labour and Capital had each withdrawn to their respective places, the distinctiveness of each was emphasised. The character of the new association, and the circumstances under which it was made – class consciousness, federation, caution, benefit, negotiation, the strictest control of labour by labour for labour, a Labour Party even – had their origins in the events of 1844. When this generation responded to the Hartley colliery disaster in 1862, it was a *Permanent* Relief Fund they helped found. Whatever its legal definition, permanence was built-into their idea of associating because, as a class, they were here to stay. When this generation founded their county unions from the 1860s, and the Miners' Federation of Great Britain from 1888, their achievements should not be underrated. These institutions' prime achievement lay in their own existence. To bring into union men who worked different seams in different ways for different markets under different ownerships, and to keep them in union, was an education in first principles.

This book set out to study social change. 'Social change' is a deceptively simple phrase, for its human meanings are complex. Prompted by Robert Owen's 1815 observation that a 'general diffusion of manufactures throughout a country generates a new character in its inhabitants', the volume has endeavoured to understand these human complexities.

'New character' may be regarded neither as an objective assessment not as a settled condition. It depends upon ways of seeing the nature of human relations, over time. In the fluidity of present experience these vary from person to person, group to group, class to class. However, it is possible, over long runs of time, to locate established and emergent patterns of perception, and even logics of perception, which are connected to social structure. It is the historian's task, and privilege, to narrate these movements.

In the northern coalfield we have seen the emergence of two major movements whose perceptions struggled for shares of control of a changing social structure – the coalowners and the pitmen. This is to offer the history of the coalfield at its starkest.

That there were other perceptions, logics, and struggles is not in doubt: between owners and magistrates; between magistrates and Home Office; between army and owners and magistrates; between engineers and pitmen; between men and women; between Trade and Metropolis; between Vend and its competitors; between union and blacklegs; between Chartists and government; between Chartists and 'middle-men'; between Methodists and the world without. The list could go on. And to go on would not be to posit some crude notion of perpetual conflict in social relations, for the reality of conflict presupposes an equal reality of association. This study has tried to account for the conflict and association of these relations but, in order to remain faithful to its subject, and because it believes that the determining relationship was infact between owners and pitmen, it has studied 'new character' in the light of how the community saw itself, in relation to how others saw it, over sixty years of structural change.

At the core of this social change was the shift from a caste of 'true-bred pitmen' to a market in labourers, from a practice of womanhood − as yet under-researched − to new formulations of femininity more personal and private. For the men, this change in productive relations was accompanied by integral changes in social relations. For the women, this reformulation of social relations was accompanied by integral ideas of desired change in productive relations. Becoming a marketed labourer, or a domiciled wife, was not only an encounter with work, or household, it was also an encounter with the self and carried with it aspects of moral worth and human dignity. Nor were these changes enacted 'one way', from those above onto those below. Those above may have initiated the changes, their's was the greater power to do so, but they by no means controlled its processes. There was a period, in the late 1840s and 1850s, with the oppositions of the past sixty years appearently weakened or destroyed, when those above were confident that they could initiate change and manipulate perceptions. This was a chimera. After 1844, as before it, social change was critically connected to crises in the balance of power. Work, culture, and protest continued to be sites of association and conflict; their forms may change but the balance of power was never the settled issue some owners thought it was in the 1850s.

The classic mining community of the late nineteenth century

took its structure – indeed it took its 'community' – from the associations and conflicts of work, culture, and protest. For the 1860s, pit village 'community', or lack of it, came to be defined in precisely these terms – schools, reading rooms, lecture halls, cooperative stores, workers' organisations. The pit village was an overwhelmingly proletarian place based upon a glaring division of Labour and Capital. It had long been such. What was different, what was 'classic', was the way in which the pit village corresponded to descriptive and prescriptive images of an English working class. The consciousness of this class could no longer be denied; few thought seriously now of razing its institutions and practices. In the northern coalfield the Methodist presence had come to dominate the imagery of the mining community. This explains Revd Christie's remarks in the Introduction. It was now seen as a community more plain and sober, more disciplined, more temperamentally suited to its function, than it had been before. This solid image was a central perception of the English working class. Also, the community's modes of protest were seen as accommodating its labourer status. A whole culture was geared to this status and afforded some protection from it. Machinery was no longer destroyed, troops were rarely required; the new accent was on union, benefit, education, the regulation of labour, by labour. Similarly with the character of the people themselves. Work, cultural, and protest relations, given that they had meaning for lived experience, were not divisible; they were the condition of each other, and the representative figure of the community represented both the unity and tension of these relations. The Methodist pitman – black-suited on Sundays, a teetotaler, self-taught, widely respected, sometimes feared, chairman of his lodge, and a Lib-Lab in politics – was such a figure. When he encountered the labour market, this man was a collectivist and a disciplinarian, in contemporary parlance, a 'labourite'. When he encountered his own self, and his soul's triumphant passage, this man was an individualist, personally culpable, standing on his own two feet. Thomas Burt was such a man. In 1893, as MP for Morpeth and a leader of his class, Burt met Gladstone. He hung on the Prime Minister's every word:

> Then, turning to me, he said: 'Mr Burt, I think on the whole matters are going very well, I take a sanguine view of the future, so far as our working men are concerned. The workmen have great power, social

and political. Their faculty for organisation is marvellous, and gives them enormous influence ... Yet there are, in my opinion, dangers ahead. While the working men of the country rightly value union, I am not sure that they recognize in the same degree the vital importance of individual liberty. That they must be taught, or they will suffer for it, and inflict grievous injuries upon themselves and others. One thing gives me unqualified satisfaction, it is that the workmen know how to select their leaders. They do not choose charlatans to represent them in Parliament'. This in substance, if not exact phraseology, was what Mr Gladstone said. My own part of the conversation I need not put on record.[5]

Burt was one of the post-1844 generation. Mr Gladstone spoke for him and he for Mr Gladstone. The meaning of his kind of 'character' awaits another history which begins where this one has ended.

Notes

Introduction

1. *The Report of the Newcastle Religious Tract Society*, Newcastle, 1817, p. 24; Revd J. Christie, *Northumberland: its History, its Features, and its People*, Carlisle, 1904, p. 110.
2. For an original discussion of the restructuring of human character to meet epochal social transformation, see: E. P. Thompson, 'Time, work-discipline, and industrial capitalism', *Past and Present*, 38, 1967.
3. R. Wilson, 'The coal miners of Durham and Northumberland: their habits and diseases', paper read before *British Association for the Advancement of Science*, Newcastle, 1863.

Chapter one

1. A. G. Kenwood, *Capital Investment in North Eastern England 1800–1913*, University of London unpublished PhD, 1962, p. 36, p. 163, p. 87. Roy Church, with A. Hall and J. Kanefsky, *The History of the British Coal Industry, 1830–1913: Victorian Pre-eminence*, Oxford, 1986, p. 108.
2. N. K. Buxton, *The Economic Development of the British Coal Industry*, London, 1978, pp. 66–8; M. W. Flinn with D. Stoker, *The History of the British Coal Industry, 1700–1830: The Industrial Revolution*, Oxford, 1984, p. 31, pp. 280–5; Kenwood, *Capital Investment*, p. 81. A. D. Knighton ('The Development of the Northumberland Coalfield: a study in the concept of cost distance', *Northern Universities Geographical Journal*, 1967) has estimated coal transport costs as dropping from 8d per ton-mile in the 17th century, to 3d per ton-mile with wagonways in the 18th century, to 1d per ton-mile with steam power in the 19th century.
3. Church, *British Coal Industry*, p. 122; Flinn and Stoker, *The History*, p. 203, p. 206; Kenwood, *Capital Investment*, pp. 91–2. The total capital estimates for the 1840s and 1850s appear to be overestimates when set alongside Church's estimates for all British coalfields whether measured in terms of replacement cost or historic total cost (pp. 102–3). Indeed, although Church and his colleagues do not address the North East specifically, by estimating average fixed-capital requirements for North East mines before 1855 at £19,000 per venture, they have radically revised total North-East capital investment in a downward direction. They do admit that requirements of between £25,000 to £35,000 were not uncommon but even these figures would continue to suggest a lower total capital investment in the area below what has previously been estimated: Church, pp. 121, 122.
4. Flinn and Stoker, *The History*, pp. 20–1; P. Cromar, 'The coal industry on Tyneside, 1771–1800; oligopoly and spatial change', *Economic Geography*, 53, 1977, p. 92.
5. Mitchell estimates trade peaks in 1825, 1836–7, 1844–6, and troughs

in 1840 and 1851: B. R. Mitchell, *Economic development of the British coal industry 1800–1914*, Cambridge, 1984, pp. 6–7.

6. J. W. House, *Population Changes since the Early Nineteenth Century*, Newcastle Kings College, 1954, p. 61. There is a decennial break in his figures for 1836–51. Calculations from 1843 tally with House's figures for 1826–36: the contemporary author was keen to show that such unprecedented growth demonstrated that a North-East coalowners' regulation was 'the best preservative against monopoly'. The monopoly referred to was that of the London factors and middlemen: Anti Monopolist, *Remarks on the Present State of The Coal Trade with a retrospective glance at its history*, Newcastle, 1843, p. 48. For estimates of North-East output, its type and distribution between 1700–1830, see: Flinn and Stoker, *The History*, p. 35. Between 1700 and 1830 the British coal industry expanded its production tenfold; between 1830 and 1913, ninefold (Church, *British Coal Industry*, p. 759).

7. Mitchell, *Economic development*, p. 317; P. E. H. Hair, *The Social History of British Coalminers 1800–45*, University of Oxford unpublished PhD, 1955, pp. 6–8; M. Sill, *Hetton-le-Hole: The Genesis of a Coalmining Landscape, 1770–1860*, University of Durham unpublished MA, 1974, i, p. 76. It is not possible to rely upon a rigid correlation between increased output and increased labour recruitment because lack of innovation in technology at the coalface did not mean that productivity did not increase, and because coalowners and their workmen were actively regulating out-put.

8. Estimates vary: Hair, *Social History*, p. 27c; House, *Population Changes*, p. 61; Mitchell, *Economic development*, p. 106. For 1844–53 the proportions above and below ground were about the same: Church, *British Coal Industry*, p. 210.

9. *Summary of the Condition of the Pitmen on the Tyne-by Mr W. Thomas of Benton Hall to Sir John Swinburne*, 1807, NEIMME, vol. Xa.

10. Hair, *Social History*, p. 27c; *Report S. C. House of Lords on State of Coal Trade*, Parliamentary Papers 1830(9), viii, p. 54; *Second Report S C on Accidents in Coal Mines,* PP 1854 (258), ix, p. 31; Mitchell, *Economic development*, p. 122, p. 106.

11. House, *Population Changes*, p. 56; Sill, *Hetton*, p. 116; W. A. Moyes, *Mostly Mining*, Newcastle, 1969, p. 100; Township of Cockfield, *Census 1851*, DCRO; Church, *British Coal Industry*, pp. 233–5; *Poor Law. Assistant Commissioner's Report, App. A, Pt I (Northumberland and Durham)*, PP 1834 (44), xxviii; *Third Report SC on Accidents in Coal Mines*, PP 1853 (820), xx, p. 47; Sill, *Hetton*, figs. 23–7.

12. 'For some kinds of labour, whose conditions did not change fundamentally as yet – again miners and seamen come to mind – the old traditions could still suffice': E. J. Hobsbawm, *Industry and Empire*, London, 1968, p. 70.

13. *Gateshead Observer*, 29 January 1842. In view of the short-distance nature of coalfield migration, it seems Embleton was being alarmist.

14. Committee of Coal Owners of the Rivers Tyne and Wear, *Minute Book*, i, October 1809, NCRO; for knowledge of the hewers, see the Complaints

and Deviations section of the book. Flinn and Stoker reckon there were 3,400 hewers for the whole coalfield in 1807–09: *The History*, p. 363.

15. 'Th. S.' [Thomas Sopwith] to *Tyne Mercury*, 7 July 1832.

Chapter two

1. E. A. Rymer, *The Martyrdom of the Mine, or a Sixty years struggle for life*, 1898, p. 5, republished in History Workshop Journal, 1, 1976.

2. George Patterson's research group found a strong impression of family interconnectedness across the coalfield, clearly a potent source of community solidarity: G. Patterson, ed., *Monkwearmouth Colliery in 1851: an analysis of the census returns*, Durham University, 1977, pp. 39–42; for an analysis of 'skill', genuine and socially constructed, see: C. More, *Skill and the English Working Class, 1870–1914*, London, 1980.

3. 'Informations of Witnesses before J. P. Stokoe, Coroner, 21 January 1811', North East Circuit Assize depositions, PRO, ASSI/45/45; Anon., *The Pits and The Pitmen*, nd, p. 22.

4. W. Hopton, *Conversation on Mines between a Father and Son*, Manchester, nd; J. Lawson, *A Man's Life*, London, 1944, pp. 46–7.

5. J. Burnett, ed., *Useful Toil*, London, 1974, p. 26; R. Harrison, Introduction, in Harrison, ed., *Independent Collier: The Coal Miner as Archetypal Proletarian Reconsidered*, Brighton, 1978, p. 4; J. R. Harris, 'Skills, coal and British industry in the eighteenth century', *History*, 61, 1976, p. 182.

6. John Buddle in, *Report SC on Accidents in Mines*, PP 1835 (603), v, p. 134.

7. W. Howitt, *Visits to Remarkable Places*, London, 1842, p. 88. Howitt was paraphrasing what pitmen had told him. It is strange that they should have scorned the 'pit-cap without even a brim' when Rymer remembered 'true-bred' pitmen wearing skull-caps in the 1840s. (fn. 1).

8. J. Peile to J. Buddle, 18 October 1823, DCRO, NCB 1/JB; Buddle to Lord Londonderry, 3 November 1823, DCRO, D/Lo/C 142.

9. W. Lowrie to J. Buddle, 8 April 1825, NCB 1/JB; for seeing 'them begin at five or six years of age, with a string tied to them for fear of losing them', see: T. Atkinson, *Report SC House of Lords on Occurrence of Dangerous Accidents in Coal Mines*, PP 1849 (613), vii, p. 527.

10. *Accidents in Mines*, PP 1835, p. vi.

11. Rymer, *Martyrdom*, p. 3.

12. J. Buddle to Lord Lambton, 28 May 1842, NCB 1/JB.

13. *Children's Employment Commission, Appendix to the First Report of Commissioners, Mines, Part 1*, PP 1842 (381), xvi, p. 514. (henceforward *CEC 1842*).

14. *Memorandum*, 18 November 1806, NCRO, DE/4/28; T. Johnston to Lord Delaval, 10 February 1801, NCRO, DE/7/6.

15. *Dangerous Accidents*, PP 1849, p. 522.

16. *Report SC on State of Coal Trade*, PP 1836 (522), xi, p. 24.

17. J. Buddle to Londonderry, 27 March 1843, D/Lo/C 142. Ashton and Sykes recognised a deterioration in labour skills, but their timing of the deterioration was mainly guesswork: (for the first half of the nineteenth century) an 'influx … of a population that had neither the professional traditions nor technical skill of colliers of the eighteenth century', in, T. S. Ashton and J. Sykes, *The Coal Industry of the Eighteenth Century* Manchester, 1929, p. 159.

18. For example, see the evidence of Martin Jude, *Dangerous Accidents*, PP 1849, p. 536.

19. See Part Three of the volume for a full account of blackleg labour.

20. *A correct Account of the Explosion at Kenton Pit on Monday October 14 1844*, Newcastle, 1844; *Miners' Advocate*, 19 October 1844.

21. *Newcastle Journal*, 5 October 1844; W. P. Roberts, *The Haswell Colliery Explosion*, Newcastle, 1844; *Newcastle Journal*, 12 October 1844. I have been unable to trace any similar outcry after the 1832 explosions.

22. *Report SC on Mines*, PP 1866 (431), xiv, p. 190; *Report SC on Coal*, PP 1873 (313), x, pp. 118, 126, 57; David Swallow, *Second Report SC on Accidents in Coal Mines*, PP 1853 (940), xx, p. 47.

23. J. H. H. Holmes, *A Treatise on the Coal Mines of Durham and Northumberland*, London, 1816, p. 30; for the seventeenth century see the account given to the Royal Society in, J. U. Nef, *The Rise of the British Coal Industry*, 1932, London, i, p. 173.

24. Report of the South Shields Committee appointed to investigate the causes of accidents in coal mines; containing an examination of safety lamps, ventilation, scientific instruments, infant labour etc, in *Second Report SC on Coal Mines*, PP 1852 (509), v, p. 160. The Shields Committee originally reported in 1842.

25. *Report SC state of the Coal Trade in the Port of London*, PP 1830 (663), viii, p. 317.

26. *Dangerous Accidents*, PP 1849, p. 190; Mitchell, *Economic development*, p. 80; for accounts of ventilation principles and history see: *South Shields Committee*, R. L. Galloway, *Annals of Coal Mining and the Coal Trade*, 1898, 1904, two vols, Newton Abbot 1971, *passim*, and Buxton, *British Coal Industry*, pp. 24–5, 70–6.

27. *South Shields Committee*, p. 175.

28. *South Shields Committee*, p. 334; *Accidents in Mines*, PP 1835, p. 13; *Dangerous Accidents*, PP 1849, p. 529, p. 141; for particular criticism of furnaces see PP 1849, p. 282. For shafts as a proportion of capital costs: Church, *British Coal Industry*, p. 111.

29. *South Shields Committee*, p. 179, p. 181.

30. J. Kenyon Blackwell, *Report on Ventilation of Mines, 25 March 1850, with Plans*, PP 1850 (1214), xxiii, p. 21; *Miners' Advocate*, 14 December 1844; *Dangerous Accidents*, PP 1849, p. 146. Fynes reckoned that between September 1817 and August 1845 there had been six explosions at Jarrow taking 135 lives: R. Fynes, *The Miners of Northumberland and Durham*, 1873, East Ardsley, 1971, p. 123. When trade unionism revived in the coalfield during the early 1860s it relentlessly campaigned against insufficient ventilation by too few shafts. The Coal Mines

Regulation Act of 1872 made the working of single shaft mines unlawful.
A second shaft could also be a vital escape route for survivors trapped
beneath the first shaft.

31. *Accidents in Mines*, PP 1835, p. 21, p. 145, p. 147, p. 282; *South Shields Committee*, p. 182.
32. Mitchell, *Economic development*, pp. 75–6, estimates a large increase in productivity, about 20%–30%, resulting from powder blasting; *Report Commissioners Accidents in Mines*, PP 1881 (3036). xxvi, p. xiii, p. 175, p. 194, p. 204, p. 211; Church, *British Coal Industry*, p. 342.
33. For a description of wedge and mallet technique, J. Brand, *The History and Antiquities of the Town and County of Newcastle upon Tyne*, London, 1789, ii, p. 681; and for a description of gunpowder and its danger, Galloway, *Annals*, i, pp. 508–11. For viewers: Thomas Crawford, 8 March 1852, *Diary 1852–5*, NCL; and Buddle, in Galloway, *Annals*, i, pp. 510–11. For Oaks disaster: J. Benson and R. G. Neville, eds., *Studies in the Yorkshire coal industry*, Manchester, 1976, p. 78.
34. *Report Inspectors use of Blasting Powder in Fiery Mines, the Secretary of State having referred back to them their Collective Report of 1875*, PP 1876 (1449), xvii, *passim; Collective Report of Inspectors of Mines relating to the Use of Blasting Powder in Fiery Mines*, PP 1875 (417), xvi, p. 15.
35. Powder is one of the main themes in the repertoire of questions put by Commissioners, *Accidents*, PP 1881.
36. Between 1815–35 the use of the Davy 'was almost solely confined to the pillar or 'broken' working; the first, or 'whole mine' working, continuing to be carried on with candles': Galloway, *Annals*, i, p. 509.
37. For full explanations of 'creep' and 'thrust' see G. C. Greenwell, *A Glossary of Terms used in the Coal Trade of Northumberland and Durham*, 1849, 1888, Newcastle, 1970, pp. 26–7, p. 29.
38. Flinn and Stoker, *The History*, pp. 82–3; Greenwell, *Glossary*, p. 61.
39. Flinn and Stoker, *The History*, pp. 88–9.
40. Evidence of John Taylor, *Accidents in Mines*, PP 1835, p. 19; of Anthony Winship, wasteman, p. 37; of John Buddle, p. 167; of George Stephenson, p. 106; of Buddle, p. 219. Evidence of Thomas Batty (aged ninety-three years, a pitman for seventy-eight years), and Ralph Hall (aged seventy-seven years, a pitman for seventy years), *CEC 1842*, p. 574; Nicholas Wood, *Accidents in Mines*, PP 1835, p. 75.
41. *Accidents in Mines*, PP 1835, p. 143; for detailed descriptions of goafs and engineering problems see *CEC 1842*, p. 545, and S. C. Crone, 'Observations on pillar working in the Northumberland and Durham collieries', *NEIMME Transactions*, ix, 1860–1.
42. John Phillips, *Report on Ventilation of Mines and Collieries*, PP 1850 (1222), xxiii, p. 4; *Accidents in Mines*, PP 1835, p. 30. By the 1880s the broken was acknowledged as extremely dangerous work. Hewers worked with deputies in propping, and received special payments: *Accidents*, PP 1881, p. 203.
43. The Dorothea pit at Philadelphia in Co. Durham, and South Hetton colliery, were judding during the 1840s, *CEC 1842*, p. 153; for roof fall

and explosion hazards of drawing the jud, *CEC 1842*, p. 149, p. 545, and Crone, 'Observations on pillar working', pp. 22–3; and for Buddle's extraction rates, *Accidents in Mines*, PP 1835, pp. 144–5; for a summary of changes in pillar working, and details of their changing depth, size, proportion, and shape, over the 18th and 19th centuries: Galloway, *Annals*, ii, pp. 230–4, and Ashton and Sykes, *Coal Industry*, pp. 14–32.

44. *Accidents in Mines*, PP 1835, p. vii; *State of Coal Trade*, PP 1836, p. 49; W. Martin, *The Philosopher's Letter to the British Government in behalf of the Poor Pitmen*, Newcastle, 23 July 1844; N. Wood, *Inaugural Address to North of England Institute of Mining Engineers*, Durham, 1852, pp. 14–15.

45. Flinn and Stoker, *The History*, p. 419; *CEC 1842*, p. 553. The 1842 Commissioners faced a dearth of records by colliery doctors and surgeons. Nor did the majority of doctors and surgeons feel free to make comment. Hetton was one of only a few collieries with consistent medical records, and their list of injuries from January 1837 to June 1840 is reproduced in *CEC 1842*, pp. 550–4; for a comparison of accidents and injuries at Haswell and East Holywell collieries for 1849–51 see: *Second Report Accidents*, PP 1854, pp. 30–1.

46. P. E. H. Hair, 'Mortality from violence in British coal-mines 1800–50', *Economic History Review*, xxi, 1968, pp. 551–2.

47. Hair, 'Mortality', p. 550, p. 560, pp. 552–3. Flinn and Stoker's section on 'Health and Accidents' (pp. 412–23) is required reading, but they badly misinterpret Hair's text by accepting figures from a *Table* which Hair disowns as 'almost valueless'. Thus their figure (p. 419) of 1.3 deaths from violence per 1000 employed per year for the late 1820s (a figure just over half the rate per English and Welsh collieries in 1873–82), can be ignored.

48. C. Storm-Clark thinks over-famous for them: 'The miners, 1870–1970: a test case for oral history', *Victorian Studies*, 15, 1971, p. 52.

49. For a contemporary account of innovations see, Matthias Dunn, *An Historical, Geographical, and Descriptive View of the Coal Trade of the North of England*, Newcastle, 1844, and report of Commissioner Mitchell for South Durham, *CEC 1842*, pp. 119–23. The serious student of technological history should look at B. F. Duckham's bibliography in, Galloway, *Anals*, i, pp. 11–15. On air currents and 'asthma': *Dangerous Accidents*, PP 1849, p. 78, p. 191, p. 202, p. 603, and *Accidents in Mines*, PP 1835, p. 167. On pneumoconiosis: A. Meiklejohn, 'History of lung diseases of coal miners in Great Britain: part 1, 1800–1875', *British Journal of Industrial Medicine*, 8, 1951.

50. R. Challinor and B. Ripley, *The Miners' Association. A Trade Union in the Age of the Chartists*, London, 1968, p. 96; *Report Commissioner State of the Population in The Mining Districts*, PP 1846 (737), xxiv, p. 10; John Robson, viewer at Hetton colliery, *Report of 1842*, D/Lo/C 142; Mr Hunter, overman at Walker colliery, *CEC 1842*, p. 627; T. Wilson, *The Pitman's Pay; or, a night's discharge to care*, Gateshead, 1830.

51. *Pits and The Pitmen*, pp. 10–11; William Anderson, viewer at St Hilda colliery, *CEC 1842*, p. 637.

52. Detailed descriptions of traditional mode in, *CEC 1842*, pp. 126–7, and *Pits and The Pitmen*, pp. 11–12; George Elliot, coalowner, and pitboy in 1831, *Sixth Report Commissioners into Organization and Rules of Trade Unions*, PP 1867–8 (3980–II), xxxix, p. 1.

53. Lord Londonderry and others, *A Letter to the Right Honourable Lord Ashley MP,* London, 1842, p. 14; for double, treble, and longer stints involving up to thirty-six hours consecutive labour see, *CEC 1842*, p. 586, p. 676, and *Children's Employment Commission. First Report of Commissioners. Mines.* PP 1842 (380), xv, pp. 116–7. George Johnson, viewer at Willington, Heaton, and Burdon Main collieries, appeared to be referring to these stints when he reckoned that only five out of every hundred collieries would be working them at any one time: *CEC 1842*, p. 567, and Commissioner Mitchell, p. 152. It is possible, however, that Johnson's 5% estimate did in fact refer to *regular* double shifts rather than stints because William Hunter, viewer at Walbottle colliery estimated 6% with the following remark: 'A regular double shift pit is not a common thing', *CEC 1842*, p. 617.

54. *CEC 1842*, p. 148, and further examples of this short double shift, pp. 155–6. Willington was working a regular three shift system of eight hours for hewers, supported by two shifts of boys on twelve hours, p. 567.

55. J. Ginswick, ed., *Labour and the Poor in England and Wales 1849–51. Letters to the Morning Chronicle from the Correspondents*, London, 1983, ii, pp. 34–5.

56. For customary differences in calculation, Mitchell, *CEC 1842*, p. 127. Evidence on approximate hours comes from *Coal*, PP 1873, p. 50, pp. 53–4, p. 111, p. 121, p. 152; *Labour Statistics from Board of Trade 1887–92*, PP 1890–1 (6455), lxxviii, p. xiii; *Royal Commission on Labour. Minutes of Evidence before Group A*, i, PP 1892 (6708–IV), xxxiv, p. 6, p. 16, pp. 32–3, pp. 131–2, p. 138, p. 182, p. 191. In 1892 eleven Durham collieries were working a three shift system, *R C Labour, Minutes of Evidence before Group A*, iii, PP 1893–4 (6894–VII), xxxii, p. 447. It should be stressed that across sources of evidence, and within them, one can find contradictory estimates of hours.

57. *CEC 1842*, p. 127, p. 152, p. 676.

58. *Accidents in Mines*, PP 1835, p. 39; *Coal*, PP 1873, p. iv, p. 153; *Board of Trade*, PP 1890–1, p. xii.

59. Longwall working advanced against a 'long' coalface as teams relieved each other in one operative process – the first team cutting and blasting, the second team filling, and the third team propping. This operation more naturally suggested a two or three shift system. In 1835 Buddle said he would use any technique he thought would fit the local geology, but longwall did not usually come into that category: *Accidents in Mines*, PP 1835, p. 145. This view was echoed, for Northumberland, as late as 1871 (*Report Commissioners on coal in the UK*, ii, PP 1871 (435–I), xviii, p. 370) but there were systematic experiments with longwalling in the 1840s which were abandoned in the 1850s and reintroduced in the 1870s: Galloway, *Annals*, ii, pp. 249–50, Mitchell, *Economic development*, p. 74. By the 1890s most of Northumberland was worked longwall,

R C Labour, PP 1892, p. 137. Longwall divided labour more than board and pillar and enabled closer supervision: Flinn and Stoker, *The History*, pp. 329–30; Mitchell, *Economic development*, p. 71.

60. See Part Three.
61. Rymer, *Martyrdom*, p. 7. The quotation is for 1858. The 1850s were defeated years for miners' unions in the two counties and although some organisation remained at colliery level, it was patchy in its influence across the coalfield.
62. A United Collier, *A Defence of the Voice from the Coal Mines in Answer to the 'Brief Observations' in reply to that pamphlet*, Newcastle, 1825, pp. 10–11; *Rules and Regulations for the formation of a society to be called the United Association of Colliers on the Rivers Tyne and Wear*, Newcastle, 1825.
63. *CEC 1842*, p. 661; *Accidents in Mines*, PP 1835, p. 169; John Buddle to Lord Londonderry, 28 May 1843, D/Lo/C 142; G. A. Cadman, *The Administration of the Poor Law Amendment Act, 1834, in the Hexham Poor Law Union 1836–1930*, University of Newcastle unpublished M Litt 1976, pp. 232–3; unidentified newspaper cutting, 30 April 1847, *Bell Collection*, NEIMME, iv; Ginswick, *Morning Chronicle*, p. 68; *Coal*, PP 1873, p. x; B. T. Hirsch and W. J. Hausman, 'Labour productivity in the British and South Wales coal industry, 1874–1914', *Economica*, 50, 1983; evidence of John Wilson MP, financial secretary of Durham Miners' Association, and Ralph Young, corresponding-secretary of Northumberland Miners' Mutual Confident Association, *R C Labour*, PP 1892, p. 34, p. 136, p. 34.
64. *R C Labour*, PP 1892, pp. 132–3.
65. John Buddle, *Accidents in Mines*, PP 1835, p. 169, and *State of Coal Trade*, PP 1836, p. 119; *CEC 1842*, p. 661, p. 649; *Miners' Advocate*, 21 September 1844.
66. *Newcastle Courant*, 11 October 1766; Robert Colls, *The Collier's Rant. Song and Culture in the Industrial Village*, London, 1977, pp. 24–56; *Monthly Chronicle of North-Country Lore and Legend*, i, 1887, p. 111.
67. SPEAKOUT of Backworth colliery, *Miners' Advocate*, 13 July 1844; *Coal*, PP 1873, p. 154; Cloughan quoted in Alan Campbell, in Harrison, *Independent Collier*, p. 78; *Miners' Journal*, 21 October 1843. For a recognition of the personal element in persuading members to restrict, John Wilson, *History of the Durham Miners' Association*, Durham, 1907, pp. 176–9.
68. 'The inclination of the seam alters the work as to difficulty; no general rule applies largely': John Harrison, viewer at Newbottle colliery, *CEC 1842*, p. 647; Thomas Taylor, owner of Earsdon colliery, p. 608. 'Cavilling' was a free system of balloting for new workplaces every quarter. Conducted by the pitmen, it was a means of equalising chances of a bad seam and can be considered as complementary with Restriction. In 1842 the thinnest seam in Northumberland and North Durham was 2' 6" at Shilbottle. The average thickness was estimated at 5'. *CEC 1842*, p. 542.
69. *Gateshead Observer*, 18 March 1843.

70. *Gateshead Observer*, 18 March 1843. As the owners introduced more short-time working, and the union insisted on Restriction, there was conflict between adequate earnings, proper safety, and union loyalty. See also: *CHRONONHONTHOLOGOS*, Framwellgate Moor colliery, *Miners' Advocate*, 6 April 1844, and the handbill, *Colliers Appeal to the Country*, Newcastle, 1844 – 'for they now have as much coal to get in *two days as formerly in three days*'.

Chapter three

1. Revd J. Hodgson, *An Account of the Explosion*, Newcastle, 1813, p. 23.
2. Wood, *Inaugural Address*, p. 18.
3. *State of Coal Trade*, PP 1830, pp. 298–9; Mitchell, *Economic development*, pp. 54–5; Flinn and Stoker, *The History*, p. 62. The first modern treatise on the practical operations of coalmining was written to advise gentlemen with money to invest, and, by inference, to safeguard them from fraud: J. C., *The Compleat Collier: Or, The Whole ART of Sinking, Getting, and Working, Coal-Mines & c*, London, 1708.
4. Flinn and Stoker, *The History*, pp. 68–9; Humphrey Jennings, ed. M. C. Jennings and C. Madge, *Panduemonium. The Coming of the Machine as seen by contemporary observers, 1600–1886*, London, 1985, p. 207; G. Johnson to J. Buddle, 6 July 1827, DCRO, NCB I/JB/1844; Wood, *Inaugural Address*.
5. Church, *British Coal Industry*, pp. 428–30; J. F. W. Johnston, *The Economy of a Coalfield*, Durham, 1838, p. 70.
6. Wood, *Inaugural Address*, p. 4; *R C Labour*, PP 1892, p. 135.
7. *Accidents*, PP 1881, p. vi, p. 165, p. 213, p. 401, p. 404.
8. *Accidents in Mines*, PP 1835, p. vi, p. 228, p. 20, p. 32, p. 81.
9. Sir Henry T de la Beche and Dr Lyon Playfair, *Report on the Gases and Explosions in Collieries*, PP 1846, (529) xliii, p. 7; *Mining Districts*, PP 1846, p. 13.
10. *Accidents in Mines*, PP 1835, p. 169; Rex v Kennedy, *Brief for Prosecution*, 2 January 1832, DCRO, D/Lo/L 21; *South Shields Committee*, p. 197.
11. *Report on Ventilation*, PP 1850, p. 25.
12. *Accidents in Mines*, PP 1835, p. 113 and p. 275. J. Kenyon Blackwell made strong recommendations for formal rules in his *Report on Ventilation*, PP 1850, p. 24. A full account of the County Regulations appears in *Third Report SC on Accidents in Coal Mines*, PP 1854 (277), ix, p. 56, and for growing pressure for such rules see, *First Report SC on Accidents in Coal Mines*, PP 1852 (691), xx, p. 54, p. 65; *Fourth Report SC on Accidents in Coal Mines*, PP 1854 (325), ix, p. 9.
13. *Third Report Accidents*, PP 1854, p. 79.
14. John Phillips, *Report on Ventilation*, PP 1850, appendix 8; *Third Report Accidents*, PP 1854, p. 79.
15. *Third Report Accidents*, PP 1854, p. 110; Kenyon Blackwell, *Report on Ventilation*, PP 1850, p. 25.
16. Tremenheere testified to managerial and supervisory incompetence,

Dangerous Accidents, PP 1849, p. 25. Jude was answering questions about a case of victimisation at Usworth colliery in 1851: *Second Report Accidents*, PP 1853, p. 3.

17. Dunn, *Third Report Accidents*, PP 1854, p. 56; Bell and Barras were expected to examine the workings for signs of danger before the first shift at 4 am, evidence of Robert Todd, hewer at Washington colliery, *Reports of Messrs Dunn, Dickinson, and Morton, Inspectors of Coal Mines*, PP 1851 (1422), xxxiii, p. 14 — Todd had recently lost two sons in an accident at the colliery; Jude, *Second Report Accidents*, PP 1853, p. 8.

18. George Parker, *Mines*, PP 1866, pp. 193—4.

19. *Dangerous Accidents*, PP 1849, p. 541, pp. 451—2, and for further union evidence, p. 528, p. 541, p. 535; Nicholas Wood, p. 222. Reasons for the failure of four private members' bills to provide the 'stern intervention' of an inspectorate between 1847—9 are given in: O. O. G. M. MacDonagh, 'Coal mines regulation: the first decade 1842—52', in R. Robson, ed., *Ideas and Institutions of Victorian Britain*, London, 1967, pp. 66—9. For Tremenheere's powerful influence see: O. P. Edwards, 'An account of the founding of H M inspectorate of mines and the work of the first inspector, Hugh Seymour Tremenheere', *British Journal of Industrial Medicine*, xx, 1963.

20. *First Report Accidents*, PP 1852, p. ix. See also *Fourth Report Accidents*, PP 1854, pp. 6—8.

21. *Report on Ventilation*, PP 1850, p. 33.

22. *Fourth Report Accidents*, PP 1854, p. 9; de la Beche, *Second Report Accidents*, PP 1854, p. 76; Mackworth, *First Report Accidents*, PP 1853, p. 117.

23. J. W. Day, chairman of Houghton Poor Law Union, *CEC 1842*, p. 719; *Second Report Accidents*, PP 1853, pp. 8—9; *Report Commissioner State of the Population in The Mining Districts*, PP 1854 (1838), xix, p. 42. For a summary of developments in this field see: D. J. Gillan, *The effect of industrial legislation on the social and educational condition of children employed in coal mines between 1840 and 1876, with special reference to county Durham*, University of Durham unpublished M.Ed 1967.

24. De la Beche, *Second Report Accidents*, PP 1854, p. 76.

25. Tremenheere, *Second Report Accidents*, PP 1854, p. 62; Thomas Sopwith, lead mining company agent, in Revd W. A. Scott, 'Education of miners' children', E. Pears ed., *Transactions of the National Association for the Promotion of Social Science*, London, 1871, p. 349; and Revd Scott, p. 348.

26. *Report Commissioner State of the Population in The Mining Districts*, PP 1849 (1109), xxii, p. 8, p. 7; *Mining Districts*, PP 1854, p. 43 — there had been unions and strikes, but the 'weeding out' of agitators was leading to 'a feeling of mutual confidence'.

27. James Mather, *Second Report Accidents*, PP 1854, p. 99; *Mining Districts*, PP 1849, p. 9.

28. *Report Commissioner State of the Population in The Mining Districts*, PP 1847 (844), xvi, p. 21; for a full account and debate on these changes of attitude see: Robert Colls, ' "Oh happy English children!" Coal, class,

and education in the North-East', *Past and Present*, 73, 1976, and A. J. Heesom and B. Duffy, *Debate*, and Colls, *Rejoinder*, Past and Present, 90, 1981.

29. *Mines*, PP 1866, p. 352; for the penetration of private insurance schemes, and permanent relief funds, in the villages after 1850: J. Benson, 'English coal-miners' trade union accident funds, 1850–1900', *Economic History Review*, xxviii, 1975.

30. De la Beche, *Second Report Accidents*, PP 1854, p. 75; William Whellan & Co., *History, Topography, and Directory of Northumberland*, London, 1855, p. 130.

31. *Second Report Accidents*, PP 1854, p. 75; Revd Street in, Scott, 'Education of miners' children', p. 353.

32. T. J. Taylor, *CEC 1842*, p. 609; Buddle to Londonderry, 16 May 1842, D/Lo/C 142.

33. B. R. Mitchell and P. Deane, *Abstract of British Historical Statistics*, Cambridge, 1962, p. 119, p. 116. Figures are for counties of Northumberland, Durham, and Cumberland.

34. Christie, *Northumberland*, p. 114.

Chapter four

1. NEIMME, ZB/4.
2. There is a bond for Lanchester Fell, Harelaw, Pontop Pike, Harperley, and Lintz pits (NEIMME, *Watson Collection*) which might be for 1757 and therefore important in a mid-century lacunae. The document is so decayed that its date is illegible, but it does bear stamps to the value of 1s 3d and the Inland Revenue explained to the NEIMME that this type of stamping lasted from July 1757 to December 1772. However, a clause in the bond stating that owners and agents 'shall order and direct without [the pitmen] sticking combining or absenting themselves' is more typical of the 1770s than the early 1760s.
3. Hylton Scott reckoned that the Bond was not longstanding then: 'The Miners' Bond', *Proceedings of the Society of Antiquaries of Newcastle upon Tyne*, fourth series, 1947. Ashton and Sykes thought that a year's hire was attractive under eighteenth-century Poor Law practice because it conferred 'settlement': *The Coal Industry*, p. 84.
4. J. Crooks to Sir J. Delaval, 12 November 1778, NCRO, DE/4/4.
5. East Denton and West Kenton *bond*, NCRO, NRO 421; Bushblades *bond*, 10 November 1766, Bill Dowding, Records Officer, NUM, Red Hill, Durham.
6. Byker and St Anthony's *bond*, 1770, *Newcastle Weekly Chronicle*, 19 August 1899; Denton and Kenton, 1804.
7. Delaval *bond*, 1770, DE/7/6; Byker Hill *bond*, 1773, NRO 421; Delaval *bond*, 1776, DE/7/6.
8. Dawson's pit, Benwell *bond*, 1703, NEIMME, ZB/4; Charlaw *bond*, 1767, NEIMME, ZB/1.
9. Burnmoor *paybill*, 1787, NCB 1/JB; Walker *bond*, 1788, NEIMME, *Watson Collection*.

10. Penshaw *bond*, 1793, NCB 1/JB.
11. Charlaw *bond*, 1767; S. Pollard, 'Capitalism and rationality: a study of measurements in British coal mining, c. 1750–1850', *Explorations in Economic History*, 20, 1983.
12. Ouston, *paybill*, 1834, NCRO, ZAN M/17/28.
13. 'the fundamental way in which the Durham miner managed to maintain an equitable system of work, and ... to stave off the competitiveness, bullying, and injustice ... it was an embryo of workers' control': D. Douglass, *Pit Life in Co. Durham*, Oxford, 1972, p. 26.
14. Bushblades *bond*, 1766.
15. *Acct. of money Payed out*, November 1762, DE/7/6.
16. J. B. Simpson, *Capital and Labour in Coal Mining during the past Two Hundred Years*, Newcastle, 1900, p. 34; Flinn and Stoker, *The History*, p. 387.
17. Simpson, *Capital and Labour*, p. 34; Flinn and Stoker, *The History*, p. 387, p. 389, p. 391; Hair, *Social History*, pp. 338–44, p. 367a; Mitchell, *Economic development*, p. 210.
18. Flinn and Stoker, *The History*, p. 390.
19. Hair, *Social History*, p. 367a.
20. Silberling's index was based on wholesale prices and did not include the cost of government duties. Also, 'the man whose scheme of expenditure conformed to that drawn up by Silberling had many idiosyncracies. He did not occupy a house, or at least he was not called upon to pay rent. He allowed himself only a moderate amount of bread and very little porridge, and he never touched potatoes and strong drink. On the other hand he got through quite considerable quantities of beef and mutton and showed a fondness for butter. Perhaps he was a diabetic'. T. S. Ashton's 'man', quoted in, B. Inglis, *Poverty and the Industrial Revolution*, London, 1972, p. 23. Church's revision spans the period 1830–1913: *British Coal Industry*, pp. 568, 573.
21. Walker *bonds*, 1780, 1781, 1783, 1784, 1788, 1791, 1792, 1793, 1795, 1797, 1798, NEIMME, *Watson Collection*.
22. Flinn and Stoker, *The History*, pp. 259–64, pp. 37–41; Mitchell, *Economic development*, pp. 54–5; Benwell Community Project Final Report Series no. 6, *The Making of a Ruling Class*, Benwell, 1978, pp. 10–14, 90–112; Church, *British Coal Industry*, p. 129; *State of Coal Trade*, PP 1830, p. 29. For an example of how litigation could define common land and common experience as rentable property, see the depositions on behalf of the Bishop of Durham, undated, for the eighteenth century; *Papers* relating to the ownership of Birtley Common for rents and royalties due, DCRO, NCB I/X/243.
23. *State of Coal Trade*, PP 1830, *passim*; Flinn and Stoker, *The History*, pp. 273–79.
24. Flinn and Stoker, *The History*, pp. 279–85; W. J. Hausman, 'Market power in the London coal trade: the limitation of the Vend, 1770–1845', *Explorations in Economic History*, 21, 1984. London selling had long been a notoriously corruptible practice: Anon., *A Pleasant Discovery of the Coosenage of Colliers*, 1591, reprinted Newcastle, 1845.

25. *State of Coal Trade*, PP 1836, p.xv. The evidences of Messrs R.W. Brandling, chairman of United Committee, J. Buddle, and T. Wood to this select committee form a valuable account of the Vend; for the power of the Vend to raise prices by about 2s per chaldron, see Hausman, 'Market power', p.295. This price-raising propensity was small compared to the weight of State taxation carried by the coal consumer up to 1831.
26. *State of Coal Trade*, PP 1836, p.12.
27. This is Brandling at his most bland. He makes the Vend appear like a gentleman's club to enable the market to indulge its expensive taste for best coals − 'Your Committee are assured it could not be undertaken under less favourable circumstances than at present exist' (p.17): *State of Coal Trade*, PP 1830, pp.6–10, p.259.
28. *State of Coal Trade*, PP 1836, p.3; evidence of Brandling, p.12; evidence of Wood, p.148.
29 *Memorandums respecting the Coal Trade & c*, c.1821, NEIMME, *Watson Collection; Coal*, PP 1873, p.160; Mitchell, *Economic development*, p.11; combinations of coal-producers were unlawful under Acts of 1711 (9 Anne, c.28), 1730 (3 Geo. II, c.26), 1731 (4 Geo. II, c.30), but were never tried and were effectively removed under the Act of 1836 (6 & 7 Will. IV, c.109).
30. *House of Lords State of Coal Trade*, PP 1830, p.55; *State of Coal Trade*, PP 1836, p.23.
31. Thomas Wood, then co-partner and manager of Thornley colliery, *State of Coal Trade*, PP 1836, p.147; *House of Lords State of Coal Trade*, PP 1830, p.40.
32. *State of Coal Trade*, PP 1830, pp.258–9, pp.280–2.
33. *State of Coal Trade*, PP 1836, p.179.
34. Buddle, *State of Coal Trade*, PP 1830, p.281.
35. The committee noted how these two functions acted together to raise the price of 'best Stewart's Wallsend' from 26s 6d to 28s 6d per chaldron in 1834: *State of Coal Trade*, PP 1836, p.vii. Brandling said that the grades of coal were never mixed but Buddle contradicted him: *State of Coal Trade*, PP 1830, p.259, p.287. On the effect of best 'to force the inferior coal on the market' see Thomas Wood, *State of the Coal Trade*, PP 1836, p.149, and the report, p.x.
36. *State of Coal Trade*, PP 1830, p.299.
37. Brandling, *State of Coal Trade*, PP 1830, p.13; Hugh Taylor, coalowner and agent, *House of Lords State of Coal Trade*, PP 1830, p.82; Buddle, *State of Coal Trade*, PP 1830, p.283.
38. *House of Lords State of Coal Trade*, PP 1830, p.13. In the second half of the century the growing demand for coke, new coal-washing processes, and more sophisticated retailing brought expanding markets for small coals. The underground separation of small coals ended in 1872.
39. Revd Dr William Buckland at Oxford called the wastage a 'national calamity', and Dr Johnston at Durham called for 'a due subordination of private interests and profits to the public welfare': *State of Coal Trade*, PP 1830, p.240; Johnston, *Economy of a Coalfield*, p.20.
40. *Remarks relative to a regulation of Vends for 1819*, NEIMME, *Watson*

Collection; C. Hiskey, 'The Third Marquess of Londonderry and the regulation of the coal trade: the case re-opened', *Durham University Journal*, xliv, June 1983, pp. 3–8.

41. D. J. Williams, *Capitalist Combination in the Coal Industry*, London, 1924, p. 41.
42. Church, *British Coal Industry*, pp. 170–1; *House of Lords State of Coal Trade*, PP 1830, p. 31; Matthias Dunn, *An Historical, Geological, and Descriptive View of the Coal Trade in the North of England*, Newcastle, 1844, p. 213.
43. Church, *British Coal Industry*, p. 131; *State of Coal Trade*, PP 1830, pp. 262–3.
44. Buddle, *State of Coal Trade*, PP 1830, p. 302. He said the coalfield was producing at about half its capacity; previously he had reckoned that the Tyne could double its output, and the Wear produce half as much again: *House of Lords State of Coal Trade*, PP 1830, p. 30.
45. Brandling, Cochrane, Buddle, *House of Lords State of Coal Trade*, PP 1830, p. 11, p. 36; Metcalf, Fawcus, *State of Coal Trade*, PP 1830, pp. 323–6, p. 337.
46. *State of Coal Trade*, PP 1836, p. xl.
47. *Great News! Great News! A full, true, and particular account of the Life, Character, and Death of that Monster, the LIMITATION COAL VEND*, Newcastle, 1829.
48. Brandling, *State of Coal Trade*, PP 1836, p. 10. Tyne and Wear increased their capacity 1829–36 by an estimated 36.9% and while, for instance, Hetton colliery had a capacity of 150,000 chaldrons in 1833, it was regulated at 110,000 chaldrons, a figure which it did not accept (p. xv). The table's information comes from P. M. Sweezy, *Monopoly and Competition in the English Coal Trade*, Harvard, 1938, p. 112, p. 110. For figures on the decline in 'issues' between 1824–44, see Sweezy, p. 119.
49. See monthly prices of best coal, London market, 1807–44: Sweezy, *Monopoly and Competition*, p. 155.
50. Londonderry to Buddle, 13 September 1828, NCB 1/JB; Londonderry to Buddle, 5 June 1825, D/Lo/C 142.
51. *State of Coal Trade*, PP 1836, p. 173; M. Dunn, *Manuscript Journal 1831–5*, NCL, 26 January 1833, 13 July 1833.
52. *State of Coal Trade*, PP 1836, pp. 174, 177.
53. Benwell, *Ruling Class*, p. 11; Wood, *State of Coal Trade*, PP 1836, p. 174; Buddle, *State of Coal Trade*, PP 1830, pp. 297–8; Mitchell, *Economic development*, p. 303; Church, *British Coal Industry*, p. 519; R. Sturgess, *Landowners and Coal in Co Durham, 1815–50*, NCL, T/S, pp. 95–6 (Sturgess and Church both draw attention to contemporary defectiveness in accounting methods); Flinn and Stoker, *The History*, pp. 324–5, 319, 326 – but for the selected collieries beware of problems of typicality and periodisation; Mitchell, pp. 306–7; Hiskey, 'Regulation of the coal trade', p. 9.
54. *State of Coal Trade*, PP 1830, p. 303.
55. Vend apologetics were that free competition might reduce prices in the short-run, but would close collieries, create heavy unemployment, cause

social unrest, and make for a more narrowly based monopoly in the long-run. Dunn had previously worked for Wood at Hetton. During the lock-out of 1832 the two men had quarrelled about the treatment of the pitmen: 'suffice it to say that his Conductives was so brutal that it is impossible I can again associate with him in the management of the Colliery'. (*Journal*, 17 May 1832). Afterwards, Dunn's smaller North Hetton colliery was being badly squeezed by Wood's bouts of unregulated production.

56. '... continual croaking about evils which are, after all, only the penalty of Adam'. (Anon., *A Few Friendly Words to The Pitmen of Durham and Northumberland by one who is well acquainted with them*, Newcastle, 1844.)

57. Buddle, *House of Lords State of Coal Trade*, PP 1830, p. 33; letter of T. J. Taylor to Tremenheere, *Mining Districts*, PP 1846, pp. 10–11; Anon., *Few Friendly Words*. The surplus labour argument was used to defend Vend practices on humanitarian grounds. Here, the committee was told that 'fighting' trade seriously reduced wages: 'at present it is very low; there is such a surplus of hands, it is very low'. (Buddle, *State of Coal Trade*, PP 1830, p. 274).

58. Dunn, *View of the Coal Trade*, p. 225. He saw only 'gloomy and dispiriting' prospects ahead 'as the quantum of vend, under the reduced prices, will not yield a profit' (p. 228).

59. Committee of Coal Owners, *Minute Book*, i, 1 October 1805.

60. In Buddle's experience, robbing the broken was a nineteenth-century practice: in the 1790s '... working the pillars was not contemplated; the maximum produce of the coal was taken in the first working ... 10 chaldrons out of 11, were best coals ... only about a tenth part skreened ... there was no waste whatever at that period'. (*State of Coal Trade*, PP 1830, p. 294). The setting of differential export duties on large and small coal in 1816 encouraged the export of small – rising to 310,000 annual tons by 1830: Flinn and Stoker, *The History*, p. 226. Wages as a percentage of costs comes from Mitchell, *Economic development*, p. 287.

61. Byker and St Anthony's *bond*, 1770; Committee of Coal Owners, *Minute Book*, i, 16 January 1811.

62. These crises, and the episodic growth of coalfield collective bargaining they engendered, is covered in the next chapter.

63. *Newcastle Chronicle*, 12 January 1811; John Rule, *The Experience of Labour in Eighteenth-Century Industry*, London, 1981, pp. 124–46.

64. *Newcastle Chronicle*, 12 January 1811.

65. *A Voice from the Coal Mines addressed to the coal owners, their head agents, and a sympathizing public by the Colliers of the United Association of Durham and Northumberland*, South Shields, 1825, p. 13.

66. Anon., *Brief Observations in Reply to 'A Voice from the Coal Mines'*, Newcastle, 1825.

67. *A Voice*, p. 14, pp. 21–2; *A Candid Appeal to the Coal owners and viewers of Collieries on the Tyne and Wear*, Newcastle, 1826, p. 1.

68. *House of Lords State of Coal Trade*, PP 1830, p. 67; *State of Coal Trade*, PP 1830, p. 274; Galloway, *Annals*, i, p. 465; Church, *British Coal Industry*, pp. 260–1.

69. Philanthropos, *The Two Subjects which Remain in Dispute Between The Coal-Owners And The Pitmen candidly considered, in a Letter Addressed To The Pitmen Of The Tyne and Wear*, Newcastle, 1831, p. 7.
70. Challinor and Ripley, *Miners' Association*, p. 103. Details of excessive fining at Thornley are given in *Miners' Advocate*, 2 December 1843, and Anon., *Account of the Thornley Strike Trial*, Newcastle, 1843; for further examples of litigation over idle-time and other issues: Challinor and Ripley, pp. 94–110; Galloway, *Annals*, i, p. 174.
71. *Miners' Journal*, 18 November 1843; *Miners' Advocate*, 15, 29 June 1844.
72. *Report of the Special Committee appointed by the Coal Owners ... Read at the General Meeting of the Trade*, Newcastle, 27 April 1844.
73. *Report of the Miners' Committee in answer to the one drawn up by The Coal Trade Committee*, Newcastle, May 1844.
74. *Miners' Advocate*, 13 July 1844.
75. *CEC 1842*, pp. 535–6; *Miners' Advocate*, 21 September 1844.
76. *Report by the Committee of the Coalowners Respecting the present Situation of the Trade*, Newcastle, 10 March 1832, and the *Report of the Special Committee*, Newcastle, 27 April 1844.
77. Lord Londonderry to Home Office, 4 March 1843, PRO, HO/45/349; for details of the reduction: *Coal Trade, Meeting of the United Committee*, Newcastle, 27 February 1843.
78. Sir F. Eden, *The State of the Poor*, London, 1798, 1928 ed., p. 268; p. 271; *Poor Law. App. A, Pt I*, PP 1834, p. 161; *Miners' Advocate*, 21 September 1844; Adam Smith, *The Wealth of Nations*, London, 1776, 1980 repr., p. 206.
79. Joseph Oxley to Sir John Delaval, 25 December 1777, 10 January 1778, 18 February 1778, 8 February 1778; John Crooks to Delaval, 17 March 1778, NCRO, DE/4/11.
80. Oxley to Delaval, 29 April 1778, 14 June 1778; Crooks to Delaval, 12 November 1778, DE/4/11. Troubles with his coal mines were not Sir John's chief preoccupation, however. The letter of 14 June has more information on his newly built glasshouse than his troublesome pitmen.
81. *Newcastle Chronicle*, 21 September 1765.
82. John Wood to Buddle, 21 March 1826, D/Lo/C 142; *Address from the North Hetton Pitmen to the Public*, May 1832, and similar trouble at Burdon Main, *To the Public*, 7 May 1832, PLL, *Coal Trade Collection*; *CEC 1842*, p. 141, p. 152, p. 151.
83. Easington Union Board of Guardians, 25 April 1843, *Minute Book*, 1837–47, DCRO MH/Poor Law Union Papers.
84. *Miners' Advocate*, 18 May 1844.
85. *Mining Districts*, PP 1846, p. 25, p. 10, p. 16, p. 20.
86. *Second Report Accidents*, PP 1853, p. 3; Rymer, *Martyrdom*, p. 9. There were partly successful attempts to reintroduce the annual Bond in Durham in 1854 and to extend it in 1862. These attempts stimulated the revival of organised trade unionism in the county, which finally terminated the Bond in all its forms in 1872. The fierce resistance to an annual Bond in the later period must be seen in the light of radical Liberal ideology

and changes in English labour law in favour of trade unions, granting them the first modern 'immunity' in 1871.

87. Dawson's pit, Benwell *bond*, 1703.
88. Extract, *Account*, 'Wrot. at the Bounder Pit in the Main Coal with a 20 Peck Corfe', DCRO, D/X 26/1. 'xx' refers to a 'score' which was twenty corves on the Tyne and twenty-one on the Wear.
89. William Thomas, 19 October 1805, *Viewer's Diary, Denton Colliery 1802–12*, NEIMME, ZB/19(c).
90. Crooks to Delaval, 17 September 1779, DE/4/11.
91. Committee of Coal Owners, *Minute Book*, i, 12 March 1812.
92. Flinn and Stoker, *The History*, p. 375; P.E.H. Hair, 'The binding of the pitmen of the north east 1800–09', *Durham University Journal*, lviii, 1965; *Newcastle Journal*, 28 September 1765.
93. This will be considered more closely in Chapter five.
94. Hetton and Elemore *bond*, 1829, DCRO, D/X 36/2; Ouston *bond*, 1835, NEIMME, ZB/8.
95. *A Candid Appeal*, 1826; George Johnson to Buddle, 21 March 1826, NCB 1/JB.
96. *Newcastle Chronicle*, 12 January 1811; *CEC 1842*, p. 538, p. 603.
97. *To the Public*, 18 April 1831, NEIMME.

Chapter five

1. Ashton and Sykes, *The Coal Industry*, p. 133.
2. *Acct. money Payed out*, 1762; for summary of 1765 dispute, *Annual Register*, 1765, p. 130; Bushblades *bond*, 1766.
3. John Allen to Sir John Delaval, 26 September 1772, NCRO, DE/6/4; Thos. Yelloley to Wm. Dobson, 20 September 1773, DE/7/6; Allen to Delaval, 25 April 1775, DE/6/4; anon., *memorandum*, 10 September 1776? 1777? DE/7/6.
4. *Viewer's Diary*, 6 March 1789; Walker *bonds*.
5. Henry Grey MacNab, *Report from the Committee Appointed to inquire into the State of the Coal Trade of this Kingdom*, p. 41, NEIMME, *Bell Collection*. A further 1,597 men from these ports had volunteered.
6. George Johnson to Lord Delaval, 3 October 1797, 27 September 1798, NCRO, DE/6/6.
7. Hewers, two pecks a fortnight, wives and children, one peck: *order*, Hartley office, 5 May 1800, NCRO, DE/4/24.
8. John Bryers to Delaval, 24 September 1800, DE/4/24.
9. *Observations on the probable consequences of even attempting by Legislative Authority to obtain a Large Supply of Coal from Staffordshire to the Metropolis*, pp. 33–4, NEIMME, *Bell Collection*; Bryers to Delaval, 9 October 1801, DE/4/24.
10. Bryers to Delaval, 26 September 1802, DE/4/24; John Brotherick to Delaval, 1 October 1802, NCRO, DE/4/40.
11. Paul Forster to Delaval, 17 October 1803, NCRO, DE/6/5, gives a chronological report from 30 September.
12. Bryers to Delaval, 6, 3 March 1805, NCRO, DE/4/27. The demand for

pitmen multiplied the competition for labour in adjacent trades: agricultural labourers were being offered 15s to 18s per week, and seamen up to seven guineas per voyage. Bryers to Delaval, 7, 14 October 1804, NCRO, DE/4/26.

13. Bryers to Delaval, 18 October 1804, DE/4/26; *Viewer's Diary*, 18 October 1804. Consider the prudent Willington pitman who left his family 'The interest of Seventy pounds which is in the Hands of Mr John Watson [viewer] ... payable half yearly', and furniture, cow, and provision for his children's education: *Last Will & Testament, Robert Campble*, 1814, NEIMME, *Watson Collection*.

14. *Viewer's Diary*, 18 October 1804; Bryers to Delaval, 24, 25 October 1804, DE/4/26.

15. Committee of Coal Owners, *Minute Book*, i, 10 September 1805. Bryers was sceptical about the chances of binding in a colliery office rather than in a public house, now that 'the pitmen think themselves of so much more consequence': Bryers to Delaval, 11 September 1805, DE/4/27. He was also sceptical about being able to stop corn supplies. He talked of compensatory wage payments – directly against the spirit of the Committee's resolution: *ibid.*

16. Committee of Coal Owners, *Minute Book*, i, 1 October 1805; *Viewbook* of George Johnson, pp. 21–3, 25, NEIMME, *Johnson Collection*.

17. 'Complaints and deviations from the resolutions of the Coal Trade for Hiring the Workmen Oct. 1805 with Answers made by the different Agents etc., to the Charges made against them', Owners' *Minute Book*, i, examples from Percy Main, Holywell, Walker, South Moor, Temple Main, and Hartley collieries.

18. Bryers to Delaval, 13, 18 October 1805, DE/4/27.

19. Bryers to Delaval, 27 October, 3, 10 November 1805, DE/4/27: 'Many Young Hewers & stout Horse drivers (that might have hewed Coals this Year) have gone to Sea on Account of great wages'.

20. Committee of Coal Owners, *Minute Book*, i, 18 September 1806. A tribunal was set up the following week to monitor special claims and cases; *Viewer's Diary*, 16 October 1806.

21. *Memorandum*, 8 November 1806, and *minutes* laid before Coal Committee, 20 November 1806, DE/4/28; Committee of Coal Owners, *Minute Book*, i, 1 November 1806.

22. Committee of Coal Owners, *Minute Book*, i, 24 September 1807, for corvers 17 September 1807, for cheating 5 November 1808, 30 September 1809.

23. Committee of Coal Owners, *Minute Book*, i, 22 December 1810; Wallsend *bond*, 1810, NEIMME, ZB/5; Tanfield Moor *bond*, 1810, NEIMME, ZB/20.

24. *Newcastle Courant*, 3, 10, 17 November 1810. Tyneside men (no figures) were put in Morpeth gaol; see the *Articles Agreed to by Members of the Brotherly Society in Painshaw, New Winning, in the County of Durham*, Sunderland, 1810, PRO, FS/1/116. Friendly societies often acted as covers for combinatory practices during the Combination Acts, 1799/1800–1824.

25. Committee of Coal Owners, *Minute Book*, i, 22 November 1810; *Newcastle Chronicle*, 12 January 1811.
26. Committee of Coal Owners, *Minute Book*, i, 16 January 1811.
27. See G. A. Williams, Introduction, in J. Gorman, ed., *Banner Bright*, London, 1976, p. 3. There is no talk of any prosecution under the Combination Acts. The Coal Trade might have been too conscious of its monopolistic odour in London to attract any extra government attention.
28. Deposition of Thomas Morrison, 'Informations of Witness', 1811.
29. *Articles, Rules, & c. To be observed and kept by the Members of the Colliers' Fund*, Newcastle, 1810; *Articles ... of the Brotherly Society*, Sunderland, 1810.
30. J. L. and B. Hammond, *The Skilled Labourer*, London 1919, p. 24; *Articles ... of the Colliers' Fund.*
31. Committee of Coal Owners, *Minute Book*, i, 10 December 1811, 12 March 1812, the comparative table had been drawn up by 29 February 1812.
32. Home Office and War Office papers at the Public Record Office have a low incidence of North-East news compared with the disturbed areas. This 'silence' is corroborated by a low incidence in local record office and Trade papers. The record increased with crisis – 1815, 1819, 1825, 1831–2, 1838–9, 1844.
33. Committee of Coal Owners, *Minute Books*, vols. i–xi.
34. General Meeting of Owners, *Minute Book*, i, 8 April 1814. There was a serious strike of Tyne seamen in October 1814 which was broken by regular soldiers and marines: Nathaniel Clayton, Town Clerk of Newcastle, to Viscount Sidmouth, 22 October 1814, PRO, HO/42/141.
35. N. McCord, 'The Seamen's strike of 1815 in north east England', *Economic History Review*, xxi, 1968; Sunderland magistrates to Sidmouth, 21 March 1815, PRO, HO/42/143.
36. Revd W. Nesfield to William Hutchinson, High Sheriff of Co. Durham, 6 June 1816, PRO, HO/42/151; unidentified newspaper cutting, NEIMME, *Bell Collection*, vol. ii; Robert Green JP to Sidmouth, 26 May 1816, PRO, HO/42/150; General Meeting of Owners, *Minute Book*, ii, 16 April 1816; anon. letter to Home Office, 15 April 1817, PRO, HO 42/163; *Minute Book*, 7, 10 March 1818.
37. The keelmen's strike was the major action, but seamen, ironmen, pitmen, and shipwrights were all involved: N. McCord, 'Tyneside discontents and Peterloo', *Northern History*, ii, 1967; D. J. Rowe, 'The strikes of the Tyneside keelmen in 1809 and 1819', *International Review of Social History*, xiii, 1968.
38. R. G. Collingwood, of Sunderland, to Sidmouth, 30 October 1819; Archibald Reed to Sidmouth, 17, 20 October 1819; Collingwood to Sidmouth, 30 October 1819; PRO, HO/42/197.
39. At Percy Main colliery, Reed to Sidmouth, 20 November 1819, PRO, HO/42/199.
40. Committee of Coal Owners, *Minute Book*, vi, nd 1820.
41. General Meeting of Owners, *Minute Book*, vii, 26 February 1822; Buddle to Londonderry 13, 24 March 1822, D/Lo/C 142; Owners, *Minute Book*, viii, 9 November 1823; Buddle to Londonderry, 3 November 1824.

42. Buddle to Londonderry, 20 March 1825, D/Lo/C 142, for trouble-free binding; also, Committee of Coal Owners, *Minute Book*, x, January 1825 – April 1826; *A Voice*, 1825.
43. Robert Green to Sidmouth, 26 May 1816, HO/42/150.
44. Revd Charles Thorp to Samuel Marsh Phillips, Home Office, 25 October 1819, HO/42/197.
45. Buddle to Londonderry, 21 March 1822, D/Lo/C 142.
46. *A Voice*, p. 34.
47. At Hetton: Buddle to Londonderry, 22 July 1825, D/Lo/C 142; at Jarrow, Committee of Coal Owners, *Minute Book*, x, 12, 16 November, 24 December 1825. On 23 March colliery carpenters, smiths, masons, and brakesmen asked for 1s per week rise, and on 25 March it was conceded: Buddle to Londonderry, 23 March 1825.
48. Buddle to Londonderry, 13 December 1825, D/Lo/C 142; *The Brotherly Society of Rainton Colliery* to Londonderry, 20 February 1826, PRO, HO/40/19.
49. Buddle to Londonderry, 31 October 1825, 25 February 1826, D/Lo/C 142.
50. *Rules and Regulations for the formation of a society, to be called THE UNITED ASSOCIATION OF COLLIERS, on the Rivers Tyne & Wear*, Newcastle, 1825, articles iv, xiv, xvi, vii, xiii, xii, vi, xvii, iii.
51. Londonderry to Home Office, 28 July 1826, HO/40/19; Buddle to Londonderry, 26 November 1825, D/Lo/C 142.
52. Committee of Coal Owners, *Minute Book*, x, 6 January 1826; Buddle to Londonderry, 26 March 1826, D/Lo/C 142.
53. Buddle to Londonderry, 19 February 1828, D/Lo/C 142.
54. Duke of Wellington to Londonderry, 11 November 1830, DCRO, D/Lo/C 113.
55. Committee of Coal Owners, *Minute Book*, x, 17 November 1830.
56. Broadside address, *To the Public*, delegate meeting, Black Fell, 6 April 1831; broadside, *The Pitmen of the Tyne & Wear*, Durham, 1831.
57. Revd R. Brandling to Buddle, 7 April 1831, NCB 1/JB.
58. Committee of Coal Owners, *Minute Book*, x, 26 March 1831.
59. For Hetton men as, 'chief instigators of the mischief', Buddle to Londonderry, 29 March 1831, D/Lo/C 142; for the Cock, Reports of Messrs Hunter and Forster, 10 April 1831, *ibid*. For Hepburn, J.M. Bellamy and J. Saville, eds., *Dictionary of Labour Biography*, London, 1976, iii, pp. 99–101. The union's open membership corrects Clegg, Fox, and Thompson, and Church who cautiously follows them, in their assertion that the Miners' Federation of Great Britain (f. 1888) was the first mass miners' union: H.A. Clegg, A. Fox, A.F. Thompson, *A History of British Trade Unions since 1889*, i, Oxford, 1964, pp. 110–11; Church, *British Coal Industry*, p. 714.
60. *Rules and Regulations of the Coal Miners' Friendly Society, in the counties of Northumberland and Durham*, Newcastle, 1831; Buddle to Londonderry, 29 March 1831, D/Lo/C 142.
61. Buddle to Londonderry, 2, 4 June 1831, *ibid*.
62. *Ibid.*, 8 May 1831.

63. This binding was said to have put Tyne unionists 'in the worst humour possible', and on the evening of the binding 'a party of the Newbottle Men [Lambton's employees] went to Pensher Office to abuse and intimidate our Men, and to stop the Binding, but they were repulsed by the Pensher men': *ibid.*, 13 May 1831.
64. *Ibid.*, 18, 15, 18, 20 May 1831.
65. *Ibid.*, 20 May 1831.
66. *Ibid.*, 19 May, 4 June 1831.
67. *Ibid.*, 13, 18 June 1831.
68. *Ibid.*, 6 June 1831.
69. On production, *ibid.*, 29 May, 4 June 1831; on labour market, *ibid.*, 21 June 1831; on union expansion, *ibid.*, 13, 25 June, 7 July; on a typical day, *ibid.*, 8 July 1831; 14 July 1831. Church and his colleagues make a rare error in their reference to the 1831 dispute. They say it 'collapsed after two weeks': Church, *British Coal Industry*, p. 677.
70. Dunn, *Journal*, 12 January 1832; Committee of Coal Owners, *Minute Book*, x, 21 January 1832; Buddle to Londonderry, 5 May 1832, D/Lo/C 142; Dunn, *Journal*, 10 March 1832. The 'keeker' counted the filled tubs and assessed pitmen's pay.
71. Dunn, *Journal*, 16 November, 1 December 1831; 25 January, 23 February 1832 (Hetton disputes); 16 December 1831, 16, 21, 23, 28 January, 22 February 1832 (Coxlodge and Kenton dispute).
72. Dunn, *Journal*, 17, 24 March, 14, 30 April, 5 May 1832; Committee of Coal Owners, *Minute Book*, x, 12 May 1832; Buddle to Londonderry, 30 May 1832, D/Lo/C 142.
73. Dunn, *Journal*, 14 April 1832; Committee of Coal Owners, *Minute Book*, x, 7 April 1832; Maj. Gen. H. Bouverie to S. M. Phillips, 1 June 1832, PRO, HO/40/30/2; Dunn, *Journal*, 16 June 1832; James Losh, chairman of Joint Committee of Coal Trade, *Memorandum*, 23 June 1832, D/Lo/C 142; Bouverie to Phillips, 2 May, 1 June 1832, *ibid.*
74. Dunn, *Journal*, 17 March 1832.
75. Dunn, *ibid.*, 19 March, 10, 19, 21, 23, 24 April; 'the main point now hinges on the non employment of Delegates'. (30 April, 1832); Committee of Coal Owners, *Minute Book*, x, 16 June 1832.
76. Dunn, *ibid.*, 11 April – 26 June, *passim*; 26, 28 June 1832; 3, 14 May, 7 June, 30 May, 11 July, 8 August 1832.
77. Buddle to Londonderry, 25 May 1832, D/Lo/C 142; Bouverie to Phillips, 12 June 1832, HO/40/30/2; Dunn, *Journal*, 16 June 1832; Brandling to Bouverie, 12 June 1832, HO/40/30/2.
78. In May 1832 there were two cavalry troops at Houghton le Spring, near Hetton colliery; one troop at Shields, one at Jarrow, two at Newcastle, and one on its way. There were infantry companies at Hetton, Jarrow, and Shields. By the end of May there had been a shift of cavalry strength from Shields and Jarrow to Newcastle and Bedlington, and by then there were infantry companies at Durham Gaol, Hetton, Rainton, Shields, Jarrow, Tynemouth, and Bedlington. Bouverie to Phillips, 2, 26 May 1832, HO/40/30/2; Bouverie to Phillips, 22 June 1832, *ibid.*; Buddle to Londonderry, 21 June 1832, D/Lo/C 142; for warnings to their labour

recruiter in Wales to be more selective in his choice, Committee of Coal Owners, *Minute Book*, x, 19 June 1832; Buddle to Londonderry, 28 July 1832, *ibid.*; Bouverie to Phillips, 8 July 1832, *ibid.*

79. Buddle to Londonderry, 26 May, 24, 25 June, 9 August 1832, *ibid.*

80. Bouverie to Phillips, 30 July 1832, HO/40/30/2; Buddle to Londonderry, 11 August 1832, *ibid.*; Bouverie to Phillips, 5 September 1832, *ibid.*; for a full account of the epidemic, R. J. Morris, *Cholera 1832*, London, 1976.

81. Bouverie to Phillips, 12 August 1832, *ibid.*; Buddle to Londonderry, 6 November 1832, *ibid.*, Dunn, *Journal*, 20 September 1832.

82. Buddle to Londonderry, 16 February 1833, *ibid.*

83. Bouverie to Phillips, 22 March, 26 August, 10 June 1833, HO/40/31/1; Buddle to Londonderry, 17, 30 March 1833, *ibid.*

84. Committee of Coal Owners, *Minute Book*, xi, for 1834; Buddle to Londonderry, 17 April 1834, *ibid.*; Owners, *Minute Book*, xi, 11 March 1835; *Coal Trade Circular*, 5 March 1836, NCB 1/JB. Some mention of the strikes is made in J. Latimer, *Local Records; or, Historical Register of Remarkable Events 1832–57*, Newcastle, 1857, p. 66, p. 70, but Tremenheere does not rate the 1836 actions in his list of 'great' strikes in, *Mining Districts*, PP 1846, p. 6.

85. Church, *British Coal Industry*, p. 568; Committee of Coal Owners, *Minute Book*, xi, 3 March 1838.

86. Committee of Coal Owners, *Minute Book*, xi, 20 March 1841, 'Wages to the Following Officers and Workmen'; Buddle to Londonderry, 26 February 1843, D/Lo/C 142. Buddle's remarks are, quite literally, borne out by Church's statistical findings. 1842–3 was a very bad year: *British Coal Industry*, pp. 568, 573.

87. Hepburn and others' efforts to revive the union in 1834 'proved a complete failure' according to Maj. Gen. Bouverie, to Phillips, 1, 12 January 1834; the revivalists are named, Buddle to Londonderry, 10 February 1834, *ibid.*; and for quote on Parkinson, Buddle to Londonderry, 21 June 1832, *ibid.*

88. Buddle to Londonderry, 19 July, 27 August 1835, *ibid.* Only three lads survived the Wallsend explosion.

89. Richard Fynes, *Miners of Northumberland and Durham*, p. 36; '[Hepburn] ... applied at Backworth Colliery last Thursday to be employed as a Shifter or Stone-workman but was told that we only employed Coal-hewers there', Buddle to Londonderry, 17 March 1833, *ibid.* Challinor and Ripley (*Miners' Association*, p. 17, p. 11) say that Hepburn peddled tea for five years before accepting the stated conditions of work. This might suggest that this exit from trade union agitation was in 1837. Hepburn's significant absence from the evidence after 1835 implies that his exit was earlier. See Bellamy and Saville, *Dictionary*, 1976, iii, pp. 99–101.

90. *The Miners's Monthly Magazine*, April 1844. The events of the 1844 dispute will be closely examined in Part Three.

Chapter six

1. For lines of victory and defeat in capitalism see, Stephen Yeo, 'Socialism, the state, and some oppositional Englishness', R. Colls and P. Dodd, ed., *Englishness 1880–1920*, London, 1986, p. 328.

2. We are now in the realm of 'invented tradition'. For essays on this see papers by E. J. Hobsbawm, P. Morgan, T. Ranger, and J. Keegan, *The Invention of Tradition*, Past and Present Society, 1977, and E. J. Hobsbawm and T. Ranger, eds., *The Invention of Tradition*, Cambridge, 1983.

3. Colls, *Collier's Rant*, pp. 24–96.

4. John Bryers to Lord Delaval, 24 September 1800, DE/4/24.

5. John Brotherick to Delaval, 1 October 1802, DE/6/11; Paul Forster to Delaval, 10 October 1803, DE/6/5; John Allen to Sir John Delaval, 26 September 1772, DE/6/4.

6. Bryers to Delaval, 13 October 1805, DE/4/27; 9 November 1804, DE/4/26; 26 September 1802, DE/4/24; 24 September 1800, *ibid.*; *Observations on the probable consequences*; John Buddle to John Iveson, 15 March 1820, D/Lo/C 142. At the height of their market power in 1805 Delaval's men were trying to make the Monday following 'pay Saturday' on optional holiday as well: Bryers to Delaval, 19 May 1805, DE/4/27.

7. Committee of Coal Owners, *Minute Book*, i, 10 September 1805; underviewer of Benwell colliery, *CEC 1842*, p. 620; Mr Nicholson, *Poor Law. App. A, Pt I*. PP 1834, p. 122. For an interesting comparison on the subject of mine owning and drink: Charles van Onselen, 'Randlords and rotgut 1886–1903: an essay on the role of alcohol in the development of European imperialism and southern African capitalism', *History Workshop Journal*, ii, 1976.

8. Committee of Coal Owners, *Minute Book*, i, 10 September 1805.

9. Joseph Oxley to Sir John Delaval, 29 May 1779, DE/4/11; John Crooks to Delaval, 3 January 1781, DE/4/4.

10. *Newcastle Chronicle*, 2, 9 May 1795; Hair, 'Binding of the Pitmen', p. 6; Mr Hunter, overman at Walker but a trapper in 1798, *CEC 1842*, p. 627; Buddle to Joseph Smith, London Corn Exchange, 10, 3 February 1800, D/Lo/C 142.

11. George Culley to Warren Hastings, 23 May 1800, NCRO, ZCU/38.

12. John Sykes, *Local Records; or, Historical Register of Remarkable Events*, Newcastle, 1865, ii, 23 April 1810; *Tyne Mercury*, 10 September 1822; Sykes, 6 February 1829.

13. *A Voice*, p. 29, p. 36; anonymous letter to *Gateshead Observer*, nd. 1844, newspaper cutting, *Strike Collection*, WCL; *Pits and the Pitmen*, pp. 28–9. The NMA's alternative bond in 1844 wanted colliery houses to be removed from the contract and rented for £4 per year.

14. Thomas, *Summary of the Condition*, 1807. A. W. Coats, in his 'Changing attitudes to labour in the mid-eighteenth century', *Economic History Review*, ii, 1958, argues for a gradual shift away from these mercantilist attitudes to labour, from the mid-eighteenth century, but in the northern coalfield these attitudes persisted well into the 1840s.

15. *Rules and Regulations*, 1831.
16. Arthur Young, *A Six Months Tour through the North of England*, London, 1771, iii, pp. 320–2; Eden, *State of the Poor*, pp. 268–71; Smith, *Wealth of Nations*, i, p. 202, 206.
17. *Newcastle Courant*, 17 November 1810. Raymond Williams' treatment of the word 'mechanical' (*Keywords*, London, 1976, p. 167) neglects the romanticisation of manufacture, and the early nineteenth-century assimilation of the term 'mechanic' for a person working in manufacture at a higher level than a labourer; for skilled engineers, the Friendly Union of Mechanics was founded in Manchester c. 1824 (G. D. H. Cole and A. W. Filson, *British Working Class Movements*, London, 1965, pp. 289–90). Also the Mechanics' Institutes from 1824 were aimed at the more skilled and prosperous.
18. *Brief Observations*, pp. 6–7; *A Defence of the Voice*, p. 9.
19. Edward Smith to Thomas Hepburn, nd. 1831–2, D/Lo/C 142; Philanthropos, *Two Subjects*, p. 6; Edward Hughes, ed., *The Diaries and Correspondence of James Losh*, publications of the Surtees Society, clxxiv, 1962–3, ii, 7 April 1831.
20. Sir James Walsham, *Report to Her Majesty's Principal Secretary of State for the Home Department, from the Poor Law Commissioners, on an inquiry into the Sanitary Condition of the Labouring Population of Great Britain; with Appendices*, PP 1842 (HL) xxvii, p. 431, p. 419.
21. *Durham Chronicle*, 5 July 1844.
22. George Hunter to Londonderry, 21 December 1843, DCRO, D/Lo/C 149.
23. Nicholas Hindhaugh to Lord Londonderry, 11 March 1844, DCRO, D/Lo/C 148; *Coal*, PP 1873, p. 304.
24. Handbill, 31 August 1765, PRO, SP/37/4.
25. Sir James Graham, Home Secretary, to Londonderry, 29 March 1844, DCRO, D/Lo/C 80. On 18 May 1844 a *Miners' Advocate* editorial asked the Trade why it refused to speak to them.
26. United Colliers Association, *A Candid Appeal to the Coal Owners and Viewers of Collieries on the Tyne and Wear*, Newcastle, 1826; Brotherly Society to Lord Londonderry, 20 February 1826, HO/40/19; Buddle to Londonderry, 11, 13 April, 9 May 1831, D/Lo/C 142; Handbill, *Durham. Sunday Morning*, 8 May 1831, NEIMME, *Watson Collection*; Buddle to Londonderry, 6 March 1833, *ibid.*
27. For a version of Londonderry's industrial relations: A. J. Heesom, 'Entrepreneurial paternalism: the third Lord Londonderry (1778–1854) and the coal trade', *Durham University Journal*, 66, 1974.
28. Londonderry to Graham, 3 June, 29 May 1844, PRO, HO/45/644.
29. Londonderry to Graham, 21 July 1844, *ibid.*
30. J. R. Leifchild, *CEC 1842*, p. 516; S. Tremenheere, *Mining Districts*, PP 1846, p. 7; *Address from Special Committee of Coal Miners to Coal Owners of Northumberland and Durham*, Newcastle, 10 July 1844; *Memorandum* of Agreement, 2 April 1855, DCRO, D/Lo/B6.
31. For popular Political Economy in government circles by the 1820s, Inglis, *Poverty and the Industrial Revolution*, ch. 4; H. Martineau, *Strikes and Sticks*, nd. 1832, PLL, *History of Coal Trade Collection*.

32. *Brief Observations*, pp. 4–5; *Newcastle Journal*, 20 June 1843.
33. Harrison, *Independent Collier*, p. 2.
34. *Poor Law. App. A, Pt I*, PP 1834, pp. 119–23, p. 139. Northumbrian labourers were less than perfect: see 'An Old Steward', *Northumberland Bondage by a Union of Hinds*, 6 March 1837, Dept. Palaeography, University of Durham, NCRO ref., A 229.
35. Colls, 'Oh happy English children', for school building.
36. See Asa Briggs, 'The language of "class" in early nineteenth-century England', in Briggs and J. Saville, eds., *Essays in Labour History*, London, 1967.

Chapter seven

1. Part Two will be about the *Primitive* Methodists, but occasionally I have used Wesleyan evidences as indicated. I have used my judgement in each case whether there was likely to be any qualitative difference in experience. It may be noted that contemporaries often referred to Methodism and its works without distinction, in a generic sense.
2. *Mining Districts*, PP 1846, p. 24.
3. *CEC 1842*, pp. 726–30, p. 647, p. 649, p. 647.
4. *Ibid.*, pp. 655–6, p. 665.
5. *Miners' Advocate*, 24 August 1844.
6. *Mining Districts*, PP 1846, p. 64, p. 20, pp. 25–6, p. 21; *CEC 1842*, p. 676, p. 648, p. 669, p. 601, p. 613.
7. *Mining Districts*, PP 1846, p. 30.
8. For sunday schools, *CEC 1842*, p. 629, p. 658, pp. 674–5; for colliery controls, p. 649.
9. Elliot was viewer at Washington and Belmont collieries, *CEC 1842*, p. 641; Reay was agent at Wallsend colliery, p. 716; Buddle, p. 625; *Mining Districts*, PP 1846, p. 19; W. Fordyce, *The History and Antiquities of the County Palatine of Durham*, Newcastle, 1855, i, p. 183; Mather was a South Shields merchant and philanthropist, *CEC 1842*, p. 670; 'Former Trapper Boy', *Gateshead Observer*, 10 August 1842.
10. Thomas, *Summary of Condition*; Thomas Burt, union leader, *Mines*, PP 1866, p. 6.
11. Bishop of Durham to Graham, 15 April 1844, HO/45/644.
12. Revd Broughton, of Washington, *CEC 1842*, p. 530; John Mackey, underviewer, St Lawrence Main colliery, p. 622; Dr Elliot, p. 667; George Elliot, chief agent to Lord Londonderry, *Second Report Accidents*, PP 1854, p. 17; J. R. Leifchild, *CEC 1842*, p. 568; T. A. Cockin, colliery manager at Auckland, p. 151; William Hunter, viewer of Walbottle colliery, p. 617; Dr R.S., p. 6; John Young, putter at Seghill, p. 611.
13. *Mines*, PP 1866, p. 12, p. 334, pp. 353–4.
14. For instance, descriptions of South Hetton and Clarence Hetton, *CEC 1842*, pp. 149–50.

Chapter eight

1. Hair, *Social History*, pp. 24–5, p. 27a.
2. Fordyce, *History and Antiquities*, ii, p. 381, p. 386.
3. Sill, *Hetton*, pp. 148–9.
4. Robert Surtees, *The History and Antiquities of the County Palatine of Durham*, London, 1816, i, p. 120, p. 83.
5. E. Mackenzie and M. Ross, *An Historical, Topographical, and Descriptive View of the County Palatine of Durham*, Newcastle, 1834, i, p. 419, p. 380.
6. Fordyce, *History and Antiquities*, ii, for South Hetton, p. 361, for Thornley, pp. 382–5; W. Page, ed., *The Victoria History of the Counties of England. Durham*, London, 1907, ii, pp. 269–70.
7. Major male occupations in the Easington Poor Law Union in 1851 were coal (2742), seafaring (387), and farming (185 farmers, 71 labourers): Fordyce, *History and Antiquities*, ii, pp. 355–6. For a smaller and older mining constituency, the village of Cockfield, the major occupations in 1851 were coalmining (69) and agricultural labouring (33) with farming (16): *Census 1851*, Cockfield Township, DCRO.
8. In 1840 HMI Allen was pleased to report on the ease of travel: *Instructions respecting an Inquiry into the State of Elementary Education in the Mining Districts of Durham and Northumberland*, PP 1841 (317) xx, p. 52. See also, B. Eccles, *The Development of Internal Transport in Northumberland*, University of Manchester dissertation for BA (Hons) 1969.
9. See Chapter one for details. After 1851 Northumberland and Durham were the fastest growing counties in a country where the 'excess of births over deaths accounted for by the greater part of population change in almost every region': E. H. Hunt, *Regional Wage Variations in Britain 1850–1914*, Oxford, 1973, p. 220, p. 225.
10. Hair, *Social History*, p. 37; with one year, three year, five year, and ten year tests for Walker colliery between 1780 and 1795, there was a labour stability of approximately two-thirds over one year, 40% over three years, 30% over five years, and 20% over ten years – but these are tacit results from what was, given the nature of the evidence, and assumptive piece of research (Walker colliery *bonds*, 1780, 81, 83, 84, 88, 1791, 92, 93, 95, 97–98, NEIMME).
11. These proportions are based on Hair's statistics (*Social History*, p. 112a) which were in turn based upon the careful use of the *Appendix to the Ninth Annual Report of the Registrar General of Births, Deaths, and Marriages*, PP 1849 (1087) xxi. Hair's North-East 'mining districts'' proportion of children under fourteen years out of total population: 38.5% (England and Wales, 35%); proportion of young adults out of total population: 58.8% (England and Wales, 55.6%); proportion of older female adults out of total population: 20.5% (England and Wales, 23.2%); proportion of older male adults out of total population: 20.8% (England and Wales, 21.2%).
12. In Hetton le Hole in 1851 the average mean family size for coal miner

heads of household was 4.45; for Hetton's total population, 4.03: Sill, *Hetton*, p. 102. For mining families having the highest fertility rates in the second half of the nineteenth century see: M. R. Haines, 'Fertility, nuptuality, and occupation: a study of coal mining populations and regions in England and Wales in the mid-nineteenth century', *Journal of Interdisciplinary History*, viii, 1977–8.

13. Hair, *Social History*, tables 6, 9, 8. It may be added that if County Durham's average infant mortality rates were appalling (174.6 per 1000 male, 154.1 per 1000 female, 1838–44), and England's were worse (205.1 male, 154.4 female), Merthyr's were horrific (248.7 male, 204.8 female) and the town appears to have known worse in 1820s: table 6, cohort nil to one years; G. A. Williams, *The Merthyr Rising*, London, 1978, p. 50; for the later century, returns from the medical officers of health suggest mining communities suffered higher rates of mortality than local agricultural labourers: J. Y. E. Seeley, *Coal Mining Villages of Northumberland and Durham: a study of sanitary conditions and social facilities 1870–1880*, University of Newcastle unpublished MA 1973, p. 17.

14. T. J. Taylor, coalowner, *CEC 1842*, p. 609.

15. *Poor Law. App. A, Pt I*, PP 1834.

16. Easington Union Board of Guardians, *Minute Book 1837–1847*, 21 June 1842, DCRO.

17. There was a mass meeting of the Northern Political Union on 1 January 1838 to protest about the Poor Law and Canada. There were important speakers (J. P. Cobbett, Feargus O'Connor, John Taylor, and Stephens), but the crowd was not large and did not contain organised pit contingents: *Northern Liberator*, 6 January 1838.

18. *Suggestions for imprisoning convicts in Coal Mines*, 1786, ms, PRO, HO/42/7.

19. W. A. Chatto, *Rambles in Northumberland and on the Scottish Border*, 1835, p. 38; Revd W. Pearson and R. Atkinson, *A Journal of an Excursion to the North of England*, 1838, ms diary, NCL; Buddle to Londonderry, 9, 14 May 1842, D/Lo/C 142; *Mining Districts*, PP 1846, p. 27.

20. In 1800 about a quarter of the nation's magistracy were clergymen: W. R. Ward, *Religion and Society in England 1790–1850*, London, 1972, pp. 2–3. In 1792, twenty-three out of forty-nine Northumberland incumbents were non-resident: G. Neasham, *North Country Sketches: notes, essays, and reviews*, Durham, 1893, pp. 133–9; in 1807 the pitmen were reported as almost completely outside the orbit of the Church, Thomas, *Summary of the Condition*, and from the 1830s the Anglican National Society made significant attempts to wean the mining community off Methodism and other disorders by building schools: *Annual Report of the Society for the Encouragement of Parochial Schools in the Diocese of Durham and Hexham*, 1832, p. 6, PRO, Ed. 7/25, 7/26, and Duffy, 'Debate', pp. 142–51.

21. J. R. Leifchild, *CEC 1842*, p. 533; Buddle to Londonderry, 13 June 1842, NCBI/JB.

22. *Statement illustrative of the amount of Spiritual Destitution in the Diocese*

of Durham, relative to the recently formed Durham Diocesan Society for the Employment of Additional Clergy, November 1859, DCRO, D/Lo/C 176; Neasham, *North Country Sketches*, p. 34. Between 1837 and 1843 Cathedral revenue for Durham was £183,809, 17s 11d, and most of it came from coal rents and royalties: Fordyce, *History and Antiquities*, i, p. 136.

23. *CEC 1842*, p. 530.
24. The Irish in particular were contrasted as a destabilising element compared with leadminers and Northumbrian 'peasants': *Poor Law. App. A, Pt I*, PP 1834, p. 126, pp. 138–9, p. 122. For Irish Roman Catholic problems in the 1860s see, R. J. Cooter, 'Lady Londonderry and the Irish Catholics of Seaham Harbour: "No Popery" out of context', *Recusant History*, 13, 1975–6, pp. 288–98.
25. Revd J. Nichol, *CEC 1842*, p. 718; Dunelm to Lords Council, 9 January 1840, in *Minutes of Proceedings of the Committee of Privy Council on Education*, PP 1839 (177) xli; *Report of the National Society*, 1843, p. 6; Duffy, 'Debate', p. 143. State inspectors were highly critical of the standards of unreformed educational provision and often represented it as a moral risk to children. Of course, in some eyes, to be working class was a moral plight in itself: *State of Elementary Education*, PP 1841, pp. 52–68.
26. Dr Mitchell, *CEC 1842*, pp. 142–3; Tremenheere, *Mining Districts*, PP 1846, p. 26.
27. Chief Constable's *Reports*, presented to County Quarter Sessions, Winter 1842 and 1847, DCRO, Q/S/OB 25. In 1841 there were eighty-one constables in County Durham, one hundred in Newcastle, and fifty-four in Sunderland: Michaelmas Sessions, 1841.
28. Anderson was viewer at South Shields colliery, *CEC 1842*, p. 637. See also corroborating evidences of underviewer at Felling, p. 635, and head viewer at Monkwearmouth, p. 642, and Leifchild the commissioner who thought the moral order of a pit village was a function of its distance from a town, 'especially of a sea port town', p. 533.
29. *Gateshead Observer*, 7 September 1849.
30. *Newcastle Courant*, 22 January 1785, 11 June 1785; *Newcastle Journal*, 16 February 1788; Revd W. Walters, *The History of the Newcastle on Tyne Sunday School Union: from its formation, to the close of its fiftieth year*, London, 1869; *Newcastle Journal*, 14 February 1835. The first sunday school was opened in Gloucester in 1780; by 1850 the national sunday schools had an attendance of two million children and just under a quarter of a million teachers. There were initial difficulties in Newcastle, of which we know little. Schools opened in 1785 with 'a very great overflow of applications'; five years later there were serious attendance problems: *Newcastle Courant*, 22 January 1785, 27 November 1790.
31. *Newcastle Courant*, 11 June 1785. For the developing class consciousness of Newcastle's bourgeoisie see *Gentleman's Magazine*, June 1737; David Harker, Introduction, *Rhymes of Northern Bards*, Newcastle, 1812, 1971 repr., pp. xxxv–xxxvi; Sydney Middlebrook, *Newcastle Upon Tyne: Its Growth and Achievement*, Newcastle, 1968, p. 195.

32. Walters, *Sunday School Union*, p. 43; *Second Annual Report of the Newcastle Sunday School Teachers' Association for Promoting the Due Observance of the Lords Day*, 1836, p. 4, p. 5, p. 10.

33. *Tyne Mercury*, 4 November 1817; *Report of the Newcastle Religious Tract Society for the Year 1817*, 1817; *First Reports of the Committees of the Adult School Society, formed for the Instruction of the Uneducated Adult Poor of Newcastle On Tyne*, 1815; E. Mackenzie, *A descriptive & historical account of the town & county of Newcastle Upon Tyne including the Borough of Gateshead*, Newcastle, 1827, ii, p. 573.

34. Thomas Oliver, *A New Picture of Newcastle Upon Tyne*, Newcastle, 1831, pp. 40–2. For Sunderland's missions and tract societies: W. Parson and W. White, *History, Directory, and Gazetteer, of the counties of Durham and Northumberland*, Newcastle, 1827, p. 333; *Newcastle Journal*, 21 December 1833.

35. Revd Donaldson to Lord Sidmouth, 3 January 1820, PRO, HO/42/203.

36. Thomas, *Summary of Condition; Newcastle Religious Tract Society*, p. 24; G. A. Cooke, *Topographical and Statistical Description of the County of Durham*, London, 1824, p. 54; Governor of Durham gaol, *CEC 1842*, p. 660, and further p. 637, p. 663, p. 152; Chief Constable's *Report*, Winter 1840.

37. Walters, *Sunday School Union*, p. 34, pp. 204–5, pp. 110–12, p. 305; Revd J. Everett, *The Walls End Miner: or a memoir of William Crister*, London, 1835, dedication. For Mechanics' Institutes as allies in civic order: Revd J. Davies, *Mechanics Institutions as Affecting the Character of the People*, Gateshead, 1848, p. 14.

38. Walters, *Sunday School Union*, pp. 104–5; A Well-Wisher to Society, *The Colliers Friend*, North Shields, 1825, p. 7, and many years later there was a report of aid for Primitive chapel building schemes at Seghill and Cramlington in 1838–9, W. M. Patterson, *Northern Primitive Methodism*, London, 1909, pp. 347–9; *Primitive Methodist Magazine*, 1884, p. 287; letter to General Committee, 22 January 1836, Sunderland Primitive Methodist Circuit, *Local Preachers and Committee Meeting Minutes*, 1831–42, DCRO, M/Sus 80; Patterson, *Northern Primitive Methodism*, p. 278.

39. Colls, 'Oh happy English children!' for 1840s and 1850s, and Seeley, *Mining Villages*, for dates of later colliery schools.

40. *State of Elementary Education*, PP 1841, p. 57; *Mining Districts*, PP 1846, p. 26. For South Hetton, *CEC 1842*, p. 149.

41. Chief Constable's *Report*, Winter 1842, for Wingate; for Hetton regulations, *CEC 1842*, p. 649, and Auckland, p. 159.

42. Poster, Thomas Forster, viewer, South Hetton Colliery Office, 15 July 1852, NCRO, ZFO/1; Patterson, *Northern Primitive Methodism*, pp. 99–100.

43. *Statistical Tables of nine principal Collieries ... dedicated to the British Association for the advancement of science*, Newcastle, 20 August 1838; *State of Elementary Education*, PP 1841, p. 57.

44. W. D. Cooper's dissertation was useful on the spread of teetotal societies, *The Teetotal Movement with particular reference to the North East of*

England, 1835–60, University of Durham dissertation for BA (hons) 1968, pp. 58–9; *Northern District Temperance Record,* October 1838; Cooper, *Teetotal Movement,* p. 8; *NDTR,* March 1839; Newcastle Teetotal Society, *Fifth Annual Report,* 1840.

45. State of Elementary Education, PP 1841, p. 57. For Methodist domination, and Primitive numbers in the North Durham mining district: *CEC 1842,* p. 533; *Mining Districts,* PP 1846, p. 27; *Primitive Methodist Magazine* (henceforward PMM), 1837, p. 339 – Sunderland 180 pupils; Hopper Street, Sunderland, 130; Monkwearmouth 78; Middle Rainton 70; Hetton 310; Easington Lane 96; South Hetton 100; Southwick 70; Durham City 43; Thornley 200. With the Primitive Newcastle Circuit at 540, and Darlington Circuit at 548, note the relative strength of Primitive Methodist sunday schooling in the mining towns and villages. There had been sunday schools in the pit villages since the turn of the century but a stable momentum does not seem to have been reached until the 1820s: Walters, *Sunday School Union,* pp. 110–12, p. 155, pp. 185–88; *CEC 1842,* pp. 143–44; *State of Elementary Education,* PP 1841, p. 63.

46. Mr Brown, agent, Cowpen colliery, *CEC 1842,* p. 165; Leifchild, p. 717; Charles Carr, coalowner, *Mining Districts,* PP 1846, p. 27 and *CEC 1842,* p. 613; *Mining Districts,* PP 1846, p. 121; 'An Eminent Engineer', *CEC 1842,* p. 151.

47. There appears to have been benefit and friendly society insurance at every colliery: *Second Report Accidents,* PP 1853, p. 27; *CEC 1842,* p. 724. 'Eminent Engineeer', *CEC 1842,* p. 151.

48. W. Morrison, *CEC 1842,* pp. 726–30; Mr Boyd, agent, Urpeth colliery, p. 716; John Buddle, p. 625. See also, Mr Robson, viewer, Hetton, p. 648; T. J. Taylor, p. 609.

49. *Gateshead Observer,* 30 July 1842. The illustrations of female and child workers in the Report made an impact; for new sensibilities in the social reportage of women and children, particularly in metropolitan journalism: C. Fox, 'The development of social reportage in English periodical illustration during the 1840s and early 1850s', *Past and Present,* 74, 1977. The pitwoman as the opposite of Woman's 'true nature': A. V. John, *By The Sweat of Their Brow. Women Workers at Victorian Coal Mines,* London, 1980, p. 11.

50. For above ground women at Newbottle and Burnmoor colliery, 'Eliz. Hall & Sist.' and others, *Pay bill,* 1787, NCB 1/JB. In 1807 there was a reference to North-East employment of girls in sorting work, at bank, Thomas, *Summary of the Condition;* for later century, in 'Newcastle' and 'Durham' districts: Home Office, *Women and Girls and Men and Boys Employed in Connection with Mines,* House of Commons return, 11 May 1887, pp. 2–3.

51. *CEC 1842,* p. 154 fn; Mackenzie, *Newcastle upon Tyne,* ii, p. 731; *Poor Law. Assistant Commissioners' Reports. App. B, Answers to Rural Queries. Pt I,* PP 1834 (44) xxx, p. 165, p. 147, p. 150, p. 164; Emily Davies, *Thoughts on some questions relating to Women 1860–1908,* Cambridge, 1910, p. 30 for quote on factories in 1860.

52. *CEC 1842*, p. 584; *Poor Law. App B, Pt I*, PP 1834, p. 147, p. 154, p. 165; *Poor Law. Assistant Commissioners' Reports. App. C, Communications. Pt I*, PP 1834 (44) xxviii, p. 120; Eve Hostetler, 'Women farm workers in 18th and 19th century Northumberland', *Bulletin NE Group for Study of Labour History*, 16, 1982; Hunt, *Wage Variations*, p. 122; *Poor Law. App. C, Pt I*, PP 1834, pp. 51–3; George Culley to Dr Fuller, 29 June 1801, NCRO, ZCU/44.

53. D. J. Rowe, 'Occupations in Northumberland and Durham 1851–1911', *Northern History*, viii, 1973, p. 124.

54. Sill, *Hetton*, p. 136, pp. 139–40; there were dressmakers at Barrington and Sleekburns colliery village in 1873, *Newcastle Weekly Chronicle*, 26 April 1873; Patterson, *Monkwearmouth*, p. 44, p. 57; Fordyce, *History and Antiquities*, ii, pp. 355–6.

55. *CEC 1842*, p. 156, p. 663; evidences on house work, in detail, only came much later – K. Armstrong and S. Wilson, *Miners' Wives*, Peterlee, 1984, Mrs McWaters, DCRO, D/MRP/3/4, Mrs Hodges, D/MRP/60/5, T. T. Ayer, *Cornsay Colliery*, 1975, ts, DCRO, p. 21; *CEC 1842*, p. 648, p. 669; *Hints to Husbands and Wives*, Newcastle, nd 1840s, NEIMME, *Watson Collection*; Mrs Hodges, p. 107.

56. John, *Women Workers*, p. 25; *State of Elementary Education*, PP 1841, p. 2, p. 5, p. 54; *Report Commissioner State of the Population in The Mining Districts*, PP 1853 (1679), xl, p. 26; Leifchild, *CEC 1842*, p. 519.

57. Dr Morrison, *CEC 1842*, pp. 662–3; Clarissa Hurd, *An Address to Women*, Demerara, 1862, p. 8; Barbara Taylor, *Eve and the New Jerusalem*, London, 1983, p. 126.

58. *Statistical Queries regarding pit villages*, enclosure, J. W. Johnston to Buddle, 28 April 1829, ('Can you do anything *to for* or *with* this ...?') NEIMME, *Bell Collection*; Incumbent, *A Few Brief Observations, Illustrations, and Anecdotes respecting pitmen in a northern colliery village*, Sunderland 1862, p. 10; *Sanitary Condition* PP 1842, p. 421, p. 419, pp. 426–8, p. 441, the quotation is from Cockermouth, p. 434; *State of Popular Education in England*, ii, PP 1861 (2794–II) xxi, p. 321.

59. W. Scott, *An Earnest Address and Urgent Appeal*, Newcastle, April 1831, p. 9.

60. *The Plain Speaker*, 19 May 1849; T. Doubleday, *A Defence of the Colliers*, Darlington, 1864; L. Simonin, *Mines and Miners; or underground life*, London, 1869, p. 238.

61. *First Report of Commissioners*, PP 1842, p. 266.

62. The sexual ideology centred on the physical and psychological maturation of children, for childhood was represented as the period when society's future hung in the balance, *First Report*, PP 1842, p. 268; *ibid.*, p. 25, and unidentified cutting, 4 May 1844, NEIMME, *Watson Collection; Newcastle Journal*, 11 June 1842, *Provincial Medical and Surgical Journal*, 11 June 1842, *Gateshead Observer*, 21 May 1842, *The Times*, 15 July 1842; *Gateshead Observer*, 30 July 1842, *Newcastle Journal*, 11 June 1842.

63. *Report Commissioner State of Population in The Mining Districts*, PP 1856 (2125), xviii, p. 27. This marked a change of opinion over twelve years. In 1844 Tremenheere had been far more sympathetic to the plight of discharged female surface-workers, and had not drawn his lines of sexual demarcation so strongly: *Report Commissioner State of the Population in The Mining Districts*, PP 1844 (592) xvi, pp. 1–3, p. 55.
64. *First Report*, PP 1842, p. 25.
65. Angus Bethume Reach, in, Ginswick, *Morning Chronicle*, ii, p. 39.
66. Dr Elliot of Newcastle Medical School, *CEC 1842*, p. 668–9; Mackenzie and Ross, *Durham*, i, p. cxv; E. Mackenzie, *An historical, topographical, and descriptive view of the county of Northumberland*, Newcastle, 1825, i, p. 203, p. 202; Mackenzie and Ross, *ibid.*
67. Buddle to Londonderry, 14 May 1842, D/Lo/C 142; C. W. Vane, *A Letter to Lord Ashley on the Mines and Collieries Bill*, London, 1842; Buddle to Bishop of Durham, 6 June 1842, DCRO, NCB I/JB/948.
68. Londonderry to Buddle, 21 June 1842, DCRO, NCB I/JB/1791; *Newcastle Journal*, 11 June 1842, *The Times*, 15 July 1842. Lords and Commons debates can be found in: *Hansard*, 3rd series, lxiii, 195–8, 1352–61; *Hansard*, 3rd series, lxiv, 538–44, *Hansard*, 3rd series, lxv, 101–24.
69. Matthias Dunn to Buddle, 26 April 1825, DCRO, NCB I/JB/431.
70. Buddle to Londonderry, 16 May, 13 June 1842, D/Lo/C 142.
71. 'Laimed in the Pit' was a common application, and for examples of sanctions, checks, and encouragements, see: Select Vestry, 23 April 1823, 20 August 1821, and 'Temporary Relief etc. paid Sundries' 1827 in, *Usworth township, poor rates, overseers accounts 1819–36*, DCRO, UD/Wa/3, 4.
72. Joseph Little of Stanhope, *Poor Law. App A, Pt I*, PP 1834, p. 160 d; Chester le Street Poor Law Union *correspondence*, 1843–6, DCRO, MH/12/2968–9; Clerk to Guardians to Lord Commissioners, 26 October 1852, Easington Poor Law Union *correspondence*, MH/12/3053.
73. F. W. D. Manders, *The Administration of the Poor Law in the Gateshead Union 1836–1930*, University of Newcastle unpublished M. Litt. 1980, p. 11.
74. See aspects of Chartist feminism in Eileen Yeo, 'Some practices and problems of Chartist democracy', in D. Thompson and J. Epstein, eds., *The Chartist Experience*, London, 1982, and Taylor, *New Jerusalem*, pp. 267–9.
75. *Miners' Advocate*, 13 July 1844; *Miners' Journal*, 18 November 1843.
76. *Log*, 14 November 1879, Consett British Mixed, DCRO E/NW/6.
77. Thomas, *Summary of the Condition*, 1807; *Penny Magazine of the Society for the Diffusion of Useful Knowledge*, 25 June 1836.
78. For a glowing example at Coxhoe, see Commissioner Mitchell, *CEC 1842*, p. 136; Dr Morrison, pp. 662–3, pp. 726–30; Edward Boyd, viewer, Urpeth colliery, p. 661; Mitchell, p. 144; Dr Elliot, p. 669.
79. *Mining Districts*, PP 1856, p. 28.
80. William Patterson, secretary, Durham Miners' Assocaition, *R C Labour*, PP 1892, p. 13.

81. *Sixth Report Trade Unions*, PP 1867–8, p. 5; *Newcastle Weekly Chronicle*, 18 January 1873, 21 February 1874.
82. R. Nelson Boyd, *Coal Pits and Pitmen*, London, 1892, p. 59; *India Office, East India. Employment of Women and Children in Mines*, House of Commons return, 20 March 1893, pp. 1–9. 1890 apologetics for Indian female miners were close both to the arguments of those who resented the 1842 Act and to the practices of those who were affected by it: Indian women did not mind nudity, they needed the income, the work was no more tough or 'masculine' than other work such as agriculture, they generally worked alongside men of their own family, their labour was cheap, they were well treated.

Chapter nine

1. In 1851 there were 106,074 Primitive Methodists (302, 209 Wesleyans), accounting for 0.51% (1.45%) of population: Robert Currie, *Methodism Divided*, London, 1968, p. 87, p. 90; for the Chester le Street, Castle Ward, Easington, and Houghton mining districts, 5% of the population attended Primitive worship (8% Wesleyan, 11% Anglican) on Census Sunday: Hair, *Social History*, p. 293.
2. Houghton le Spring Wesleyan Methodist Circuit, *Circuit Schedules 1836–1847*, 13 March 1846, DCRO, M/Ho/54.
3. Seeley, *Mining Villages*, p. 317.
4. Currie, *Methodism Divided*, p. 95.
5. Robert Moore, *Pit-Men, Preachers and Politics*, Cambridge, 1974, p. 25; James Obelkevich, *Religion and Rural Society, South Lindsey 1825–1875*, Oxford, 1976, p. 256; Currie, *Methodism Divided*, p. 94. E. P. Thompson made mighty efforts to penetrate the relationship between social change and Methodist growth in his *The Making of the English Working Class*, London, 1963, and in the second edition, made clear the need for detailed, chronological, analysis, Harmondsworth, 1968, pp. 917–23.
6. N. Curnock, ed., *The Journals of the Rev. John Wesley AM*, London, 1938, iii, pp. 68–9.
7. Revd F. Young, *Early History of Methodism around Houghton le Spring*, Hetton, 1927; Sunderland Wesleyan Methodist Circuit, *List of Members 1782–1836*, four volumes, DCRO M/Sus/147–50; North Shields Wesleyan Methodist Circuit, *Names of Members 1811–1873*, DCRO, M/SS/1; Houghton le Spring Wesleyan Methodist Circuit, *Circuit Schedules 1836–1847*, M/Ho/54.
8. Sunderland Town Mission, *Committee minutes*, 3 July 1839, DCRO, H/Sus/205.
9. J. W. Fawcett, *Memorials of Early Primitive Methodism in the County of Durham 1820–1829*, 1908. For the seditiousness of Primitive and 'Tent Methodists' see 'J. S.' to Home Department, 6, 23 April, 2 May 1821, PRO, HO/40/16.
10. Memberships of Philadelphia, Lumley, South Shields, and Sunderland Wesleyan Societies, 1816–1823, *Names of Members 1811–1873*, M/SS/1, for Wesleyan revivals 1820–1, 1822–3.

11. Journal of Bro. J. Gilbert, N. Tyne, July 1823, *PMM 1823*, p.279; South Shields, March–April 1824, *PMM 1824*, p.228; Rev. Branfoot, Hebburn, November 1823, *PMM 1824*, p.255; see also July 1823 successes of Bro. J. Spencer at Newcastle, and February–March on North Tyne, *PMM 1824*, pp.250–1; and Bro. G. Wallace's successes, July 1823–February 1824, *PMM 1824*, pp.222–6.

12. *PMM 1825*, pp.69–72; Rev. H.B. Kendall, *The Origin and History of the Primitive Methodist Church*, London, 1905, i, p.202. This is an abridged account from Nelson's journal.

13. From journal of Nathaniel West, 15 October 1823, Kendall, *Origin and History*, p.203; Sunderland Primitive Methodist Circuit, *Baptisms solemnized in the Parish of Monkwearmouth 1843–1953*, DCRO, M/SUS/68; Durham Primitive Methodist Circuit, *Register of Baptisms 1841–1850*, DCRO, M/Du/25; Patterson, *Northern Primitive Methodism*, p.14.

14. *PMM 1832*, p.149.

15. Buddle to Londonderry, 19, 29 December 1831, Nathaniel Hindhaugh to Buddle, 20 January 1832, D/Lo/C 142; Maj. Gen. Bouverie to S.M. Phillips, 30 July 1832, HO/40/30/2; Buddle to Londonderry, 11 August 1832, D/Lo/C 142; Bouverie to Phillips, 5 September 1832, HO/40/30/2.

16. *PMM 1832*, p.48, pp.227–9, p.385.

17. Buddle to Londonderry, 23 November 1832, D/Lo/C 142.

18. *PMM 1832*, pp.227–9.

19. *PMM 1832*, p.385, pp.227–9; for 'terror of cholera' in South Hetton, Thomas Beatty, surgeon, Easington Poor Law Union, to Commissioners, 15 November 1849, MH/12/3053; M.C. Dixon, *An Affectionate Address to the inhabitants of Newcastle and Gateshead*, General Union of Newcastle Religious Tract Society, 1832.

20. Revd J. Brewster, *A Sermon preached in the Parish Church of Boldon*, 1812, p.11; Revd J. Hodgson, *An Account of the Explosion which killed ninety-two persons*, 1813, p.72; Liverpool Religious Tract Society, *Narrative of a Dreadful Occurrence at Felling Colliery*, 1812, p.11. See also, T. Lessey, ed., *Short Account of the Life and Christian Experience of John Thompson, One of the persons killed by the explosion which took place in the Felling Colliery*, 1812, in PLL, *Coal Trade Collection*.

21. SPCK, *Colliery Tale; or Village Distress*, 1835, p.15; Great Northern Advertiser, *Letter from the Dead to the Living; or the Colliery Boy and his Mother*, 1841; for sunday school teacher who had gathered his class round him as they choked to death, Everett, *Walls End Miner*, p.162; on explosions as subject of popular music and doggerel: *Descriptive Poem on the late Lamentable Occurrence which took place at Wallsend Church Pit*, chapbook, Newcastle, 1835; *The Collier; Or, the dying hour of William Johnson*, 1836; also, see the amendments to the printer's proof of *The Willington Colliery Explosion*, nd, in NEIMME, *Bell Collection*, xix, p.304, where 'Willington' is replaced by 'Wrekenton', and the dates, number of survivors, and predominant families are all amended.

22. The mining community had its own responses to make, as well as, or with, the responses of the SPCK, Tract Societies, and Methodists; for

customary rituals after Penshaw's loss of fifty-nine in 1823: Buddle to Londonderry, 3 November 1823, D/Lo/C 142.

23. *PMM 1840*, p. 278, p. 277, p. 297.
24. Sunderland Primitive Methodist Circuit, *Quarterly, Local Preachers', and Committee Meeting Minutes 1831–1842*, 15 March, 10 September 1832, M/Sus/80; *PMM 1833*, pp. 376–7; *1835*, pp. 313–4; *1836*, pp. 310–11; *1837*, p. 266; *1838*, pp. 381–2; *1839*, p. 449.
25. *Quarterly ... Minutes*, 16 September 1833; *PMM 1837*, p. 267; *PMM 1839*, p. 449.
26. *Accounts of Monies and Members 1828–1836*, DCRO, M/Du/34, *Minute Book*, M/Du/25.
27. There are different growth patterns between Wesleyan and Primitive societies at Newbottle (1829–31), Houghton (1829–30, 1832–35), and Hetton (1829–35), and similar patterns at Moorsley (1836–41); there is evidence of greater Primitive volatility at Hetton (1830–35) and Moorsley (1836–39). However, one must note that Wesleyan figures were for full members and Primitive figures for full and trial; and there are gaps in recorded membership; and there is the possibility of unrecorded volatility between quarter days; for Newbottle, Houghton, and Hetton comparisons: *Accounts of Monies and Members 1828–1836*, M/Du/34; Sunderland Wesleyan Circuit, *Lists of Members 1782–1836*, M/Sus/147–50. For Moorsley: *Account Book*, M/Du/25; Houghton Wesleyan Circuit, *Circuit Schedules 1836–1847*, M/Ho/54.
28. *PMM 1838*, pp. 99–103; *PMM 1843*, pp. 217–8; Westgate Primitive Methodist Circuit, *Reports to District Meeting 1836–1932*, 4 March 1837, DCRO, M/We/93; for gaps in trialists: South Shields Primitive Methodist Circuit, *Accounts of Monies and Members 1837–50, Quarterly Lists of Members 1832–41*, DCRO, M/SS/29, M/SS/23. For children, Sunderland Primitive Methodist Circuit, *Quarterly, Local Preachers', and Committee Meeting Minutes 1831–1842*, 16 September 1833, M/Sus/80.
29. *PMM 1842*, p. 135; *PMM 1843*, pp. 141–4.
30. Durham Primitive Methodist Circuit, *Quarterly and Circuit Committee*, 16 March 1840, M/Du/25.
31. *Ibid.*, 13 April 1844.
32. *Northern Liberator*, 26 January, 23 February, 2 February, 4 May 1839.
33. For Sherburn Hill and Haswell, Graph III; for Moorsley Wesleyans, fn. 27.
34. *Northern Liberator*, 23 February, 2 March 1839.
35. *Northern Liberator*, 16 March 1839.
36. Sunderland Primitives minuted in 1839 'That the Circuit has Suffered by the influence of Chartism' (*Quarterly Minutes*, 16 September 1839). Did this refer to Chartism as a rival organisation, or was it a reference to coalfield disruptions after the Chartist July–August peak of a similar but smaller kind which followed Hepburn's Union defeat in 1832?
37. There are very few Chartist references to religious opposition. Chartist special praise of Thornley Primitives was obviously intended as criticism of other religious groups. At Hetton, local missionaries tried to lessen attendance at a Chartist meeting, without success, but it was not recorded

who they were (*Northern Liberator*, 16 March 1839). In April there were references to pro-Chartist Wesleyan sermons at Auckland and Aycliffe (*Northern Liberator*, 13 April 1839). Ten years previously, Winlaton, an iron making village by the Tyne and a Radical-Chartist centre for nearly thirty years, had been a Primitive circuit in its own right with twenty societies. The discovery of this in 1909 was said to have surprised Edwardian Methodists: Patterson, *Northern Primitive Methodism*, p. 204.

38. *Northern Liberator*, 16 March 1839.
39. Durham Primitive Methodist Circuit, *Quarterly and Circuit Committee*, 24 June 1844; Darlington Primitive Methodist Circuit, *Accounts of money and members*, September 1844, DCRO, M/Du/25, M/Da/35.
40. Durham, *ibid.*, 24 March 1845, 22 June 1846. See also South Shields Primitive Methodist Circuit, *Monies and Members*, September 1843, 1844, M/SS/29.
41. Durham, *ibid.*, 19 June 1847, and Graph IV.
42. For makeshift premises from the 1830s: Rev. W. Brown, *Centenary of Primitive Methodism in the Hetton Circuit*, Durham, 1923; and W. H. Walton, *Centenary Celebration, Primitive Methodist Church, Jarrow on Tyne*, So Shields, 1922; the pitman John Bell had offered his home at three colliery villages, *PMM 1870*, p. 422. For a spurt of chapel building after 1850 at South Hetton, Seaham, Murton, Middle Rainton, Newbottle and Hetton: Sunderland Primitive Methodist Circuit, *Circuit Schedules 1838–1850*, DCRO, M/Sus/75. Anglicans considered themselves at a serious disadvantage when they compared their lone parson and their need to build and consecrate against Methodist lay officialdom and the flexibility of the meeting room.

Chapter ten

1. C. N. Wawn, *Thomas Curry, the Pious Keelman*, Newcastle, 1822, pp. 10–12.
2. Young, *PMM 1847*, p. 457; Colling, *1856*, p. 401; Birkbeck, *1865*, pp. 115–6 – see also James Potts, *1857*, pp. 184–5, Betsy Goodchild, *1846*, p. 188, Sarah Lowther, *1850*, p. 249; with other groups – William Hindhaugh, *1843*, pp. 322–3, James Pyburn, *1862*, p. 593; privately taken – Matthew Raisbeck, Hetton miner converted 1834, *1862*, p. 253; its attainment – Timothy Hackworth, Wylam colliery blacksmith converted 1811, in W. D. Lawson, *Wesleyan Local Preachers*, Newcastle, 1874, p. 155.
3. W. R. Cross, *The Burned-over District: the Social and Intellectual History of Enthusiastic Religion in Western New York 1800– 50*, Ithaca, 1950; J. F. C. Harrison, *Robert Owen and The Owenites in Britain and America*, London, 1969, p. 102, p. 138.
4. For direct evidence of such plots, this time directed against American communists in 1929: Liston Pope, *Millhands and Preachers. A Study of Gastonia*, Yale, 1942.
5. Robert Southey, *The Life of Wesley and the Rise and Progress of*

Methodism, London, 1820, i, p. 298, p. 246; John Walsh, 'Methodism at the End of the Eighteenth Century', in R. Davies and G. Rupp, eds., *A History of the Methodist Church in Great Britain*, London, 1965, i, pp. 313–4. To be fair to Walsh, his essay is about eighteenth-century experience.

6. Fawcett, *Memorials*, pp. 17–18, p. 20; Kendall, *Origin and History*, p. 142, p. 147. Wesley was usually embarrassed by hysteria at his meetings – 'How fond he is of the word "calm"': R. A. Knox, *Enthusiasm*, Oxford, 1950, p. 452. The problem of a professional ministry and its ability to relate to the emotions of poor people (and the workings of the Holy Spirit) was always present in Methodism; '"Whence are the people to look for their Revivalists? Not, alas! to a College"' – quoted in Currie, *Methodism Divided*, p. 48. See also, G. E. Milburn, *A School for the Prophets. The Origins of Ministerial Education in the Primitive Methodist Church*, published by the author, Sunderland, 1981.

7. See fn 3.

8. A. Ure, *Philosophy of Manufactures*, London, 1835, p. 417, pp. 423–5. See Thompson's cogent argument on religious submission and factory discipline, *The Making*, 1968, pp. 385–440.

9. Kendall, *Origin and History*, p. 298.

10. Thompson, *The Making*, pp. 428–9, p. 919. Thompson's theory oscillates between the bold and the tentative, and both features have tended to harden under criticism. His suggestions of reasons for chiliastic 'despair' range from the Industrial Revolution in general, to War and Counter Revolution, to millenarial expectancy, to industrial and political unrest, to 'above all' 'misery and war weariness' (pp. 417–29 *passim*). In addition, he adds the endemic instabilities of the village, and the various possibilities for self-induced revivalism (p. 919). Given such a range of potential reasons – from general contexts to direct external factors to internal generation – the theory can lose some of its startling force when applied to specific cases. There is also the problem of chronology and location. The theory applies to the years 1780 to 1820; or to the French War years in particular, with possibilities in rural-mining areas 'long continued'; or up to 1832; or beyond 1832, considering the attributed Methodist influence on factory discipline (pp. 918–21). Sometimes, Thompson's worker, when faced with Buntingite Wesleyanism, loses that capacity for reinterpretation according to experience, which is retained when in contact with Radicalism or Owenism (eg. p. 402). At other times in other places, Methodism is held as being softened and modified by this experience manifest in the mutuality of working-class community (p. 416). This sort of difficulty is sub-divided by Thompson's contrast between Primitive and Wesleyan Methodism: 'We can scarcely discuss the two Churches in the same terms' (p. 436).

11. R. Currie, A. Gilbert, L. Horsley, *Churches and Churchgoers. Patterns of Church Growth in the British Isles since 1700*, Oxford, 1977, p. 42; Church, *British Coal Industry*, pp. 568, 570.

12. Thompson, *The Making*, p. 919; Hazlitt, *ibid.*, p. 406; Southey, *Life of Wesley*: W. James, *The Varieties of Religious Experience: a study in*

human nature, London, 1904, p. 95; for taking the approach beyond reasonable knowledge: N. Cohn, *The Pursuit of the Millennium*, London, 1957, and G. R. Taylor, *The Angel Makers. A Study in the Psychological Origins of Historical Change 1750–1850*, London, 1958.

13. Kendall, *Origin and History*, pp. 145–6; *PMM 1824*, pp. 212–14; *PMM 1825*, pp. 32–4.

14. *PMM 1824*, pp. 212–14; Fawcett, *Memorials*, p. 34; for comparisons in rationality and irrationality of morning and evening services, for farm labourers: M. K. Ashby, *Joseph Ashby of Tysoe 1859–1919*, London, 1974, p. 170.

15. *CEC 1842*, p. 588.

16. See John Walsh's 'Enthusiasm' in *History Workshop Journal*, 5, 1978, p. 207.

17. Frances Bevan, *The Story of John Wesley*, London, nd 1860s?, pp. 102–3; Kendall, *Origin and History*, p. 203; *New Moral World*, 28 July 1838, in Harrison, *Robert Owen*, p. 133.

18. Thompson, *The Making*, p. 437.

19. Kendall, *Origin and History*, pp. 220–1.

20. *PMM 1850*, p. 647, obituary of preacher Jane Curry, and *PMM 1884*, p. 28; *PMM 1829*, pp. 175–8; *PMM 1884*, p. 285, Patterson, *Northern Primitive Methodism*, p. 325, p. 232, p. 288; the coffee and sandwich allegations were made at Sacriston after a former lay preacher, Thomas Carr, had left the union and joined an evicting squad. Carr had previously been a Chartist speaker, teetotal lecturer, and seeker after a position in the union: *Miners' Advocate*, 24 August 1844.

21. SDUK, *Penny Magazine*, 5 August 1837; Obelkevich, *Religion and Rural Society*, pp. 259–312; Dr Morrison thought it would prove 'endless' to give examples of village superstition, a frame of mind which 'often sets the dictates of reason at defiance' and in which he included Primitive Methodism: *CEC 1842*, pp. 726–30; Kendall, *Origin and History*, p. 119; Patterson, *Northern Primitive Methodism*, p. 238; *PMM 1825*, pp. 213–5.

22. Kendall, *Origin and History*, p. 136; *PMM 1824*, pp. 58–61; *PMM 1870*, pp. 423–7.

23. Patterson, *Northern Primitive Methodism*, pp. 207–8. Working-class associational life appeared to favour performance over print, and there is reason to believe that strong dialects and oral traditions served as defences to working-class culture: *Penny Magazine*, 5 August 1837; Lady Anon., *Life Amongst the Colliers*, 1862, pp. 12–13, p. 153; *Northern District Temperance Record*, August 1839. For preachers' pay, Sunderland Primitive Methodist Circuit, *Quarterly ... Minutes*, 16 February 1837, M/Sus/80.

24. Kendall, *Origin and History*, pp. 32–3; Everett, *Walls End Miner*, p. 133; J. Ritson, *The Romance of Primitive Methodism*, London, 1909, p. 268.

25. There was a fall in Wesleyan growth 1816–17, membership, and funds 1820: J. S. Werner, *The Primitive Methodist Connexion. Its Background and Early History*, Wisconsin, 1984, p. 13, and pp. 6–21, p. 87, p. 135, p. 124.

26. J. Kent, *Holding the Fort. Studies in Victorian Revivalism*, London, 1978, pp. 11–12, p. 17.

27. John Wesley, *An Earnest Appeal to men of Reason and Religion*, Bristol, 1771; *A Farther Appeal*, London, 1778 (sixth and fifth editions); *The Principles of a Methodist*, London, 1796.

28. For modes of discourse I found Raymond Williams very helpful: *Marxism and Literature*, Oxford, 1977, part III.

29. Werner, *PM Connexion*, p. 49; W. F. Swift, 'Women itinerant preachers of early Methodism', *Proceedings of the Wesley Historical Society*, xxviii, xxix, 1952, 1953.

30. Philotheos, *Letter to the People called Methodists, on their unscriptural mode of addressing God at their prayer meetings, with brief remarks on females speaking and praying in public*, Manchester, 1826; Revd A. Rees, *Reasons for not cooperating in the alleged 'Sunderland Revivals'*, Sunderland, 1859; Werner, *PM Connexion*, p. 21, p. 84.

31. Durham Primitive Methodist branch, *Minutes of Preachers' Meetings*, 5 September 1838, M/Du/25; Durham Primitive Methodist Circuit, *Quarterly and Circuit Committee*, March 1839, March 1840, M/Du/25.

32. Werner, *PM Connexion*, p. 140.

33. As essay of this title won the Norrisian Theological prize at Cambridge, *Newcastle Chronicle*, 2 May 1795; Southey, *Life of Wesley*, p. 481; T. Trotter, *An Essay ... on Drunkenness*, Newcastle, 1810, p. 33; *PMM 1884*, p. 156; *PMM 1851*, p. 67.

34. J. R. Featherston, *Weardale Men and Manners*, Durham, 1840, pp. 45–7; comments of Wesleyan Dr Adam Clarke in Everett, *Walls End Miner*, p. 31; Mackenzie, *Northumberland*, i, pp. 205–6, William Andrews ed., *Bygone Durham*, London, 1898, p. 261.

35. Eleanor Wall of Pittington, *PMM 1855*, pp. 633–4; for fixations with last moments of life: R. Lonsdale, leadminer, *1849*, p. 698; A. Young, pitman, *1861*, pp. 517–8; R. Grieves, pitman, *1879*, pp. 243–4; Mary Foster, Castle Eden colliery, *1888*, p. 308. Wawn's biography of Curry devotes eleven out of twenty-six pages to his death, *Thomas Curry, the Pious Keelman*.

36. On the preachers' books, Ritson, *The Romance*, p. 114.

37. *PMM 1861*, pp. 520–3; *1870*, pp. 246–8; *1849*, p. 641; *1870*, pp. 423–7; from 'Memoir of W. Bramwell', 1839, quoted in Kent, *Holding the Fort*, p. 26; see also R. Punshon, pitman, *PMM 1853*, p. 719; R. Clasper, keelman, *1852*, p. 574; R. Young, pitman, *1847*, p. 457; Phoebe Longman of Easington, *1854*, pp. 30–2; W. Grieves of N. Shields, *1854*, p. 129; J. Featherstone, leadminer, *1848*, pp. 132–4; W. Bell, pitman, *1858*, pp. 129–30.

38. *PMM 1878*, pp. 121–2; *1869*, p. 628; *1865*, pp. 685–6; *1888*, p. 632; *1826*, pp. 265–9; see also: Eleanor Goodchild, of Sunderland, *1848*, p. 759; Eleanor Wall, of Pittington, *1855*, pp. 633–4; Jane Curry, of Washington, *1850*, p. 647; Jane Hetherington, of Weardale, *1832*, pp. 27–8; John Durham, at Sunderland, *1832*, p. 329; E. Gray at Earsdon, *1832*, p. 398; W. Thompson, pitman, *1894*, pp. 391–2.

39. *PMM 1842*, pp. 292–4; *1867*, pp. 316–7; *1855*, p. 383; *1853*, pp. 634–5;

1847, pp. 257–8; *1862*, p. 593; *1832*, p. 330: for further cases of moving from Wesleyans to Primitives: J. Robinson, leadminer, *1883*, pp. 310–11; Mary Porteous, domestic servant, *1861*, pp. 520–3; Mary Cosens, of Birtley, *1832*, pp. 451–5.

40. *PMM 1890*, p. 311; see also, George Clough, pitman, *1878*, pp. 121–2; Ben Robson, pitman, *1886*, p. 55.
41. *PMM 1866*, p. 41; *1855*, p. 382. See also, W. Aisbit, pitman, *1851*, p. 124; J. Tulip, pitman, *1890*, p. 311; J. Quilt, soldier, *1848*, p. 638.
42. *PMM 1871*, p. 434; *1841*, p. 239; *1859*, p. 120; see also, J. Lonsdale, leadminer, *1856*, p. 700; Jane Cooper, of Hetton, *1848*, p. 62; O. Ferguson, seaman, *1850*, pp. 123–4; Jane Halliday, of Hetton, *1852*, pp. 124–5; W. Fairley, pitman, *1852*, p. 712; J. Dixon, pitman, *1853*, p. 255; Eleanor Goodchild, *1848* p. 759; Mary Jackson, of Weardale, *1850*, p. 251.
43. *PMM 1857*, pp. 190–1; *1874*, p. 559; *1853*, p. 440. John Weatherston, pitman, in 1832 after his move to Hetton, *1850*, p. 573; and Ralph Punshon, pitman, in 1838 after his move from Hetton to St Helen Auckland, *1853*, p. 719.

Chapter eleven

1. Quotations come from Richard Baxter, *The Saints' Everlasting Rest*, London, 1809 ed., p. 37, p. 54. Baxter, a seventeenth-century Presbyterian Divine, was prescribed theological reading for all Primitive preachers.
2. Baxter, *Rest*, p. 191, p. 161.
3. Everett, *Walls End Miner*, pp. 12–13. 'Let sinners be convinced that you speak not of your own head', Baxter, *Rest*, p. 159.
4. Revd D. McAllum, *The Substance of the first Sermon, preached in the New Chapel, Chapter Row, South Shields 26 February 1809*; Durham Primitive Methodist Circuit, *Quarterly and Circuit Committee*, 19 June 1848, M/Du/25.
5. For a discussion of ideological theory in this way, L. Althusser, *For Marx*, London, 1977, pp. 232–4. Marx understood religion as ideology within the problematic of 'alienation'. For a classic statement: K. Marx, *Introduction to A Critique of Hegel's Philosophy of Right*, 1844, London, 1975, p. 244.
6. Werner, *PM Connexion*, p. 13, p. 19, pp. 135–9, p. 161; *Rules, Regulations Arrangements, and Orders, for Sunday Schools*, nd 1832?, p. 2; *General Consolidated Minutes of the Primitive Methodist Connexion*, London, 1850.
7. Durham Primitive Methodist Circuit, *Quarterly and Circuit Committee*, 20 December 1841; Sunderland Primitive Methodist Circuit, *Quarterly ... Minutes*, 10 September 1838, M/Du/25, M/Sus/80.
8. Kendall, *Origin and History*, p. 35, and Ritson, *The Romance*, p. 12; *PMM 1832*, p. 330; Houghton le Spring Wesleyan Methodist Circuit, *Local Preachers' Meeting Minutes 1836–38*, 24 December 1838, DCRO, M/Ho/58; Revd J. Parker, *A Preacher's Life*, London, 1899, p. 6.
9. Pioneer theorising into what he calls the historical reality of the soul is in M. Foucault, *Discipline and Punish. The Birth of the Prison*, London,

1977; for the late nineteenth century the main social aspect of membership was the 'consequential' aspect of open ethical behaviour: Moore, *Pit-Men*, p. 119.

10. Durham Primitive Methodist Circuit, *Quarterly and Circuit Committee*, 2 December 1841, 22 March 1847, M/Du/25; *PMM 1865*, pp. 492–3; Durham PMC, *Quarterly*, 18 June 1842, 18 December 1848, 24 October 1842; Sunderland PMC, *Accounts of Monies and Members 1828–36*, Durham branch and Circuit, *Account Book 1836–48*, for selected colliery villages, M/Du/34, M/Du/25.

11. Durham Primitive Methodist Circuit, *Quarterly and Circuit Committee*, 5 November 1841, *Account Book*, 10 September 1841, 16 March 1840, M/Du/25.

12. *PMM 1848*, pp. 132–4; *1852*, p. 574; *1871*, p. 234.

13. See Chapter eight; for the diary records of rich women trying to achieve a moral unity of their time: *Diary of Lady Cecilia Ridley 1835–6*, NCRO, ZRI/32/6; *Diary of Henrietta Trotter*, 29 April 1829, DCRO, D/X/277/1.

14. South Shields Primitive Methodist Circuit, *Quarterly Meeting Minutes 1833–45*, 1 July 1842, 9 June 1841, DCRO, M/SS/13,14.

15. Houghton le Spring Wesleyan Methodist Circuit, *Local Preachers*, 28 September 1848; Sunderland Primitive Methodist Circuit, *Quarterly … Minutes*, 12 September 1836, DCRO, M/Sus/80.

16. South Shields Primitive Methodist Circuit, *Quarterly Meeting*, 8, 22 February 1834, 25 June 1842, M/SS/13,14; Sunderland Primitive Methodist Circuit, *Quarterly … Minutes*, 1 April 1836, M/Sus/80. A notorious, and unpleasant, local case of Methodist intimacy, oversight, and gender relations, concerned the Wesleyan minister, Revd T. Hill, and Miss Bell: *The Cause of Truth defended; … the two trials of Revd T. Hill … for the defamation of character of Miss Bell*, North Shields, 1827.

17. There appeared to be a high proportion of pit boys, perhaps a quarter, who regularly attended village sunday schools. Attendance seemed to be as ordinary a part of their lives as accident and injury: *CEC 1842*, p. 570, p. 661.

18. Curnock, *Journals*, v, p. 469; *PMM 1847*, pp. 379–80; Everett, *Walls End Miner*, p. 127; Isaac Watts, *Songs Divine and Moral for the use of children*, Alnwick, 1840, p. 12, p. 23, pp. 27–8; *PMM 1842*, pp. 292–4; *1849*, p. 319.

19. Houghton le Spring Wesleyan Methodist Circuit, William Street Methodist Church, *Sunday School Teachers' Meetings 1827–34*, and *Rules*, and *Rules, Attendance, and Notes of Wesleyan Sabbath School, 1839*, DCRO, M/Ho/98, M/Ho/99.

20. *Rules, Regulations*, pp. 11–12.

21. S. D. Waddy, *Report on Sunday and Other Schools, presented to The Conference of 1837* [–43], London, 1871; Monkwearmouth Wesleyan Sabbath Schools, *A Narrative of Facts*, Bishopwearmouth, 1851. For a Primitive split in Sunderland also caused by insensitive central administration: G. E. Milburn, 'Tensions in Primitive Methodism

in the 1870s', *Proceedings of the Wesley Historical Society*, xI, February 1976.

22. For Anglican institutions: Fowberry Sunday School, *Rules and Proceedings 1823*, NCRO, Z/CU/38; Felton Sunday School Teachers' Meeting *Minute Book 1819—1821*, NCRO, 347/121.

23. George Parkinson, *True Stories of Durham Pit-Life*, London, 1912, pp. 30—3, pp. 65—72.

24. T. Garbutt, *Substance of an Address ... at a Social Meeting of the teachers and friends of the Methodist Sabbath School, Howden*, Howden, 1834, p. 9.

25. Newcastle Nelson Street Anniversary, *PMM 1846*, p. 504.

26. Garbutt, *Substance*, p. 7.

27. Curnock, *Journals*, iii, p. 73; *PMM 1832*, pp. 451—5; *1849*, p. 641; *1848*, p. 638; *1843*, pp. 322—3; *1856*, p. 401; *1853*, pp. 634—5. Bowling was described as the pitman's favourite 'diversion' in *Newcastle Chronicle*, 5 October 1805, and see, A. Metcalfe, 'Organised sport in the mining communities of south Northumberland 1800—89', *Victorian Studies*, 25, 1982. For sabbatarian instincts, see admonitions on Sunday pleasure trips: Sunderland Primitive Methodist Circuit, *Leaders' Meetings*, 2 June 1842, 3 July 1845, DCRO, M/Sus/111.

28. *Miners' Advocate*, 23 March 1844; Patterson, *Northern Primitive Methodism*, p. 285; *PMM 1826*, pp. 265—9. Methodism was famous for its music. There can be little doubt that its musical enthusiasm, and skill, benefited from its interaction with the culture of the Poor. The northern coalfield's musical excellence was recognised by the Brighton impressario George Fox, although his judgement was not disinterested '[pitmen were] The only group of persons of the lower Class who have hitherto devoted their Leisure hours to music ... have often set a good example, particularly when aided, as they used to be by such practical patronage as yours' (Fox to Buddle, 5 April 1842, NCB I/JB).

29. Wilson, *Habits and Diseases*, p. 4.

30. South Shields Primitive Methodist Circuit, *Quarterly Meeting*, 15 June 1839, M/SS/13, 14; *PMM 1833*, p. 77; Kendall, *Origin and History*, p. 473. In 1834 Co. Durham had the fourth highest concentration of British and Foreign Temperance Society members (10.4 per 1000 population): B. Harrison, *Drink and the Victorians*, London, 1971, p. 109. For the circumstantial relationship between ale houses, gambling sport, and assault: North East Circuit, *Depositions*, 1784—86, PRO, ASSI/45/35.

31. The Coal Trade and the Drink Trade were structurally connected by the tradition of paying men in public houses. Many lessees had money in local brewing and some overmen owned beershops. In 1807 the coalowners tried to persuade each other to pay 'at private houses, avoiding the temptation to intemperance', Thomas, *Summary of the Condition*; for holidays and celebrations with drink supplied by owners: *Newcastle Courant*, 16 December 1786, *Newcastle Chronicle*, 9 June 1802. Newcastle dockers swore by ale for their health, strength, and wind, T. F. Dibdin, *A Bibliographical, Antiquarian, and Picturesque*

Tour in the Northern Counties of England and in Scotland, London, 1838, p. 330.

32. Sunderland Primitive Methodist Circuit, *Quarterly ... Minutes*, 14 September 1835, M/Sus/80; *PMM 1854*, p. 129.
33. *CEC 1842*, p. 143, p. 163, pp. 160–1; *PMM 1857*, pp. 394–5; Revd J. Dawson, *Peter Mackenzie. His Life and Labours*, London, 1896, p. 55, p. 85.
34. *PMM 1873*, pp. 175–6; *1854*, p. 129; Kendall, *Origin and History*, ii, pp. 193–4.

Chapter twelve

1. Thomas Crawford, viewer, to Maj. Gen. Bouverie, 8 June 1831, PRO, HO/40/29/1; *Mining Districts*, PP 1846, p. 8, p. 25.
2. *Mining Districts*, PP 1846, p. 8; owners and viewers at Wallsend, *CEC 1842*, p. 625; *ibid.*, p. 608–9; *Durham Chronicle*, 16 April 1831.
3. Crawford to Bouverie, 8 June 1831, *ibid.*; Bouverie to S. M. Phillips, 26 May 1832, HO/40/30/2; George Johnson, viewer Willington colliery, *CEC 1842*, p. 568; Revd J. Miller, Pittington, to Londonderry, 19 June 1844, HO/45/644; Messrs Nicholson, Tulip, Archer and Dixon at South Hetton teetotal pledging, *Northern Temperance Advocate*, February 1843; prayers, Sunderland Primitive Methodist Circuit, *Quarterly ... Minutes*, 15 March 1832, M/Sus/80 and *Mining Districts*, PP 1846, p. 8; *Plan*, January 1844, WCL; publicans, Thornley area, *Miners' Advocate*, 14 December 1844; sunday schoolroom, *Miners' Advocate*, 8 February 1845.

   See also *Pits and The Pitmen* for their 'rude energy and picturesque fluency' as 'the natural leaders and encouragers of every popular movement' (pp. 5–6, p. 22); Ginswick, *Morning Chronicle*, ii, for their 'deepest influence' and 'homeliest patois' (p. 78); and R. F. Wearmouth, *Methodism and the Working Class Movements of England 1800–1850*, London, 1937, pp. 221–38.
4. *Mining Districts*, PP 1846, p. 8; Chas. Carr, owner Seghill, *ibid.*, p. 25; Seaton Delaval owner, *ibid.*, Buddle to Londonderry, 27 April 1832, D/Lo/C 142.
5. R. Elliot, underviewer Penshaw, *Mining Districts*, PP 1846, p. 16; *Miners' Advocate*, 13 July 1844; *Newcastle Journal*, 13 April 1844; Wesleyan preacher, *Mining Districts*, PP 1846, p. 26.
6. *Newcastle Journal*, 22 June 1844.
7. *Durham Chronicle*, 14 May 1831; Buddle to Londonderry, 21 June 1832, D/Lo/C 142; Mr Liddell, *CEC 1842*, p. 593; George Johnson, *ibid.*, p. 568; T. J. Taylor, *ibid.*, pp. 608–9.
8. Tremenheere, viewers, and managers, *Mining Districts*, PP 1846, p. 8, p. 28, p. 20, p. 23, p. 25; for a dawn raid on Thornley by twenty-five policemen and the arrest of three leaders: Londonderry to Home Secretary, 29 November 1843, Col. Wemyss to Londonderry, 29 November 1843, PRO, HO/45/349.
9. R. A. S. Redmayne, *Men, Mines, and Memories*, London, 1942, p. 26; *CEC 1842*, p. 591; *Mining Districts*, PP 1846, p. 29.

10. The charisma mainly belonged to W. P. Roberts, the Radical solicitor from Bath and attorney to the union. Roberts became a coalfield hero after his successful defence of the Thornley strikers in 1843 and early 1844. Other charismatic leaders were William Daniells, editor of the *Advocate*; William Beesley, a journalist and Chartist who attached himself to Daniells, and received the greatest vituperation from the bourgeois press – a sure sign of influence; and, in the early phase, Feargus O'Connor, whose *Northern Star* was an instigator of the union through 1842–43.

11. Meetings as reported in the *Miners' Advocate*. Not all the major meetings could be included in the count because from August 1844 the strike was losing support and working pitmen faded from the scene as they went back to work or were victimised. Only meetings up to 30 July 1844 have been included.

12. Preachers composed half or nearly half the platform, for instance, at Shadon's Hill, near Wrekenton, on 2 March, 8 April 1844. Preachers Dent, Haswell, Pratt, and Charlton shared platform with Roberts at Shadon's Hill on 2 March; preachers Bell and Parkinson with Beesley at Wallsend on 10 April; preachers Dent, Archer, and Pratt with Daniells on Newcastle Town Moor 30 July 1844; for information on Tommy Ramsey: Bellamy and Saville, *Dictionary*, 1972, i, p. 280. George Charlton presents us with a problem of identification. The most famous 'George Charlton' in the region during the period was Alderman George Charlton (1808–85), butcher, businessman, Primitive Methodist preacher, teetotaler, Liberal politician, Mayor of Gateshead in 1873–4, alderman 1876. When he died the Gateshead Constabulary Band led the *cortege* and 50,000 turned out (*PMM 1889*, pp. 370–2). Another 'George Charlton' was the man so prominent in the NMA – a leading speaker, a district delegate, a member of the Miners' Committee in May 1844, and a scourge of the coalowners. (See for example *Miners' Advocate*, 13 January, 9 March, 18 May, 27 July 1844.) Given such prominence in the union one would have expected this George Charlton to have been a miner, but non miners and ex miners did figure in the union's organisation, and the *Northern Star* 20 May 1843 names him as a sail maker from Sunderland. Most of the *Advocate's* references to him say he was a South Shields man. Moreover, although the PMM obituary makes no mention of the 'first' George Charlton's involvement in miners' unionism, we know from Kendall that this Charlton was an extreme 'Democrat' and frequent speaker at miners' meetings in the 1840s. (Kendall, *Origin and History*, ii, pp. 193–4).

13. *Coal and Iron Miners' Journal*, 10 June 1843; Robert Forbes' 'prize essay', *Miners' Advocate*, 19 October 1844; letter of John Hall, *Journal, ibid.*

14. *A Defence of the Voice*, and for the United Colliers' disgust that the Vend expected pitmen to 'work like irrationals', p. 11; Forbes, *Miners' Advocate*, 19 October 1844; *ibid.*, 1 June 1844.

15. *Miners' Advocate*, 27 January 1844; *Coal and Iron Miners' Journal*, 10 June 1843; for knowledge, *Miners' Advocate*, 6 April 1844, and *Manchester Guardian's* reference to the delegates, 'a credit to the class', *Miners' Advocate*, 27 January 1844.

16. Forbes, *op. cit.*; *Miners' Advocate*, 2 December 1843.
17. *Poor Law. App. A, Pt I*, PP 1834, p.130; Burt, *Mines*, PP 1866, p.6.
18. A. Pitman, *A Dialogue between Jack and Tim upon Reform and the Duties of Pitmen and Proper Remuneration for their Labour*, Newcastle, 1831, pp.8–9; *A Defence of the Voice*; praise for 'eloquent' speeches of northern delegates at NMA Glasgow Conference, two of whom were preachers, *Miners' Advocate*, 6 April 1844.
19. Buddle to Londonderry, 28 September 1821, D/Lo/C 142.
20. *Miners' Advocate*, 24 February, 9 March, 1 June, 24 August 1844.
21. Wawn, *Thomas Curry*, p.28; for condescension: Sunderland Wesleyan Methodist Circuit, *Quarter Meeting Minutes*, 6 January 1820, DCRO, M/Sus/142.
22. *Miners' Monthly Magazine*, June–July 1844.
23. *Mining Districts*, PP 1846, p.30; Buddle to Londonderry, 22 February 1826, HO/40/19; *Second Report Accidents*, PP 1853, p.6; Earsdon official and Chas Carr, *Mining Districts*, PP 1846, p.25. For more studied differentiation – *Report from Select Committee on Mines*, PP 1863 (431) xivl, and *Seventh Report of Medical Officer of Privy Council*, PP 1864 (3416) xxviiil, p.516.
24. *A Kind Word to the Pitmen from a Friend in the Country*, Newcastle, 1832, p.7.
25. Selection from WCL, *Strike Collection*, for 1844.
26. *Newcastle Journal*, April 1844 (cutting in *Strike Collection*); *Miners' Advocate*, 21 September 1844; letter from Beta, Percy Main colliery, *ibid.*, 23 March 1844; letter, Ouston Miner, *ibid.*, 24 August 1844; Strike Committee, *To the Deceived and Deluded Workmen now employed on the collieries*, Durham, nd. 1844. A correspondent from Framwellgate Moor colliery called for 'moral and social redemption', *ibid.*, 6 April 1844.
27. John Bryers to Lord Delaval, 11 September 1805, DE/4/27.
28. 'Explanation of the Colliery Allowance Bill', Buddle to Londonderry, 24 May 1824, D/Lo/C 142.
29. Fairley, *PMM 1867*, pp.316–17; Gibson, *1840*, p.278; Hepburn, *1865*, pp.546–7 – he had attended sunday school, could read his Bible at eight years, was converted aged twenty-six in 1822, lost his faith in 1832, recovered 'the long lost pearl of great price' in 1850, and died, to receive an obituary, in 1864.
30. *Miners' Advocate and Manx Intelligencer*, June 1847.
31. Some historians, like Richard Johnson ('Educating the educators: "experts" and the state 1833–9', in A.P. Donajgrodzki, ed., *Social Control in Nineteenth Century Britain*, London 1977, p.91) have used Gramsci's sense of the word 'hegemony' to describe this process. The hegemonic concerns ways other than 'economic' that a ruling class maintains power – ways Gramsci labelled 'ethico-political'.

Chapter thirteen

1. Buddle to Londonderry, 16 December 1825, D/Lo/C 142.
2. This section will not try to count protests during the period. It is a difficult, if valid, exercise (see R. Wells, 'Counting riots in eighteenth-century England', *Bulletin of Society for Labour History*, 37, 1978), and can lead to misapprehensions (see J. Stevenson and R. Quinault, eds., *Popular Protest and Public Order*, London, 1974, p. 29, p. 50).
3. *Depositions* of Potter and Hobson, 26 November 1731; Johnson, Woodmass, and Sellar, 26 November; Cooper, Jackson, Thompson, and Watson, 2 December; Harrison the staithman before Hedworth, the magistrate and owner of the staith, 26 November; Nicholas, Galloway, and Harrison, 24 November; Tinn, 18 November, PRO, SP/36/25. 'Staithes' were coal depots in the eighteenth century, and erections for the transfer of coal into keels and collier-ships in the nineteenth. 'Wear Water Men' is not a reference to keelmen, but to pitmen producing coal for Wear shipment. There is no record of this protest in the Assize depositions: PRO, ASSI/45/19.
4. Durham Quarter Sessions, *Order Books*, October 1754, DCRO, Q/S/OB 11; Matthew Ridley to Earl of Northumberland, 13 September 1765, SP/37/4; *Annual Register*, 1765, p. 130; John Oxley to Delaval, 14 June 1778, DE/4/11; *Newcastle Chronicle*, 14 March 1789; *deposition* of Turner, 14 March 1789, North East Circuit Assizes, PRO, ASSI/41/36 pt. ii, *deposition* of Gascoyne, 16 March 1789, *ibid.; House of Lords State of Coal Trade*, PP 1830, p. 69.
5. *Newcastle Journal*, 21 September 1765; Ridley to George Ward, 14 June 1771, NCRO, ZRI/38/L; Thomas Barnes, viewer Walker colliery, 23 February 1793, PRO, HO/42/23; Bryers to Delaval, 29 April 1800, DE/4/24.
6. JPs and others to Duke of Grafton, 16 September 1765, PRO, WO/1/872; Durham, *Order Books*, July 1766, 1775, DCRO, Q/S/OB 13; Bryers to Delaval, 6 March 1805, DE/4/27.
7. Durham, *Order Books*, July 1775, Q/S/OB 13; Oxley to Delaval, 29 May 1779, Crooks to Delaval, 3 January 1781, DE/4/11, DE/4/4; *Newcastle Courant*, 24 May 1800; *Viewer's Diary*, 12 March 1789 *et al*; *Newcastle Courant*, 14 March 1789.
8. *CEC 1842*, p. 646, p. 669; informer to Home Office, 15 April 1817, HO/42/163; Howitt, *Remarkable Places*, p. 88; Maj. Gen. Bouverie to Lord Fitzroy Somerset, 1 April 1832, HO/40/30/2; marching order, War Office to Col. Burgoyne, Lincoln, 6 September 1765, PRO, WO/5/53; Buddle to Londonderry, 22 October 1830, D/Lo/C 142.
9. Sykes paid due attention to both; he recorded keelmen's direct actions in 1709, 1710, 1794, 1803, 1815, 1819, 1822; and seamen's in 1768, 1775, 1793, and 1815. There were, of course, far more than these dates suggest. John Sykes, *Local Records*.
10. Ridley to Ward, 29 April 1768, 28 June 1771, ZRI/38/L – in 1800 the mere 'apprehensions' of riot were enough to win a pay rise (*Newcastle Courant*, 15 February 1800); Cooper Ahhs to Rowland Burdon MP,

January 1793, Thomas Sanderson to Burdon, 23 February 1793, PRO, HO/42/24; J. Beckett, Home Office, to Mayor of Newcastle, 8 November 1809, PRO, HO/43/17.

11. Release of comrades: Ridley to Ward, 29 April 1768, NCRO, ZRI/38/6; Sanderson to Burdon, 18, 20 February 1793, HO/42/24; Mayor of Newcastle to Home Office, 11 November 1809, PRO, HO/42/99. River negotiations: Allen to Delaval, 11 March 1775, DE/6/4; Brotherick to Delaval, 2, 5, 11 May 1785, NCRO, DE/4/32; *Newcastle Courant*, 24 October 1789. 1787 quotation from *deposition* William Wake, December 1787, North East Circuit Asssizes, PRO, ASSI/45/36 pt. i.

12. Duke of Northumberland to Viscount Weymouth, Home Office, 12 April 1768; Edward Mosley, Mayor of Newcastle, to Viscount Barrington, War Office, 2 April 1768, PRO, SP/44/142.

13. Northumberland to Earl of Bute, Home Office, 12 March 1761, PRO, SP/37/1; *Petition*, 10 June 1785, PRO, HO/42/6.

14. Mayor of Newcastle to Henry Dundas, Home Office, 28 March 1793, PRO, HO/42/25; for reports of combined actions on river and land at this time: J. Bulmer to Burdon, 1 November 1792; Thomas Powditch to William Pitt, 3 November; Burdon to Home Office, 3 November; Hon. Capt. Cochrane, HMS Hind, to Dundas, 20 November, PRO, HO/42/22, and, *Newcastle Chronicle*, 3 November, 1 December 1792, 23 February, 2, 9, 23 March 1793.

15. John Williamson to Bishop of Durham, 10 June 1740, Cuthbert Fenwick to Home Office, 20 June 1740, PRO, SP/36/51; Bouverie to Somerset, 1 April 1832, HO/40/30/2.

16. For the causal relationship of hunger and protest, D. E. Williams, 'Were "hunger" rioters really hungry? Some demographic evidence', *Past and Present*, 71, 1976.

17. *Monthly Chronicle*, iv, 1890, p. 83; Joyce Ellis, 'Urban conflict and popular violence. The guildhall riots of 1740 in Newcastle upon Tyne', *International Review of Social History*, xxv, 1980; *Newcastle Journal* 21 June, 30 August 1740; *MS* account, NCRO, ZRI/27/8. For crowd actions and moral traditions, E. P. Thompson, 'The moral economy of the English crowd in the eighteenth century', *Past and Present*, 50, 1971.

18. Cuthbert Fenwick, Mayor of Newcastle, to Bishop of Durham, 20 June, to Duke of Newcastle, 19 June 1740; Fairles Smith of Sunderland to John Hedworth JP, 20 June 1740, SP/36/51; *MS* account; Mackenzie, *Newcastle upon Tyne*, ii, p. 52; *Newcastle Journal*, 5, 19 July 1740; Fenwick to Home Office, 27 June 1740, SP/36/51.

19. *Newcastle Journal*, 26 July, 16 August 1740.

20. Mackenzie, *Newcastle upon Tyne*, ii, p. 72; *Newcastle Chronicle*, 2, 9 May 1795; Richard Chambers, Mayor of Newcastle, to Home Secretary, 6 January 1795, PRO, HO/42/34; Home Secretary to Bishop of Durham, 1 August 1795, PRO, HO/43/7; *Newcastle Courant*, 31 October 1795; *Newcastle Chronicle*, 14 November 1795. There was a further major crowd action for wheat in Sunderland in 1801, *Newcastle Courant*, 4 April 1801.

21. *Marching Book*, 24 February 1761, PRO, WO/5/48; *Newcastle Journal*,

21 February 1761; *Monthly Chronicle*, iii, 1889, p. 557; R. B. Turton, *History of the North York Militia*, 1907, Stockton, 1973, repr., p. 44; A. J. Hayter, *The Army and the Crowd in Mid-Georgian England*, London, 1978, p. 177. For the poor's mistaken beliefs that full-time military conscription was to follow: H. T. Dickinson, 'The Hexham militia riot of 1761', *Durham County Local History Society*, 22, 1978, p. 3. The army and the militia were unpopular institutions in eighteenth-century England.

22. *MS* Sermon, 1761, NCRO, ZAN/M/16/B.8.

23. *Newcastle Courant*, 7, 14 March 1761. For occupations of dead and wounded, diary of Capt. John Dawson in, Surtees Society, *North Country Diaries*, Durham, 1910, i, pp. 254–7.

24. Ralph Heron to Sir Matthew White, 10 March 1761, NCRO, ZAL/40/12; diary of Lt. Allen in, *Monthly Chronicle*, iii, 1889, p. 558.

25. Contemporary estimates of the dead include 120 (Robin Hymers, a servant: Capt. Dawson's diary, fn. 23); forty-five (Lt. Allen's diary, fn. 24); thirty (letter of Ralph Heron, fn. 24); twenty-one (letter of Holdernesse, below). Stanley Palmer ('Calling out the troops', *Journal of Society for Army Historical Research*, lvi, 1979, p. 213) accepts George Rudé's figure of forty-two (*The Crowd in History*, New York, 1964, p. 35), whereas J. R. Western put it at 'twenty dead at least' (*The English Militia in the Eighteenth Century*, London, 1965, p. 298) which refers to Turton's account (*North York*, p. 45). However, Turton acknowledges William Allen's diary (fn. 24) which estimates forty-five. Dickinson (fn. 21) reckons eighteen were killed on the spot and quotes a Hexham attorney for a final tally of fifty-two; for the King's attention: Lord Holdernesse to Lord Ligonier, Commander in Chief, 12 March 1761, PRO, SP/44/139. For the 'butchers': Turton, *North York*, p. 45, p. 58. Regular soldiers did not arrive until May: letter book, 4 May 1761, PRO, WO/4/64.

Chapter fourteen

1. 'Riotous' assemblies of twelve or more not dispersing after proclamation, was made treason, 2 & 3 Edward VI, 1548–9. The contemporary *Riot Act* was passed 1 George I, 1714. Thompson's 'great risings' are in 1709, 1740, 1756–7, 1766–7, 1773, 1782, 1795, 1800–1 ('Moral economy', p. 79). Hayter categorises three types of riot–brawls, predictable affrays as at fairs, and great risings – but it was quite possible for one type to become another (*Army and the Crowd*, pp. 39–41).

2. *Newcastle Courant*, 11 June 1763; *Tyne Mercury*, 10 September 1822.

3. *Newcastle Courant*, 10 January 1801; *Tyne Mercury*, 31 December 1822; Mackenzie, *Newcastle upon Tyne*, ii, p. 88; *Newcastle Courant*, 17 October 1767, 18 September 1779; *Articles of South Shields Friendly Society*, submitted 1794, PRO, FS/1/115.

4. For naval victory, and Tory election parade, *Newcastle Journal*, 30 May 1741, 27 December 1740.

5. *Newcastle Journal*, 23 April 1768; G. T. Brown, 'Riding the stang',

Antiquities of Sunderland, xi, 1910, pp. 23–36; Sykes, *Local Records*, i, 13 February 1783 – and Shields shipwrights who threatened to stang a dockowner, Joseph Bulmer to Burdon, 19 March 1793, HO/42/25; *Newcastle Chronicle*, 3 November 1792.

6. *Newcastle Chronicle*, 23 February 1792; Sanderson to Burdon, 18 February 1793, HO/42/24, Thomas Powditch to William Pitt, 3 November 1792 (quoted A. Aspinall, *Early English Trade Unions*, London, 1949, p. 13), *Newcastle Courant*, 3 August 1793; North East Circuit Assizes, information of Gamble and Rowland, 30 July 1833, PRO, ASSI/45/63; *Newcastle Chronicle*, 23 February 1792.

7. Bulmer to Burdon, 1 November 1792, HO/42/22; *deposition* of William Coppin, 17 October 1815, PRO, HO/42/146.

8. *MS* account; Duke of Northumberland to Viscount Weymouth, 12 April 1768, SP/44/142.

9. Lord Barrington to Weymouth, 13 April 1768, SP/44/142. The War Office were reluctant to call out troops. They told the magistrates 'it is not without some inconvenience': to Mayor of Newcastle, 5 April 1768, PRO, WO/4/83.

10. Edward Mosely, Mayor of Newcastle, and city and county magistrates, to Viscount Barrington, 2 April 1768, WO/4/83; *minutes of application* of Layton, Forrester, Wilson, before magistrates, 9 December 1819, PRO, HO/42/200; magistrates to Northumberland, 13 December 1819, PRO, HO/42/201; *Tyne Mercury*, 12 October, 7 September 1819.

11. There is a growing literature on all of these groups and their methods; for efforts to integrate popular sanctions into a cohesive, plebeian 'class' culture, see: E. P. Thompson, 'Eighteenth century English Society: class struggle without class?' *Journal of Social History*, iii, 1978.

12. Van Mildert, Bishop of Durham, to Londonderry, 25 October 1831, DCRO, D/Lo/C 108; Buddle to Londonderry, 16 April 1831, D/Lo/C 142.

13. Buddle to Londonderry, 15, 17 April 1834, D/Lo/C 142; J. P. Cobbett, in *The Charter*, 17 February 1839.

14. Central reading: D. Hay, 'Property, authority, and the criminal law', in Hay, Linebaugh, Thompson, eds., *Albion's Fatal Tree*, London, 1975; for a local example of the gallows spectacle, the Newcastle tract, *A Particular Account both of the Private and Public Behaviour of William Alexander while in Prison and at the Place of Execution*, 1783.

15. Nelson Boyd, *Coal Pits*, pp. 4–6.

16. Hayter, *Army and the Crowd*, pp. 166–86; Palmer, 'Calling out the troops', p. 200; W. Napier, *Life and Opinions of General Sir Charles James Napier*, London, 1857, ii, p. 39, p. 14, p. 59.

17. J. Keegan, 'Inventing military traditions', *Past and Present Conference*, 1977, p. 99; Anon., *The Spirit of Despotism. Dedicated to Lord Castlereagh*, London, 1821, p. 42; John Shield, 'Bob Cranky's Adieu', in, John Bell, ed., *Rhymes of Northern Bards*, Newcastle, 1812. For military presence: *Newcastle Magazine*, March 1760, *Newcastle Journal*, 26 July 1740, *Newcastle Courant*, 26 September 1761, 8 June 1799, *Newcastle Chronicle*, 9 June 1804.

18. *Spirit of Despotism*, p. 53.
19. Nathaniel Clayton to Charles Brandling, 23 December 1793, HO/42/23; Lord Grenville, War Office, to Col. Delaney, 13 November 1792, PRO, HO/51/147; *Petition*, Sunderland magistrates, 10 June 1785, HO/42/6.
20. Turton, *North York*, pp. 53–4.
21. *MS* account.

Chapter fifteen

1. For the eighteenth century there was usually not more than 20,000 troops available for domestic policing, Palmer, 'Calling out the troops', p. 198, p. 206; except for a brief period in 1766 when magistrates took *ad hoc* responsibility, troops were called by communications from magistrates to Secretary of State, Secretry to War Office, War Office to stations, troops to magistrates, Palmer, p. 204; Hayter, *Army and the Crowd*, pp. 20–6.
2. Blackstone quoted in Palmer, p. 202. Namier co-related the small and uninfluential army to the strength and coherence of central government, and both to Britain's uninvaded island position: L. B. Namier, *England in the Age of the American Revolution*, 1930, London, 1970 ed., p. 7.
3. Turton, *North York*, pp. 34–5, pp. 50–1, pp. 63–4; Stevenson, *Popular Protest*, pp. 47–9; J. Kinsley ed., *The Poems of John Dryden*, Oxford, 1958, iv, pp. 1741–57.
4. James Rudman to Dundas, 13 February 1793, HO/42/23; Sanderson to Burdon, 1 February 1793, Brandling to Burdon, 5 February 1793, HO/42/24.
5. Hayter, *Army and the Crowd*, pp. 9–11, p. 19; Palmer, 'Calling out the troops', p. 207, pp. 210–11.
6. J. Williamson, Sheriff of Durham, to Home Office, 24 May 1740, PRO, SP/36/50; *Marching Book*, 29 May 1740, PRO, WO/5/34; Williamson to Bishop of Durham, 10 June 1740, PRO, SP/36/51.
7. Williamson to Bishop, 15 June 1740, PRO, SP/63/403.
8. For examples, G. Holmes, 'The Sacheverell riots', *Past and Present*, 72, 1976, pp. 68–9; 1795 popular pricing in Newcastle was done 'in presence of the town's officers', Mackenzie, *Newcastle upon Tyne*, ii, p. 72, and Thompson, 'Moral economy', pp. 83–98; Rudé, *The Crowd*, pp. 47–65, pp. 135–48, Curnock, *Journals*, iii, p. 81, and Anthony Steele, *History of Methodism in Barnard Castle*, London, 1857, p. 32.
9. Edward Hughes, *North Country Life in the Eighteenth Century*, London, 1952, pp. 262–3; Anon. to Viscount Sidmouth, 14 October 1819, HO/42/197; Buddle to Londonderry, 28 September 1821, 24 March 1831, D/Lo/C 142. A 'fitter' arranged sales between coalowner and shipowner.
10. William Hutton to Thomas Wallace, 7 September 1820, NCRO, ZM1/S76/48.
11. Turton, *North York*, p. 44; Fenwick to Bishop of Durham, 20 June 1740, SP/36/51; *MS* account. Sir Walter Blackett, Tory MP for Newcastle (1734–77) was famed in 1741 as a 'Father of the Poor', 'never perhaps did the poor of Newcastle ... receive more support', L. B. Namier,

Structure of Politics at the Accession of George III, 1929, London, 1963 ed., p. 95.

12. Hayter, *Army and the Crowd*, p. 29.

13. *Handbill*, 31 August 1765, SP/37/4; magistrates and others to Duke of Grafton, 16 September 1765, WO/1/872; Grafton to Secretary of War, 17 September 1765, PRO, SP/44/194; Ridley to Ward, 8 April 1768, NCRO, ZRI/38/L; Lt. Col. Morrison, *report*, 18 April 1768, WO/4/83; *Newcastle Courant*, 26 August 1786.

14. Durham Quarter Sessions, *Order Books*, July 1766, 1775, 1800, Q/S/OB/13/14/16, and *Newcastle Courant*, 27 September 1800; Revd Nesfield arbitrated for the seamen in 1816 as he had for the pitmen in 1810 (Robert Gray to Sidmouth, 3 November 1815, PRO, HO/42/147), James Losh had advised the pitmen and seamen (Hughes, *Diaries and Correspondence*, 24 October 1815), a solicitor Harvey was hired by the keelmen in 1768 (Ridley to Ward, 29 April 1768, ZRI/38/L); Capt. Rothes, Impress Service, to Philip Stephens, Admiralty, 30 January 1793, PRO, HO/28/9.

15. *Newcastle Journal*, 28 September 1765; Revd Miller to Londonderry, 19 June 1844, HO/45/644. See A. W. Coats, 'Changing attitudes to labour in the mid-eighteenth century', *Economic History Review*, ii, 1958.

16. Northumberland to Sidmouth, 18, 19 December 1819, HO/42/201.

17. *Tyne Mercury*, 8 October 1822; George Douglas to Delaval, 21 March 1775, NCRO, DE/4/8; Londonderry to Sir James Graham, 19 June 1844, D/Lo/C 80.

18. Lady Jane Allgood to Sir Lancelot Allgood, 10, 13 March 1761, ZAL/40/12. Lancelot Allgood (1710–82), High Sheriff Northumberland 1746, Tory MP for county 1748–53, knighted 5 December 1760; Jane Allgood (1721–78), relative of Lancelot, heiress of Robert Allgood of Lambley and Simonburn. Lancelot came to his Simonburn, Shitlington, Lambley and Seghill estates on marriage. Nunwick House was new; building began in 1749.

19. Lady Allgood to Sir Lancelot, 10 March, nd., after 10 March, 13 March 1761, ZAL/40/12. Lady Jane's account was not without sting for her husband; she implored the magistracy to come out of Newcastle and show itself – 'the sooner you show your courage the better'. Her husband and his friend Christopher Reed were lampooned for their cowardice in *The Will of a certain Northern Vicar*, quoted in, R. Welford, *Men of Mark 'twixt Tyne and Tweed*, London, 1895, p. 42.

20. *Spirit of Despotism*, p. 62, p. 56.

Chapter sixteen

1. State repression came principally through the 'Two Acts' of 1795 (36 Geo.III c. 7&8); the Combination Acts of 1799–1800 (39 Geo.III, c. 81, 39&40 Geo.III, c. 106); and the 'Six Acts' of 1820 (60 Geo.III & 1 Geo.IV, c. 1, 2, 6, 8, 9, 13). *Habeas Corpus*, 'next in importance to *Magna Charta*' (*Blackstone*), was suspended for specified periods in 1794, 1799, 1801, and 1817. In the North East there were major labour disputes in 1792,

'93, '95, 1800, '04, '09, 1810, '14, '15, '16, '18, '19, 1822, '24, '25. See: N. McCord and D.E. Brewster, 'Some labour troubles of the 1790s in NE England', *International Review of Social History*, xiii, 1968; McCord, 'The seamen's strike of 1815 in NE England', *Economic History Review*, xxil, 1968; D.J. Rowe, 'The strikes of the Tyneside keelmen in 1809 and 1819', *International Review of Social History*, xiii, 1968; Rowe, 'The decline of the Tyneside keelmen in the 19c', *Northern History*, iv 1969; McCord, 'Tyneside discontents and Peterloo', *Northern History*, ii, 1967.

2. Mackenzie, *Newcastle upon Tyne*, ii, p.730, p.731.
3. C. Blackett to Home Office, 22 November 1792, HO/42/23 – he did remark however that one thousand 6d copies of Paine's *Rights of Man* had been sold the previous summer; list 'where from the appearance of the Lower Orders of the People Disturbances may be expected', 1817, PRO, HO/40/9/4; *Report* of secret committee, 1818, PRO, HO/40/3/7.
4. *Full Account of the General Meeting ... for the purpose of taking into Consideration the late Proceedings in Manchester*, Newcastle, 1819, p.14; Mackenzie, *Newcastle upon Tyne*, ii, pp.81–3.
5. Duke of Northumberland to Sidmouth, 1 October 1819, PRO, HO/42/196; Nicholas Fairles to Sidmouth, 30 September 1819, PRO, HO/42/195; East Division Castle Ward to Northumberland, 2 October 1819, Earl of Darlington to Sidmouth, 13 October 1819, HO/42/196.
6. Archibald Reed to Sidmouth, 20 October 1819; Northumberland to Sidmouth, 24 October 1819; Charles Thorp to Phillips, 25 October 1819; W.S. Hawks to Sidmouth, 27 October 1819 (one month later fifty small cannon were reported found at Hawks' Iron Foundry – Magistrates Askew and Collinson to Sidmouth, 27 November 1819, HO/42/99); Mr Riddell to Sidmouth, 27 October 1819; Reed to Sidmouth, 29 October 1819; R.G. Collingwood to Sidmouth, 30 October 1819, HO/42/197; Robert Gray to Sidmouth, 2 November 1819, PRO, HO/42/198; Northumberland to Sidmouth, 30 October 1819, HO/42/197; Buddle to John Iveson, 15 October 1819, DCRO, D/Lo/C 150.
7. Mr Clark to Sidmouth, 10 November 1819; Thorp to Sidmouth, 15 November 1819; Reed to Sidmouth, 11, 17, 20 November, 6, 10 December 1819, HO/42/198; Maj. Gen. Byng to Home Office, 8 December 1819; Maj. Gen. Barnard to Sidmouth, 10 December 1819, HO/42/200; Thorp to Lords Strathmore and Sidmouth, 6 December 1819, HO/42/198; newspaper cutting, NEIMME, *Bell Collection*, ii, p.77.
8. It seemed to be important to know the extent of political infiltration above all else: on the Tyne keelmen's disputes of 1822, and Sunderland shipwrights' of 1824 – Northumberland to Home Office, 29 October 1822, Mayor Bell of Newcastle to Home Office, 7 December 1822, PRO, HO/40/17; Lt. T.P. Hawkins to Gen. Byng, 30 May 1824, PRO, HO/40/18.
9. Thomas Powell, Hartlepool, to Lord Russell, 18 July 1839; magistrates Fawcett, Fenwick, Spearman, Durham City, to Russell, 21 July, 15 August 1839, PRO, HO/40/42.
10. Capt. Rothes to P. Stephens, Admiralty, 30 January 1793, HO/28/9; Bulmer to Burdon, 19 March 1793, HO/42/25; Robert Green, South

Shields, to Home Office, 8 October 1815, HO/42/146, 1 November 1815, HO/42/147; Mayor of Newcastle to Sidmouth, 12 December 1815, HO/42/147; Fairles, South Shields, to Sidmouth, 13 November 1815, HO/42/147; Northumberland to Sidmouth, 16 September 1816; clerk to magistrates, Castle Ward, to Sidmouth, 12 September 1816, PRO, HO/42/153; Forster to Sidmouth, 6 October 1818, PRO, HO/42/18.

11. Newspaper cutting, NEIMME, *Bell Collection*, ii, pp. 71–4; Revd Nesfield J.P. to William Hutchinson, High Sheriff of Co. Durham, 6 June 1816, HO/42/151; *Newcastle Chronicle*, 1 June 1816.

12. Mayor Blackett, Newcastle, to Home Office, 12 September 1765; Matthew Ridley to Northumberland, 13 September 1765, SP/37/4; Fenwick to Delaval, 5 May 1800, DE/4/24.

13. Capt. Cochrane to Dundas, 20 November 1792; Powditch to William Pitt, 3 November 1792; Burdon to Home Office, 8 November 1792; Bulmer to Home Office, 9 November 1792, HO/42/22.

14. Burdon to Home Office, 13, 14 November 1792; Burdon to Mayor of Newcastle, 19 November 1792; Col. Delaney to Lord Grenville, 21 November 1792 (Grenville had infact moved to the Foreign Office in April 1791); Cochrane to Dundas, 20 November 1792; Burdon to Home Office, 20 November 1792, HO/42/22.

15. Mayor and magistrates to Dundas, 28 March 1793, HO/42/25; Thomas Barnes, viewer Walker colliery, to Home Office, 23 February 1793, HO/42/23.

16. General Committee of Shipowners to Home Office, 10 November 1815, HO/42/147. At the beginning of the action they had talked directly with the Admiralty. In 1818 magistrates were still trying to recover £500.00 spent in raising 500 special constables for this dispute. The shipowners refused to contribute. (Northumberland magistrates to Home Office, 26 January 1818, PRO, HO/42/173.)

17. Mr A. H. Robertson to Sidmouth, 6 October 1816, HO/42/153.

18. Buddle to Iveson, 15 October 1819, D/Lo/C 150; Bulmer to Sidmouth, 28 September 1819, HO/42/195. See also: N. McCord, 'The government of Tyneside 1800–50', *Transactions of the Royal Historical Society*, xx, 1970, p. 9, p. 12, p. 19.

19. Correspondence on North East Volunteers and Armed Associations, 1794–1813, PRO, HO/50/333; *List of Officers ... Yeomanry Cavalry and Volunteer Infantry*, War Office, 1 October 1804 – for Co. Durham's seventeen units and Northumberland's thirteen units, pp. 225–32, pp. 535–42; *Newcastle Chronicle*, 9 June 1804.

20. *Newcastle Courant*, 10 May 1800; *Newcastle Chronicle*, 25 October 1806; Nathaniel Clayton, Town Clerk Newcastle, to Sidmouth, 22 October 1814, HO/42/141; *Tyne Mercury*, 31 October 1815; Bulmer to Burdon, 22 February 1793, Sanderson to Burdon, 23 February, 18 February 1793, HO/42/24.

21. *Newcastle Chronicle*, 23 March 1793, 15 March, 17 May 1794, and 4 May 1793; Mayor Rudman to Dundas, 2 December 1793, HO/42/22.

22. *Newcastle Courant*, 2 February 1811. Not all those in authority regarded the Impress as a means to discourage disputes. The Coal Trade needed

keelmen's labour and feared the tenacity of their resistance: N. McCord, 'The impress service in north east England during the Napoleonic War', *Mariners' Mirror*, 54, May 1968, pp. 163–74.

23. The Newcastle Impress 'rendezvous' was dismantled; the Volunteers faded after 1805 and many were absorbed by the Local Militia in 1808; the Militia were run down after 1815 till their revival in 1852; in August 1819 the North East had only two troops of Dragoon Guards: McCord, 'impress service', p. 177; J. W. Fortescue, *The County Lieutenancies and the Army 1803–14*, London, 1909, pp. 214–9; Turton, *North York*, pp. 121–32; Correlli Barnett, *Britain and Her Army 1509–1970*, London, 1970, p. 258, p. 278; *Troop Placements*, 2 August 1819, PRO, HO/42/191.

24. Speech of E. Mackenzie at Radical demonstration: *Tyne Mercury*, 2 November 1819.

25. *Report*, October 1816, PRO, HO/42/154; Earl of Darlington to Sidmouth, 15 October 1819, HO/42/196; Reed to Sidmouth, 6 November 1819, HO/42/198; Buddle to Londonderry, 11 December 1830, D/Lo/C 142.

26. R. H. Saunders, Additional report on the coal district, government *MS*, 4 February 1833, PRO, HO/44/26. They had been encouraged by the respect accorded to the six Metropolitan constables stationed at Hetton during the strike.

27. Durham Quarter Sessions, Chief Constable's *Report*, Michaelmas, Winter 1841, Q/S/OB/25; Londonderry to Graham, 6 October 1844, D/Lo/C 80.

Chapter seventeen

1. Deputy Mayor of North Shields to Home Office, 19, 20 July 1819, PRO, HO/42/189.

2. Revd R. Gray to Sidmouth, 18 September 1819, HO/42/195; Mr Collingwood to Sidmouth, 11 October 1819, Gray to Sidmouth, 14 October 1819, HO/42/196. There were arms searches at Winlaton and Swalwell which found nothing: Revd C. Thorp to Sidmouth, 21 October 1819, HO/42/197.

3. W. Richardson JP to Sidmouth, 14 December 1819, HO/42/201; Buddle to Revd H. Phillpotts, 25 October 1819, HO/42/197.

4. Thorp to Sidmouth, 4, 6 October 1819, HO/42/196; Buddle to John Iveson, 8 October 1819, D/Lo/C 150.

5. Buddle to Phillpotts, 25 October 1819, HO/42/197; Buddle to Iveson, 8, 15, 20, 25 October 1819, D/Lo/C 150; Buddle to Londonderry, 10 October 1819, D/Lo/C 150.

6. Buddle to Iveson, 25 October 1819, D/Lo/C 150; December meeting of North Durham magistrates identifying Radical strength at Jarrow, Sheriff Hill, Penshaw, Rainton, Houghton, Newbottle, Hetton, Hebburn, Washington, Fatfield, Mount Moor, Winlaton, Team, Felling, Sunderland and Shields – newspaper cutting, NEIMME, *Bell Collection*, ii, p. 77; Archibald Reed to Sidmouth, 27 October 1819, Buddle to Phillpotts, 25 October 1819, HO/42/197; Buddle to Iveson, 21 October 1819, D/Lo/C 150.

7. Buddle to Iveson, 12, 17 November 1819, D/Lo/C 150; Reed to Sidmouth, 15, 24 December 1819, HO/42/201; R. G. Collingwood to Sidmouth, 30 October 1819, HO/42/197; Revd R. Donaldson, Morpeth, to Sidmouth, 3 January 1820, HO/42/203.

8. Buddle to Phillpotts, 25 October 1819; Thorp to Phillips, Home Office, 20, 25 October 1819, HO/42/197. Mackenzie, a leading city Radical, reckoned that 'the principles of Radical Reform were spread, and espoused "with all the fervour of a moral or religious feeling"': *Newcastle upon Tyne*, ii, p. 81.

9. *Declaration and Rules of Political Protestants*, October 1819, HO/42/197; *Declaration of Political Protestants of North and South Shields*, 2 October 1819, HO/42/196; Mr Ranney, North Shields, to Sidmouth, 26 August 1819, PRO, HO/42/193: Thorp to Sidmouth, 4 October 1819, HO/42/196; Anon. to Home Office, October 1819; Buddle to Phillpotts, 25 October 1819, HO/42/197.

10. Thorp to Phillips, 25 October 1819, HO/42/197; Thorp to Sidmouth, 4 October 1819, HO/42/196; Buddle to Phillpotts, 25 October 1819, HO/42/197; Buddle to Iveson, 8, 17, 25 October 1819, D/Lo/C 150.

11. *Declaration and Rules*; Mackenzie, *Newcastle upon Tyne*, ii, p. 81.

12. *Tyne Mercury*, 2 November 1819; Mackenzie, *Newcastle upon Tyne*, ii, p. 82; *Report*, 12 October 1819, HO/42/196.

13. Buddle to Londonderry, 20, 23, 25 March, 22 July, 31 October 1825, D/Lo/C 142; *Sunderland Echo*, 18 February 1960.

14. *Rules and Regulations for the formation of a society to be called the United Association of Colliers on the Rivers Tyne and Wear*, Newcastle, 1825; for their democratic structure, see reply of General Committee to owners' proposals for a joint relief fund: Thomas Herron, Cock Inn, to Buddle, secretary, 28 January 1826, Committee of Coal Owners, *Minute Books*, vol. x.

15. *Rules and Regulations*, no. xv; *A Voice from the Coal Mines ...*, 1825.

16. We do not know to what extent cooperative and labourist political economy influenced the United Colliers. Certainly, the Colliers' statements suggest an influence, and cooperative propaganda was well-timed to raise the possibility of connection around 1825: the Cooperative and Economical Society (f. 1821), the London Cooperative Society (f. 1824), and Thomas Hodgkin's famous *Labour Defended* (1825). Richard Fynes' 1873 *Miners of Northumberland and Durham* refers to a pitman named Mackintosh at Hetton colliery who was an active cooperator in 1825, and who 'Like Galileo ... lived before his time'. (p. 16) Mackintosh, Fynes says, was victimised and forced to emigrate. *The Collier's Friend*, by 'A Well-Wisher to Society', previously cited, was published in 1825, and is clearly a cooperative work. Although mainstream political economy always stressed market forces, there were signs of a softening in its attitudes to the independence-through-prudence role of combinations: Society for Diffusion of Useful Knowledge, *A Short Address to Workmen on Combinations to Raise Wages*, London, 1831; Nassau Senior and Thomas Tomlinson, *Report*, presented to Viscount Melbourne, 21 August 1832, PRO, HO/44/56.

17. Buddle to Londonderry, 22 February 1826, HO/40/19; John Wood, Mount Moor colliery, to Buddle, secretary, Committee Coal Owners, 21 March 1826, D/Lo/C 142; Hetton and Elemore *labour force*, 1829, D/X/36/2.
18. Buddle to Londonderry, 6, 29 March 1831, D/Lo/C 142; *Rules and Regulations of the Coal Miners' Friendly Society in the Counties of Northumberland and Durham, established June 4 1831*, Newcastle 1831; *Poor Law. App. A, Pt I*, PP 1834, p. 131.
19. Buddle to Londonderry, 14 April 1831, 6 November 1832; *Report from Coal Trade Office*, 13 April 1831; Buddle to Londonderry, 1 January 1833, D/Lo/C 142.
20. 'Castor', *A Letter on the Disputes ... Addressed to the Editor of the Tyne Mercury*, Newcastle, 29 February 1832; *Newcastle Journal*, 23 June 1832.
21. Buddle to Londonderry, 12 May, 23 April, 4, 29 May, 13, 25 June, 7, 14 July, D/Lo/C 142; Thomas Crawford to Bouverie, 8 June 1831, HO/40/29/1; Buddle to Londonderry, 20, 29 May, 6, 19 June 1831, D/Lo/C 142.
22. Crawford to Bouverie, 8 June 1831, HO/40/29/1; Buddle to Londonderry, 20 May, 4, 21 June, 8, 30 July 1831, D/Lo/C 142.
23. Bouverie to Phillips, 2 May 1832, HO/40/30/2; Bouverie to Maj. Gen. Fitzroy, 7 April 1831, HO/40/29/1.
24. Bouverie to Phillips, 6, 30 April, 8, 22 May 1831, HO/40/29/1.
25. Bouverie to Phillips, 7 May 1832, HO/40/30/2; Buddle to Londonderry, 5 May 1832, D/Lo/C 142; Bouverie to Robert Brandling JP, 6 May 1832, HO/40/30/2.
26. Col. Sir Henry Rofs to Bouverie, 4 April 1831, HO/40/29/1.
27. *Poster*, 7 April 1831, PLL, *History of Coal Trade Collection*; Buddle to Londonderry, 10, 11, 13 April 1831, D/Lo/C 142; Bouverie to Phillips, 12 April 1832, HO/40/30/2; R. H. Saunders, Additional Report on Coal District, 4 February 1833, HO/44/26.
28. Durham Assizes, July 1831, newspaper cutting, NEIMME, *Bell Collection*, ii, p. 388; *Report of Trial of Pitmen for The Riot at Waldridge Colliery*, Durham 1832; *Report of Trials of Pitmen and Others Concerned in late Riots, Murders etc., in the Hetton and other Collieries*, Durham 1832.
29. *Pitmen and Others ... including a full report of Mr Justice Parke's Charge to The Grand Jury*; deposition of N. Fairles JP, 15 June 1832, PRO, HO/44/29.
30. *Newcastle Courant*, 28 July 1832; *Pitmen and Others*; Fynes, *Miners of Northumberland and Durham*, pp. 33–4. Jobling's body was quickly removed by a secret gang led by his brother-in-law, Robert Turner: G. B. Hodgson, *The Borough of South Shields*, Newcastle, 1903, p. 377.
31. See for instance, Thomas Taylor to Buddle, 10 March 1832, D/Lo/C 142.
32. Bouverie to Phillips, 27 May, 12, 20 April 1832, HO/40/30/2.
33. Brandling to Bouverie, 12 June 1832; Bouverie to Fitzroy Somerset, 17 June 1832, HO/40/30/2.
34. *Account of the Great Meeting of the Pitmen ... on Newcastle Town Moor, 21 March 1831*, Newcastle 1831.
35. Buddle to Londonderry, 29 March 1831, D/Lo/C 142; Scott, *An Earnest Address*; union broadsheet, *The Coal Owners and the Pitmen*, Newcastle, May 1831.

...cott, *Earnest Address; Account of the Great Meeting of the Pitmen ... at Black Fell, 14 April 1832*, Newcastle 1832; Buddle to Londonderry, 27 June, 12, 15 May 1832, D/Lo/C 142; 'A Pitman', *Dialogue between Jack and Tim upon Reform and the Duties of Pitmen and Proper Remuneration for their Labour*, Newcastle 1831; 'Carbonarius', letter 6 August 1832 to *Newcastle Chronicle*, NEIMME, *Bell Collection*, ii, p. 551; *Pitmen of Tyne and Wear*, Durham, 16 April 1831 and *To the Public*, Newcastle, 18 April 1831, addresses; *Newcastle Journal*, 2 June 1832.

37. *Reports* of Messrs Hunter and Forster, enclosures, Buddle to Londonderry, 10 April 1831, D/Lo/C 142.

38. Newspaper cutting, 26 April 1831, NEIMME, *Bell Collection*, ii, p. 297; Buddle to Londonderry, 18, 19, 28 May 1831, D/Lo/C 142.

39. Buddle to Londonderry, 25 June, 30 July 1831, D/Lo/C 142; 'Vindex', *Coalowners and Pitmen*, Newcastle, June 1831.

40. Letter, 9 January 1832, *Newcastle Chronicle*, NEIMME, *Bell Collection*, ii, p. 388; Bouverie to Phillips, 26 May, 1, 12, 22 June, 8 July 1832, HO/40/30/2.

41. Bouverie to Phillips, 2 April 1832, HO/40/30/2; newspaper cutting, 12 April 1832, NEIMME, *Bell Collection*, ii, p. 419; as told to Lowery by Hepburn 'years after', B. Harrison and P. Hollis, eds., *Robert Lowery. Radical and Chartist*, London, 1971, pp. 76–7.

42. Bouverie to Brandling, 6 May 1832, Bouverie to Phillips, 7 May 1832, HO/40/30/2; Buddle to Londonderry, 5 May 1832, D/Lo/C 142; *Pitmen and Others*; depositions of Constables Raine and Falcus, Northumberland Summer Assizes, 1832, ASSI/45/63.

43. Buddle to Londonderry, 13 June 1832, D/Lo/C 142; *To the Miners & Pitmen of the Principality of Wales, 1 June 1832, General Description of Hetton and Elemore Collieries, 20 April 1832*, NEIMME, *Watson Collection*; attack on coach in Leeds carrying Chesterfield colliers bound for Hetton, *Leeds Mercury*, 2 June 1832.

44. *Rules of Hetton Colliery Agents and Workmen's Friendly Society*, 11 February 1832, *Rules of the Rickleton and Harraton Outside Collieries Relief Fund*, 23 September 1833, *Percy Main Colliery Relief Fund*, 6 December 1834, PRO, FS/120; *Hetton Coal Co. Relief Fund Notice*, 1834, DCRO, D/X/126/2; *CEC 1842*, p. 724; *Newcastle Journal*, 18 January 1834; Asst. Commissioner Wilson, *Poor Law. App. A, Pt. I*, PP 1834, p. 131; T. J. Taylor, *CEC 1842*, p. 609.

45. Bouverie to Phillips, 17 February 1834, PRO, HO/40/32/1; Mackenzie and Ross, *Durham*, i, p. cxvi; *CEC 1842*, p. 646; Walters, *Sunday School Union*, p. 236.

46. *Newcastle Journal*, 9 June 1832; *Reports of Durham Assizes*, 30 July 1832, NEIMME, *Bell Collection*, xi.

47. 'General' Jane Bogey led women in the first incident of the 1740 riots in Newcastle; in 1793 the Sunderland keelmen's strength was counted, 'exclusive of their Wives and Daughters'; in the year of the Wideopen pitched battles, women were also involved in shipwrights' affrays on the Tyne: Ellis, 'Urban Conflict', pp. 340–7; Sanderson to Burdon, 1 February 1793, HO/42/24; deposition of Parker Gamble, 30 July 1833, ASSI/45/63.

48. *Reports of Durham Assizes*; information of Job Davies, February 1833, ASSI/45/63.

49. For women as recipients, see for example, Manders, *Gateshead Union*, p. 20; K. Gregson, *The Operation of the Poor Laws in the Hartlepool Poor Law Union 1859–1930*, University of Newcastle unpublished M. Litt. 1976, pp. 76–7, p. 102.

50. Chester le Street Union, 'List of Queries', 8 May 1843, Board Circular, 23 April 1844, MH/12/2968; Easington Union, 'Report', 25 March 1846, clerk's return, 18 March 1844, DCRO, MH/12/3053/3052; 'Average expenditure for the three years ending 25 March 1840', MH/12/3052.

51. R. G. Barker, *Houghton-le-Spring Poor Law Union 1837–1930*, University of Newcastle unpublished M. Litt 1974, p. 46.

52. Chester le Street Union, James Gray to Poor Law Board, 12 April 1845, 17 March 1846, MH/12/2968/2969; 'list of widows and their families', August 1852, Easington Union, MH/12/3053.

53. Manders, *Gateshead Union*, p. 61; G. A. Cadman, *The Administration of the Poor Law Amendment Act, 1834, in the Hexham Poor Law Union 1836–1930*, University of Newcastle unpublished M. Litt. 1976, p. 207; Easington Union, Report of R. Richardson, 30 October 1843, MH/12/3052, Richardson to Poor Law Commissioners, 8 September 1847, MH/12/3053.

54. *Poor Law. App. A, Pt. I*, PP 1834, p. 131.

55. Cadman, *Hexham Poor Law Union*, pp. 230–3; Easington Union, Revd Liddell to Commissioners, 24 April 1844, MH/12/3052.

56. Easington Union, John Dote to Commissioners, 26 October 1852, MH/12/3053; P. A. Wood, *The Activities of the Sunderland Poor Law Union 1834–1930*, University of Newcastle unpublished M. Litt. 1975, pp. 85–6. The Houghton le Spring Guardians had opposed the philosophy of the 1834 Act almost from its inception in their area; see the reply, Houghton Union, Commissioners to Guardians, 1 June 1838, DCRO, MH/12/3147.

57. Manders, *Gateshead Union*, pp. 49–52; for Chester le Street, *Poor Law. App. B, Pt. I*, PP 1834, p. 147.

58. Patterson, *Monkwearmouth*, pp. 19–21; Barker, *Houghton ... Union*, p. 25, and p. 44.

59. Buddle to Londonderry, 29 March 1829, D/Lo/C 142.

60. The grander societies registered with the Registrar General of Friendly Societies. For County Durham there were relatively few registrations until the 1850s; but before then, from 1814 to the mid 1820s, and from 1838 to 1842, there were spurts of female registration only slightly less than male. Male societies are far in excess of female societies from the 1850s: PRO, FS/2/3 'Index of Societies 1784–1875'.

61. 15 October 1825, FS/1/116; 7 March 1840, PRO, FS/1/22; newspaper cutting on male embezzling treasurer of women's society, DCRO, NCB/I/RS/467; Brother Leighton, *Regulations and General Laws of the United Order of Female Rechabites*, Newcastle 1841.

62. For careless paternalism regarding a widows' trust, John Gregson to Londonderry, 2 August 1837, DCRO, D/Lo/C 504; for a poor widow's appeal, E. and M. Hepplewhite to Viscountess Vane, April 1872, and

uttal, 'This woman has nothing to complain of ...', J.B. Eminson ɔ Earl Vane, 12 April 1872, DCRO, D/Lo/C 626.
Letter of Messrs Jordan and Certs, 12 February 1892, letters to Secretary, Hartley Relief Fund, NCRO, 488/A/1/8.

64. G.L. Campbell, *Miners' Insurance Funds*, London, 1880, NEIMME Tracts, vol. 121, pp. 287–304; *RC Labour*, PP 1892, pp. 150–4, p. 21, p. 18.

65. M.J. Daunton, 'Miners' houses: South Wales and the Great Northern Coalfield 1880–1914', *International Review of Social History*, xxv, 1980. When sanitary improvements had to be made under instruction from the local inspectors of nuisances there could be arguments about levels of ownership and responsibility between colliery companies and private landlords. At Hetton, miners had rented twenty-two private cottages through the colliery: *Notices*, from Inspectors ... to Thomas Wood, DCRO, NCB/13/216.

66. *Sanitary Condition*, PP 1842, pp. 419–20; Ginswick, *Morning Chronicle*, pp. 38–9. Church has found overcrowding and inadequate sanitation to be endemic features of North-East colliery housing for most of the century: *British Coal Industry*, pp. 606–11.

67. Household size, compared with Irish (5.9), and Scots (4.4), Sill, *Hetton*, pp. 127–30; *Sanitary Condition*, PP 1842, p. 420; Houghton Union, letters to Board of Health, January 1855, DCRO, MH/13/222; Barker, *Houghton ... Union*, p. 174, *CEC 1842*, p. 667; *Sanitary Condition*, PP 1842, p. 421.

68. *Newcastle Weekly Chronicle*, 28 June 1873; *Poor Law. App. A, Pt. I*, PP 1834, p. 119, p. 122, for importance of fuel and fire; Ginswick, *Morning Chronicle*, p. 40, for coldness of cottages from open 'loft' area; *North Eastern Daily Gazette*, 13, 15 September, 1 October, 14 November 1892 for water and Ludworth; 13, 15, 27 September for examples of damp and smoke; Ginswick, *Morning Chronicle*, p. 40, for damp and smoke.

69. Chester le Street Union, 'Report of medical officer on sanitary condition of district', 1897, DCRO, MH/12/2985; Houghton Union, Edward Welford's petition of ninety-eight rate-payers to Board of Health, 20 September 1853, John Legge for Guardians to Board of Health, 1 October 1852, DCRO, MH/13/94; Easington Union, Thomas Beatty, surgeon, to Commissioners, 15 November 1849, MH/12/3053; Houghton Union, Revd D. Haslewood to Spencer Walpole, 29 January 1867, MH/13/222; *North Eastern Daily Gazette*, 3 November 1892; W.W.E. Fletcher, *Reports of Medical Inspectors of Local Government Board*, HMSO, 1907, p. 21, p. 3.

70. *Newcastle Weekly Chronicle*, 1 March, 15 November, 18 October, 26 April, 16 August 1873.

71. *Ibid.*, 13 December 1873, 30 November, 26 October 1872, 20 December 1873.

72. *North Eastern Daily Gazette*, 27, 28, 13, 15 September, 1, 3, 12 October, 14 November 1892.

73. *Newcastle Weekly Chronicle*, 5, 26 October 1872; Ernst Dückershoff, *How the English Workman Lives*, London, 1899, p. 40.

74. *Newcastle Weekly Chronicle*, 9 November 1872.
75. As Barbara Taylor does for Owenite Socialism in *Eve and the New Jerusalem*, London, 1983.

Chapter eighteen

1. W. Burdon to Home Office, 12 October 1833, HO/44/26; Bouverie to Phillips, 20 May 1834, HO/40/32/1; Latimer, *Local Records*, p. 66, p. 70; *Northern Liberator*, 29 December 1838.
2. *Northern Star*, 9 March 1839.
3. *Sunderland and Durham County Herald*, 12 July 1839; Mr Headlam to Lord John Russell, Home Secretary, 13 July 1839, PRO, HO/40/46, and Richard Pemberton, and Messrs Fawcett, Fenwick, Spearman to Russell, 19, 20 July 1839, HO/40/42; John Kidson, clerk to Sunderland JPs, to Russell, 13 July 1839, *ibid.*
4. *Northern Liberator*, 13, 20 July 1839: depositions, Newcastle Spring Assizes 1840, PRO, ASSI/45/65; Phillips to Sir John Fife, Mayor of Newcastle, 22 July 1839, PRO, HO/41/14; Fife to Russell, 15 August 1839, HO/40/46; Phillips to Fife, 17 August 1839, HO/41/14; John Rowland, 'Physical force Chartism on Tyneside in 1839', in M. Callcott and R. Challinor, eds., *Working Class Politics in North East England*, Newcastle, 1983; Sir Hedworth Williamson to Russell, 22 July 1839, HO/40/42.
5. *Newcastle Journal* 27 July 1839; Fife to Russell, 19 July 1839, HO/40/46; Thomas Kidd was arrested for selling the handbill *General Strike* in Newcastle on 10 August, deposition, Spring Assizes; Fife to Russell, 12 August 1839, HO/40/46; Marshall Fowler to Russell, clerk to JPs, East Division Castle Ward, to Russell, 14 August 1839, HO/40/42.
6. Buddle to Londonderry, 12, 13, 14, 18 August 1839, D/Lo/C 142; clerk to JPs, Castle Ward, to Russell, 24 August 1839, HO/40/42.
7. *Northern Liberator*, 6 December 1839; Marquis of Normanby, Home Secretary, to Duke of Northumberland, 19 December 1839, Normanby to Earl Talbot, 23 June 1840, PRO, HO/41/15; Buddle to R. A. Douglas Grisley, 11 July 1840, NCL, *Durham Collieries*.
8. Clerk to JPs, Stockton, to Russell, 17 July 1839, Thomas Powell, Hartlepool, to Russell, 18 July 1839, HO/40/42; Phillips to Messrs Shippenden and Fawcett, Durham, 18 July 1839, HO/41/14; Pemberton to Russell, 19 July 1839, Fawcett, Fenwick, Spearman to Russell, 20 July 1839, HO/40/42.
9. Messrs Bainbridge and Spurrier to Home Office, 31 July, 2, 3, 13 August 1839, clerk of JPs, Castle Ward, to Russell, 14 August 1839, HO/40/42; Phillips to Fife, 24 July, 1 August 1839, HO/41/14; Napier, *Life and Opinions*, ii, p. 22.
10. Summary of answers to circular sent to colliery managers, Fawcett, Fenwick, Spearman to Russell, 20 July 1839, HO/40/42; *Newcastle Weekly Chronicle*, 27 September 1873; Thomas Burt and Aaron Watson, *Thomas Burt, Pitman and Privy Councillor*, London, 1924, p. 24; Charles Bigge to Russell, 25 July 1839, Matthew Ridley to Duke of Northumberland, 15 August 1839, HO/40/46.

51. Challinor and Ripley, *Miners' Association*, pp. 88–9; *Northern Star*, 24 February 1844; Executive Council, *Address to Members*, 1, 6 March 1844, WCL. Roberts and Beesley started their independent *Miners' Magazine* in March 1844 which ran alongside the *Advocate* as a more didactic journal. First Beesley and then Roberts edited the *Journal* before withdrawing. William Daniells succeeded them as editor of the *Journal's* successor, the *Advocate*.

52. *Newcastle Journal*, 6 April 1844; *Miners' Advocate*, 6, 20 April 1844.

53. *Newcastle Journal*, 18 May 1844; and 13 April, 11 May.

54. *The Bye-Laws of the Miners' Association of Castle Eden*, WCL; Challinor and Ripley, *Miners' Association*, pp. 82–4; *Gateshead Observer*, 27 July 1844; evidence of William Brown, *Rules of Trade Unions*, PP 1867–8, p. 29; *Rules and Regulations of the Miners' Association*, 1843, NEIMME Tracts, 66, pp. 77–80. On its open membership, see Part One, Ch. 5, n. 59.

55. T. Wood to R. Burdon, 8 April 1844, HO/45/644; unidentified correspondent to Londonderry, 29 July 1844, Londonderry to Graham, 21 July 1844, D/Lo/C 80.

56. *Posters*, 30 July, 6 August 1844, WCL; *Miners' Advocate*, 24 August 1844; Rymer, *Martyrdom*, p. 3.

57. *Miners' Monthly Magazine*, June–July 1844.

58. *Miners' Advocate*, 2 December 1843, 24 February, 21 September 1844.

59. Revd Duncombe Shafto, vicar of Houghton le Spring, to Londonderry, 7 June 1844; Wemyss to Londonderry, 12 June 1844, HO/45/644; Duke of Northumberland to Graham, 2 August 1844, PRO, HO/45/646. Northumberland praised all parties, even the pitmen, who had 'shown an endurance worthy of a better cause'. The Duke took little part in the struggle, sending only two letters to the Home Office – one to say it had begun and another to say it had nearly ended. The *Gateshead Observer* remarked on the triviality of breaches of the peace early in the strike, on 26 April 1844.

60. Buddle to Londonderry, 2 July 1843, HO/45/349; *Appeal of Wingate Grange Colliery*, 4 July 1843, D/Lo/C 142.

61. *Northern Star*, 16 September 1843, 27 January 1844; *Miners' Advocate*, 24 February, 10 March 1844.

62. See N. W. Thompson, *The People's Science. The popular political economy of exploitation and crisis 1816–34*, Cambridge, 1984, pp. 31–77; Church, *British Coal Industry*, p. 536.

63. Summary of Pratt's letter, *Miners' Advocate*, 4 May 1844.

64. 'Garwin Grumbler', Sacriston colliery, *Miners' Advocate*, 2 December 1843; *Miners' Journal*, 21 October 1843; Church, *British Coal Industry*, p. 454.

65. *Miners' Advocate*, 30 December 1843; song, *Owners' Vend and Miners' Union*, handbill WCL.

66. *Miners' Advocate*, 30 December 1843, 24 February 1844.

67. *Miners' Journal*, 4 November 1843, *Miners' Advocate*, 30 December 1843; Special Committee NMA, *Miners' Advocate*, 27 July 1844, *Miners' Advocate*, 24 February 1844.

68. Flinn and Stoker, *The History*, p. 311. In London, falls in the retail price (average of 0.3% per year, 1770–1845) were 'almost entirely determined' by the removals of State taxes: Hausman, 'Market power', p. 391.
69. Mitchell, *Economic development*, pp. 34–8; Church, *British Coal Industry*, p. 61.
70. Mitchell, p. 43; Flinn and Stoker, p. 365; Mitchell, pp. 317–18; Church, p. 472. All of these authors put tons per man year North-East productivity well ahead of UK average productivity, but there are discrepancies. There is a discrepancy in these authors' estimates for the North East in the early nineteenth century: Flinn and Stoker estimate 290 tons (p. 365), Mitchell between 225 tons (1800) and 265 tons (1816), (p. 317). There is a further discrepancy between Mitchell and Church's estimates of comparative North East and UK average productivity in 1840–41: Church's is 323: 284 tons for 1841 (p. 472), Mitchell's is 343: 238 tons for 1840 (p. 317).
71. Ginswick, *Morning Chronicle*, p. 69. This was said at a pit which in 1849 was operating a Restriction policy.
72. *Miners' Advocate*, 13 July 1844. The NMA made appeals for help to other trades, and got it from glass cutters, quarrymen, sail-weavers, chain-makers, brass workers, iron workers, shoemakers, sawyers, leadminers, coachbuilders, timbermen, boilermakers, carpet-weavers, and mechanics (*Miners' Advocate*, 18 May 1844).
73. Buddle's contempt for trade unions had been compounded by the NMA's political connections: to Londonderry, 28 May 1843, D/Lo/C 142, 11 June 1843, HO/45/349.
74. Buddle, *State of Coal Trade*, PP 1830, p. 274, Taylor to Tremenheere, *Mining Districts*, PP 1846, pp. 10–11, Dunn, *View of the Coal Trade*, p. 225; Ginswick, *Morning Chronicle*, p. 40; *Hints to Husbands and Wives*, NEIMME, *Watson Collection*; Well-Wisher, *Colliers Friend*, pp. 4–5.
75. *Poor Law. App. A, Pt. I*, PP 1834, p. 130. For high marrying rates and youthful communities, see Patterson, *Monkwearmouth*, p. 26, p. 32, and Flinn and Stoker, *The History*, p. 338 who discovered that 70% of the Felling colliery work-force in 1812 was under thirty years.
76. Hodgson, *Account of the Explosion*, p. 23; J. Baillie, *Advice to Mothers, on the best means of promoting the health ... and intellectual improvement of their Offspring*, Newcastle, 1812, p. vi.
77. Scott, 'Education of miners' children', p. 351.
78. *Poor Law. App. A, Pt. I*, PP 1834, p. 131, p. 130.
79. *Poor Law. App. C, Communications*, PP 1834, p. 399; Taylor, *New Jerusalem*, p. 201; Wood, *Sunderland Poor Law Union*, p. 29; Cadman, *Hexham Poor Law Union*, p. 257.
80. Graham to Londonderry, 29 March 1844, D/Lo/C 80; Londonderry to Graham, 27 May 1844, George Hunter, viewer, to Londonderry, 27 June 1844, HO/45/644. In June the Coal Trade suggested a policy of mass eviction, but Londonderry blocked it: Londonderry to Graham, 27 June 1844, HO/45/644.
81. Wemyss to Londonderry, 25 May 1844, HO/45/644.

82. Londonderry to Sir Robert Peel, 6 February 1844, DCRO, D/Lo/C 96; Londonderry to Graham, 15 April 1844, HO/45/644.
83. Hindhaugh to Londonderry, 17, 23, 24 April 1844, D/Lo/C 148.
84. Londonderry to Graham, 29 May, 3 June 1844, HO/45/644; Hindhaugh to Londonderry, 14 June 1844, D/Lo/C 148; Reply of Special Committee of Coal Trade, 8 June 1844, HO/45/644.
85. Hindhaugh to Londonderry, 4 July 1844, D/Lo/C 148; Revd Miller, vicar of Pittington, and Revd Shafto, vicar of Houghton le Spring, to Londonderry, 3, 6 June 1844; Londonderry to Graham, 20 June 1844, HO/45/644.
86. R. Burdon, Chairman Durham City JPs, to Graham, 8 April 1844, HO/45/644; Phillips to Burdon, 12, 16 April 1844, PRO, HO/41/18; Chief Constable's Reports to Quarter Sessions, Midsummer, Michaelmas, Winter 1844, DCRO, Q/S/OB 26; Resolution, Coal Trade Committee, 3 June, and nine JPs to Graham, 4 June 1844, HO/45/644, and Graham to Londonderry, 11, 20 June 1844, HO/41/18; Londonderry to Graham, 19 June, 5, 21 July 1844, HO/45/644.
87. Thomas Hood to Burdon, Resolution of Coal Trade Committee, 8 April 1844; nine JPs to Graham, 4 June 1844, HO/45/644; deposition of Thomas Harrison, Northumberland Summer Assizes 1844, PRO, ASSI/45/67; Wemyss to Burdon, 8 April 1844, HO/45/644; Chief Constable's Report to Winter Session 1844, Q/S/OB 26 – squads at Shiney Row, Castle Eden, Trimdon, Thornley, Coxhoe, Kelloe, South Hetton.
88. *Miners' Advocate*, 27 January 1844; Graham to Londonderry, 29 March 1844, D/Lo/C 80; Graham to Londonderry, 23 July, Phillips to Arbuthnot, 14 June 1844, HO/41/18.
89. *Miners' Advocate*, 20 April 1844.
90. Burdon to Graham, 12 April 1844, HO/45/644 – and the following correspondence on laying-in the pits: E. Potter to Burdon, 8 April; Thomas Wood to Burdon, 9 April; Hunter to Burdon, 9 April; Thomas Foster to Burdon, 10 April; deposition of Cuthbert Allison, 10 April; M. Seymour to Burdon, 10 April; statement of Anthony Brydon, 13 April, HO/45/644. There was no case of direct action against plant except for the cutting of railway wire at Tanfield: E. Shipperdson to Graham, 24 April 1844, HO/45/644.
91. For Durham recruitment: Wemyss to Durham JPs, 8 April; Burdon to Graham, 22 April; JPs of Durham and Gateshead to Londonderry, 24 May 1844, HO/45/644. For Northumberland recruitment: letters of JPs to Home Office, 1, 2, 27, 28 May 1844, HO/45/646, and for Bedlingtonshire (technically a part of County Durham, 'geographically' in Northumberland), Messrs Carr and Lorraine to Graham, 14 May 1844, HO/45/644.
92. Hunter to Londonderry, 30 May 1844, HO/45/644; *Durham Chronicle*, 6 July 1844 reports of Midsummer Sessions, for long quotation on Stormont Main colliery; depositions of Harrison and Steel, Northumberland Summer Assizes 1844, ASSI/45/67; *Durham Chronicle*, ibid.; depositions of Clough, Defty, Wearmouth, Bones, Craddock, 13 February 1844, HO/45/644.

93. *Newcastle Journal*, 11 May, 1 June 1844; letter from *Rebeckah* to Thomas Johnson, reprinted *Durham Chronicle*, April 1844, cutting in WCL; letter from *Swing*, 6 April 1844, HO/45/644.

94. *Newcastle Courant*, 19 April 1844; *Durham Chronicle*, 6 July 1844; *Courant, ibid.*

95. *Durham Chronicle*, 6 July 1844; *Newcastle Courant*, 19 April 1844; *Chronicle, ibid.*; Wood to Burdon, 8 April 1844, HO/45/644; *Chronicle, ibid.*

96. Burdon to Graham, 9 June 1844; Londonderry to Graham, 27 May 1844; Reply of Special Committee, 8 June 1844, HO/45/644.

97. Wemyss to Londonderry, 9 June 1844, HO/45/644; *Newcastle Journal*, 18 May, 1, 8 June 1844.

98. Hunter to Londonderry, 12 June 1844, HO/45/644.

99. Information, complaints, of owners and agents, 5, 6 June 1844, HO/45/644.

100. Miller to Londonderry, 19 June 1844; Coal Trade Office, *Circulars*, 13, 20, 27 July 1844; Londonderry to Graham, 21, 29 July 1844, HO/45/644.

101. *Newcastle Journal*, 11 May 1844; Easington PL Union, Hawley to Commissioners, 9 May 1844, MH/12/3052; *Newcastle Journal*, 22 June 1844.

102. *Miners' Advocate*, 24 August, 16 November 1844.

103. *Miners' Advocate*, 11 January, 8 February 1845; *Durham Chronicle*, 4 April 1845; *Mining Districts*, PP 1846, p. 64.

Conclusion

1. Speech of Binns, HO/40/42.

2. *Mining Districts*, PP 1850, pp. 43–8; *Rules of Trade Unions*, PP 1867–8, p. 85; *Mining Districts*, PP 1854, pp. 40–1; *Newcastle Weekly Chronicle*, 17 May 1873; *Manchester Guardian*, 30 April 1847.

3. *Coal*, PP 1873, p. 297; Taylor, 'Combination', pp. 29–30; Mitchell, *Economic development*, p. 264. The steam coal collieries continued to foment owners' desires to reunite in some form. In 1852 the Northumberland Steam Collieries Association was organised to settle prices, but failure to do this led to attempts to settle wages with the Steam Collieries Defence Association in 1864. Similar groupings existed in County Durham.

4. *Miners' Advocate*, 24 August 1844.

5. Burt and Watson, *Thomas Burt*, pp. 137, 301.

Index